oreign Policy in World Politics

oy C. Macridis, editor

FOREIGN POLICY

in

World Politics

FOREIGN

POLICY

in

Gabriel A. Almond
PRINCETON UNIVERSITY

Vernon V. Aspaturian
PENNSYLVANIA STATE UNIVERSITY

George I. Blanksten
NORTHWESTERN UNIVERSITY

Bernard C. Cohen
PRINCETON UNIVERSITY

Karl W. Deutsch
MASSACHUSETTS INSTITUTE OF
TECHNOLOGY

Lewis J. Edinger
MICHIGAN STATE UNIVERSITY

Leon D. Epstein
UNIVERSITY OF WISCONSIN

Dankwart A. Rustow
PRINCETON UNIVERSITY

Robert A. Scalapino
UNIVERSITY OF CALIFORNIA
BERKELEY

Kenneth W. Thompson
ROCKEFELLER FOUNDATION
NEW YORK CITY

Allen S. Whiting
RAND CORPORATION
SANTA MONICA, CALIFORNIA

World Politics

ROY C. MACRIDIS, *Editor*

PROFESSOR OF POLITICAL SCIENCE
WASHINGTON UNIVERSITY, SAINT LOUIS

1958

PRENTICE-HALL, INC.

Englewood Cliffs, N. J.

FOREIGN POLICY IN WORLD POLITICS
Roy C. Macridis, Editor

LIBRARY OF CONGRESS CATALOG CARD NUMBER: 58-9833

PRINTED IN THE UNITED STATES OF AMERICA

32654

PREFACE ...

The study of comparative government has dealt traditionally with the parallel descriptive analysis of the political institutions and processes of individual countries, with particular reference to domestic politics. At the same time the study of international relations has been primarily concerned with relations between states—power relations, ideological conflicts, and the resolution of conflicts through treaties, various international organizations, and, ultimately, war. Thus the study of one of the most significant aspects of policy—foreign policy—has remained in something like a no man's land. Comparative government texts usually ignore it and international relations texts assume a knowledge both of the processes through which foreign policy is made in various countries and of its substance, that the student rarely possesses. It is the purpose of this volume, at a somewhat modest level, to attempt to fill this gap in our approach to both comparative government and international relations and to provide the missing link that should logically connect the two fields of our discipline. This link is the comparative study of foreign policy-making and of the foreign policies of various countries.

It was not our purpose to develop a general theory in which the complexity of our material could be conveniently "fitted in." Given the state of political science today many of the recent efforts made to develop comprehensive theories and conceptual schemes have become Procrustean beds and the subject treated emerges sometimes without any feet to stand on and more often without a head and sense. Our purpose is simply to study the foreign policy of a number of political systems and thus to supplement our existing knowledge, and to show the characteristics of foreign policy both in terms of the contextual elements of a given political system and in terms of the existing balance of international relations. The one naturally affects the other.

v

It is regretted that a projected section on the foreign policy of India by Professor Richard L. Park of the University of California could not be included in this edition because of its author's illness. The omission will be rectified in a future edition.

Much of the credit for this publication goes to Mr. Donald Hammonds of Prentice-Hall. It was in part his idea and he followed the project with interest and patience and gave to it his full support whenever any difficulties emerged. Professor Almond provided the outline that suggested a common approach and he and Dr. Kenneth Thompson of the Rockefeller Foundation read most of the chapters and made many helpful suggestions. I wish to thank both of them. But above all I wish to thank all the contributors for the good will and cooperation they showed every time I called upon them for modifications, reductions, additions, bibliographical references, and the like. The very fact that a symposium of this kind reached the stage of publication within a relatively short time is a tribute to their kindness and understanding.

ROY C. MACRIDIS

CONTENTS . . .

SOVIET FOREIGN POLICY (Cont.):

6

FOREIGN POLICY OF MEXICO (*Cont.*):

10

THEORIES AND PROBLEMS OF FOREIGN POLICY   351

11

AMERICAN FOREIGN POLICY   379

1 . . .

INTRODUCTORY:
COMPARATIVE STUDY OF
FOREIGN POLICY

. . . Gabriel A. Almond

I. Problems of Scope and Method

THE EVENTS of recent years have produced a revolution in the international political system. They have also produced a restlessness and a taste for innovation in three of the disciplines most directly concerned with understanding and interpreting it—international relations, comparative government, and diplomatic history. This book is a response to these profound changes and represents an effort to consolidate some of the advances that have been made in these disciplines in recent years.

The revolution in the international political system has at least three aspects that call for comment here. The first of these is a radical advance in military technology, which has raised the risks of international conflict prohibitively and has placed an enormous burden of responsibility upon our foreign policy and diplomacy. The second is the transformation of the international political system from its centuries-old Europe-centered pattern into one in which there are two primary centers of dominance and initiative—the United States and Russia—and in which Latin America, the Middle East, Africa, South Asia, and South East Asia have acquired great importance, as centers of initiative and as objects of international competition. Third, the Soviet Union operates not only as a national power in international politics but, through the international Communist movement, partici-

1

pates directly in the internal politics of nations throughout the world. Although revolutionary powers in the past have sought to penetrate and subvert the political orders of foreign countries, the Soviet Union and the Communist movement have developed and exploited this technique with extraordinary success.

The implications of these three developments for the study of foreign policy and international politics are clear. The high risk of foreign policy imparts a note of exceptional urgency to our efforts to understand the problems, issues, and potentialities of international politics. The emergence of the Communist powers and of the non-Western areas, together with the relative decline of Europe have rendered obsolete the traditional emphasis in our curricula on the conduct of American foreign policy and European diplomacy. It is perhaps as important for us today to know about the conduct and content of Turkish, Egyptian, Indonesian, and Burmese foreign policy as it is to know about that of France, Italy, and Germany. Furthermore, given the instability of most of the countries in the non-Western areas and the Communist program of penetration and subversion, our interests require that we know a great deal more about these countries than was formerly thought adequate for the study of international affairs. We would like to be able to appraise the stability of political institutions, movements, and policy tendencies in these countries, their capacity to provide for the expectations and needs of their peoples and to resist Communist efforts at penetration. Hence the study of foreign policy must not only include the new countries of the non-Western world, but it must be a depth study of social forces, the political process, and political attitudes and expectations as well as of the overt patterns in contemporary diplomatic behavior and foreign-policy decisions.

The scholarly responses to these challenges may be grouped under three headings. First, scholars have tried to describe the international political process in rigorous and systematic terms. Second, they have attempted to formulate theories of the various means or instrumentalities employed in international politics—in particular, theories of international communication and propaganda, of the use of economic means in affecting the policies of foreign countries, and of the uses and limitations of military force in the conduct of foreign policy. Third, their study of the foreign policies of the countries involved in the international political process has taken new and productive directions.

Meanwhile, the field of comparative government has escaped from its Western European parochialism to include the non-Western countries, and it has broken from its formal institutionalism to include the study of political groups and attitudes as they affect the policy-making processes of nations. The discipline of diplomatic history has moved beyond its concern with the official decisions of foreign offices and the acts of diplomats to take an interest in the impact on foreign policy of the internal politics of states and of the interplay between foreign and domestic politics and policy.

This book represents an intersection of these most recent developments in the scope and method of international relations, comparative government, and diplomatic history. Its title, *Foreign Policy in World Politics*, must be viewed more as an exhortation than as a report of accomplished research and analysis. For these newer research developments and approaches are no more than beginnings. Studies of foreign policy and the foreign policy-making process in the United States can draw on a rich and varied collection of historical and institutional studies, as well as specific case studies of foreign policy decisions, but for countries outside the United States there is only a small accumulation of research studies on the content and conduct of foreign policy, and there are relatively few scholars concerned with adding to it. To be sure, the situation varies from the United Kingdom and the European continent where basic research in politics and policy-making has begun to acquire momentum in recent years, to the situation in the non-Western countries where little if anything is known, where the tradition of scientific research on politics is lacking, and where the resources of scholarly personnel are small indeed as compared with the *terra incognita* that confronts them.

Hence the spirit in which this volume is presented is a modest one. What is offered is a framework, emphasizing what ought to be available to give our teaching in international relations and foreign policy the kind of scope and precision that the problems of the modern world require. The unevenness of this first effort reflects the state of our present knowledge. Future editions will reflect progress in empirical research and theory. But since it is always useful to appraise what we know in the light of some optimum set of goals, we ought to consider what a more thoroughly developed field of comparative foreign policy analysis would be like, and what uses it would have in the study of international relations.

Ideally the comparative study of foreign policy would have as its major goal the discovery of the most significant types of foreign policy "actors" and the conditions associated with their emergence, persistence, and transformation. It would take us beyond the crude distinctions made today between "great" and "small" powers, "imperialist" and "peaceful" powers, "have" and "have-not" nations, "revolutionary" and "conservative" powers and the like. We might still use these dichotomies in our analytical efforts, but we would base our theory upon a substantial collection of empirical studies, which would make possible a more exhaustive and logically coherent classification and a more valid body of propositions about the conditions associated with the emergence of the various types.

The development of such a field of comparative foreign policy research and analysis would contribute greatly to the two other bodies of theory that constitute the study of international relations—theories of the international political system and theories of the means or instruments of international influence (legal, organizational, diplomatic, economic, military, and symbolic). Obviously the kind of international political system in existence at any given time—whether it is stable or unstable, consensual or dissensual, bipolar or multipolar, whether it is a unified interdependent system, or whether it consists of more or less autonomous subsystems—is peculiarly dependent on the kinds of nations or actors that constitute the system. Similarly, any effort to classify and analyze foreign policy actors would have to treat the characteristic ways in which these nations employ means—their attitudes and behaviors in relations to international law, international organization, their diplomatic styles, the forms and contents of their international communications, and their modes of behavior in the employment of military and economic means. Thus the development of a productive discipline of comparative foreign policy is high on the agenda of the study of international relations, just as it is peculiarly dependent on the development of a broad study of comparative government and politics to support it.

But there is an important point to be made in this connection. Although the development of a comparative study of foreign policy depends on advances and accomplishments in the study of comparative politics, we cannot anticipate that the needs of comparative foreign policy research will be automatically satisfied by typical comparative government studies. These studies tend properly to focus on the functioning of the domestic political system, and they have commonly neglected the importance of the international situation in affecting the form of the political process and the content of domestic public policy. Hence a good program of research in comparative foreign policy not only depends on the comparative study of political systems, but it will also make a significant contribution to the understanding and characterization of these systems. We do not know until this day whether the differences in the functioning of the multiparty systems of the Scandinavian countries and those of France and Italy are to be attributed to internal differences in culture, economics, and political and governmental structure, or whether they are attributable to the differences in the "loading" of these systems with difficult and costly foreign policy problems, or whether both and in what proportions. Hence the comparative study of foreign policy has much to give to as well as much to receive from the study of comparative government. It is a "basic" as well as an "applied" field of research.

In the planning of this volume an effort was made to select countries according to criteria of significance and representativeness. These objectively desirable criteria had to be compromised in order to take account of the availability of knowledge in various countries. At the same time it is noteworthy that non-Western countries have been included in equal proportions with Western ones, that "underdeveloped" countries as well as "developed" ones are included, that almost all the major world areas are represented, that totalitarian and authoritarian countries are treated in the volume as well as democratic ones, and that among the democratic countries continental European ones are represented as well as the United Kingdom and the United States. Furthermore, although any claims of systematic comparison are premature, the participants in this effort operated from a common outline, and sought to provide basic information on the same relevant topics. Thus the framework of the volume facilitates comparison, even though it will be some time before rigorous and systematic comparison becomes possible.

Each one of the country studies includes treatments of (1) the historical background, (2) the characteristics of the foreign policy-making process, and (3) the substance of the country's foreign policy including its goals and its employment of means. The historical sections have as their purpose the identification of the main factors that have conditioned the role of the country in international affairs: its economic resources and capacities, its social stratification, its persistent cultural tendencies, its political structure and ideological tendencies, changes in its international position, and the main historic tendencies in its foreign policy.

Since the foreign policies of nations are in constant process of formulation and change, each one of the studies comments on the country's organization for foreign policy-making. Not only the executive, the relevant ministries, the legislature and the important committees, but the nongovernmental agencies and forces are included. One could hardly account for the differences in French and British foreign policy-making without reference to the important roles of political parties, interest groups, the media of communication, and the characteristics of public opinion. One could hardly arrive at judgments of the relative stability of Mexican and Turkish and Japanese foreign policy without careful analysis of the internal pattern of support for or opposition to current foreign policy tendencies on the part of significant political and social groups in those countries. Similarly, our judgments of the stability and potentialities of Russian and Chinese foreign policy must be based on careful estimates of internal pressures and impulses which exist in these overtly monolithic countries, as recent events dramatically illustrate.

Finally, each one of these studies treats the substance of the country's foreign policy. It seeks to find answers to the following two questions: (1) How does the particular country define its contemporary foreign policy interests and objectives? (2) By what means does it pursue these foreign policy objectives? In each study there is some treatment of economic foreign policy—tariffs, trade controls, foreign investments, foreign aid, and the like. Each study in some measure treats of security foreign policy problems and policies—diplomatic ties and objectives; patterns of alliance and of integration; military capacity, problems, and objectives. Each study discusses the themes of cultural and ideological foreign policy, dealing with bonds of language and culture as these affect patterns of alliance and sympathy, patterns of communication and international propaganda activities.

Where the treatments of these themes are brief, the reason is in most cases a lack of the most elementary knowledge about these problems and tendencies in most areas of the world. This may be a weakness of the present volume; however, it also has the important function of directing our attention in an orderly way to gaps in our basic knowledge, and to the significant research opportunities these gaps present. This volume is presented to students and scholars in the field of foreign policy and international relations as a report of progress, and as a chart for future research.

II.   A Common Outline

Each chapter includes three major sections: (1) a brief historical and descriptive section, (2) a section on the foreign policy-making process, and (3) a section on the substance of foreign policy.

A.   Historical descriptive section

Identification of the country in terms of its internal and external history, particularly those aspects of its history which have a significant influence on its contemporary foreign policy. Attention to be paid to:

1. Economic development.
2. Cultural and social development.
3. Political and ideological development.
4. Persistent foreign policy interests and tendencies.

This introductory section identifies some of the main factors that have conditioned the role of the country in foreign affairs: its economic resources and capacities, its social stratification, its persistent cultural tendencies, its political structure and ideological tendencies, changes in its international position, and the main historic tendencies of its foreign policy.

B. The foreign policy-making process

This section covers the following subject matter:

1. The governmental agencies:

    a. The Executive (*e.g.*, prime minister, relevant ministries, and interministerial or interdepartmental organizations).
    b. The Legislature (including relevant committees).

2. The nongovernmental agencies:

    a. Political parties.
    b. Interest groups.
    c. Media of communication.
    d. Characteristics of public opinion.

The treatment of these subtopics stresses both role and policy tendencies where relevant (*e.g.*, differences in policy tendencies among ministries, or between executive and legislative, or among political parties and interest groups).

C. The substance of foreign policy

The section on the substance of foreign policy is analytical in approach and deals with the contemporary situation. The problem might be formulated as follows: How does the given country define its foreign policy interests and objectives? And by what combination of means does it pursue these interests and objectives?

The following topics serve to some extent as an organizing structure:

1. Economic foreign policy:

   a. Tariffs.
   b. Trade controls.
   c. Investments.
   d. Foreign aid.

2. Cultural and ideological foreign policy:

   a. Culture bonds.
   b. Ties of language and communication.
   c. International ideological activities.

3. Security foreign policy:

   a. Diplomatic ties and objectives, including U.N. role.
   b. Military capacity, problems, objectives.

2 . . .

BRITISH FOREIGN POLICY

. . . Leon D. Epstein

AMONG OTHER British governmental practices, the formation and execution of foreign policy have often been regarded as models for other countries and particularly for the United States. Much of the world has been willing to admire the method if not always the substance of British policy. It has been assumed that Britain's policy-making process was well calculated to serve the national interest, and that, more than elsewhere, the wisdom and shrewdness of diplomacy prevailed over political emotions and parochial concerns. Probably this diplomatic prestige was inevitable in light of the fact that so small an island kingdom existed as a world power for several centuries. The very success of British foreign policy enhanced the reputation of the process by which that policy was made and executed. However, this reputation may not survive the present period of British adjustment to decline in status as a world power. Accommodation and retreat, not always graciously accomplished, appear less grand than the policies that established Britain's empire and leadership in world affairs.

I. The National Background

A. Economic geography

Except for Japan, whose days of glory were few, Britain is the only major power of modern times to be based on an island rather than a sizable continental area. It is easy to forget how small the British island home is. The whole of the United Kingdom, including the six counties of Northern Ireland plus England, Wales, and Scotland,

9

comes to just over 94,000 square miles—an area smaller than Oregon and only slightly larger than Minnesota. Over 50 million people now live in the United Kingdom, and about 44 million of this total are in England and Wales, which together have one of the highest population densities of any white community of comparable size. Ten million persons live in London and its immediate environs, and almost every Englishman is within a day's rail journey of London.[1] This densely populated island is separated from the northwest coast of Europe by only 21 miles of open water, but even this distance has been sufficient for British life to develop its own distinctive pattern. Although isolation from European power struggles (in the nineteenth-century American manner) has never been feasible, the British have avoided identification as a purely European power.

Britain's island location and the absence of a nearby frontier, either in Britain or on the continent, made it natural for Englishmen to seek their fortunes in faraway places. This meant sea trade as well as colonial settlement, and both ventures were highly developed before the industrial revolution. Thus almost from the start British factories supplied an established overseas trade in addition to a domestic market. By the mid-nineteenth century, the large-scale exchange of domestic manufactures for overseas raw materials and foodstuffs became the cardinal feature of the British economy. Cheap coal, only recently in short supply, provided an important base for the early British industrial supremacy. Not until 1870 did this supremacy begin to fade relative to the more rapid industrial growth of Germany and the United States.[2]

Nineteenth-century industrialization made the British almost entirely an urban people, and reduced agriculture to a decidedly secondary status. Now less than 5 per cent of the nation's gainfully employed workers are engaged in agriculture—a lower proportion than that of any other country in the world.[3] Despite recent successful efforts to increase agricultural production, the British must remain predominantly a manufacturing people and also a people largely dependent on outside sources of food and raw materials. Well over half of the nation's food is now imported, and in order to pay for the food Britain must export a very high percentage of its manufactured

[1] Demographic and economic data are published by the Central Statistical Office, *Annual Abstract of Statistics* (London: H. M. Stationery Office).

[2] W. Stanford Reid, *Economic History of Great Britain* (New York: Ronald Press, 1954), pp. 337, 377.

[3] P. Sargent Florence, *The Logic of British and American Industry* (London: Routledge and Kegan Paul, 1953), p. 5.

products. British per capita real income does stand relatively high in the world, comparing favorably with that of continental Europe, but this standard rests heavily and uneasily on the vicissitudes of international economic relations.

B.   Social structure

Class differentiation, on various bases, is treated more openly as a fact of life in Britain than it is in the United States, and this treatment may lead to an exaggerated estimate of the importance of class conflict in British politics. However, there is some significance in the fairly definite conception of a working class that has prevailed in British society. Despite the social rise of many Englishmen in each generation,[4] folkways have frankly reflected the assumption that most children of workers would themselves become workers. The acknowledgment of class status has been associated with a sense of solidarity among British manual laborers, expressed in industrial unionism as well as political movements. This class-consciousness is at least partly a legacy of the very uneven distribution of the benefits of nineteenth-century industrialism. In recent decades, and especially since World War II, egalitarian governmental policies have done much to blur strictly economic distinctions between workers and middle-class people.[5] Status is now more than ever identified with occupation rather than income, and also with intangibles like style of life or manner of speech.[6]

A striking example of the preservation of class distinctions on a basis other than purely economic is provided by the educational system. The famous "public schools," really private boarding schools, have remained by far the most prestigious secondary institutions, attracting almost all children whose parents can afford to send them. More revealing of conscious policy, however, is the existence side by side of different types of publicly supported schools. One type is the grammar school, intended for students who (in examinations at age 11) display academic promise and who therefore are deemed qualified for an education leading to professional careers. The other types, called modern and technical schools, are intended for less promising students. Only recently have there been experiments with comprehensive schools designed, like the American high school, to give courses

---

[4] D. V. Glass, ed., *Social Mobility in Britain* (London: Routledge and Kegan Paul, 1954), p. 20.

[5] Dudley Seers, *The Levelling of Incomes Since 1938* (Oxford: Basil Blackwell, n.d.).

[6] T. H. Pear, *English Social Differences* (London: Allen and Unwin, 1955).

under one roof for students of different abilities. The standard separation at age 11, it should be emphasized, is based on demonstrated ability, and not on wealth or inherited social status. Environmental handicaps there must be, but in principle there is nothing to prevent a child of working-class parents from qualifying for the best grammar school, and subsequently for one of the many government scholarships to a university. Thus British public education is designed to provide a high-level training for an intellectual elite.[7] The tradition here represented may also be observed in the particularly wide gulf between the elite press (the *Times* and the *Manchester Guardian*) and the poor-quality mass-circulation newspapers.

On the other hand, there are many ways in which British society is markedly homogeneous. The population is almost entirely white and overwhelmingly of a "British stock," formed by successive invasions of long ago. The Scots and the Welsh preserve some distinctions, but their national background is assuredly British. Irish immigrants must be noted separately, but they, along with smaller numbers of continental refugees, are decidedly exceptional minorities. The great bulk of Britain's inhabitants, unlike Americans, have no national background save their present one. Also the British have a considerable religious homogeneity. The nation is largely Protestant. There are fewer than four million Roman Catholics, and fewer than a half-million Jews.

C. Political experience

Not only are the British old as a people, but they are also old as a nation. The unity of England and Wales goes back to the middle ages, and even the union with Scotland dates from the beginning of the eighteenth century. The island was small enough to be dominated early by a single political authority, mainly representing the numerically superior English population. National political institutions are of long standing—so long that loyalty to those institutions can be taken for granted in a way that is difficult for a people who have created their nation in recent times. Furthermore the supremacy of Parliament, in relation to the monarch, has been constitutionally established since 1688. Traditionally, however, the parliamentary regime was liberal and aristocratic: it was liberal in the sense of standing for the liberty of individuals and of property, and it was aristocratic in that relatively few were eligible to choose parliamentary

---

[7] H. C. Dent, *Growth in English Education 1946-1952* (London: Routledge and Kegan Paul, 1954).

representatives. Like British society in general, the political system was non-egalitarian until late in the nineteenth century, when the vote was extended to the mass of the population. That the political institutions, managed over centuries by a special ruling class, should thus have been democratized without revolution distinguishes British history from so much of the European continent's. But that history is also distinguished from America's by the fact that Britain had a long predemocratic political experience, and adapted universal suffrage to an old institutional pattern.

The liberalism of the British tradition has been associated particularly with the toleration of dissenting and unpopular opinions. Although there have been exceptions, respect for individual liberty of expression has been characteristic of modern British history. To some degree this reflects the heritage of Protestant religious differences which, since the seventeenth century, have been tolerated for the sake of internal peace. Whatever the source, there is no doubt about the vitality of the tradition in political as in religious matters. Sometimes it has meant toleration of eccentrics and even of those regarded as subversive elsewhere in the democratic world.

D.   Persistent external concerns

Historically Britain has had two major international concerns. The first has been to maintain ocean access to the Empire. The second has been to prevent any one power from dominating the continent of Europe. Both concerns have been vital to the national interest. Without overseas connections, Britain would be cut off not just from imperial possessions or Commonwealth partners, but also from the world trade sustaining British life. Even more directly would Britain be adversely affected if any single nation controlled Europe and so threatened to dominate Britain as well.

In the days when the British Empire was at its zenith, and when most of the now equal partners in the Commonwealth were imperial colonies, the simplest way to maintain overseas access was for Britain itself to command the seas. This is just what Britain did on its own until about the time of World War I. As long as "Britannia ruled the waves" the nation's trade routes were secure and so were military communications with the Empire. The growth of American naval power ended exclusive British control of the seas, but the advantages of that control remained because the United States became an ally and not an enemy. The most direct threat first came from a German navy, and especially from German submarines in both world wars. For the first time in modern history an enemy was equipped with a force that could just possibly cut the British lifeline to the outside world. And this was not yet all. The airplane threatened the island even more dramatically during World War II. Ruling the waves, even if still within the power of Britain joined by the United States, was no longer enough to provide security for the island and its people.

The classic British concern with the European balance of power has sometimes been explained as a corollary of the nation's general position in the world. In his famous Foreign Office memorandum of 1907 Eyre Crowe assumed that Britain's capacity to command the seas, which he regarded as essential, would inspire fear and jealousy among other countries. To avert an anti-British combination based on such fear and jealousy, Crowe thought that Britain needed to make special efforts to develop a policy that harmonized with the interests of other nations. First among these interests, Crowe said, was independence, and therefore Britain had rightly championed (and should continue to champion) the independence of nations against any single powerful and ambitious state. In practice, this policy meant a grouping of forces against first one strong European power and then another, "but ever on the side opposed to the political dictatorship of the strongest single State or group at a given time." [8] So explained, Britain's policy in Europe is a striking instance of high-mindedness coinciding with national self-interest.

II.   The Policy-Making Process

In discussing the conduct of British foreign affairs, observers sometimes hold that there has been a sharp change from control by a nineteenth-century executive elite to control by a twentieth-century legislative democracy.[9] This seems to overstate what has happened. Now as before the initiative remains in the hands of the executive branch. It may be granted that the contemporary executive, in exercising its initiative, responds to a broader public than did nineteenth-century statesmen, whose concern was limited to an upper- and middle-class electorate. But the concern to secure support for a given foreign policy was no less real for a popular and successful nineteenth-

[8] Memorandum by Mr. Eyre Crowe in *British Documents on the Origins of the War 1898-1914*, Vol. III, ed. by G. P. Gooch and Harold Temperley (London: H. M. Stationery Office, 1928), p. 403. On the balance of power, see also Harold Nicolson, *Diplomacy* (London: Oxford University Press, 1950), p. 135.

[9] The belief that such a change has taken place is accepted, admiringly, by many left-wing writers, but it is also accepted as a fact, though an unfortunate one, by a conservative critic like Walter Lippmann, *The Public Philosophy* (Boston: Little-Brown, 1955), p. 24.

century Foreign Secretary like Lord Palmerston just because his public was smaller than that of present-day democratic Britain.[10]

A. Governmental agencies

1. *The executive authority.* The basic constitutional principle is that the Crown is responsible for British policy. In modern times this means that responsibility is exercised by ministers of the Crown—that is, by the Government. Although ministers hold office only by having the confidence of a majority in the House of Commons, the conduct of foreign policy is firmly in their hands and subject but rarely to concessions necessary to retain that parliamentary confidence. Policy is not conceived as the product of legislative deliberation, but only as matter for debate after it has been submitted by the Government. Practically speaking, the Government usually consists of a cabinet of fifteen to twenty ministers, chosen by the Prime Minister from among his party's most important political leaders. Together the members of the cabinet share executive responsibility in a way that an American administration does not. The Prime Minister is not so dominant as is a President in relation to his cabinet.

Nevertheless, the Prime Minister himself assumes a special responsibility in all major foreign policy matters even though ordinarily—and always since 1924—the foreign secretaryship is entrusted to another member of the cabinet. The Foreign Secretary is much more than the Prime Minister's agent, but he is by no means free to make policies without the approval of his chief and, more generally, of the cabinet. Contrary to general impressions, the foreign secretaryship has not always, especially in recent years, gone to a man greatly experienced in international affairs. Sir Anthony Eden did, it is true, have such an orientation even before he first became Foreign Secretary, but Labour's two postwar appointees, Ernest Bevin and Herbert Morrison, had both been concerned almost exclusively with domestic matters before assuming the Foreign Secretary's duties. Considerations other than experience in foreign affairs evidently guide the selection. It may be just as important to find a man—like the trade unionist Ernest Bevin—who is well equipped to lead party members, or a man in whom the Prime Minister can have great personal confidence. The latter is illustrated by the combination of Prime Minister Churchill and Foreign Secretary Eden, and by Eden and Selwyn Lloyd in 1956.

---

[10] Sir Charles Webster, *The Foreign Policy of Palmerston,* Vol. I (London: G. Bell and Sons, 1951), pp. 44-51.

Other members of the executive beside the Prime Minister and the Foreign Secretary deal with foreign affairs. In the Foreign Secretary's own department, below the cabinet level, there are additional political appointees: two ministers of state, one in the Commons and one in the Lords, and also two joint under-secretaries of state. Beyond the department itself other ministers have work that is closely related to foreign affairs. This is especially true of the Chancellor of the Exchequer and the Minister of Defense, and of the secretaries for Commonwealth Relations and for Colonial Affairs. What must be said of all ministers dealing with foreign affairs, whether or not they are directly assigned to that sphere, is that they are primarily politicians and only secondarily specialists in the subject-matter of their ministries. The Foreign Secretary, like any minister, exercises executive authority as a member of his Government, and the Government represents the political leadership of the nation.

2. *The foreign service.*   Deliberately and carefully differentiated from the political level in the conduct of foreign affairs is the career service. As a distinguished retired career officer explained, "The Foreign Service is an instrument of Government; it does not formulate policy." However, it is granted that the Foreign Service, by presenting all the material facts, "advises the Secretary of State on what his policy should be." [11] Obviously the giving of advice in this manner contains an element of influence even though the power to make policy remains in the hands of the political authority. Thus the description of the Foreign Service's role as limited to the carrying out of policy must be qualified in view of the inevitable indefiniteness of a line between formulation and execution.

A sense of profession is highly developed and of long standing in the Foreign Service. Admission to the Foreign Office itself as well as to the diplomatic service has been firmly based on open competitive examinations since the 1870's, when a similar procedure was adopted in the British civil service generally. Recruitment, then as now, was separate from recruitment of members of the home service, and the development of special standards of competition gave the Foreign Service a prestige of its own. Until after World War I there was even a separation between diplomatic personnel and Foreign Office (or headquarters) personnel. Not only has this separation disappeared, but since the large-scale reorganization of 1943 the Foreign Service now includes the formerly distinct Consular and Commercial-Diplo-

---

[11] Frank T. Ashton-Gwatkin, *The British Foreign Service* (Syracuse: Syracuse University Press, 1950), p. 49.

matic Services plus some auxiliary services. The whole of this enlarged Foreign Service, however, remains distinct from the bulk of civil service employees.

The traditionally prestigious elements of the Foreign Service have been the diplomats and the top-level personnel of the Foreign Office. It is they who occupy the positions for which independent means and social status were once requisites, and for which the intellectual and personal standards have been so high as to favor those with the very best educational backgrounds. Ordinarily this meant high-ranking graduates of Oxford and Cambridge, but recently the class bias which this implies has been mitigated by the greatly enlarged state scholarship program at British universities. Intellectually the method of selection has remained as rigorous as ever, and possibly it has become more elaborate through the postwar use of an interview conducted during a candidate's 48 hours of residence in a town or country house.[12]

Real career opportunities have been afforded by the Foreign Service because the very top positions, with rare exceptions, have been reserved for members of the Service. With respect to diplomatic assignments, British practice has differed notably from the once-prevalent American custom of giving the best foreign posts to politicians and businessmen as rewards for their contributions to successful presidential campaigns. It is equally important to appreciate that the British promotional ladder also includes the extremely important positions involving administrative direction of the Foreign Office, particularly the post of Permanent Under-Secretary for Foreign Affairs. The word "Permanent" in this context distinguishes the civil service position from those secretaries and under-secretaries who are political appointees of the Government of the day. Among career officers, the Permanent Under-Secretary is the main official adviser to the Foreign Secretary, and he is also the administrative head of the Foreign Service. His advice on policy matters may be ignored or overridden, as it was by the Chamberlain Government of the 1930's, but this is hardly regarded as normal or desirable in the British system.

Members of the Foreign Service have vigorously defended their position as *the* British specialists in international matters. For example, there have been strong protests against the Treasury's effort during the interwar years to maintain the same control over Foreign Office personnel procedure as was exercised by the Treasury over the do-

---

[12] *Ibid.*, pp. 85-88. Also on recruitment see Lord Strang, *The Foreign Office* (New York: Oxford University Press, 1955), chaps. 4-5.

mestic civil service. Such control by outsiders, it has been argued, was so serious as to contribute to the ineffectiveness of British foreign policy during the 1930's.[13] Since World War II the independence of the Foreign Office has been secured, at least in the sense that the authority of the Secretary of the Treasury, as Head of the Civil Service, does not extend to Foreign Service personnel. No doubt much can be said for the spirit with which the Service guards its own standards, but this very spirit has caused outsiders to suspect that the Foreign Service might have too much confidence in its own members. In particular, it has been suggested that the Service was slow in recognizing serious faults in the records of two subsequently notorious members, Maclean and Burgess, who defected to the Communists.[14]

One last point about the Foreign Service deserves notice. Its members, even the Permanent Under-Secretary, do not assume public responsibility for governmental policy even if their advice has helped to formulate it. The responsibility is the minister's and the Government's. So well established is this principle, in custom as in law, that career officials remain entirely outside the arena of political debate over policy. Any attack on the Government's policy is directed to political ministers, not to Foreign Service officers. Mistakes, if there are any, have to be accepted by politicians.

3. *Parliament.* To say that the British legislative authority does not make foreign policy is not to say that in this area it has no influence at all. As the most significant focal point for British debate and controversy, Parliament exerts a great influence, but the whole context of the British political system limits Parliament to an indirect role. The principle that the cabinet holds office only as long as its policies are supported by the votes of a majority in the Commons must be understood in light of the fact that the Commons does not exercise its power to reject Government policy. Plainly the Commons contains a majority of a given party which regularly supports the Government and its policy. Although not all members of a parliamentary party always like all of their leaders' policies, only rarely does any one of them vote against the leadership on a parliamentary question involving confidence in the Government. If individual members of the majority do directly influence their Government's policies, it is through intra-party discussion and pressure. In parliamentary voting the party is

---

[13] Ashton-Gwatkin, pp. 26-27.

[14] Ernest Davies, "The Foreign and Commonwealth Services," *The Civil Service in Britain and France,* ed. by William A. Robson (New York: Macmillan, 1956), p. 67.

cohesive and disciplined.[15] The minority party, or parties, provides the opposition vote in the Commons, but by definition it always loses.

Since the Parliament is not an independent center of authority, there is nothing comparable to the loci of power represented by American congressional committees and their chairmen. Individual M.P.'s do not share in policy-making in foreign affairs, or ordinarily in any other area, unless they are also members of the Government, and particularly of the cabinet which is *the* significant committee of the House of Commons. Nor with respect to the administrative conduct of policy can M.P.'s outside the responsible executive authority exert the direct influence that is within the capacity of American legislators.[16]

Freed, it might be said, from independent decision-making, Parliament exists to debate the policies of the Government. It does so vigorously and significantly. The popularly elected Commons is the main forum, but occasionally there are important foreign affairs debates in the House of Lords as well. Always, however, it is in the Commons that the Government is expected to make the principal defense of its policies against the Opposition. Although each parliamentary party contains a variety of individual views, which find expression in debate if not in voting, major attention is ordinarily focused on the give-and-take between party leaders. On an important occasion the Government's policy will be presented and defended by the Foreign Secretary, one or two of his political aides, and the Prime Minister; the Opposition will then be represented by appropriate members of its "shadow cabinet"—that is, particularly by its prospective foreign secretary and its prospective prime minister (the Opposition leader). Thus a Commons debate is mainly between those responsible for policy and those who would like to be and might well become responsible. It is a discussion between a Government and its alternative.[17]

The question may be raised about how much a debate really matters. Although a bad governmental showing does not modify majority approval in the immediate circumstances, it can weaken the position of the cabinet leaders within their own party and so possibly lead

---

[15] This subject is treated at some length in the author's "Cohesion of British Parliamentary Parties," *American Political Science Review*, Vol. L, pp. 360-77 (June 1956).

[16] Max Beloff, *Foreign Policy and the Democratic Process* (Baltimore: Johns Hopkins Press, 1955), pp. 25-26.

[17] A good example is provided by the debate on Labour's censure motion against the Conservative Government's armed action in Egypt. *Weekly Hansard,* 26 Oct.–1 Nov. 1956, cols. 1635-1748.

to future changes in personnel or policy. And it can strengthen the Opposition before the country, thus influencing future elections. Similarly a weak Opposition case can damage the leadership of the minority party. There is not much doubt that British politicians place great store by performance in debate, and no minister is likely to survive if his own supporters find him a poor spokesman for the Government and the party.

Foreign policy debates in the Commons occur, in one form or another, with considerable frequency. Usually they are scheduled in order to discuss some currently controversial policy or subject, and accordingly the interval between debates varies with the number of international crises. However, there is at least one foreign affairs debate every three or four weeks. The politically conscious members of the community may follow the proceedings in the full reports of the nation's quality newspapers, and also in the columns of critical comment carried by the serious intellectual weeklies. Although little parliamentary news is carried in the popular dailies for the benefit of the mass of the population, the serious press does very well in keeping the sizable educated minority informed as to the course of parliamentary discussion.

In addition to full-fledged debates on foreign affairs, the Government is subject to attack during the regularly scheduled Commons question period—the first hour of each of the first four meeting days of the week. During this period questions are addressed to ministers concerning their various policies. Foreign affairs receives its share of questions, both from Opposition members and from the majority party's own followers. Sometimes the questions are directed to the Prime Minister instead of the Foreign Secretary and his political aides. More often than is possible for other subjects, foreign affairs questions can be turned away on the ground that to answer would violate national security. However, there are many questions, sometimes difficult and embarrassing, that Government spokesmen do attempt to handle. Politically it is unwise for ministers to dodge too many questions. The question period as well as the general debate serves to exemplify the usefulness of Parliament's role with respect to policy-making: to question and criticize, but not to defeat the Government.

Apart from strictly party criticism, designed to embarrass the Government for the Opposition's benefit, there are some parliamentary remarks that, although not unrelated to party considerations, reflect an individual M.P.'s concern with a particular aspect of world affairs. The leading case in point is the parliamentary performance of Winston Churchill in the 1930's. As a nonministerial member of the governing

Conservative party, Churchill used the Commons as the principal forum for his views on the dangers of British military weakness in relation to Hitler's Germany. Much less famously, the left-wing Labour critics of Britain's postwar anti-Soviet alliance with the United States tried to employ parliamentary speeches as a way of gaining attention and support for their protests against the policies first of their own Labour Government and later of the Conservative Government.

B. Nongovernmental agencies

1. *Political Parties.*   Although there are wide areas of agreement on some critical occasions, as illustrated by wartime coalitions, it is normal and legitimate for the party out of power to attack either the substance or the execution of the foreign policy of the party in office. Outside of Parliament, both major parties maintain large mass organizations with rather loosely defined relations to the respective parliamentary parties and their leaders. These extraparliamentary organizations are not simply cadres of office-holders and prospective office-holders.[18] Nor are they skeletonized structures to be filled out only during election campaigns. Rather they contain large numbers of regular dues-paying members. On this score, the Conservative structure is simpler than Labour's. Conservative membership is entirely individual and direct. The member joins a Conservative constituency association, which is affiliated to the National Union of Conservative and Unionist Associations. Total membership has risen to about three million in the postwar years. Labour's more complicated structure allows both direct and indirect memberships. In addition to nearly one million who belong to constituency Labour associations, over five million are counted as members because they belong to trade unions that are affiliated to the Labour party and that pay dues to the party out of the union dues of their members.

From the viewpoint of each party's parliamentary leadership the principal purpose of the mass membership is undoubtedly to help win elections. Advice, let alone direction, on policy questions is hardly desired, but this does not prevent the organized membership from offering and even urging such advice. Regular dues-paying members have often become active in the first place in order to have a role affecting policy. There are two levels at which rank-and-file members can try to influence decisions. The first is through the constituency organization, which in each case, Conservative or Labour, selects its parliamentary

---

[18] The fullest account of the relationship of mass to parliamentary parties is by R. T. McKenzie, *British Political Parties* (London: Heinemann, 1955).

candidate, and would therefore appear to have the means to influence decisively the position of an M.P. Yet this channel is of limited importance. It is very infrequent that a constituency association threatens to reject the candidacy of an incumbent M.P. as a way of getting the representative to follow any policy line beyond that established nationally by the party. Although leading constituency-association activists do have ready access to their M.P. for purposes of pressing their opinions, their political consequence is restrained by the centralized character of British politics. The views of a particular constituency association are unlikely to prevail over those of a party's national leadership backed by a majority of a parliamentary party.

The second level for rank-and-file influence is the national conference held annually by each major party. The conference seems designed for this purpose, and avowedly so in the Labour case. Delegates to each conference are chosen by the various units of the national party, and they have the opportunity to present, discuss, and vote on policy resolutions. On foreign affairs as on other matters the mass membership of each party has had distinctive views which it has sought via conference resolutions to persuade or pressure party leaders to adopt. The Conservative conference has done so without claiming the power to fix the parliamentary leadership's policy, but the Labour conference has often acted as though it and the executive committee elected by the conference did have such power. The record, especially when Labour was in office, does not support this claim. Rather it appears from the 1945-1951 period that the Labour Government succeeded in getting the party conference to support foreign policy positions already adopted by the Government. Always, it should be stressed, the parliamentary leadership is an important element in conference decision-making of the Labour party as well as the Conservative party.

Regardless of their disputed role in determining policy, organized parties do serve, much more regularly than in the United States, as media for the expression of public opinion and thus as agencies of popular pressure if not of popular control. Although the international view of neither party has been monolithic, it is fair to say that the tendency of activist pressure, Labour or Conservative, has been ideologically more doctrinaire than that of actual British policy as supported by moderate opinion. Best known in the postwar years has been the left-wing advocacy of many constituency delegates at Labour conferences. Although ordinarily defeated by the bloc vote of the largest trade union delegations, the constituency representatives have been joined by enough unionists to register substantial objections to the line of the parliamentary leadership and occasionally, after Labour was in Opposition, to secure what looked like concessions in the form of compromise resolutions. The source of the left-wing view has been both socialist and pacifist. Proposed resolutions have reflected suspicion of the Anglo-American alliance against the Soviet Union, of German rearmament, of the course of American policy in the Far East, and of the manufacture of the hydrogen bomb.[19] To a large extent this advocacy within the Labour party coincided with Bevanism—the general movement, headed by Aneurin Bevan, that sought to take the Labour party to the left on both domestic and foreign issues. The persistence of a left-wing tendency in foreign affairs is linked also to the party's traditional opposition to "power politics" and "imperialism," and to its old faith in a distinctive socialist foreign policy. This perspective may still be observed in the party as a whole when it opposes the use of British power for "imperialist" purposes.

Among Conservatives there is a contrary ideological tendency in foreign policy that derives from party tradition. Generally the tendency is right-wing, but it is more accurately called imperial. "Empire" is the emotive word for zealous Conservatives as "socialist" is for Labour. Without so openly challenging established party leadership as has the Labour Left, the Conservative imperialists have used the annual conference to urge various measures to preserve the Empire— a term that Conservatives often prefer to Commonwealth even when they mean the latter. Speeches and resolutions have ordinarily been general and exhortative, but occasionally the party has been asked to take a specific stand. A case in point is opposition to the General Agreement on Trade and Tariffs (GATT) on the ground that free trade would sacrifice the Imperial Preference system. Also, in one way or another, delegates to Conservative conferences have demonstrated their uneasiness about how well the Empire was being protected, and a desire that the Conservative leadership adopt a tougher line against Britain's enemies than has been typical of postwar governmental policy, Conservative or Labour.[20] In particular, there is a rank-and-file Conservative element, though not always a dominant one, that prefers the use of military force to the surrender of British interests, and so rallies readily to support the kind of action taken by Eden's Government in Suez in 1956.

Rank-and-file pressures in constituency organizations and in party

---

[19] For examples, see the *53rd Annual Report of the Labour Conference (1954)*, pp. 69-89, and the *54th Annual Report of the Labour Conference (1955)*, pp. 137-51.

[20] See the *74th Annual Report of the Conservative Conference (1954)*, p. 51, and the *75th Annual Report of the Conservative Conference (1955)*, pp. 27, 33.

conferences are often closely related to differences of opinion within the parliamentary parties. It is really the M.P.'s composing these parties who are the direct objects of whatever influence the external organizations can bring to bear. Despite the advantages, already described, of the party's leadership in maintaining parliamentary cohesion—especially when holding governmental office—the fact remains that the few hundred M.P.'s composing a majority party do have a final authority. Their backing for a policy has to be secured by a Government. And when a party is out of power there is even room for some initiative by the parliamentary party membership. Labour formally gives control of its Opposition policy to the parliamentary party as a whole, and the Conservative party maintains an equivalent though less clear-cut means for backbench M.P.'s to express their opinions, which may also be the opinions of their constituency followers.

Finally in discussing the role of parties it should be pointed out that, despite opposing extremists within each party, the moderate Conservative and the moderate Labour leaders have occupied a good deal of common ground with respect to Britain's postwar foreign policy. Rearmament and the American alliance, to take two leading examples, have not been at issue between the two parties. Actually it has been unusual for there to be so significant an interparty division as was reflected by Labour's virtually united opposition to the Conservative Government's Egyptian campaign of 1956.

2. *Interest Groups.*   Lately the standard view of the unimportance of interest groups in the British political process has been subject to question, and the beginning of the study of such groups has disclosed a large role at least in domestic matters. Nor does anyone doubt that on such questions as tariffs British manufacturers, unions, and farmers have means of effectively conveying their preferences to governmental authority. However, it is evident that British interest groups, though as multifarious as those anywhere else, operate differently from their American counterparts. The very fact that political parties are national in character and cohesive in parliamentary organization limits the usefulness of pressuring legislators, directly or through constituents, for individual votes. To affect the main lines of governmental policy, certainly in foreign affairs, a British interest group would have to influence a party's leadership, or more remotely the bulk of a parliamentary party. Neither of these avenues seems feasible except for the biggest interest groups, although on lesser matters, particularly those involving administrative decisions, it may be assumed that smaller groups exert influence.

Major British interest groups tend to have direct connections with a political party. The outstanding example is that of the trade unions, most of which are affiliated to the Labour party and thus share directly, often dominantly, in that party's policy-making. The unions also have a general organization, the Trades Union Congress, which is not affiliated to the Labour party and which does confer with Governments of either party in behalf of union interests. Somewhat similarly the cooperative movement works both within and outside the Labour party. The Conservatives have no precise organizational counterparts, but industrial leaders maintain close connections with the party.

No large groups are organized specifically to influence foreign policy. This excludes the Royal Institute of International Affairs, whose concern is mainly research. Between the wars there was a large League of Nations association carrying on a large-scale propaganda campaign, but there is no contemporary parallel. The churches should not be ignored as an influence in matters directly affecting peace or war, since many have traditionally represented considerable pacifist sentiment. Veterans' organizations, it might be added, play no appreciable part in affecting general policy. What is also missing, from an American standpoint, is the presence of substantial ethnic blocs. Although there are European refugees in Britain, they are not numerous enough to subject British foreign policy-making to serious pressure. Even the Jewish population of half a million cannot be said to be an electoral factor in determining British policy toward Israel, despite a vigorous Zionist movement that has had a role within the Labour party. Likewise the Irish minority, largely centered in a few manufacturing cities, is not a decisive influence even though it too has a few parliamentary spokesmen.

Generally interest groups, with the notable exception of the trade unions, do not publicly present resolutions designed to influence the foreign policy of the Government. Many organized groups may be consulted in a nonpublic way, but this is a part of the decision-making process about which there exists little detailed information. At most there are rumors or vague references, suggesting for example that commercial interests in British Hongkong had something to do with the British recognition of Communist China.

3. *Mass Media of Communication.*   The most basic point to note about British mass media is their national character. Strictly local and regional newspapers are minor in relation to the media centered in London. The British audience is essentially national for newspapers, magazines, radio, and television. Opinion concerning foreign policy,

as that concerning most domestic policy, is formed nationally and not regionally.

British communication has also been given a special character by the continued monopoly of radio broadcasting by the government-owned British Broadcasting Corporation, and by a similar television monopoly until 1955 when closely supervised commercial television was allowed to compete with the B.B.C. The government-owned service has avoided the editorializing news commentary typical of American radio and television. The news is reported straight and without dramatization by the B.B.C., and a similar standard is expected of the new commercial television. However, B.B.C. facilities are used by Government spokesmen, particularly the Prime Minister and the Foreign Secretary, for official expositions of foreign policy. The importance of this means of communication with the nation was firmly established by the successful wartime speeches of Winston Churchill. Some radio and television time is divided, according to an agreed-upon formula, between political parties for a presentation of their views on international as well as other issues. Occasionally, too, there are discussion programs involving foreign policy. In no case is there any purchase of time for the presentation of opinions.

Neutrality in British radio and television contrasts with sharply partisan attachments on the part of the press. Except for Labour's London *Daily Herald,* whose policies are controlled by its trade union owners, this partisanship is solely a matter of choice by ordinary private publishers. Most papers lean to the Conservatives, but the largest London paper, the *Daily Mirror,* is pro-Labour. Although none of the mass-circulation dailies, like the *Mirror* and its several pro-Conservative counterparts, give much serious editorial or news attention to international affairs, it is through their headlines, often slanted by partisan considerations, that a large share of the British population forms its perspective with respect to international policies. Nevertheless the quality press, even with its small circulation, deserves more attention as a molder of opinions.[21] A few papers reach most Englishmen who have opinion-making roles. Except in Scotland, where there are equivalent newspapers, almost every person seriously concerned with national and international affairs reads either the quasi-official *Times* of London or the liberal *Manchester Guardian.* Just possibly, if "seriously concerned" is defined broadly enough, the category should include the readers of the Conservative *Daily Telegraph,* which

---

[21] An excellent study emphasizing the role of the quality press in opinion formation is R. Bassett, *Democracy and Foreign Policy, A Case History: The Sino-Japanese Dispute, 1931-1933* (London: Longmans, 1952).

is unusual in that its news presentation stands between the popular press and the quality press. Just as striking as this daily newspaper situation is the fact that either one of two Sunday papers, the *Observer* or the *Sunday Times*, is read by virtually the whole of the serious English public. In addition, the special importance of the weekly *Economist* should be noted; more than other intellectually oriented weeklies, like the *Spectator* and the left-wing *New Statesman*, the *Economist* reaches the influential. Although these various papers and periodicals often present divergent views, there is an intimacy about the English circle of discussion that is absent in a larger and less centralized political community.

Less highly organized media of communication than those so far mentioned also play an important role in Britain. Pamphlets, for instance, are still widely used by party and party-affiliated groups to reach the public. A good example was the Bevanite circulation in 1951 of a series of pamphlets outlining the left-wing's opposition to Britain's foreign policy. Furthermore, in a nation that does more book-reading than the American, it is worth mentioning that both scholarly and popular volumes on foreign policy reach the public. Nor should speeches at public meetings, even though declining in popularity as a result of television competition, be neglected as a means of influencing political audiences. A speech by a major public figure remains an important occasion at least for the membership of a political party.

C.   General role of public opinion

Many of the agencies just discussed under the heading of "nongovernmental" are often conceived as representing public opinion in contrast to the official agencies of governmental policy-making. For analytical purposes it has been useful to adhere to this distinction, but there is another approach lately employed by English critics. The term "Establishment" is used to refer loosely to an inner circle of important ministers, top civil servants, editors of the serious press, and a miscellany of persons, many academic, who informally consult with the others. Based on common social and intellectual backgrounds, the members of this Establishment overlap governmental and nongovernmental agencies. They not only make policy; they also expound it through the quality papers and in university halls.

No doubt there is more divergence among the British influential than the concept of an Establishment conveys. But with or without the term, the British community frankly recognizes the leadership groups that, in Gabriel Almond's phrase, "carry on the specific work of policy formulation and policy advocacy." As Almond has also pointed out, though in reference to the United States, an elite of this sort does not operate independently of "certain policy criteria in the form of widely held values and expectations." [22] The British public, like publics elsewhere, sets such criteria, and the policy-makers are limited thereby—as, for instance, by the public's manifest desire for peace. The subtlety of these relations was well described by Kenneth Younger, a former Minister of State for Foreign Affairs. Control of foreign policy, he said, was more oligarchic than control of domestic policy, and on first reflection he thought of no occasion when he or his superiors "had been greatly affected by public opinion in reaching important decisions." But this first impression he realized was misleading because public opinion did affect ministers in a general way. "The Government," he wrote, "tends to identify itself almost unconsciously with a vaguely sensed general will, and no clear formulation of the pressure of public opinion upon Government policy ever occurs." [23] Especially, Younger believed, a Government identified with its own supporters.

III.   The Substance of Foreign Policy

Ordinarily it is assumed, whatever respective party positions happen to be, that major elements in British foreign policy are not subject to drastic change.[24] No such change was evident, for example, in the transfer of office from Conservative to Labour in 1945, or from Labour to Conservative in 1951. The definition of the national interest remains fairly stable, and the world situation allows a Government only limited choices, often confined to methods, tone, and timing.

A.   Commonwealth relations

Properly speaking, Britain's imperial policy may not belong in the sphere of foreign affairs, and the details of that policy cannot be specified here. However, in international matters the British themselves view the Commonwealth (or Empire as it is still called by its oldest champions) as an overseas extension of the British nation and thus as an

---

[22] Gabriel Almond, *The American People and Foreign Policy* (New York: Harcourt, Brace, 1950), pp. 5, 6.

[23] Kenneth Younger, "Public Opinion and Foreign Policy," *British Journal of Sociology*, Vol. VI, pp. 169, 171 (June 1955).

[24] Basic material on British policy of the recent past may be found in *Documents on British Foreign Policy 1919-1939*, ed. by E. L. Woodward and Rohan Butler (London: H. M. Stationery Office, 1947-1954), and a general historical account in *The Cambridge History of British Foreign Policy 1783-1919*, ed. by A. W. Ward and G. P. Gooch (London: Cambridge University Press, 1922-1923).

entity through which Britain can play a larger role in the world than it could as an island kingdom standing alone. As a recent British ambassador to the United States has declared: "It would be misleading to talk about the British contribution to the free world solely in terms of the efforts and the economy of the fifty million people in the British Isles. Britain lies at the heart of the Commonwealth, and the Commonwealth contains over six hundred million people, more than a third of the population of the free world." [25]

The Commonwealth is a unique institution. Its members (as of 1958) are ten sovereign states without fixed political obligations. They regularly consult each other, and often reach agreement even though there is no legal need to do so. Each of the ten states has some kind of British heritage, if not from immigration at least from a period of years under British rule. Each finds it convenient, economically at any rate, to maintain the Commonwealth tie. The symbol of free association is the Queen, acknowledged by all as Head of the Commonwealth and by some member nations as their own crowned head. In the latter category are Britain itself and those other Commonwealth members closest to Britain in ethnic origin, language, and customs: Australia, New Zealand, Canada, and (marginally) South Africa. Significantly, the first new postwar members, India, Pakistan and Ceylon, became republics, and in their different view of the Queen as in other more substantial ways these nations, containing two-thirds of the Commonwealth's six hundred million people, cause the whole structure to appear less united than the British would prefer. However, to hold the Asian members within the Commonwealth, Britain has been willing to make the structure even more flexible and informal than it was when originally developed in the interwar period. Similar accommodation was possible for Ghana and Malaya as they became member nations in 1957.

In addition to its ten present members the Commonwealth contains other countries that are not fully self-governing and are not therefore "members." [26] Mainly these countries are British dependencies, with a total population of about 75 million. In some instances they are now on the verge of self-governing status, and so they are likely additions to the number of member nations. A special instance is provided by the Federation of Rhodesia and Nyasaland, which although still subject to British supervision is treated for some purposes as a Common-

---

[25] Sir Roger Makins, "The Commonwealth in World Affairs," *Labor and Industry in Britain*, Vol. XIV, p. 116 (Sept. 1956).

[26] K. C. Wheare, "The Nature and Structure of the Commonwealth," *American Political Science Review*, Vol. XLVII, p. 1025 (Dec. 1953).

wealth member. As other various dependencies in Africa, Asia, and the Caribbean do become fully sovereign, the British hope that each will choose to join the Commonwealth. Thus there is envisioned a multiracial body of self-governing nations largely coinciding with the world-wide expanse of the old British Empire. Within the new Commonwealth, substituting for power formerly exercised over colonial dependencies, the British would like to provide a leadership freely accepted as one based on experience and mutual interest. On the intangibles of Commonwealth cooperation rests whatever aspiration Britain still has to play the role of a great power in the contemporary world.

Most interesting of Britain's postwar Commonwealth relations has been that with India, the largest member nation and a prime claimant to Asian leadership. Agreement with India is really essential if there is to be a Commonwealth policy, but such agreement has been difficult because the Indian view of the world over the last decade has in fact been so different from Britain's. Thus the common front of Commonwealth members has often been fictional. Unlike Britain, India has been persistently neutralist with respect to the American-led Western effort to contain Russian aggression. And India, along with other Asian Commonwealth partners, has been anti-colonial (that is, anti-Western colonial) and therefore often anti-British in matters reaching the United Nations.

Gaining the Commonwealth membership, even if not the policy agreement, of former dependencies like India, has provided one justification for Britain's postwar withdrawal from former imperial possessions. The problem has been to withdraw at just the right time: when a colonial population was sufficiently prepared for self-government, so as to resist Communists, and yet before a population was so aroused against British rule as to make subsequent Commonwealth membership politically unfeasible. With some exceptions, the British have succeeded pretty well. In India, Pakistan, and Ceylon, the British did manage to withdraw in a manner regarded as seemly. In Africa, at least where the problem is not complicated as it is in Kenya by large-scale white settlements, the British have been following a general policy similar to that pursued in Asia during the earlier postwar years.

The exceptions to graceful British withdrawal have attracted considerable attention. In Malaya, an expensive fight against Communists was conducted so that the foundations of independent self-government could painfully be constructed. Another type of problem has been presented by the island of Cyprus, just offshore from Turkey in the Mediterranean and within striking distance of the Suez Canal.

Here the British have wanted to maintain a principal Middle Eastern military base, and for this purpose to hold the island under British sovereignty despite violent protests from some inhabitants who want the island joined to Greece. The majority of Cypriots are Greeks, but there is a substantial minority of Turks who prefer British to Greek rule of the island. Some constitutional compromise is being sought; meanwhile, the British Government (in 1956) met terrorist attacks with strong repressive measures—over the objections of British Labour. Evidently the British Government considered the cost of maintaining the British position on Cyprus to be worth while on the assumption that Greek sovereignty would lessen the security of the base and also antagonize Turkey. The British stand was unpopular, in and out of Britain, but it involved operations on a small enough scale for the nation to finance. Cyprus's chief significance, however, is not to exemplify Commonwealth or colonial policy, but rather to show British determination to maintain a position of strength somewhere in the Middle East. All other considerations in Cyprus were subordinated to military ones, as in the case of smaller dependencies like Gibraltar.

Some other legacies from the era of European expansion are difficult for contemporary Britain either to liquidate or transform. Nevertheless, in the light of the whole postwar development toward self-governing Commonwealth units, it is no wonder that the British feel sadly misunderstood when they are denounced as a colonial power. Their past expansion seems, in British eyes, to have made the nation peculiarly and unfairly vulnerable to American and Asian criticism based on the salt-water fallacy: that overseas expansion is evil in a way that continental expansion is not. On this score, Britain can expect more understanding from other European nations, particularly France, than from the United States. Whereas once the European powers were imperial rivals, now in their retreat from empire they can stand together in appreciating the problems of fighting rear-guard action.

B. Cultural and ideological ties

Of a different sort but not necessarily less strong than the Commonwealth bond are Britain's noninstitutional ties based on culture and ideology. These ties cut across the line between Commonwealth and non-Commonwealth countries. Canada, Australia, New Zealand, and (to a lesser extent) South Africa would be regarded as kindred nations even without a Commonwealth structure. Their populations are heavily British in origin, their language is English (though with large exceptions in Canada and South Africa), and their political institutions are direct adaptations of the British model. Together with Britain and the

United States they constitute the nongovernmental entity that Englishmen, and Sir Winston Churchill in particular, like to call the "English-speaking peoples." [27] The term is partly a euphemism for an inappropriate and offensively exclusionary phrase like "Anglo-Saxon world," and yet it conveys much of the feeling associated with a racial or ethnic bond.

Within the English-speaking world the British recognize the United States as a very special case. Although similarities in many matters, including a common (that is, an English) political heritage, are acknowledged and even overstated, relations are complicated by those differences which are found to exist between American and British customs.[28] Sometimes these differences are regarded as unfortunate deviations from a British norm, as in the case of American government preserving the separation-of-powers principle instead of adopting the parliamentary-cabinet system. More significantly, in postwar years the British have found it difficult to get accustomed to American predominance, militarily and economically, in relation to Britain and much of the Western world. The United States, as the newcomer in international affairs, sometimes appears to Englishmen as a brash usurper of Britain's former leading role, particularly in the Middle East. Irritation with American ways, however, has not prevented the broad central sector of British opinion from considering the postwar alliance with the United States to be natural and right. Ideologically, the Anglo-American alliance has been uncongenial only to left-wing socialists who objected to American capitalism, and to imperialist Conservatives who saw American criticism of the British Empire in terms of nationalist rivalry. Even many of these ideological critics objected mainly to the terms of the alliance, admitting, though bitterly, Britain's overriding need for American power.

Beyond the United States and the English-speaking members of the Commonwealth, Britain's cultural and ideological ties are less definite. A general attachment to political democracy causes Englishmen to identify more readily with some nations than others, and a minority in the Labour party sympathizes particularly with professedly socialist countries and with the ideological neutralism of Nehru's India. There is a cultural link with the nations of Western Europe, especially France, but its strength appears less than that of an English-speaking

---

[27] As, for instance, in Churchill's famous Fulton speech. *New York Times,* March 6, 1946, p. 4.

[28] The problems of the Anglo-American relationship, as seen by Englishmen, are treated in the author's *Britain—Uneasy Ally* (Chicago: University of Chicago Press, 1954), chap. 2.

Atlantic community. This is in spite of the heavy volume of British travel to the continent, and in spite of the communion in an old and threatened culture which British intellectuals share with their continental counterparts. Apparently for most Englishmen the barriers of language and unstable continental politics outweigh geographic proximity. Germany presents a particular difficulty; its aggressive enmity is too recent for popular links to be easily established.

With respect to all of Britain's broad ties with other countries, the claim is often made that foreign policy has been developed apart from such considerations, particularly of ideology, and solely on the basis of a calculated national interest.[29] But even if it is true that policy is arrived at independently of ideological preferences, there can be no doubt that support for a given policy can be more readily obtained when that policy is in line with the attachments of the British community.

C.   Foreign economic policy

Britain's dependence on overseas trade means that economic matters are always in the forefront among foreign policy issues. Since World War II the most constant national worry has been to maintain a sufficient volume of exports to pay for needed imports of food and raw materials. During much of the last decade Britain required outside help in the form of loans and Marshall Aid in order to bridge the dollar gap. That is, Britain had to be given dollars, over and above those earned, so as to allow the purchase of goods from the United States and Canada. More recently American aid has been for military purposes, but this too involves a degree of dependency.

The general postwar economic policy of seeking to increase exports has been complicated by Britain's leading role among the nations associated in the sterling bloc. Within this bloc free exchange is encouraged, and earnings of gold and dollars are pooled for dealing with non-sterling countries. The sterling bloc consists of all parts of the Commonwealth except Canada, plus Burma, Iceland, Iraq, Ireland, Jordan, and Libya. It is not Britain alone, but this bloc as a whole that seeks a balance of trade with the rest of the world. Britain serves as banker for the bloc. In this arrangement there are advantages for both British trade and British prestige. Besides helping to maintain London as a major center of international exchange, the sterling bloc facilitates the exchange of British manufactured goods for food and raw

---

[29] Note, for example, Churchill's rejection of the ideological case against Franco Spain. *The Second World War,* Vol. 5 (Boston: Houghton Mifflin, 1951), p. 627.

materials produced in Commonwealth countries. To assist in the economic development of the bloc's non-Western sections, some of which, like Malaya, are large dollar-earners, Britain has sought to encourage investment of the relatively small amount of capital that the nation now has available for export. Investment on a larger scale within the sterling bloc has been envisioned and even projected in what is known as the Colombo Plan, but Britain itself now finds it difficult to produce the surplus needed to reestablish its prewar status as an overseas investor. That status was largely lost as a result of forced wartime sale of British assets.

One of the obvious marks of an economic policy geared to postwar scarcity has been Britain's severe control over foreign exchange. Englishmen have been closely limited as to how much of their own currency they could exchange even for other European currencies, and individuals have been practically banned, during most of the postwar period, from exchanging pounds for dollars. The domestic consumption of certain goods suitable for export has been either prohibited or stringently curtailed by high purchase taxes in the home market. Altogether British policy has involved a major national effort, most austere in the immediate postwar years, to sell abroad in order to live. Especially has Britain wanted to sell in the American market, although before World War II a relatively small volume of British goods was shipped to the United States. The increase since 1945 has been impressive, but still short of what Britain wants.

Given the national need for external trade, it might be expected that Britain would have a low tariff policy. Of course, this was Britain's nineteenth-century position. Then Britain was able to compete in terms of price and quality of manufactures with almost any other country, and it was willing to encourage importing food from abroad both because it was cheaper and because the nations that sold Britain food could buy its manufactured products. Thus there was no high protective tariff for industry or agriculture. However, in the twentieth century this free-trade formula ceased to seem so evidently to Britain's net advantage. British manufacturers now encountered difficulties in foreign markets from newer industries of other countries; some of these newer industries were more efficient, some employed cheaper labor, and some were protected in their own markets by tariffs. Furthermore, the general terms of trade were not always to Britain's advantage—that is, world prices of food and raw materials, especially in the 1940's, rose in relation to prices for manufactured goods. Additional cause for the British to reexamine their trade policy was provided by the problem

of importing food during two world wars. The result of all these circumstances has been a substantial revision of British trade policy during the last several decades. Although more than ever concerned that
other countries, particularly the United States, should not have high
tariffs against British manufactured goods, Britain has nevertheless re-
treated from free trade. Even apart from the stringent but evidently
temporary control over imports since World War II, Britain has for
some time protected agriculture and selected manufacturing industries.

Closely linked to Britain's limited protective system is Imperial
Preference. Under this arrangement, largely the product of the 1930's,
Britain and other Commonwealth nations have negotiated reciprocal
tariff advantages. The object is to encourage intra-Commonwealth
trade, and from the British standpoint to provide a protected non-
domestic market for manufactured goods in exchange for discrimination in favor of Commonwealth agricultural products in the home
market. An extension of this arrangement, in the direction of strictly
Commonwealth free trade, is often suggested as a major alternative
for British economic policy. It is particularly popular among rank-
and-file Conservative believers in the closer imperial ties advocated as
long ago as the turn of the century by Joseph Chamberlain. However,
not all Commonwealth nations find it in their interests to extend Imperial Preference on a broad front, and Britain itself finds that special
Commonwealth preferences often conflict with a desire for more American trade, as negotiated through the General Agreement on Tariffs
and Trade (GATT).

Similarly, Imperial Preference has not always seemed strictly compatible with increased British engagement in efforts to establish special trade relations with Western Europe. Britain has deliberately held
back from European supranational economic schemes, such as the
Schuman Plan for a common market in coal and steel, on the ground
(among others) of special British economic relations with the Commonwealth. Although a member of various postwar agencies designed
to aid European recovery, especially the Organization for European
Economic Cooperation, Britain has been reluctant to join moves
toward European free trade. Only in 1956 was there some sign of
British reconsideration. The discussion at that time of a European
common market by France, Western Germany, Italy, and the Benelux
countries elicited a much more favorable British response than had
any previous suggestion. The Chancellor of the Exchequer granted the
advantages of a European free-trade area, and seemed to regard it as
feasible provided foodstuffs, livestock feed, drink and tobacco could

still be protected by individual nations within the trading area.[30] He meant that Britain would have to be allowed to discriminate not only in favor of its own domestic production of those items, but also in favor of Commonwealth production.

Although it must be recognized that a decision to join even a partial free-trade area in Europe would represent a substantial change in British policy, such a decision could not cause Britain to diminish its concern with world trade generally. No continental source can supply the wide range of materials that Britain draws from all parts of the world. In fact, the continent too is dependent on many of the same non-European supplies. Oil, for instance, must be imported in large quantities from overseas. Britain is thus bound to try to maintain its ocean trade routes, and to regard any threat to a key point like the Suez Canal as a threat to the national economy.

D. Security policy

Britain alone cannot protect itself against aggression. The island's location, vulnerability, and limited resources require protection in the form of collective arrangements with other nations, and would so require even without the special hazards of nuclear weapons. Strictly speaking it may be said that modern Britain never relied solely on its own military capacities. The traditional effort to maintain a European balance of power necessarily involved joining some nations against others. However, before World War I this policy, combined with command of the seas, allowed Britain considerable freedom of action and certainly a sense of having the national destiny in its own hands. The change in Britain's relative position may not have been fully appreciated until World War II, but in 1940 even the magnificent stand against Hitler could not conceal Britain's inability to protect its far-flung interests without the aid of a stronger power.

After World War II, and partly as its consequence, Britain appeared distinctly less imposing than either of the super powers, Russia and the United States. Britain's old problem of preventing an aggressive enemy from dominating the continent was made more difficult than ever. Against Russia after 1945, even more apparently than against Germany in the 1930's, no British-led combination of European states was strong enough to maintain a balance of power. Security against Russian domination of the continent required American participation. Accordingly the cornerstone of Britain's postwar European policy has been to obtain an American commitment, of a sort denied before

---

[30] *Weekly Hansard,* 23-25 Oct. 1956, col. 462.

World War II, to defend Western Europe, and by this means to deter aggression. American involvement in the North Atlantic Pact is thus viewed as a prime diplomatic success. As a leading British diplomatic historian has written of the treaty, "It is indeed in one sense the culmination of British policy during the last half century." [31] That is, Britain has at last, through an outside ally, succeeded in righting the European balance of power which, in the twentieth century, Britain was unable to maintain. From this viewpoint, British participation in the military arrangements of the Western European Union, though a sharp departure in British policy, is decidedly subordinate to membership with America in the North Atlantic Treaty Organization.

Status as a junior partner in an alliance is a new experience for Britain, and the relation is maintained with misgivings. The British have usually tended, since 1947, to be fearful that American policy toward Russia would be too provocative, too zealously anti-Communist, and too uncompromising. Reaching a high point in 1950-51, this suspicion has since that time declined but not vanished. It is the British who have pressed for conciliatory meetings of the Big Four. Also there have been fears that the United States, as it assumed more and more responsibility for checking Asian Communism, might not concentrate sufficiently on European defense. In particular, Britain has not shared the hostility of the United States to Communist China, whose government the British recognized in accord with their traditional diplomatic practice and also in accord with their postwar policy of accommodation to new regimes in Asia. In late 1950, when the Korean War threatened to involve a major American commitment, Winston Churchill was surely expressing general British feelings when he said that the sooner "the Far Eastern diversion" could be stabilized the better. It is in Europe, he said, that the world cause will be decided. "Perhaps," Churchill noted, "we are biased by the fact that we all live there or thereabouts. But none the less, one cannot conceive that our natural bias has in any way distorted the actual facts." [32] The subsequent American decision to strengthen the North Atlantic Treaty Organization met with a strongly positive British response. Britain's substantial contribution to European defense, as part of the price for greater American efforts, left no doubt about the primacy of British concern.

Toward the Middle East, British attitudes vis-à-vis American have

---

[31] Sir Charles Webster in *United Kingdom Policy*, ed. by Sir Charles Webster (London: Royal Institute of International Affairs, 1950), p. 26.

[32] 481 *H. C. Deb.* 1336 (30 Nov. 1950).

been very different from those relating to the Far East. Britain's involvement in the Middle East, traditional because of the area's geographic relation to sea routes to India and Australia, has increased in recent decades because of a dependence on the oil resources of the Persian Gulf. The need to secure the Middle Eastern oil supply added to the strategic reasons requiring Britain to safeguard the Suez Canal. In the words of a distinguished British soldier, "It has been an axiom of British policy that no hostile Power should be allowed to establish itself within striking distance of Suez, and we have fought immense campaigns in support of this policy." [33] At the end of World War II the Middle East appeared to have been secured, but Britain's general influence in the whole of the Mediterranean was visibly weakened by 1947 when the problem of defending Turkey and Greece against Communist aggression had to be turned over to the United States. Britain's inability to solve the postwar Palestinian problem, together with the rise of Arab nationalism, created difficulties for the established British policy of supporting friendly Middle Eastern governments with economic and military aid. This policy has gradually been crumbling under the impact of anti-Western nationalist movements. By 1956 only remnants of British tutelage remained in the Arab world.

Britain's choice in deciding how to deal with Middle Eastern nationalism has been hard. At least until 1956 British policy tended to be accommodating. For example, the seizure of the Anglo-Iranian oil company prompted no military response. And Britain long refrained from siding with Israel against its Arab enemies. Britain went so far as to yield, in 1954, to Egypt's demands that British troops be withdrawn from the Suez Canal Zone. It was only the subsequent seizure of the Suez Canal Company by the Egyptian dictatorship—six weeks after the last British troops were withdrawn—that was too much for Britain. Finally in 1956, along with France, Britain used force in an attempt to reassert control over the future of the canal. The failure of this move may well mark the end of British influence in the Middle East, and thus the transfer to the United States of responsibility for checking Russian infiltration in the region and for dealing with an increasingly intransigent Arab nationalism. Nevertheless, so far in the postwar years Britain has persisted in exercising some of this responsibility despite limited resources and limited backing. The fact that the United States has often stood apart from British involvement has troubled Britain, and particularly Conservative Governments.

---

[33] Ian Jacob in *United Kingdom Policy, ibid.,* p. 51.

The difficulty in the way of British action in the Middle East, or of independent action anywhere, has been that the nation's military potential requires American help for any major campaign. Anything that risks war against Russia, or against Russian "volunteers," needs American support, and even many a lesser risk needs American economic assistance. This is so despite the respectable strength and fighting quality of Britain's military establishment, and the fact that Britain has manufactured its own hydrogen bomb. None of Britain's considerable preparedness—achieved, incidentally, with American help —is thought sufficient for the nation alone, or with Western European allies, to risk war against a major enemy. This makes understandable the Government's moves in 1957 to reduce the size of the armed forces.

A point that remains to be discussed is British membership in the United Nations. As one of the founding Big Five, Britain is a permanent member of the Security Council and a prominent participant in U.N. affairs generally. Except in the Suez altercation, Britain has tended to join in majority decisions of the organization. However, official British policy has never relied primarily on the United Nations as the agency for maintaining national security against aggression. Although many Englishmen, particularly liberals and Labour party members, display a considerable emotional attachment to U.N. ideals, British policy-makers have understandably found alliances like the North Atlantic Treaty Organization sturdier shields than the U.N. Charter. Britain has been anxious primarily to maintain the United Nations as a gathering place for all nations, including Communist nations, so that opportunities for discussion, negotiation, and compromise are available.

IV.   Summary

The best way to summarize recent British foreign policy is to say that it seeks to meet immense responsibilities with severely limited resources. The diminution of British power, relative to the rest of the world, is a cardinal feature of the international situation in the twentieth century. It is only less noticeable than such other international phenomena as new superpowers or Asian nationalism because Britain has been going down and not up. The consequence for the rest of the world, as well as for the British themselves, may be just as serious even if not so obvious.

A drastic alternative, which the British have not accepted and which perhaps could not be consistent with national survival, is to drop out entirely as a world power and assume the "Little England" role that was advocated once before, in the mid-nineteenth century. The model might be the Netherlands, Switzerland, or Sweden. For the present, however, Britain's intentions do not involve an abdication of power and influence, and certainly not a surrender of the international policies enabling an island population of fifty million to survive. Even the accommodations that Britain has made to nationalist elements in the Commonwealth have been designed to retain British status in a revised form. Furthermore, the British have maintained a considerable share of the responsibility of defending themselves and others from Communist aggression. Neutralism as between East and West has so far been well in the background of British consciousness. Most Englishmen have been able to view the United States as a powerful ally brought in to help a common cause, and not as a nation using Britain for its separate purposes.

Whatever frustrations postwar British policy has encountered flow from limited British power in the contemporary world. It is unreasonable to attribute recent difficulties to the policy-making process itself. As before, British decisions are made by an executive authority advised by specialists in foreign affairs. Allowing for the fact that the fear of modern war, in Britain as elsewhere, involves popular pressure for peace-making governmental policies, there seems nothing novel about the present need of the British executive to obtain public support against a partisan opposition. Much more stringent limits on the freedom of decision-making arise from a world situation in which Britain cannot afford the consequences of an independent foreign policy.

Selected Bibliography

Churchill, Sir Winston, *The Second World War* (Boston: Houghton Mifflin, 1951).

Jennings, W. Ivor, *The Commonwealth in Asia* (London: Oxford University Press, 1951).

Nicolson, Harold, *Diplomacy* (London: Oxford University Press, 1950).

Strang, Lord, *The Foreign Office* (New York: Oxford University Press, 1955).

Ward, A. W., and G. P. Gooch, eds., *The Cambridge History of British Foreign Policy, 1783-1919* (London: Cambridge University Press, 1922-23).

Webster, Sir Charles, *United Kingdom Policy* (London: Royal Institute of International Affairs, 1950).

Woodward, E. L., and Rohan Butler, eds., *Documents on British Foreign Policy, 1919-1939* (London: H. M. Stationery Office, 1947-54).

3 . . .

FRENCH FOREIGN POLICY

. . . Roy C. Macridis

Introduction

The dilemma confronting French foreign policy today may be stated in rather simple terms. France, incontestably one of the great powers of the nineteenth century, has found her position in the world progressively declining. The aspiration and the illusion of greatness and strength, however, have persisted.

France emerged from World War II without a navy and with an army of only a few divisions; with her economy seriously undermined after some four years of occupation; drained of manpower; facing urgent problems of economic and social reconstruction at home. Her situation was such that her aspirations to remain a great power could not possibly be realized without a clear perception of the heavy mortgage that underlay her position—namely her dependence upon Britain and, primarily, the United States.

This dependence called for a retrenchment in her foreign commitments and for a careful choice, among the many alternatives, of a course of action that was consistent with the realities of the French position and strength. If one were to use Walter Lippman's axiom that commitments in foreign policy must be commensurate with strength, it was very clear that there were few commitments that France could undertake and carry out successfully without Anglo-American support. France's liberty of action, therefore, was limited. Her position in the world was a borrowed one, with the lender free to maintain it or to withdraw it.

So the dilemma involved either the acceptance of the realities of the post-World War II situation, or a continuation of France's "vocation of greatness" without the physical and economic resources to implement it. The dilemma runs throughout the years after the Liberation and may continue to plague the country in the future. Neither the political system nor the political parties and the press have managed to present it to the public in clear-cut terms. There has been no "great debate" and no "agonizing reappraisal" for the purpose of redefining the French position and status in the world. Lip service continues to be paid to nineteenth-century myths and no political party has ever dared reexamine them critically and frankly. And while France continues to act in terms of her nineteenth-century myths, her position in the new power structure created after World War II is becoming increasingly difficult. As the gap between ideology and reality grows, the strains upon the social and the political system become greater. The latter, unable to clarify issues and formulate new perspectives, becomes in a real sense the captive of the prevalent ideology, so that the gap is still further widened instead of being bridged!

To explain the nature of the dilemma and to indicate how and why the political system has failed thus far to face up to it will be the purpose of this chapter, which, it is hoped, will also bring to light some interesting material for comparative analysis, especially when the position of France is compared with that of Great Britain and Germany. We shall first discuss briefly the most important factors that have shaped French foreign policy—its geographic position, its economic and social development, its cultural influence, and some of its more persistent interests. Next we shall discuss the French political institutions and their role in the elaboration and the formulation of foreign policy. Finally, we shall discuss the basic patterns of foreign policy pursued by France, especially in the last decade. Throughout our discussion we shall bear in mind the fundamental problem we have posed—the discrepancy between aspiration and reality—inquiring into the reasons why this discrepancy has been allowed to persist.

I.   Background Factors

A number of interacting factors constitute the setting in which foreign policy operates. Some of these factors are objective ones—they can be easily measured and compared; others are subjective and constitute the image a community has of itself in the world. Among the objective factors the most important are the nation's economic strength, its geographic position, its military potential and technological know-how, its culture, and the diffusion of its culture in other parts of the world. The subjective factors are primarily ideological; they can be studied with reference to the various elites of the system and to the particular conception the elites have of their country's role in the world. Important among those elites is, of course, the political leadership. Subjective and objective factors constantly interact to give to foreign policy a dynamic and ever-changing pattern; however, such interaction may be impeded for various reasons, so that the "reality," *i.e.* the objective factor, may be at variance with "ideology," *i.e.* the subjective factor. As we pointed out, this might be a tenable hypothesis to explain French foreign policy in the twentieth century.

A.   The French economy

In the early part of the nineteenth century France had one of the most highly developed economic system in the world. Her population was one of the most numerous and, like Great Britain, the country was going through a process of rapid industrialization. Her agriculture was the most prosperous in Europe. Throughout the century the French economy continued to develop. In the period of Napoleon III (1851-1870) industrialization continued, capital investment increased rapidly, the accumulation of capital and the rate of urbanization were accelerated and the demographic ratio between the town and farm was accordingly modified—though the agricultural population remained larger than the urban population.

In the latter part of the nineteenth century French economic development continued, but the rate of growth began already to show a slackening while investment assumed some peculiarities that are worth observing. French savings grew at a remarkable rate, but they were not reflected in the growth of internal capital investment. The French became lenders, but not investors, and they invariably preferred foreign markets to their own market. Huge loans were made to various East European and Balkan nations, particularly to Russia, which paid a good interest. World War I wiped out most of these loans.

By the end of the century, and more particularly in the years between the two world wars, the French economy showed signs of decline. Its rate of growth fell below that of Germany, England, and the United States; the productivity of the French worker was low in comparison to that of the British, the American, or the German worker; the ratio between town and farm continued to show an increase of urbanization, but the rate of growth remained far below that of these three countries. Even today more than 40 per cent of the gainfully employed persons in France can be classed as farmers. What is more, agricultural productivity in France declined because of the fragmentation of farms and the resulting inability of the French farmer to use mechanical equipment and fertilizers. By the turn of the century agriculture had become in a sense a liability in France and an impediment to industrialization. The farmers demanded protection for their high-priced products and they got it. France evolved a protectionist tariff policy, which maintained a highly inflated domestic price structure. At the same time, agricultural production found a number of outlets that were both economically and socially wasteful. The production of wine and alcohol was so much in excess of the needs of the domestic market that the state, under the pressure of powerful lobbies, was forced to buy and stock at considerable expense the excess quantities.

Between 1918 and 1940, capital investment was practically nil. In fact a number of economic historians refer to the period as one of disinvestment, which in nontechnical terms means that the factories and the machines, the roads and the buildings of the nation were going through a period of deterioration. The French capital goods were being used faster than they were rebuilt!

The demographic situation also had been rapidly changing. The population by the end of the nineteenth century reached a stationary level at some forty million. The number of babies born was about equal to the number of old people dying every year.

The end of World War II brought into light the weaknesses of the country and accentuated a number of them. For instance, the greater part of the foreign assets and investments of France had been wiped out; millions had lost their lives or health as a result of the war and the enemy occupation; the industrial equipment of the country had reached a state of obsolescence. The tasks ahead were heavy indeed: to stop inflation and put the currency back on a healthy basis; to rebuild the communications, the schools, the factories and homes; to improve the productive resources so as to bring production up to the prewar level and surpass it; and to rationalize and reorganize the agriculture. One factor can be given on the positive side of this rather discouraging picture—the demographic situation improved and the birth rate for the first time moved ahead of the death rate.

B. Geographic position

France's geographic position accounts for certain apparent contradictory interests and commitments. On the one hand, she has been a continental power with frontiers that include to the east, Belgium, Germany, Switzerland, and Italy, and to the southwest, Spain; on the other hand, she has had an Empire with possessions throughout Northern Africa and in the Pacific, the Indian, and the Atlantic oceans. As the French Empire developed and was consolidated by the end of the nineteenth century, France, unlike England, had to assume heavy burdens in order to maintain herself as a continental power and at the same time rule her far-flung Empire.

On the continent the Spanish frontier presented no problem, nor was Belgium or Switzerland a threat. The threat came from Germany —a Germany that after 1870 had been unified and after 1930, despite its defeat in 1918, confronted France once more with a population of over 70 million and an economic and industrial system far more powerful than her own. The Empire, on the other hand, required everlasting vigilance against potential marauders, particularly England, and against nationalist independence movements. This position called for a strong fleet and heavy economic sacrifices. The position of France, therefore, involved heavy burdens. It required the maintenance of a strong army at home and a strong navy to "protect" the Empire.

This position of France accounts for the existence of two distinct mentalities within its political leadership. The one tended to emphasize the imperial commitment of France, to plead for a strong navy and a *rapprochement* with Germany. It was clearly anti-British, since the traditional obstacle to French imperial ambitions and naval power had been Great Britain. The other mentality tended to emphasize the continental position of France, to plead for a strong army and to underplay her imperial commitments. It tended to be pro-British and anti-German. However, neither point of view could or did prevail. Germany was naturally in favor of encouraging France's imperial commitments, in exchange for a free hand in Europe, particularly in Eastern Europe and also in the Middle East; this free hand ultimately could not but endanger France's position in Europe. England, on the other hand, was anxious to encourage France in her continental policy, with the full realization that a strong French army would deter Germany and hence would allow it to concentrate on its naval strength and the development of its own Empire, ultimately at the expense of the interests of France in the world.

From whichever point of view one looks at the situation as it developed in the latter part of the nineteenth century, one cannot help but realize that the French predicament was a serious one. France, more than any other country of the world, had to assume the heavy burdens of a continental power and of an Empire. The end of World War II and the subsequent developments indicate, as we shall see, that France stubbornly attempted to preserve both.

C.   Cultural diffusion

It would hardly be an exaggeration to say that France was in the nineteenth century the cultural home of the world. From a political, artistic, literary, and educational point of view, French thought radiated everywhere. The French Revolution had given to the cause of freedom a clear-cut formulation and was carried to all the parts of Europe by Napoleon's armies; the French Napoleonic code was plagiarized by almost every Latin American and European nation; the French language was the medium of communication in international conferences and the second language of all the educated classes of the world; France's philosophers, her intellectuals, her scientists pioneered the cause of human and scientific knowledge. No other country could count on so many friends and potential sympathizers.

Innumerable cultural ties linked France with the world. Such links constituted, without any doubt, a capital that, like the Marseillaise, was just as important as ships and soldiers, or the investment of the British merchants and storekeepers in the British Empire. But it was the kind of capital whose logic calls for continuous reinvestment. It was also the kind of capital that tends to pervert the lender! With the relative decline of the French economy in the twentieth century, other nations began to attract scientists and intellectuals. The use of the French language in diplomacy and in other aspects of international relations began to be challenged. The French political system itself showed signs of strain; and some of the system's manifestations, particularly in the Empire, revealed obvious incompatibilities with the universal ethical postulates that the French Revolution had introduced in the world. The colonial elites who had studied in France and for whom French was a second language, chose to engage her in a dialogue in which the lessons they had learned became increasingly embarrassing for the teacher. But at the very moment the dialogue was engaged—particularly between the members of the Empire and the metropolis—French cultural preeminence had become permanent and incontrovertible in the minds of the French elites. It became a myth, an *idée fixe*, to which no exception could be allowed and no argument permitted. French cultural supremacy was taken for granted. From this, as we shall see, flowed innumerable reflexes which account for some of France's present actions: her unwillingness to change her policy with regard to the Empire; her extreme sensitivity to criticisms from abroad; a blind pride in her own system which is considered to be superior to that of any other nation in the world;

and finally a strong belief in the unique "mission" of France—to educate, to cultivate, to humanize.

D. The development of the political system

Perhaps one of the most surprising aspects of the development of France in the nineteenth century is the great discrepancy between her internal political instability and her stable position as a world power. Internally, the French political system has been a prey to contradictions, divisions, and conflicts that sapped the energy of the nation and rendered a coherent domestic policy impossible. As a world power, on the other hand, France grew in strength throughout the nineteenth century. Her policy showed a remarkable continuity, at least in the two basic foreign policy considerations that we have mentioned earlier: her imperial vocation—she assumed control of Algeria, Morocco, and Tunisia and extended her rule throughout equatorial Africa; she conquered Indochina and Madagascar; and her continental vocation —she created what was reputedly the strongest army of the world and became the cornerstone of the Entente Cordiale.

Internally, however, the picture was quite different. Despite the French Revolution and the great influence it exerted throughout the world, it was not before 1875 that France managed to set her own house into some kind of order and to translate many of the political aspirations of the Revolution into reality. It was only after 1875 that universal franchise became part of the system; that freedom of association and freedom of the press were realized. It was only after 1875 that education was extended to include those who could not pay, at both the primary and the secondary level. It was only after 1875 that administrative interference in elections was abandoned and a modicum of communal freedoms established. But what was particularly characteristic was the division of opinion, the sharpness of the conflict between classes and ideologies, and the inability of the political system, as such, to transcend these conflicts and to command respect and loyalty.

The French political scene has been one of division and of conflict. First, there has been conflict between the individual and the State. For numerous reasons, the Republican philosophy has been associated with an extreme form of individualism of which the antisocial and probably apolitical posture of the individual is the mainspring. Second, the Republic involved a continuous conflict between the State and certain groups. A good segment of Catholics, for instance, never admitted the claims of a secular State to educate their children, to allow for divorce, to perform marriages. Third, the workers' coming of age precipitated them in 1870 into a revolutionary adventure—the Commune—and exposed them to severe reprisals from the State and the army. Since then, and particularly after the October Revolution and the foundation of the Third International, a great part of the workers have sought to satisfy their aspirations outside or against the Republic.

The Republic has been based upon a complex of multiple negations on the part of a great many of its social groups. This negation is translated into every election in a protest vote, in which the voters vote against the Republican State rather than for a party or for positive policy-measures. Since the period of the Liberation, this protest movement has represented 40 to 48 per cent of the ballots cast for non-Republican or clearly anti-Republican parties—the Communists, the Gaullists, and the Poujadists.

If the conflict between the State and the various groups that constitute the body politic were to emerge as a direct and frontal antinomy, it is obvious that the Republic, or for that matter any government, could not survive. This is averted by the divisions that exist within the body politic among the various groups. The groups that are either indifferent or hostile to the Republican State are even more hostile to each other! Catholics and laity, Communists and partisans of free enterprise, the town and the farm, the bourgeoisie and the working classes are much more at odds with each other than they are with the Republic. Such divisions involve every aspect of policy—social legislation, educational policy, economic policy, the reform of the political institutions and, of course, foreign policy.

Until very recently, however, the government and the administration were given considerable freedom in foreign affairs, primarily because the divisions of the body politic revolved around domestic matters. Relatively few governments fell in the Third Republic over issues of foreign policy. The Ministry of Foreign Affairs preserved a great autonomy vis-à-vis the Cabinet and the Prime Minister, who was often shielded from the many ministerial crises and remained in office for a long period of time. Foreign policy was made in the Department of Foreign Affairs; it remained largely beyond the control of the legislature. Being fashioned by civil servants, it assumed a continuity that contrasted with the instability of the government. This situation, however, produced a number of peculiarities with unfortunate consequences that are becoming apparent today:

1. It fostered a spirit of seclusion in which the civil servants of the Ministry of Foreign Affairs assumed great powers and responsibilities.

2. It helped accentuate the legalistic mentality of the Foreign Office, already imparted to them by their training in the law schools. For them, foreign policy-making was in the nature of a continuous lawsuit in which argument, precedent, and proof were given priority. Thus, the very nature of international relations—the changing balance of power relations—was largely lost from sight. Even today, the debate over the various interests of France, both in the United Nations and outside, is carried out in terms of law rather than in terms of expediency.

3. It alienated public opinion from a healthy discussion of foreign policy. In turn, the political parties themselves, so vocal and articulate on matters of domestic policy, tended to gloss over questions of foreign policy.

4. Finally, the seclusion of those responsible for foreign policy strengthened the myths with which they had been brought up. The principle of imperial vocation and of continental power, the position of France as a great power, the assumption that cultural supremacy meant political strength, became stereotypes that undermined healthy scepticism, criticism, and reexamination of goals and trends.

E.   Persistent patterns

We might say in conclusion that a number of patterns underlie the conception of French foreign policy. In the nineteenth century such patterns reflected France's strength, but they slowly crystallized into dogmas and myths that were ultimately separated from twentieth-century reality. It is nonetheless in terms of such myths that France's post-World War II foreign policy is being shaped rather in terms of the new factors that developed partly as a result of the war and partly as the result of a number of social, economic, and ideological forces that stirred the world.

The French dogmas were (1) the continuation of France's imperial position and (2) continental strength. The first meant, as we have seen, the maintenance of the far-flung Empire with all the financial difficulties and obligations it entailed. Not for a moment was the notion of federalism and self-government seriously entertained. The Empire was conceived as a part of France's mission and as a continuous challenge to French culture and influence. The resurrection of France as a continental power was also an automatic reflex. No political leader doubted it. The end of World War II and the defeat of Germany was in a sense the *revanche* for the German occupation of France. Victory, it was thought, simply reestablished the prewar balance! To implement France's continental position the same alliances with the West and with the East were contemplated—all of them directed against a Germany that lay prostrate and divided. The fact that the Soviet Union had gained a foothold in the heart of Europe seemed in no way to alter the traditional French reflexes. Germany was the enemy of France. A weak Germany and a Franco-Russian Alliance remained the condition of French security. When General de Gaulle visited Moscow and signed the Franco-Russian treaty in December 1944, he was preserving French security according to the best traditions of the nineteenth century. Underlying all these actions was the belief that France, with her Empire, secure from the resurrection of German might and German attack, was once more a great power ready to fill the power vacuum that lay in the heart of Europe and to throw her weight on one side or the other on the scale of the power conflict that emerged between the Soviet Union and the United States.

II.   The Machinery of Foreign Policy-Making

Foreign policy-making in a democratic system involves the formulation of policy after the careful analysis of a great number of factors by a government that has the support of the legislature and the public. It involves the reconciliation of a welter of domestic interests and the consideration of certain limiting factors that are external to the system and cannot be modified by the system.

Today, foreign policy involves economic and social issues, labor relations, permanent international organizations, and a host of international technical bodies. International relations affect, therefore, every aspect of national life. Foreign policy has become an extremely complex phenomenon that cannot be encompassed and understood by the Department of Foreign Affairs alone. It requires collective thinking and planning in which goals and alternatives are carefully assessed before a "policy-line" is formulated. In turn, such a policy-line must be flexible enough to be modified in terms of changing circumstances as they are noted by the political leadership. Finally, the freedom of the government to decide is always qualified by the right of the legislatures to inquire, to be informed, to consider the broad aspects of policy, and, ultimately, to accept or reject specific governmental formulations.

The Constitution of the Fourth Republic and the practice that has developed in the last decade present some innovations, but substantially the practice of the Third Republic has been duplicated.

A.   The constitutional setting

The preamble of the Constitution of the Fourth Republic states in somewhat grandiloquent terms:

> The French Republic, faithful to its traditions, conforms to the rules of the public international law. It will undertake no war for the object of conquest and will never employ its forces against the liberty of any people. . . . On condition of reciprocity, France will accept those limitations of her sovereignty which are necessary for the organization and defense of peace.

The principle now stated, we may turn to the specific articles that deal with the organization of foreign policy-making. They involve the role of the Prime Minister and the Cabinet, and their relations to the Parliament (the National Assembly and the Council of the Republic). The most relevant provisions are the following:

> "War cannot be declared without the vote of the National Assembly and the previous advice of the Council of the Republic" (Art. 7). [It should be noted that the advice of the Council of the Republic need not be favorable. This, together with the fact that the Prime Minister and his Cabinet are not responsible to the Council of the Republic, might lead us to believe that the second Chamber does not participate in the formulation of foreign policy.]

> "The President of the Republic is kept informed of international negotiations. He signs and ratifies treaties" (Art. 30). [Since the President of the Republic is not politically responsible, all his actions in negotiating and ratifying treaties are carried out in his name by the Prime Minister and the Cabinet.]

However, it should be noted that the President of the Republic (i.e. the Prime Minister) cannot sign and ratify all treaties. Article 27 provides that:

> "Treaties relating to international organization, peace treaties, commercial treaties and treaties which commit the finances of the State, those which concern the personal status and property rights of French citizens abroad; those affecting internal French laws, and those which carry with them the cession or the acquisition of territory, are final only after having been *ratified by law*." [In such cases, the Prime Minister signs treaties but the ratification requires legislative approval. It should also be noted that the government tends to give a very wide interpretation to Article 27 and prefers to associate both the National Assembly *and* the Council of the Republic with all actions that involve ratification by law.]

Finally, Article 28 provides that the "abrogation or the amendment of a treaty cannot take place by the government without prior authorization by the National Assembly."

The paucity of constitutional specifications on the limits and the manner in which foreign policy is formulated is due to the tacit acceptance of the principles that have prevailed since the establishment of the Third Republic. They are the following:

1. The Prime Minister and the Cabinet formulate foreign policy and sign certain treaties.

2. Such a formulation is always subject to legislative scrutiny.

3. Certain treaties and the declaration of war must be authorized or ratified by the legislature. In this connection, the ratification of treaties "by law" involves both the National Assembly and the Council of the Republic, since the latter participates in the legislative function.

4. The formulation of foreign policy, like the formulation of any other policy, engages the political responsibility of the Prime Minister and the Cabinet.

5. The Parliament may utilize all the constitutional prerogatives it has in order to hold the government responsible. It can ask questions, interpellate the government, pass motions of censure and resolutions, introduce prejudicial motions, establish prior conditions limiting the freedom of the government to negotiate. In other words, it has adequate means at its disposal, not only to control the government, but to associate itself with the conduct of foreign policy.

6. The Prime Minister and the Cabinet can at any time make an issue of foreign policy a matter of confidence and force the National Assembly to accept it or else to overthrow the Cabinet. The right of dissolution that the British Prime Minister possesses in such a case, however, is available to the French Prime Minister only under specific conditions.

B.   The governmental process

The formulation of foreign policy, like the formulation of any other policy at the governmental level, involves the cooperation of the Prime Minister and his Cabinet with the Parliament. As a result, its formulation suffers probably more today than in the past because of certain inherent weaknesses of the governmental process in France. These weaknesses are (1) the coalition character of the Cabinet, and (2) Cabinet instability.

1. *Coalition Cabinet.* In France the Cabinet is generally composed of the leaders of a number of political parties. Ever since the establish-

ment of the Third Republic hardly ever a party or a combination of two parties has managed to provide a majority in the legislature. So the Cabinet is a coalition of the leaders of many parties and groups. As a result, the desired homogeneity of views upon policy in general and upon foreign policy in particular is lacking. Very often the members of one and the same Cabinet hold opposed views on matters of foreign policy. That happened, for instance, between 1952 and 1954 when members of the same Cabinet were in favor and against the European Defense Community. The coalition Cabinet produces, therefore, a number of adverse consequences at the level of foreign policy formulation:

a. Policy on a number of issues cannot be formulated because of the incompatibility of views held by Ministers of the same Cabinet.

b. Lack of Cabinet homogeneity gives undue power to the permanent administrative services (the bureaus) of the Department of Foreign Affairs and of other Departments to deal with issues of foreign policy on a day-to-day basis.

c. A coalition Cabinet makes it very difficult for the public to allocate responsibility on matters of foreign policy. Very often, policy is the result of pressures and counterpressures and compromises within the Cabinet so that no single political leader or party can be held responsible.

2. *Cabinet Instability.* In France the average life of a coalition Cabinet has been short. In the last two decades of the Third Republic the average life of a Cabinet hardly exceeded eight months. From the establishment of the Fourth Republic to the beginning of 1958 there were 18 Cabinets. The succession of Cabinets at this rate is responsible for the following consequences:

a. Lack of continuity in foreign policy-making.

b. Lack of planning on policy-goals.

In the past both these evils were to a great degree compensated by the independence of the Minister of Foreign Affairs and by his continuity in office. In the years between the two wars, Poincaré, Briand, and Paul Boncour occupied the positions of Secretary of Foreign Affairs for a long time. In the first decade of the Fourth Republic Shuman and Bidault were Foreign Affairs Ministers for eight consecutive years, during which more than ten cabinets held office.

However, if continuity in office of the Minister of Foreign Affairs compensated the evils of Cabinet instability in the past, it no longer does so today, simply because issues of foreign policy can no longer be dissociated from other issues of policy. They are part of a whole that engages the Cabinet and, as a result, calls for a common Cabinet policy and planning.

With these general considerations in mind, we may proceed now to describe briefly the governmental organization. Under the Prime Minister and subject to the collective direction of the Cabinet, which, as we have indicated, is theoretical rather than real, the Minister of Foreign Affairs directs the foreign policy of the nation; he is responsible for over-all initiation of policy and for its implementation. Under him, the civil servants, the Director General of the Department of Foreign Affairs, the heads of the various bureaus, the ambassadors and consuls and the various attachés of the Embassies abroad constitute the network of information and implementation.

The influence of these career diplomats and civil servants has been great. They had evolved an *esprit de corps* that until 1945 made entry into the foreign service the prerogative of influential and wealthy families, so much that foreign service career was passed from father to son. It was only in 1945 that entry into the Department of Foreign Affairs was opened effectively to competitive examination. The *esprit de corps* of the Department has not been broken yet, nor is it likely that those recently admitted by virtue of competitive examinations will be able to change it in the near future.

The strength of the Departmental bureaucracy, however, and, with it, the autonomy of the Ministry, has been undermined in the last decade for a number of other reasons. As we pointed out, foreign policy involves a number of factors and interests that can no longer be represented by the Department. This change has led to two very important consequences:

1. There has been a proliferation of new agencies, outside the Department, dealing with foreign affairs. They are located in the Ministry of Finance, the Ministry of Economic Affairs, the Ministry of Industry and Commerce, the Ministry of Agriculture, the Merchant Marine, the Ministry of National Defense, the Ministry of the Overseas Territories, the Ministry of National Education, the Ministry of Health, the Ministry of the Interior, and the Ministry of Justice. Although these Departments are being constantly reorganized and their participation in foreign policy constantly redefined, the above listing gives a fair sample of the participation of many Ministries in matters of foreign policy.

2. At the same time, as the nature of foreign relations changes to include economic and social considerations and as the number of

permanent international organizations increases, the very problem of the representation of the country takes a functional and specialized character and calls for knowledge that the members of the Department of Foreign Affairs do not have. France participates in a great many such organizations, notably the European Payments Union, the NATO, the OEEC, the European Coal and Steel Community, the European Pooling of Atomic Energy, and the European Common Market. These are on-going international organizations of vital importance to France's economic, social, and military interests.

Two more general observations are in order. First, the proliferation of agencies dealing with international relations requires some coordinating and planning agency. Such coordination takes place at the level of interdepartmental committees entirely on an *ad hoc* basis. The only two semipermanent coordinating cabinet committees are: (1) the "general secretariat attached to the Organization of European Economic Cooperation (OEEC)," composed primarily of civil servants of the various economic Ministries; and (2) the "permanent secretariat of the National Defense," operating under the Ministry of the National Defense—staff organization with rather limited functions and a turbulent history of continuous reorganizations. All the other existing coordinating organizations operate either at the administrative level and are composed of civil servants or are *ad hoc* organizations to deal with a particular problem. As Professor Duroselle points out, "there are no coordinating agencies between the different bureaus of the *Quai d'Orsay* [the Ministry of Foreign Affairs] and the other Ministries." [1] There are some ministerial committees, but, because of the instability of the Cabinet, they are just as short-lived as the Cabinet itself. Furthermore, there is no permanent planning agency. To quote again Professor Duroselle, "the most striking fact is the complete absence of planning organisms. French policy is organized exactly as if decisions are to be taken on a day-to-day basis." [2]

The only planning agencies that exist, it may be argued, are the Ministry of Foreign Affairs and the Cabinet as a whole. But the first, as we have pointed out, is unable to cope with the volume and the complexity of the work involved, while the instability of the latter makes planning in foreign policy impossible. It is generally admitted that since the Liberation France has had no foreign policy

---

[1] Jean Baptiste Duroselle, "L'Elaboration de la politique étrangère française," *Revue Française de la Science Politique,* Vol. VI, No. 3, Juillet-Septembre 1956, p. 418.

[2] *Ibid.,* p. 516.

on many and grave matters that concerned her. There were many
Algerian policies, a number of European policies, a great number of
North Africa policies, succeeding each other, but never forming a whole
and never followed in terms of a coherent plan. In other words,
foreign policy-making has exhibited the same traits that every aspect
of policy-making had exhibited in the past: inability to reach decision,
competition among many points of view within the Cabinet, rapid
changes in policy-goals, and absence of a coherent program.

Such a situation can not but invite growing parliamentary interference, which aggravates the situation. Disagreements on foreign
policy inevitably reach the Parliament and become in turn matters
over which political parties and parliamentary groups take sides, thus
intensifying party warfare in the National Assembly, causing frequent
dislocations of the existing majorities and accentuating Cabinet instability.

C.   Parliament at work [3]

Repository of the national sovereignty, the National Assembly has
wide powers. It can impose certain limitations and conditions, interpellate the government, and suggest policy in the form of resolutions. It can demand explanations during negotiations, or it can wait
until negotiations are finished and then either reject or accept the
policy of the government. The National Assembly acts either as a
body or through its Committee on Foreign Affairs.

1. *The Committee on Foreign Affairs.* The Committee, like all
the other Committees of the National Assembly, is composed of 44
members chosen by the Assembly on the basis of proportional representation, so that the political composition of the Committee is a
replica of the political configuration of the National Assembly. It
elects every year a President and appoints a *rapporteur* to study and
report to the Committee and to the Assembly the various measures
submitted to it. The Committee has only a small staff and its work
depends primarily on the zeal and often the political ambition of its
rapporteurs. Unlike the American Committee, it holds only "closed"

---

[3] Very few studies on this subject have appeared. I am indebted to the material
that has appeared in mimeographed form in connection with a round table conference of the French Political Science Association in 1956. More particularly the
paper of Alfred Grosset, "L'Action parlementaire sur la politique étrangère en
France" is invaluable. Also, Edgard S. Furniss, Jr., *Weaknesses in French Foreign
Policy-Making* (Center of International Studies, Princeton University, 1956) is
worth consulting. The best available work is *La Politique étrangère et ses fondements,* J. B. Duroselle, ed. (Paris: Armand Colin, 1954).

hearings and hears only Cabinet officials. Very rarely civil servants of the Department of Foreign Affairs, and other governmental officials or experts, are invited. Its means of information are quite limited, since only its President is allowed to see personally and in confidence the information at the disposal of the Ministry of Foreign Affairs. On the other hand, he is not allowed to see the outgoing instructions and directives, nor to take cognizance of policy plans. For instance, the Schuman Plan for the establishment of a Coal and Steel European Community was elaborated by a small group of men around the head of the Planning Commission, Jean Monnet, and the Committee on Foreign Affairs learned about it for the first time through the press after the Minister of Foreign Affairs had endorsed the plan.

The secrecy of debates, the lack of information, the lack of well-defined channels of communication between the Committee and the Ministry of Foreign Affairs, and the lack of staff have tended to reduce the Committee's role and significance. Internally divided in a manner that reflects the party divisions of the Assembly, the Committee has been unable to make any significant contribution in the development of foreign policy. As an instrument of legislative control it has exercised an activity without coherence and imagination and has accentuated the inherent governmental instability and lack of over-all planning.

2. *The National Assembly.* The lack of coordination and planning that we discussed with reference to the government is of course emphasized when we observe the Parliament at work. As Professor Duroselle points out, "the lack of continuity and coordination . . . reappears at the parliamentary level." [4] The old practice, which he rightly considers to be consistent with the Constitution, and according to which foreign policy decisions were submitted before the Assembly only after they had been formulated by the Cabinet, has been abandoned. The National Assembly participates at all levels and stages of the foreign policy-making process. It does so in a number of ways that go far beyond its constitutionally accepted powers of ratifying or rejecting a treaty.

a. *Interpellations.* Interpellations are questions leading to a debate and involving frequently a vote of censure or a vote on the question of confidence. Any member of the National Assembly may demand to interpellate the government. Although, as Professor Grosser points it

---

[4] Duroselle, *op. cit.*, p. 519.

out, only nine interpellations on matters of foreign policy were introduced in the period 1947 to 1953, the weapon remains a potent one.

b. *Resolutions.*   A resolution is a general statement of purpose that reflects the orientation of the National Assembly. For instance: "the government is in favor of trade between East and West." Or a demand may be made in favor of: "a governmental initiative for the purpose of proposing a substitute solution to the European Defense Community." Resolutions are not very effective instruments of control, but they tend to indicate the general orientation of the National Assembly, which no Cabinet can afford to ignore.

c. *The decision of the "ordre du jour."*   The National Assembly fixes through a rather cumbersome mechanism its own agenda every week. It may therefore refuse to accept a discussion on a foreign policy issue in order to express its disapproval of the Cabinet, or it may decide to include such a debate against the will of the Cabinet. Though practiced rather infrequently, this device is extremely embarrassing to the government, especially when the latter is unwilling, for reasons of secrecy, to expose its plans prior to negotiations.

d. *Debates on ratification.*   These are the normal debates on foreign policy that follow the governmental negotiations and the presentation of a treaty before the National Assembly. What should be the normal constitutional procedure, however, has become the exception. The government, in order to avoid the possibility of parliamentary disapproval, attempts to associate the Parliament in its activities *before* the actual signing of the treaty that will have to be submitted for ratification. This procedure takes a number of forms:

1. *"Propositions of law."*   A general statement embodying the main principles of the projected treaty is passed giving to the Cabinet the assurance that the Parliament will later ratify the Treaty.

2. *Preratification.*   The National Assembly is asked to approve a given treaty before it is actually signed. The Schuman Plan provides such an illustration.

3. *Engagements before the Committee and the National Assembly.* The Minister of Foreign Affairs, in presenting his policy before the Foreign Affairs Committee or the National Assembly, receives their approval but often accepts a number of specific engagements that limit his freedom.

Parliament, therefore, is beginning to participate in the formulation of foreign policy. At the state of preratification, the discussion of a general legislative authorization, or the demand for an authorization of the Committee of Foreign Affairs, both the National Assembly and the Committee of Foreign Affairs introduce in a variety of ways a number of limitations and conditions that bind the government and impose upon it a given course of action. "Parliament tries constantly to intensify its role in matters of foreign policy." [5] Given the instability of the government, such action cannot but add to the general lack of direction, leadership, and coordination.

There is an even more important consideration that we should discuss in assessing the present relationship between the National Assembly and the Cabinet in foreign policy-making. The importance of economic factors in foreign policy and the existence of many international organizations have led, as we have seen, to the gradual displacement of the decision-making focus from the Ministry of Foreign Affairs to the whole Cabinet and, in turn, to the Parliament. Interest groups activate parliamentary groups and the political parties. Hence, the very phenomenon that accounts for the by-passing of the Ministry of Foreign Affairs accounts also for the increased parliamentary activity, interference, and initiative. Matters such as the Free Trade Zone, the European Common Market, the European pooling of atomic energy, and the Organization of European Economic Cooperation affect economic interests so directly that they are bound to interest the parliamentarians.

The French political system, however, seems to have taken no steps to adjust itself to the situation described above and to develop new organisms to cope with it. On the contrary, the maintenance of the mechanisms of the Third Republic is not only incompatible with the needs of the times, but also seems to be the indirect cause of the aggravation of the situation. Decision-making is progressively displaced from the Minister of Foreign Affairs to the Cabinet and the Prime Minister and, ultimately, to the National Assembly. Each step corresponds to a progressive diffusion of responsibility, to a progressive fragmentation of effort, and to a progressive weakening of the central decision-making authority. More specifically, the lack of any organisms for over-all planning at the executive level, the lack of any similar organisms at the parliamentary level to provide for continuity in policy-making, the inherent weakness of coalition Cabinets and the exploitation of this weakness by the growing parlia-

---

[5] *Ibid.*

mentary interference are the typical characteristics of the general setting within which foreign policy is made in France. There are no institutions to give it a common pattern and direction and undertake a constant examination of goals and relate them to means.

D.   The nongovernmental agencies

The discussion of the role of Parliament in foreign policy would be incomplete if we did not include a brief analysis of the role of political parties, pressure groups, the press, and public opinion.

1. *Political parties.*   Political parties are organs of opinion-formation and ultimately of policy-formulation. They not only reflect public opinion but also educate it by presenting to it policies and alternatives. They not only reflect antagonisms and different points of view that exist within the body politic, but they also tend to bridge differences and suggest areas of compromise.

The French party system, however, does not perform such functions. Parties, to begin with, are extremely numerous. When election time comes, there are literally hundreds of "lists" and it is only the expert who can reduce the different labels to ten or twelve political organizations. The French party structure is not simply a multiparty one, like that of Sweden or Holland. It is normally a ten- or twelve-party system.

Second, the parties are not, with the exception of the Communist and the Socialist parties, disciplined. Once the election is over, members of the same party often form separate political groups in the National Assembly; the center and the right-wing parties do so frequently.

Third, there are invariably parties that are *against* all Cabinets and all decisions taken. The Gaullist movement, with some 107 deputies, voted against all government before it broke up; the Communist Party, between 1947 and 1953, voted against all governments; the Poujadist group voted against almost all governments during 1956 and 1957. Such a situation accentuates the instability of the Cabinet and makes the taking of decisions a very arduous process. A coalition Cabinet that faces the continuous opposition of 150 to 250 deputies out of a total of 627 (in 1951) or 596 (in 1958) cannot have a high life expectancy.

Fourth, the French parties are committed to certain ideological positions that divide them very sharply. A foreign policy may fail to receive a majority because two parties that agree on it vote differently —simply because they disagree on other issues.

Finally, the formation of a Cabinet involves a number of compromises and pledges, the formulation of conditions and reservations that limit the Prime Minister's freedom of action. The basic disagreements are so sharp that when a Cabinet is formed it often commits itself not to take action on certain issues on which no agreement exists. Such issues often are foreign policy issues, with the incongruous result that a Cabinet is formed committed in advance *not* to take any action on a matter of foreign policy.

As a rule, political parties have not shown great interest in foreign policy on election day. Their electoral platforms carry vague general statements of purpose. Unless there is a matter of great electoral significance, the parties avoid declaring their position. Hence, the public is not properly informed, does not have an opportunity to assess responsibility and to vote for or against a policy. More and more in the last five years, however, political parties have taken a stand on issues of foreign policy. The MRP (Popular Republican Party) has been consistently in favor of political and economic integration of Western Europe, even to the extent of advocating important limitations upon French sovereignty. At the same time, it has been pro-Empire, in favor of the war in Indochina and the preservation of the integrity of the Empire in Africa. The Communist Party has been consistently against European integration and the NATO, in favor of a neutralist position, against the maintenance of the Empire and favorable to self-government and independence of the colonies. The Socialist Party, like the MRP, appeared to be pro-European, but broke in two when confronted with the problem of the European Defense Community. As for the other parties, no clear-cut commitment can be found. Attitudes change depending upon the circumstances. The Radicals are divided on every issue involving European integration or the French Empire. The right-wing groups are all in favor of maintaining the Empire, but divided when it comes to the questions of European integration. In each case and for each issue we find different patterns of voting in the National Assembly.

2. *Interest and pressure groups.* Pressure groups have been active primarily in domestic policy problems. Operating much like the American pressure groups, they exert a strong influence over all aspects of domestic policy-making. In contrast, their participation on matters of foreign policy has been negligible until recently—first, because the Ministry of Foreign Affairs remained and continues to remain impervious to the pressures of particular interests, and second because,

as we have pointed out, most issues of foreign policy did not directly affect organized interests. Only in the last decades has the changing nature of foreign policy and its direct impact upon economic and social interests produced a growing involvement of pressure groups.

Trade unions, despite their syndicalist orientation, came under the influence of left-wing political parties, particularly the Socialist Party and, since the Liberation, the Communist Party. Their tactics of direct action were used quite often to express political claims. Strikes in favor of the Spanish Republic or against American economic aid, and stoppage of work as a protest against the NATO have been calculated to directly press the government in favor of or against a particular policy. Trade unions are also concerned with all foreign policy measures that affect indirectly the position of the workers: tariff policies, commercial treaties, immigration policies, the activities of the International Labor Office of the League of Nations or the United Nations.

A number of other pressure groups have also become active. In all cases, however, they limit their form of action to the traditional pressure-group techniques. Among these groups we should note the CNPF (Conseil National du Patronat Francais), the most important organization of business and industry; the PME (Confédération Générale des Petites et Moyennes Entreprises), an organization that until the advent of the Poujadist movement claimed to represent the small and medium business establishments; the FNSEA (Fédération Nationale des syndicats d'exploitants agricoles), particularly vigilant in all matters affecting agricultural interests. All these interest groups have become increasingly articulate over issues involving European economic cooperation and American financial aid. They have been scrutinizing carefully the activities of the OEEC, the European Payment Union, the pooling of atomic energy, the Schuman Plan, and the European Common Market.

3. *Public Opinion.* The French public opinion, so deeply concerned with issues of domestic and economic policy, has been generally rather indifferent to matters of foreign policy. In fact, if we divide public opinion into two broad categories—(1) the passive, including all those who are entirely unaware of foreign matters, who are not interested, do not discuss them, do not read about them, do not listen to the radio and who voluntarily admit that they are not interested; and the active, composed of those who are interested, who debate and participate, including the "opinion-forming" groups

(newspaper men, educational leaders, political leaders, and various civic groups)—we find in France that the number of those belonging to the passive group is extremely large. Furthermore, the dividing line between the active and the passive group is so sharply drawn that there is often little intercommunication between the two. The active group tends to remain self-contained and is very rarely able to pierce the wall of apathy and ignorance of the passive group. To be sure, such a generalization must be accepted with caution, but there is adequate evidence to support it. For instance, the number of persons who refuse to express any opinion and who admit ignorance on matters of foreign policy since the period of the Liberation—which is hardly a period of normalcy—is astonishingly high.

Public-opinion polls show that the French continue to be primarily concerned with domestic issues. In September 1951, while the Korean war was still in progress and the Indochinese war was a serious problem for France, to the question "Which are the problems that interest you most?" 33 per cent indicated it was the price of meat; 15 per cent the remilitarization of Germany; and 4 per cent the events in Korea.

Public opinion is badly informed. A distinction should be made, however, between the urban population and the rural population, the first being better informed and more interested in foreign matters. All the polls indicate, however, a great percentage—ranging from 20 to 40 per cent—of persons who do not answer questions related to issues of foreign policy. No problem concerned French public opinion more than that of the rearmament of Germany. Yet, polls conducted by the French Institute of Public Opinion in 1952 showed a great degree of apathy and confusion. To quote the authors, "Four-fifths of the public had heard of the project (the European Defense Community), but they did not know whether the project had been voted or not . . . The project of an European Army, as it is proposed, embarrassed many because it is not known well at all . . ." [6]

The apathy and ignorance of the masses is sharply contrasted, however, with the deep involvement of the active groups. Foreign policy matters are discussed in detail in the leading newspapers and periodicals. A number of organizations, political leaders, educators, and intellectuals are engaged in a continuous dialogue. But the discussion hardly goes beyond this small group and their newspapers, which do not reach more than a million readers, mostly in the urban

---

[6] Sondages, Suppléments au no. 2, 1953. Quoted in *La Politique étrangère et ses fondements,* "L'Influence de l'opinion publique et des partis," p. 87.

centers. What is very characteristic, therefore, is the isolation of the "active" groups. Civic associations that in the United States and in England perform the function of a "transmission belt" between the active groups and the people are very weak in France.

Elaboration, discussion, and ultimate formulation of foreign policy is the preserve of a relatively small group of citizens. The disagreements within this group are so sharp as to accentuate the divisions and the lack of continuity that we have noted in discussing foreign policy-making at the governmental and parliamentary level.

III. The Substance of Foreign Policy: Trends and Problems

France has followed two basic foreign policy objectives ever since the eighteenth century. The first is the policy of *natural frontiers* and the second is the policy of what might be called *European status quo,* or *balance of power* in Europe.

According to the first objective, the natural frontiers of France have been on the Rhine and on the Alps. They include Belgium, Holland, and Luxembourg and the German territories that lie west of the Rhine. This was interpreted to mean that France's strategic and military interests extended to those areas and no other power could set foot there without jeopardizing her interests. The continuity of this policy is remarkable. Danton stated in 1793: "The frontiers (of the Republic) are marked *by nature.* . . . They are the Rhine, the Alps and the Pyrennean mountains." Clémenceau affirmed in 1919: "The move towards the Rhine was the tradition of our ancestors . . . It was the tradition to create a frontier, a *true* frontier marking the French territory. . . ." General de Gaulle in 1944 demanded in the name of a weak and defeated country: "The Rhine *is* French security and I think the security of the whole world. But France is the principal interested Party. . . . She wishes to be solidly established from one end to the other of her *natural frontier.*" [7]

The policy of *status quo,* on the other hand, was based upon three assumptions that have become in turn three basic policy-objectives.

1. France is not interested in any European conquest.
2. France must see to it that no single power can gain preponderant

---

[7] *La Politique étrangère et ses fondements.* The excellent article by J. Raoul Girardet, "L'Influence de la tradition sur la politique étrangère de la France," pp. 143-163.

strength in Europe. The status quo—consisting of a number of competing political units, small if possible—should be maintained so as to give France the role of an arbitrator. From this, a third and obvious consequence flows:

3. France must become the protector of small states throughout Europe, since it is only thanks to the existence of many of them that she can effectively play the role of arbitrator and maintain her position of supremacy in Europe.

The "natural frontier" policy put too much emphasis upon military strength and ignored the development of European nationalism that France herself helped to spread in Europe and throughout the world. The policy of the status quo, on the other hand, has been a policy primarily of security through negotiation and diplomacy. France, behind her frontiers, preventing changes in the balance of power of Europe, ready to help the small nations and in fact ready to see small nations gain their independence, assumed a permanent defensive posture and was ready for war only when her security was at stake. "France, placed in the center of Europe, has the right to influence all the great developments. Her King, like a supreme judge, can consider his throne as a tribunal established by Providence to guarantee the respect for the rights and properties of the sovereigns," [8] wrote Vergennes in 1777. This providential role of France in the maintenance of peace in Europe has been restated many times.

In 1919 the two policies converged. The theory of natural frontiers led to the demilitarization of the Rhine area, to the control of the Saar, and to the military hegemony of France over the Low Countries. The policy of the status quo, as redefined, led to an effort to divide Germany, the break-up of the Austro-Hungarian Empire, and the establishment of a number of new nations all over Eastern and South-Eastern Europe, with which France established close political, economic, and military ties. Of course, a number of other factors entered into the picture. The Wilsonian idea of self-determination encouraged the establishment of small states and France was only too pleased to take them under her protection, while the creation of a number of small states east of Germany formed a *cordon sanitaire* against the Soviet Union and at the same time prevented Germany from moving east.

By 1919, then, the two traditional French foreign policies had found a happy reconciliation. Despite a number of difficulties—the

---

[8] Quoted by J. Raoul Girardet, *op. cit.*

dismemberment of Germany didn't take place, for instance—the general settlement reached gave France both a position of preponderance in Europe and a great degree of security and safety. If only the world had stood still, France would have maintained that position!

It is perhaps not unfair to say that the policy of balance of power and security, which we discussed briefly in connection with Europe, slowly became France's world-wide policy. The Empire had been consolidated by the end of the nineteenth century and World War I. The imperial and with it the world vocation of France continued side by side with its continental vocations in the years after World War II—years that we intend to discuss now. We shall divide our discussion into three parts: (A) France and Europe, (B) France and the Empire, (C) France and the World.

A. France and Europe: the insoluble dilemma

The immediate reaction of France after the Liberation was to attempt to reestablish her traditional position of security in Europe and of independence as a world power. From 1944 until mid-1947, a policy was followed that for all practical purposes was identical to that of 1919. France proposed the following:

1. The dismemberment of Germany and prolonged occupation of the country.
2. Heavy reparations and tight control of German industrial output.
3. The reestablishment of French control in the area west of the Rhine by the detachment of these territories from Germany.
4. A prolonged occupation, if not annexation, of the Saar.
5. The independence of the small nations of Europe.
6. An alliance with Russia directed against a threat to her security from Germany.
7. An alliance with Great Britain.

Under the government of General de Gaulle this policy was pursued with great tenacity. Almost immediately after the Liberation in December 1944 a Treaty of Mutual Assistance was signed with the Soviet Union. The two countries agreed to take "all the necessary measures in order to eliminate any new menace coming from Germany and to take the initiative to make any new effort of aggression on her part impossible." (Art. 3.) Immediately after the signature of the pact General de Gaulle gave assurances that it was not the intention of France to "isolate" Great Britain and the United States. "Because two of the principal powers of the world—free from any conflict of interest in any part of the world—decide to unite under specific conditions, it does not mean that either the one or the other envisages to organize the world and even its security without the help of other nations," he declared.[9]

But one might ask whether the haste with which General de Gaulle went to Moscow to sign the treaty was not motivated by considerations other than the security of France from an attack by Germany, which lay literally prostrate before the Anglo-American and Russian armies. By the treaty with Moscow, France was indeed serving notice to her former Anglo-Saxon allies that she intended to pursue an independent policy. In July 1946 for instance, General de Gaulle, though retired from the government, insisted that it was the duty of Western Europe to assure the equilibrium of the world endangered by the emergence of Russia and the United States as world powers.

Throughout 1946 every effort was made by France to gain the support of either the Soviet Union or the United States and Great Britain in the implementation of her German policy. Neither of her two allies, however, responded favorably, since they both hoped to see ultimately an economically and politically unified Germany *on their side,* something that would have meant the end of French aspirations for European security and leadership. When the Soviet Foreign Minister, Molotov, in July 1946 declared himself in favor of a politically unified Germany, the author of the *Année Politique,* one of the foremost scholars on international relations, wrote: "There was reason for France, which could count on the support of her ally in the East *against* the Anglo-Americans, to be disappointed." [10]

There were more disappointments to come. The Soviet Union feared that France would ultimately become part of the Anglo-Saxon camp and refused to support her aspirations to see the Ruhr and the Rhine provinces detached from Germany. The Soviet-American conflict at the time revolved around the control of the whole of Germany and the prize was to their eyes far more important than France. By the time it became quite clear that the conflict could not be resolved except by a partition of Germany, France had discovered that her policy had failed. She had failed to gain the support of either the Soviet Union or the United States; she had failed to play the one against the other and was faced with the dilemma of either accepting the division of Germany into two zones, a division that could confront France with a highly industrialized and powerful Western Germany, or of following an independent policy by main-

[9] *Année Politique,* 1944-45, p. 89.
[10] *Année Politique,* 1946, p. 400.

taining her occupation of part of South-Western Germany and the Saar.

1. *The Cold War and the development of Western Alliances.* The Cold War, whose origin can be traced to Yalta and Potsdam, erupted in the middle of 1947. Two conferences, held in Moscow and in London, had failed to produce any kind of agreement on the problems of Germany. The lines were being drawn and the division of Germany into two zones—the Soviet and the Anglo-Saxon ones—became a certainty. The conflict implied the strengthening of both zones and hence the development of a strong Western German Republic with the support of the United States and England. France managed to maintain control over the Saar, but failed in all her other claims. After June 1947 the whole of Western Europe and Great Britain received massive American aid to develop their economy. In 1948 the Brussels Pact brought together the Benelux countries, France, and Great Britain. It provided for a permanent consultative council, for negotiations for the purpose of promoting economic development of the countries concerned, and a military clause calling for immediate consultations for the purpose of taking common action against a German attack or aggression and for the purpose of coping with a situation that constituted a menace to peace, no matter where it occurred or from whence it came. In 1949 the logic of the developments called for the creation of a large military umbrella in which not only the Brussels signatories but also all the Western countries, including ultimately Greece and Turkey, participated. The United States became a permanent part of this alliance that continues in effect today under the name of North Atlantic Treaty Organization. Article 5 stipulated that an attack against any one of the signatories, either in Europe or in North America, would be considered to be an attack against all. It further provided (Art. 9) for a permanent deliberative organization and the establishment of a common military command. Western Germany was excluded from the NATO.

These developments determined France's position. She became a permanent member of a Western Alliance, under the over-all direction of the United States. Such an alliance underwrote her security and, in general terms, the integrity of her Empire. The exclusion of Germany continued to give her a strategic position in Western Europe and the semblance, if not the reality, of national power and independence. But the question of Germany's future had been only postponed. A military Western Alliance without Germany hardly represented a solution of the problems of military defense. Furthermore, as the struggle between the East and the West not only continued but was intensified after the attack against South Korea, the prize of Germany became more important for the two major opponents. For the United States the rearmament of Western Germany became, rightly or wrongly, the logical step for the construction of a strong defensive wall in the West against a potential Soviet attack, similar to the attack on South Korea.

For France, however, such a rearmament spelled the end of whatever aspirations she had to retain a position of leadership in Western Europe. German economic development and the revival of German strength across the Rhine brought forth the traditional reflexes. A German Army was an imminent threat. Yet, by 1950 or 1951, as we pointed out, there could be no question of French security. The military alliance with Great Britain, the Brussels Pact, the NATO, and the presence of American and British forces on the continent constituted adequate guarantees. It was France's notions of independence and European supremacy that were really at stake. For a Western Alliance in which an armed Western Germany participated would inevitably come under the domination of the country that was the strongest—Western Germany. It was at this stage that the conflict between independence and security became a heart-rendering one.

2. *The European Defense Community and its alternatives.* The defensive arrangements of the Western world and the Atlantic powers appeared to have developed in a satisfactory manner, except for the German problem. Western Germany was not a part of it and the Western German resources were considered indispensable by the United States. The problem, therefore, was to integrate Western Germany's power within the frame of a Western Alliance without alienating France and the signatories of the Brussels Pact.

It was, strangely enough, the French who came forth with the best answer to the problem: the creation of a Western European Army— the European Defense Community—involving a genuine integration of national forces, a unified command and, if possible, a supranational authority to make over-all decisions. The United States became convinced that such a policy was preferable to the rearming of Western Germany within the NATO. Besides, there were many tangible indications of a widespread movement in favor of European cooperation. The Council of Europe had been established in 1949, representing all the Western European nations, with a European Assembly; the Organization of European Economic Cooperation was an European body studying the resources and needs of Europe and attempting to liberalize trade relations. The Western European Payments Union was functioning in order to control and regulate the deficits in the balance of payments of various European countries, and, above all, the Coal and Steel Community, initiated by France, had become a reality that involved a supranational authority with power to make decisions on matters of investment, production, and transportation of coal and steel among the six signatory powers— Western Germany, France, the Benelux countries, and Italy. The establishment of an European Army, ambitious though it appeared to be, was welcome in the context of these developments towards European cooperation and integration.

It is not out of purpose, here, to tell in detail the story of the European Defense Community. No sooner had it been announced and formulated that it provoked a storm of protest in France. The political parties were activated in favor of or against it. Extreme right-wing and extreme left-wing parties joined hands against the Treaty, which was defended by a sharply divided center. In the eyes of French public opinion the most important trait of the Treaty was the German rearmament; the issues that were fought revolved around the question of whether Germany should be rearmed or not. A majority of the members of the National Assembly considered a German rearmament even within the EDC to be a direct challenge to French sovereignty and to spell clearly the end of France's aspirations to remain a leading European nation. To be sure, there were many other reasons. The memory of Nazi Germany was too fresh in the minds of many; the possibility that Western Germany, once rearmed, might attempt to provoke a war with Russia in order to achieve its unification, and thus might drag the whole of Western Europe and France into a war, was pointed out; the assumption by Germany, of a predominant role in Europe, at the time when France was heavily engaged in protecting her Empire, was also mentioned. Each party and each parliamentary group saw specific reasons for refusing to accept the Treaty, while its proponents defended it also for different reasons. There was no genuine majority for or against the Treaty and it was on a procedural motion that, in August 1954, the EDC was rejected by the French National Assembly. In the meantime all its prospective members had honored the signature of their governments. It was only the French Assembly that used its constitutional prerogatives and refused to ratify the Treaty. The rejection climaxed four whole years of near failure for European defense. Germany remained out of the NATO and it was only in December 1954 that the National Assembly, six months after defeating the EDC for fear of German rearmament, reversed its position and allowed Germany to become a member of the NATO and to rearm herself within the context of the NATO and under its unified military command—which had been the original intention of the United States!

The failure of the EDC and the subsequent integration of Western Germany's military forces within the NATO marked also the failure of French foreign policy to maintain a preponderant position in Western Europe. Her security was protected better than ever before against the only power that could threaten Europe—the Soviet Union. But the price paid for this was the loss of her preponderant position in Europe.

3. *Neutralism.* While the EDC was being debated and criticisms against it multiplied, the movement in favor of neutralism assumed great importance. It is hard to define or attempt to describe it briefly without doing injustice to its manifold aspects and characteristics. Essentially, it was a movement that answered the profound hopes of the French people that, in case of war, France would be allowed to remain out of it. Some 70 per cent of the French people answering a poll conducted by the French Institute of Public Opinion expressed this hope in 1951, when the cold war was at its highest. At the same time, neutralism was a movement that tended to reassert the traditional French claims of independence and balance of power. Since the world was divided between two camps, France alone, or France at the head of Western Europe, could afford to say plague upon both their houses and, if need be, to arbitrate between them. This, as we have seen, was the position of General de Gaulle and many of his followers.

The neutralist position, advanced by the Communist Party and by some left-wing intellectuals, had other motives. Essentially, they were to weaken American predominance over Western Europe. Many of the left-wing intellectuals were motivated by subtler considerations. These were: the independence of the French nation to continue to develop her own way of life; the rejection of the realities of a bipolar world in which one had to be a satellite of one of the two great powers; an emphasis upon France's cultural and intellectual vocation (which we noted in our introductory part). For some, it was mere anti-Americanism and a declaration of France's independence from American tutelage; for others, it was the belief that France had more to gain than to lose from a pro-Soviet orientation; for

many others, it was a constructive step towards the building of a
solid Western Alliance with Great Britain as a partner, which would
develop enough strength to play the role of a Third Force that France
could not play alone.

But the German problem was again an obstacle. A Third Force
in Europe without Western Germany and without whole-hearted
British commitment could not be strong enough. A Third Force with
Germany, however, was one in which Germany, rather than France,
would assume a preponderant role. The real tragedy was that France,
weak alone, found that any form of European integration and alliance
underwrote in capital letters her weakness and subordination—to the
United States, to the Soviet Union, or to Western Germany. By 1954,
therefore, France found herself, after interminable zig-zags, equivo-
cations, and soul-searching, back in the Atlantic camp to which a
fifteenth member had been added—Western Germany.

The decision was taken with reluctance. The quest for independence and greatness had not been abandoned. The Suez adventure,
in which England and France attacked Egypt without consulting
the other Atlantic powers—particularly, the United States—clearly
manifested this quest. At the same time, the hardening of the Soviet
foreign policy in Hungary reminded many that twelve years after
V-E Day, the threat to Western Europe continued to come from
the East. Perhaps, more than anything else, the Hungarian events
strengthened French opinion in favor of the reestablishment of a
Western Union with Germany as a partner and with the support of
the United States. In other words, we may be entering a period in
which French foreign policy will reconcile itself with the realities
of a bipolar world and act accordingly, even if it means an abandon-
ment of France's traditional vocation of European supremacy.

B.   France and the Empire

As we noted earlier, France emerged from World War I as one
of the three big powers. Russia lay in the throes of Revolution; the
United States still was unwilling to assume international responsibilities that involved continuous commitments abroad; elsewhere
in the world, the stirrings of nationalist awakening were making
themselves heard but not sufficiently to cause concern to the colonial
powers. Among them, England and France were the most important.

The French Empire extended over every continent of the world.
Its administration was a vestige of the Napoleonic conceptions of a
highly centralized bureaucratic system—an administration in which
Paris through the colonial officials made the ultimate decisions and

legislated for the whole Empire. Its cementing ideology was that of "assimilation"—the notion that ultimately every inhabitant would become a French citizen and be represented in the French Parliament—a notion at marked variance with the Anglo-Saxon conception according to which political and cultural evolution of the colonial peoples would ultimately bring about political autonomy and self-government.

The history of the French colonial policy since the Liberation is one in which the instability of her systems, the inability to make decisions or to implement them, and the weakness of an overburdened and highly centralized governmental and administrative machinery produced a series of shifting and often contradictory policies. It is a story of broken promises and pledges. It is also a story of a continuous warfare. Ever since 1944 France has been engaged in a war in various parts of the Empire and, in every case, she has lost. It is the story of a tremendous expenditure that has gone wasted; that has left the metropolis, at every successive stage, weaker than before, more dependent upon outside aid, more divided internally, and in a more precarious position within Europe and vis-à-vis a resurgent Western Germany.

It is not our purpose to give a detailed account of the colonial policy of France, but rather to note some of its most important characteristics: the unwillingness of the French political leaders and public opinion to face the issue of France's position *in* Europe and *in* the Empire and to make a choice. Such a choice, inevitably, involved an answer to the question of commitments and available resources. Could France continue to foot the bill of the maintenance of the Empire, especially one in which many of the indigenous populations served notice of national independence, and, at the same time, maintain her position in Europe? Anyone who surveyed her resources could not but realize the pressing need for a choice. The British example in India, Pakistan, and Ceylon was also extremely revealing. France, however, failed to make a choice.

Already, in 1944, the basic charter of colonial policy had been drafted at the Brazzaville conference. In this conference it was decided that "the purpose of the civilizing work accomplished by France in the colonies excludes any idea of autonomy, any possibility of an evolution outside of the French Empire. The establishment, even in the remote future, of 'self-government' in the colonies must not be considered." [11] In 1945, when a Trusteeship Committee was

---

[11] *Année Politique*, 1944-45.

appointed within the United Nations, the French made it quite clear that they would not accept its jurisdiction. The Empire was French and hence a matter of domestic policy. From then on, France pursued the same policy. Any concessions made to the idea of self-government were made under stress to meet emergency situations and were never implemented.

In 1945, the new French Constitution included an impressive array of some twenty articles on the establishment of the French "Union"—to replace the Empire. The President of the French Union was the President of the French Republic; the Assembly of the French Union, with only advisory powers, was composed of representatives from metropolitan and overseas departments and territories. The metropolis, however, had 50 per cent of the total number of representatives. A number of overseas territories were, and continue to be, considered as "departments" of France, and hence were assimilated to the French Departments, administratively and politically. Algeria, Guadeloupe, Martinique, Réunion, and Guyenne are Departments. Other territories, however, are simply known as "the overseas territories" in which there has been, until very recently, little political and administrative autonomy. Another group was composed of "associated states"—territories that were to be given something corresponding to dominion status without the right to have an army, however, and without the right to have their own representation in foreign affairs. Finally, there were the protectorates (and trusteeship territories) over which France had only a temporary trust to see to it that they reached a position of maturity entitling them to independent status. Tunis, Morocco, Syria, and Lebanon were in this group.

The promise of participation in the French Union, under terms that established French superiority, was not very appealing to many colonial leaders. They all, however, were willing to participate within some kind of union, in which their independence and equality would be guaranteed. In the years after the end of World War II there was not a single former colony or protectorate that claimed complete independence or that was axious to sever all relations with France. In every case, it was the French insistence upon assimilation and French sovereignty that drove them to extremes and led to prolonged warfare. In 1945, France refused to allow for the independence of Syria and Lebanon and to withdraw her army. Within a year she had to give in. In 1947, she refused to enter into negotiations with Ho-Chin-Minh and engaged upon a war that lasted until 1954, finally giving in. The war in Indochina cost France more than a billion dollars a year; drained her of resources; retarded her internal investment policy; paralyzed her alternate plans for an economic and social reconstruction of the North African territories. It was primarily responsible for France's inability to keep pace with German economic reconstruction in Western Europe.

But the Indochinese war brought other problems to a head. In Algeria, Tunis, and Morocco, the independence movements were gaining strength. These movements, however, envisaged continuous cooperation with France. The leader of the Tunisian movement, Bourguiba, for instance, had declared in 1947: "We do not want to be French. We are Tunisians and we wish to stay Tunisians, *friends of France*, if France respects our national pride." [12] Similar pronouncements were made by the Sultan of Morocco, Sidi Mohammed ben Youssef. In every case, the French political leaders and representatives and the various military leaders in command of the French troops reiterated the philosophy of the French vocation. "France could not abandon these territories to their fate." "France intends to stay in Tunisia or Morocco." Time after time, the legitimate interests of France were evoked. Time after time, the representatives of the French government and the Army intervened. By 1956, both Morocco and Tunisia became independent. The refusal to grant self-government—similar to dominion status—had left and continues to allow for only one alternative: secession.

This situation is most evident in Algeria, where there has been a very strong movement in favor of self-government since the period of the Liberation. It gained strength after the independence of Morocco and Tunisia and in 1958 a war was in progress, which was beginning to assume the proportions of the war in Indochina. There were many opportunities to cope with the Algerian situation, however, and progess had been made in 1947 when special legislation granting considerable political autonomy to Algeria had been passed. This legislation, however, was never implemented, and later claims of French sovereignty in Algeria and assertions that France "intends to stay there" sounded very much similar to the same assertions made for Syria, Lebanon, Indochina, Tunis, and Morocco.

C. France and the world: the vocation of greatness

The explanation of the predicament of the French Empire lies in the postwar vocation of France to maintain her position in Europe

---

[12] *Année Politique,* 1947, "L'Union Française, Bilan Politique de l'Année 1947."

and in the world, in the name of past memories and past greatness. The French Empire, a French commentator wrote in 1947, in an excellent but highly optimistic analysis of the prospects of the French Union, "corresponds without any doubt to the profound interest of France. . . . France cannot aspire to play an important international role except in terms of her ability to represent a powerful association of peoples." [13] Thus the interests of France, as a world power, justified for her leaders a colonial policy that was designed to maintain by all possible means her Empire. One may question this notion. Is strength to be measured in terms of the heavy economic burdens that the Empire entails? Is it to be understood in terms of a repressive policy in which the French Army has found itself involved since 1944? Is it to be measured in terms of reluctant subjects and in terms of outposts in economically backward areas? Even if one were to answer in the affirmative, another question would have to be raised: How much of an Empire did France need? There are obvious limiting conditions, for no nation can have as much as it wishes. But even then, the extent of domination depends upon one's resources. Was the maintenance of French sovereignty in Indochina, for instance, consistent with the interests of the French Empire? For that effort made it impossible for France to pursue a policy of reconstruction in North Africa which, after all, was so much closer to her Mediterranean and European interests.

But such a presentation of alternatives is perhaps too rational. The fate of the Empire and the fate of France were invariably presented in terms of the destiny of the nation in the world. This vision was, in turn, projected into the future exclusively in terms of France's past. The inevitable answer, therefore, was given in terms of traditional historical reflexes—French military power, her cultural superiority, her civilizing mission, and her Empire. The policy of assimilation, for instance, pursued for so long and with such dismal failure, appeared to be in the nature of a privilege that France extended to all colonial peoples to be part of France. That it was rejected was a matter of intense mortification.

Over and above these misconceptions the assessment of national strength was also couched in terms of the nineteenth century imperial perspectives. The equation, however, was not the same in view of the development of colonial nationalism. The British saw in it something the French refused to realize: that to maintain an Empire

---

[13] *Ibid.*, p. 275.

by force is far more expensive, far more debilitating to a nation's strength than to abandon it.

So France continues to live and act in terms of her interests as they were understood in the nineteenth century. Her European position is, however, undermined by the emergence of Western European schemes of economic, political, or military cooperation that will inevitably consecrate, for better or worse, German ascendancy. Her position as a world power has suffered not because she has lost great parts of her Empire, but because of the manner in which she has lost them. In every case, a prolonged military effort destroyed her prestige and taxed her resources at home. No other political system in the post-World War II period displays the same inability to relate commitments to resources and to appraise both in terms of an ever-changing equation of the balance of world forces, in terms of which national power can be measured and foreign policy shaped.

Selected Bibliography

J. E. Howard, *Parliament and Foreign Policy in France* (London, 1948).

Herbert Luethy, *France Against Herself* (New York, 1955).

Donald C. McKay, *United States and France* (Cambridge, Mass., 1951).

Philip Williams, *Politics in Post-War France* (New York, 1954).

David Thompson, *French Foreign Policy* (London, 1954).

D. W. Brogan, *France Under the Republic, 1870-1939* (New York, 1940).

Edgard S. Furniss, Jr., *Weaknesses in French Foreign Policy-Making* (Princeton, 1956).

J. B. Duroselle, *La Politique étrangère et ses fondements* (Paris, 1954).

Année Politique. Annual volumes published since 1944. It constitutes one of the best sources of material on French foreign policy.

4 . . .

FOREIGN POLICY OF THE
GERMAN FEDERAL REPUBLIC

. . . *Karl W. Deutsch*
and
. . . *Lewis J. Edinger*

I.   The Historical Setting and Basic Attitudes

In all countries the making of foreign policy is influenced by the *legacy of the past*. Among the small groups of influential persons as well as among the broad masses of the voters, memories of the past help to shape the images of what foreign policy is and what it could be. Such memories guide men's imagination as to what tasks any present or future foreign policy could accomplish, what persons and institutions should accomplish them, and by what methods. People turn to memories for answers to their basic questions: "Who are we?" "What do others expect of us?" and "What should we expect of ourselves?" In all countries, memories thus fashion expectations; everywhere they influence the interplay between foreign policy and the on-going process of national self-perception and self-definition. In Germany, however, these historical memories are in some respects more self-contradictory than in any other large country.

A.   The heritage of memories

From the tenth to the thirteenth century the medieval German Empire was the leading power of Europe and claimed the symbolic and, at times, the actual leadership of Western Christendom. For another three centuries, from the thirteenth to the sixteenth century,

German princes and cities, German knights and German merchants were predominant in Central and Eastern Europe without finding serious rivals. Generations of German school children have had impressed upon them those three centuries of universal greatness, and those six centuries of unchallenged German predominance in Central Europe; but they have been given a far less clear picture of the processes that were at work in the centuries of decline and catastrophe that followed.

By the sixteenth century, Germany had had no effective central government for almost three hundred years, without suffering until then any serious risk of foreign military invasions; but with the rise of more effectively organized states in Western Europe this situation changed. France, at times allied with Sweden, fought the Spanish and Austrian empires on German soil for almost two centuries, leaving the country divided into innumerable independent states. The political fragmentation of Germany was made far deeper by the religious cleavages of the Reformation of the early sixteenth century, which left the German people approximately two-thirds Protestant and one-third Catholic. In the same period the routes of world trade shifted away from Central Europe to the Atlantic coast and to the ocean lanes to the countries overseas. These economic processes were subtle and anonymous, but their results were disastrous and conspicuous, like the decline of a patient who is weakened by a serious disease of which he remains ignorant. In any case, it seemed as if the world were turning cold and hostile toward Germany. Many of the prosperous German cities declined while French and English trade centers increased in size and influence. These unfavorable economic developments left the German middle class economically and culturally backward, as well as politically weak and lacking in self-reliance, during the time when the middle classes became more prosperous and more self-reliant in the West.

Throughout the sixteenth and seventeenth centuries German states, German cities, and German politics remained on the whole petty; no effective economic or political centers for the entire area developed. In spite and because of this situation a new concept—"Germany" (*Deutschland*)—came into use, and a vague notion spread that the Germans were a single people with some sort of common identity, some common destiny, and some common need for safety and prestige.

Early in the seventeenth century, when economic decline and political frustration had become well established on the German scene, the full force of political catastrophe struck. In the Thirty Years War from 1618 to 1648 about one-third of the German people perished in a war waged essentially by foreign countries for reasons of European power politics, with no significant result for the German people other than sufferings and devastation. During the rest of the seventeenth and eighteenth centuries Germany remained a battle-field of foreign powers; in the course of these two centuries Germans acquired an image of Germany as the "land of the middle," helplessly exposed to attacks, surrounded by hostile powers, and condemned to be the perpetual victim of foreign aggressors because of her own lack of unity, organization, and concentrated military power.

By the end of the eighteenth century two major patterns of response to this situation had become widespread. One pattern consisted in accepting the political and religious division of the country, and the almost total absence of significant military power on the part of most of the petty states into which the country was divided. Resigned to view politics as hostile and evil—as already Martin Luther had pictured it—some Germans felt free to concentrate their energies on diligent productive work in trades and crafts, in economic activity, and perhaps most important of all, in the arts and sciences.

A contrasting but related pattern of response developed in the state of Brandenburg-Prussia: if politics was evil, force and cunning were its only realistic methods. This view stressed the strengthening of the state as the only organization that could safeguard the survival of the individual in a world of enemies. To make this state ever larger, stronger, more efficient, and more disciplined was believed the only way of ensuring a minimum of security and dignity for its population in a hostile world. The subjects of the King of Prussia might at least live in a state of law, with an orderly administration and some security against the arbitrary whim of foreign powers. Political passivity and military assertiveness—Potsdam, the town of the Prussian soldier-kings, and Weimar, the town of the German poets—these became two opposite and equally one-sided symbols of the Germans' response to their predicament.

In the course of the nineteenth century these two German tradi-tions were in part fused under the impact of the German industrial revolution and of the German political unification movement, which culminated in 1871 in the establishment of a united German Empire under Prussian leadership. The new political and social system linked much of the German intellectual and literary heritage to the Prussian tradition of widespread public education and instruction. The German intellectuals of the generation that reached maturity after 1809 and experienced the closing phases of the Napoleonic

Wars were receptive to nationalism and impressed with the need for national political power. It was not only the memories of the humiliating French occupation in the days of Napoleon that made national military power seem ever more important. The growth of German industry and commerce created a whole series of conflicts with the neighbors of Germany, such as disputes with the Netherlands about the shipping tolls on the lower Rhine, or with Denmark about the duchies of Schleswig and Holstein and, hence, about the territory of the future German Kiel Canal between the Baltic and the North seas. Only military power seemed likely to prevent endless frustrations in these conflicts and to resolve them in accordance with what were considered German needs.

In the course of the nineteenth century, and particularly after 1848, the German middle class and the German liberal parties turned increasingly to an alliance with their own princes, with the aristocracy and the military castes of Germany, and in particular to an alliance with the Prussian state. Bismarck's policy of "blood and iron," which accomplished the reunification of Germany in three wars between 1864 and 1871, found in the end the overwhelming support of the German intellectuals and the German middle class, as well as of most of the German people. The coming of the railroads and the triumph of industrialization and urbanization fell into the same decades as these triumphs of power politics, and Bismarck's empire was credited for all.

To this day, Bismarck's popularity has remained outstanding. In January 1955, 30 per cent of a cross-section of German adults said that among great men Bismarck had done most for Germany; five years earlier, in January 1950, 35 per cent of a similar cross-section of voters had given the same answer.[1] No other German historical figure even approaches this popularity. In popular memory, the empire that Bismarck founded, and that endured from 1871 to 1918, lives on as a golden age. Of a cross-section of German adults in October 1951, 45 per cent identified this empire as the period in which they felt Germany had been best off.

But the memories from the period of Bismarck's empire are by no means all idyllic. They include memories of the rivalries of international power politics in the age of imperialism, and images of the

---

[1] Elizabeth Noelle and Erich Peter Neumann, *Jahrbuch der öffentlichen Meinung, 1947-1955* (Allensbach am Bodensee: Verlag für Demoskopie, 1956), p. 132. (All data are for samples of the adult population—*i.e.*, above 18 years—unless otherwise indicated.) Unless otherwise specified all data concerning opinions and attitudes come from this source.

envy and resentment of foreign countries at German commercial and political successes. They include the beginning of the themes of a German bid for "living space," for a "place in the sun," and the double image of the empire-building and colony-owning Western powers, such as France and England: these countries were seen as models and reference groups whom the Germans should imitate and from whom they had to learn how to get on in the world, and at the same time they appeared as envious enemies ready to encircle Germany for her destruction. By 1914 a very large number of Germans saw themselves engaged at one and the same time in a bitterly competitive struggle for world power and a desperate defensive effort for national survival; and they welcomed the seemingly clear-cut state of open war as a long-awaited release from the tensions and frustrations of the prewar years. The outbreak of World War I was thus accepted with enthusiasm; about three million poems celebrated the event within the first nine months after its outbreak in August 1914. At the beginning, volunteers for combat duty were numerous, and the fighting morale of front-line troups remained high until close to the end. Even after 1918 many Germans refused to accept the fact of defeat; about one-quarter of the German voters continued to support parties that insisted that with better home-front morale the war would have been won.

Some of these memories of an inevitable power struggle against foreign envy and hostility were revived and reinforced by the impact of the great economic depression that hit Germany in 1929, and which by early 1933 had produced six million unemployed, almost one-third of the industrial labor force. The image of a hostile international environment, the image of a German empire, similar to what the British Empire was considered to be like, as a solution to Germany's difficulties, the image of a desperate bid for "living space" and a place among the leading imperial nations of the world—all these played their part among the appeals by which Hitler rose to power. At the beginning of the Nazi terror, in the elections of March 1933, as many as 43 per cent of the German voters supported Hitler's National-Socialist party, and another 8 per cent supported Hitler's close allies in matters of foreign policy at that time, the German Nationalist party. Fifteen years later, in October 1948, 41 per cent of a cross-section of German voters recalled that they themselves had approved of the Nazi seizure of power in 1933. In the same month, 57 per cent agreed that National Socialism was a good idea that had been badly carried out.

The German defeat at the end of World War II, so much more

shattering than that at the end of World War I, is vividly remembered. Four Germans out of every five in a cross-section of the adult population interviewed in October 1948, remembered aerial bombardments or fire at the front; almost one in four dreamed still of these experiences; about one out of every six reported these dreams as exciting, terrifying, frequent, or intense. By June 1954, almost two Germans out of every five expressed the belief that in the future Germany would be once again one of the most powerful states of the world. Another two-fifths of the same sample did not believe that this would ever again happen; the rest were undecided.

Compared to the glories and terrors of two world wars, the civilian interlude of the Weimar Republic between 1918 and 1932 is remembered as relatively colorless. Less than one-tenth of Germans interviewed in October 1951 remembered it as the best period for Germany in the twentieth century; one month later a somewhat smaller percentage named it as the worst.

The legacy of German history is thus profoundly ambiguous as a background for future German foreign policy decisions. It includes memories that counsel fear of remaining weak in a world of ruthless foreign interests, but it is also rich in memories of suffering and defeat following upon reckless bids for world power. It is rich in memories of success in fields requiring economic, technical, or scientific performance, but it lacks for much of a thousand-year period any impressive memories of sustained political successes following upon nonaggressive foreign policies and upon peaceful development of democratic and constitutional practice. Dictatorship and war are remembered by perhaps three-fifths of the German people as terrible failures; but democracy and peaceful international relations are not at all widely remembered as successes. This store of memories is likely to limit the number of German voters who will support a consistent and firm commitment to democracy and to wholehearted cooperation with the Western powers. But historical memories also influence German attitudes on foreign policy in other ways.

B.   Images of foreign policy
   objectives

Perhaps more prominently than most other large peoples, Germans view their foreign policy in terms of their own collective status and prestige in the world at large. Its tasks include not only the procurement of material advantages, or the maintenance of peace; it is expected to contribute to the respect of the world for the Germans and thus to bolster indirectly German self-respect. One out of every three Germans interviewed in a survey in July 1952 believed that the Germans were unpopular in the world at large; and one out of six believed that they were unpopular because of their good qualities, particularly their ability. On the other hand, one German in eight believed that it was their bad qualities, their loudness, lack of adaptability and their intolerance, that made the Germans unpopular abroad.

At present, the largest world power and one of the smallest—the United States and Switzerland—are among the countries most admired; 8 per cent of the persons asked in a survey in July 1954 said they would like most of all to live in the United States, another 7 per cent picked Switzerland, and another 8 per cent scattered their preferences over the rest of Europe. In November 1953 a cross-section of young people between 15 and 24 years old were asked whether the Germans could learn anything from other peoples, and if so, from what people. Almost two-thirds of the youngsters answered that Germany could indeed learn from others; 23 per cent then named as model the United States, 10 per cent named England, 7 per cent Switzerland, 5 per cent France, 3 per cent Sweden; the rest were scattered.[2]

1. *Attitudes toward the United States.*   Germany today is a country in search of friends, just as she is a country in search of herself. Clearly, the political friendship that is most popular in Germany today is that with the United States. In June 1952, and in January 1956, about three-fifths of Germans interviewed in polls felt that the United States was well disposed toward cooperation with Germany; in 1952, only 29 per cent made the same assumption about England, and only 12 per cent did so for France. In September 1954 almost four-fifths of the Germans interviewed felt that Germany should cooperate as closely as possible with United States; not quite three-fifths said the same about cooperating with England; and less than one-half advocated close cooperation with France. To questions requiring a decision between "East" and "West," or between cooperation with the United States or cooperation with Russia, more than three-fifths of the persons interviewed in surveys between 1950 and 1954 answered consistently in favor of cooperation with the United States.

2. *The appeal of neutralism.*   A majority of German voters would like to combine American military protection and friendship with the United States with the advantages of neutralism. In March 1955 almost

---

2 Karl-Georg von Stackelberg, ed., *Jugend zwischen 15 und 24: Eine Untersuchung zur Situation der Deutschen Jugend im Bundesgebiet* (Bielefeld: Emnid-Institut, 1954), p. 87.

three Germans out of four expressed unequivocally hostile attitudes toward Communism, and 96 per cent of the respondents to a poll in August 1956 were sure that conditions of life were more favorable in the Federal Republic than in the Communist-ruled Eastern Zone of Germany.[3] Yet, neutrality appears to many a prudent policy for Germany, if not for themselves. In the early days of the Korean war, in July 1950, only one person in four described his own attitude in the East-West conflict as neutral, but a year later, in August 1951, three-fifths chose neutrality between Americans and Russians as the best policy for Germany, and in June 1956 again 54 per cent preferred neutrality to "being on good terms with the Americans" (38 per cent) or "being on good terms with the Russians" (4 per cent).

To some extent, popular images of the relative strength of the United States and the Soviet Union play a part in these alignments. When asked which of these two countries they expected to be more powerful that the other "in fifty years from now," 32 per cent in August 1953 picked the United States, 11 per cent said "Russia," and 5 per cent expected them to be equally strong (9 per cent) or were undecided (48 per cent). Later, the proportion seemed to have shifted somewhat. When asked which side they considered "stronger at the moment, the Americans and the West, on the one side, or the Russians and the East, on the other," 41 per cent chose the West in August 1955, but this proportion slipped to 33 per cent in August 1956, while those who saw Russia as stronger, increased from 12 per cent in 1955 to 23 per cent in 1956. In reply to an immediately following question, 26 per cent in August 1956 also expected the United States and the West to be the stronger side "five years from now," but a slightly higher proportion—27 per cent—said that Russia and the East would be ahead by then.[4]

Policy-makers thus can count on popular approval in their efforts to maintain a general climate of friendly relations with the United States, but they must be careful not to arouse fears of dangerous commitments, which could unite a majority of voters against them. At the same time, politicians who prefer a closer approach to neutrality in international affairs must be careful not to arouse fears of a loss of American friendship. So long as the Western Alliance appears to the German voters as primarily defensive and peaceful, these two attitudes can be reconciled. A considerable amount of agreement on basic foreign policy orientations has, in fact, developed among

---

[3] Emnid Institute, Report on *Ideologies*, February 1957, pp. 1, 15.
[4] *Ibid.*, p. 3.

the major parties and among the great majority of the electorate. If, however, new and major tangible commitments should be demanded from Germany by her allies, or if the international situation should approach the brink of war, much of this consensus might disintegrate.

3. *National reunification and the eastern territories.* Other foreign policy aims on which there is a great deal of popular agreement stem directly from Germany's defeat and partition in World War II.

First of all, Germany after her defeat in 1945 was an exhausted, partly destroyed, and half-starved country, occupied by four foreign powers. Since no central government was set up for Western Germany until 1949, the tasks of procuring a minimum of food and shelter fell to the occupying powers and to new German local and provincial governments that were set up under their supervision. When a federal government for Western Germany was established, its first and basic long-range task appeared to be the gradual regaining of national independence. This goal of independence had, up to a point, precedence in the minds of voters over all others. More than two-thirds of all respondents, and more than three-quarters of all men, said in August 1949 that they were "ready to commit all their strength to make Germany self-supporting and independent, politically and economically." This goal seemed to hold precedence even over the goals of maintaining friendship with the United States and regaining a respected position among the Western powers, equal eventually at least to that of France and the United Kingdom. The fact that the Adenauer government was able to pursue all these goals at the same time between 1949 and 1957 contributed much to its strength.

Other foreign policy goals also arose directly from the German postwar situation. First of these in the minds of most West German voters was the reunification of Eastern and Western Germany, substantially on the basis of those political and social institutions that prevailed in the German Federal Republic. Next, there was the question of the German expellees from Eastern Europe and the former German territories east of the Oder and Neisse rivers. Over ten million persons of German language and sympathies were expelled from such East European countries as Poland, the Baltic countries, Czechoslovakia, Hungary, Rumania, Yugoslavia, and from those parts of prewar Germany east of the Oder and Neisse rivers which came under Polish or Russian administration after 1945. Many of these expellees wanted to regain their former lands, properties, and social positions; and their aspirations had the approval, mild or strong, of many German voters. Regaining particularly the former German

Oder-Neisse territories, including coal-rich Silesia, thus became a long-range task expected from German foreign policy

4. *The fear of war.* The fact seems to be, judging from many poll results, that a majority of Germans hold firmly to these foreign policy objectives in the abstract, but would be unwilling to fight for any of them. Asked in February 1955 whether Germans should fight to defend Europe against an armed Soviet attack, only 38 per cent favored armed resistance; 34 per cent said that above all war should be avoided, and 28 per cent were undecided.

German public opinion seems thus largely united in disliking and distrusting Communism and Communist governments; in fearing and rejecting war; in seeking at least economic and political equality with other Western powers, such as France and the United Kingdom; and in desiring to remain friends with the United States. Subject to these overriding beliefs, large majorities wish for eventual national re-unification and, less urgently, for the recovery of former German territories in the East. In the third rank of possible foreign policy goals, smaller but still appreciable majorities desire German participation in some form of a United Europe.

5. *The sympathies for Western European union.* In September 1955 more than two-thirds of Germans polled said they would vote in favor of forming a United States of Europe; almost three-fifths in the same poll considered the formation of a United States of Europe a practical possibility; only 17 per cent thought it impossible. This favorable attitude seems to have persisted, albeit somewhat weakened. In September 1956, when asked to choose between two "solutions for the future: the rebuilding of Germany as a completely independent national state with its own customs-frontiers, or Germany as an equal member of a European union," a bare majority of 51 per cent chose membership in a European union, while 43 per cent preferred an independent national state.[5]

The favorable attitude toward European integration is subject, however, to two qualifications: though not necessarily impractical, European union seems remote; and it must not take away from Germany the sovereign right of ultimate decision. Only 37 per cent of Germans questioned in January 1955 believed that they would live to see the Western European countries unite to form the United States of Europe; and of those polled in September 1955 only between 25 and 32 per cent, depending on the wording of the question, were

---

[5] Emnid, *Ideologies,* p. 9.

willing to concede to a European Parliament the right of ultimate decision in questions touching important German interests, while between 42 and 46 per cent insisted that ultimate decisions must remain with the national Parliament or government of Germany. There the matter seems to have remained.

More specific institutions of European cooperation did not become popular foreign policy goals. The number of those endorsing the ratification of the European Coal and Steel Community (ECSC) declined from 39 per cent in June 1950 to 21 per cent in January 1952; a year later, in March 1953, only 19 per cent said it had "not been a mistake" for Germany to join in this arrangement, while 75 per cent were either undecided (15 per cent) or uninformed (60 per cent).

The project of a European Defense Community (EDC), which was to include German troops under a common European command, was endorsed by 33 per cent in March 1950, and 37 per cent in September 1954 expressed regret for the failure of the project. Throughout the period, however, polls always recorded more opponents than supporters of any German troop contribution to a West European defense force, but the levels of both support and opposition usually remained below those for or against an independent German army.

The German membership in the North Atlantic Treaty Organization (NATO) seems to have had even less popular backing. In April 1954, while 48 per cent of Germans polled knew at least approximately the meaning of EDC, only 24 per cent could even approximately identify NATO.[6] It is noteworthy that, despite these low levels of popular support, the government of Chancellor Adenauer succeeded in securing parliamentary ratification of the NATO, the European Coal and Steel Community, and the European Defense Community treaties, so that the last-named treaty failed only because of French but not German opposition.

Among the popular images of major foreign policy goals one is conspicuous by its absence. This missing goal is national rearmament: no popular majority is pressing for it. In 13 polls from November 1950 to February 1955, opposition to an independent German army declined from 48 per cent to 43 per cent, but support only rose from 33 per cent to 39 per cent. By November 1956, after the Hungarian uprising, 46 per cent endorsed in principle the setting up of a German Federal Army, but another 46 per cent opposed it.[7]

What the German government does in the way of rearmament is

---

6 Emnid, *Ideologies,* pp. 7-8.
7 Emnid, *Ideologies,* p. 5.

thus a response to international considerations or conceivably to special interest groups; it is not being driven to rearmament by any domestic popular pressure.

Regardless of popular feelings on any matter of foreign policy, however, German foreign policy-makers have a great deal of leeway so far as domestic opinion is concerned. There is a long-standing German tradition of leaving such complicated matters to experts and persons of authority; and the German government may count on popular acquiescence even to relatively unpopular foreign policy moves. Thus the Adenauer government, without encountering serious domestic opposition, has been far more friendly to France on the issue of the Saar territory, and to Israel on the issue of German reparations, than public opinion would have liked it to be.

C. Ideologies and classes

The Germans of the Federal Republic are largely an urban and industrial people. By 1955, almost one-third (32 per cent) of Germans above 18 years of age lived in large cities of more than 100,000 population; another 14 per cent lived in middle-sized cities of between 20,000 and 100,000 inhabitants. This left 28 per cent for small towns (2,000-20,000 population) and 26 per cent in smaller, mostly rural communities. In part as a result of war losses, 55 per cent were women as against only 45 per cent men. As many as 20 per cent of the total were 60 years or older, while 24 per cent were under 30, and the rest were nearly evenly divided between those above and below 45 years of age.

In their occupations, almost one-half (48 per cent) were industrial workers, and another 4 per cent were rural laborers. There were also 18 per cent private white-collar employees, and 5 per cent public officials, bringing the total share of wage- or salary-earners up to 75 per cent, or three-quarters of the total. The remaining quarter were self-employed persons, made up of 12 per cent peasants or farmers, a little less than 12 per cent businessmen and artisans, and a little more than 1 per cent of persons in the free professions such as doctors, architects, or lawyers.

Educational levels are not high. Only 4 per cent of Germans above 18 years had the equivalent of a junior college education. Another 14 per cent had the equivalent (*Abitur*) of 10 grades in school (*Mittlere Reife*), while the remaining 82 per cent had no more than the equivalent of 8 school years (*Volksschule*).

No political group can win a majority in Germany without the support of at least part of these urban and industrial groups, but there are enough peasants, white-collar workers, and others of middle-class status or aspirations to permit a variety of political combinations and to reward political appeals designed to unite at least some wage- and salary-earners with some self-employed groups. This situation limits the effectiveness of class appeals and favors politicians who can present their views as serving the interests of the nation.

Other conditions likewise reduce the effectiveness of sectional or denominational politics and encourage the appeal to national interests. One-fifth of the Germans above 18 years are expellees or refugees who cannot be expected to support policies based on the interests of a single region or section.

Many among these expellees are of middle-class background, and whatever their present occupations may be, their memories and style of thinking are still at least partly middle-class. To the 47 per cent of persons who are now in middle-class or white-collar occupations there must thus be added an appreciable group of wage-earners with middle-class aspirations—all of which could lend themselves to expression in national terms. A similar consideration applies to the religious groupings. With the population above 18 almost evenly divided between 52 per cent Protestants and 44 per cent Roman Catholics (who are somewhat better organized), Germans could only expect deadlock from religious quarrels. Finally, the main ideological cleavages inherited from the days of the Empire, the First (Weimar) Republic, the Nazi dictatorship, and two world wars, all cut largely across regional, religious, and class boundaries.

The most important underlying cleavage in Germany is that between friends and enemies of the Republic—supporters of democracy and adherents of dictatorship. In practical terms, this still means the latent but persistent difference between Nazi and anti-Nazi—between those who would like to see some equivalent of the Hitler dictatorship restored and those who wish to maintain democratic institutions.

The issue of Communism plays only a minor role. Only 8 per cent of West Germany indicated a favorable view of it in a poll in April 1950; and by March 1955 this had slipped to 2 per cent. In the 1953 elections Communism gained less than 3 per cent of the vote, and the large majority of West German voters and politicians are against it as they are against sin. Nazi sympathizers still are alternately vehement in denouncing Communism or particularly ready to play with the thought of making alliances with Communists against the West, in line with the old Stalin-Hitler pact of 1939, and with some more recent "national-bolshevist" propaganda themes. But it is in their appeal to the traditions of nationalism and authoritarianism that the potential strength of the Nazis must be sought; it is here that the supporters of democratic institutions will have to resist them.

The consistent supporters of democracy seem to number about one-fourth of the adult population. On some issues they declined to one-fifth—which was the number of those polled in December 1952 who approved of resistance against Hitler even in wartime—but on the whole it has held remarkably steady. One German in four told interviewers in November 1953, "I would do everything I can" to prevent the return of a new Nazi party to power. Roughly the same proportions of 25 to 28 per cent reported themselves in October 1948 as having been "opposed to both the domestic and foreign policies" of the Hitler regime, and rejected National Socialism as an idea; the same fraction expressed in June 1952 unqualified condemnation of Adolf Hitler; favored in May 1954 the black-red-and-gold colors of the German Federal Republic as against the black-white-and-red of the Hohenzollern empire and the Nazis; said in October 1954 that men who had worked in Germany in the resistance movement against Hitler should be eligible for high governmental positions; and endorsed democracy in October 1956 in terms of implying an awareness of shared responsibility and duties as well as rights.

On the other side, there is a hard core of unreconstructed Nazis and a penumbra of their partial sympathizers. In Germany between 1950 and 1956 about one German in eight was for most political purposes a Nazi. That is, in poll after poll between 11 and 15 per cent said that they liked Hitler and Goebbels, professed race doctrines about Jews, and announced that they would welcome the return of a new National Socialist party to power. Among young people between 15 and 25 years, polls in November 1953, 1954, and 1955 showed about 10 per cent professing favorable opinions of Hitler and of National Socialism.[8]

About one German in four was an emotional supporter of the Nazis in general, professing a predominantly favorable opinion of Hitler, his deputy Hess, and the Nazi Youth leader von Schirach. About the same proportion of Germans expressed an unfriendly attitude toward democracy and toward the black-red-and-gold flag of the Federal Republic. An equal number felt that the main responsibility for the outbreak of World War II lay with the Western powers; and that Germany had lost the war mainly because of domestic sabotage and treason. Not surprisingly, almost as many (24 per cent) wished to bar from high government positions any man who had taken part in the wartime resistance against Hitler.

On many specific issues, however, a much larger number of Germans held nationalistic views that made them potential allies or supporters

---

[8] Rolf Fröhner, *Wie stark sind die Halbstarken? Dritte Emnid Untersuchung zur Situation der Deutschen Jugend* (Bielefeld: Stackelberg Verlag, 1956), pp. 119-121, 305-310.

of a revival of Nazi traditions or policies on these particular questions. Thus about one-third of Germans polled in 1952 expressed anti-Semitic views, while about two Germans out of five opposed the legal punishment of anti-Semitic propaganda and agreed that it was better for Germany not to have any Jews. A similar number opposed in 1954 the admission of former anti-Hitler refugees to high positions in the Federal Republic, and in the same year roughly the same proportion expected Germany to become once again one of the most powerful states in the world. Slightly more than one-half of Germans polled in 1951 favored the lifting of the ban on the wearing of Nazi World War II decorations with the swastika symbol (almost every second German man had at least one such decoration), and they opposed the idea of reissuing these decorations with the swastika omitted. A majority rejected the notion of German war crimes. More than one-half (55 per cent) felt in 1953 that the German soldiers of World War II had nothing to reproach themselves for in their behavior in the countries they had occupied. As many as 70 per cent of the Germans polled said that they could not consider, or could not have considered, marrying a person of Jewish descent. Finally, we may recall what we noted earlier about the image of history that Germans hold today. More than four German adults out of every five polled have favorable memories of one or the other of the two authoritarian systems of government in Germany during the twentieth century: the Hohenzollern monarchy before 1918 and Hitler's Third Reich between 1933 and 1945.

Most of the large popular majorities on particular foreign policy issues thus seem to arise in those cases where many or all of the 25-30 per cent all-weather democrats and many or all of the 20-25 per cent antidemocratic Nazi sympathizers can agree. Where they all do so, a considerable part of the usually undecided or ambivalent persons may be likely to join in. We have surveyed the main issues that tend to produce this kind of agreement between pro- and anti-Nazis, adherents of nationalistic dictatorship and of democracy, friendly and hostile critics of the United States, France, and United Kingdom. They are the familiar issues of opposition to Communism, preference for Western economic and political connections and living standards, desire for restoring and increasing national prosperity and German international prestige and bargaining power.

The nature of this consensus implies its limits: most voters will not follow nationalist goals to the brink of war; most democrats will not increase German international bargaining power to the point where extreme nationalists and militarists would actually regain major power in domestic politics; most of the right-wing extremists do not wish to deepen their alliance with the West to the point where they would have to drop their anti-Semitism, admiration for much of the Nazi system, and contempt for democracy. Wherever those limits of consent are reached, democrats and Nazi sympathizers separate again; a considerable part of their countrymen withdraw into silence or indifference, and policy decisions though sometimes delayed or compromised are carried on by the government in line with the democratic sectors of opinion and in line with what is judged to be the relevant international opinion.

D. Wanted: a foreign policy of caution

Altogether, the structure of German public opinion in the mid-1950's favored a foreign policy of firm symbolic attachment to the West, coupled with caution and a preference for limiting the extent of actual commitment. There was a clearly accepted general goal—the prosperity and prestige of the German people on the level of the leading Western nations—and there were at least four agreed-upon specific goals: (1) the exclusion of any major Communist influence from Western Germany, (2) the preservation of peace, (3) the retention of United States friendship and support for German aspirations, and (4) the reunification of Eastern and Western Germany, substantially on West German terms. Two further goals were endorsed by majorities but were perceived as less urgent for the time being, and perhaps also as less important in the long run. These less salient goals were the recovery of former German territories east of the Oder and Neisse rivers, and Western European integration.

Above all, German opinion wanted to avoid unpalatable choices. It rejected anti-Communism at the price of war, as well as peace at the price of Communist rule. It rejected national reunification at the price of either Communist penetration or the loss of Western friendship. It favored neutrality, provided it could be coupled with continuing close and friendly association with the West, but it would not favor any overt displays of neutralism that might alienate Germany's Western allies.

These preferences corresponded fairly well to the very limited range of opportunities offered to German foreign policy by the international situation of the time. The two great power blocs, led by the United States and the U.S.S.R. respectively, appeared in a position of near-stalemate. Neither side could count on a clear and certain shift of power in its favor in the immediate years ahead. At the same time, all major countries in Europe were committed to one of the two blocs. There was no effective bloc of neutral countries; only Sweden, Finland, Austria, and Switzerland were neutral in military terms, and Yugoslavia was not being firmly committed to either side. These countries could not form any effective combination that would offer any positive attractions or opportunities to Germany.

Under these conditions, some of the determinants of German foreign policy were likely to be negative: to avoid or delay any decisions that might make matters worse. So long as really attractive positive opportunities were lacking or, like Western European integration, seemed at best very slow in coming, German public opinion was most likely to favor a policy of cautious advance, designed to limit German risks and to increase quietly and steadily the extent of German bargaining power. But what any major political or economic shift, such as a major political crisis or a severe economic depression, would do to this alignment of opinion, no one could foretell.

This, then, was the popular image of the tasks of German foreign policy. What was the image of its makers? They should be experts, competent to make all necessary changes within the broad limits of the goals outlined. They should be cautious, but determined on essentials; persevering, persistent, resourceful; they should try every promising approach, but not make any major concessions or compromises at the expense of long-run goals. They did not have to be open or explicit; they should not bother the voters with the burden of decisions; above all, they should be united. If they could also be "crafty" or "foxy," so much the better; "prudence," "diplomacy," "smartness" and "foxiness" were all considered in January 1955 major traits of Chancellor Adenauer, at a time when his popularity was high.

There was less public concern about the constitutional, legal, and administrative details of the way in which foreign policy was supposed to be made. Nevertheless, these arrangements are important, and it is to them that we must now direct our attention.

II.   The Role of Governmental and Nongovernmental Institutions in the Making of Foreign Policy

Under the Constitution of the German Federal Republic foreign policy is the responsibility of the federal government. The ten constituent states of the Republic and their governments are bound by federal actions in the realm of foreign policy; if required, they are expected to pass enabling legislation to incorporate into state law commitments undertaken by the federal government toward foreign governments. To a limited extent, the states participate in the formation of foreign policy through the upper house of the federal legislature (*Bundesrat*); this house is composed of representatives of the ten state governments, and each state has from three to five votes according to the size of its population. This chamber has an absolute veto over all constitutional changes, but only a suspensive veto over ordinary legislation. Prior to the conclusion of treaties affecting the particular interest of one or more states, the state governments have the right to make their views known, but these opinions are not binding on the federal government and may formally be ignored by it, though political considerations may induce the federal government to take them into account in deciding a course of action. As under the constitution of the Soviet Union, and diverging from our own system, the states have the right to conclude treaties of their own with foreign nations—subject to the approval of the federal chancellor—when these deal with matters not specifically reserved for federal jurisdiction or with subjects of concurrent jurisdiction not yet preempted by the federal government. These, however, are minor matters; in the main, foreign policy is federal in theory and practice.

A.   The key role of the chancellor

Within the federal government, the federal chancellor (*Bundeskanzler*) is constitutionally the principal decision-maker in the realm of foreign policy. His cabinet, the federal president, the two chambers of the federal legislature, and the federal constitutional court may under certain circumstances share in the decision-making process, but constitutionally the final source of authority is the chancellor, who alone has the power and responsibility for determining public policy.

The framers of the "Basic Law" of 1948—the constitution of the federal republic—deliberately endowed the chancellor with considerable power in the hope of avoiding the sort of governmental instability that is common in many countries where an all-powerful legislature is divided into many bitterly antagonistic factions. At the same time, they wanted to prevent a recurrence of the sort of irresponsible executive absolutism that had prevailed in Germany before 1918 and in the early 1930's. Designed for the traditional German multiparty system, the Basic Law strives for executive responsibility by providing for a chief of government elected by and responsible to a majority of the popularly elected lower house of the federal legislature. It strives for governmental stability by providing that a chancellor remains in office until (1) a majority, or at least a plurality, of the lower house agree on a replacement, or (2) a new lower house is elected, or (3) the incumbent chancellor dies, resigns, or is convicted of certain criminal acts. The chancellor cannot be impeached. Thus, it was hoped by the fathers of the constitution, neither the disintegration of a coalition nor the opposition of a parliamentary majority unable to agree on a replacement should force the fall of a government. "Chancellor Government" ("*Kanzlerregierung*") is intended to make the head of the government less dependent upon the legislature than under a pure parliamentary system, yet more so than under our own presidential form of executive leadership.

In accordance with these principles, the chancellor alone—and not the entire government—is supposed to determine government policy, see to its execution, and account for it to the legislature. There is no collective responsibility of the entire government. Accordingly, the chancellor in effect appoints and dismisses the members of his cabinet; his recommendations are binding on the federal president who has the formal power of appointment and dismissal. In turn, the ministers of the chancellor's government are solely responsible to him as his advisors and subordinate administrators, and their tenure ends automatically with his.

Constitutionally, neither the president nor the legislature can compel the chancellor either to include anyone in his government or to dismiss any minister. Chancellor Adenauer successfully maintained this point in 1955, when one of the parties in his coalition broke with him and sought to withdraw its representatives from the government. The ministers, Adenauer insisted, were his agents once they joined the government, and not those of their party. Subsequently, he dropped some cabinet members on his own because their presence in the government apparently no longer seemed politically advisable to him. Adenauer's actions underlined the fact that a strong chancellor who commands a majority in the lower house of the legislature can afford to defy suggestions concerning the composition and size of his government. On the other hand, a weak chancellor—that is one who did not command such a majority or even a plurality—presumably would have to be far more considerate toward the leaders of parties whose support he sought in connection with the make-up of his cabinet. In order to gain such support he might be forced to accommodate them, to give ministerial portfolios to representatives of parties whose support he wanted, perhaps to create new portfolios or appoint ministers without portfolios. He might have to offer important ministries to powerful political leaders who were not necessarily qualified for these posts but would bring him the parliamentary support he needed.

B.   Other offices and officials

Individually, the members of the chancellor's government are supposed to administer the affairs of their ministries in accordance with the general policy determined by their chief. As in the case of the chancellor himself, the personality, experience, and qualifications of the incumbent play an important part in determining the actual role he plays in the decision-making process and the extent to which he relies upon subordinate officials.

Chief among the ministries concerned with foreign policy is, of course, the Foreign Office (*Auswärtiges Amt*). It is officially charged with "attending to foreign affairs," and unless the chancellor makes special exceptions (as in the case of the Minister for Economic Co-operation in the second Adenauer Government), other ministries may deal with foreign governments and international organizations only with its approval. Jurisdictional conflicts are resolved either by the entire cabinet or by the chancellor alone. Other ministries directly or indirectly concerned with foreign policy decisions are those of Defense (*Bundesministerium für Verteidigung*); Finance (*Bundesministerium für Finanzen*); Economics (*Bundesministerium für Wirtschaft*); the Ministry for Expellees, Refugees, and Victims of War (*Bundesministerium für Vetriebene, Flüchtlinge und Kriegsbeschädigte*)—which was especially created to attend to the interests of some twelve million citizens who fled or were expelled from German and East European territories now dominated by the Soviet Union; and the Ministry for All-German Affairs (*Bundesministerium für Gesamtdeutsche Fragen*)—whose special responsibility are matters pertaining to the reunification of divided Germany. The second Adenauer Government (1953-57), as previously mentioned, also included a Minister for Economic Cooperation (*Bundesminister für Wirtschaftliche Zusammenarbeit*) who dealt with questions pertaining to European economic cooperation.

Collectively, the ministers form the chancellor's cabinet and, as such, are supposed to advise him on matters of general policy decisions and to decide upon government proposals to be submitted to the legislature. The actual role of the cabinet and its individual members in decision-making would also appear to depend very largely upon the personalities and relative political power of the chancellor and of his minister. A strong chancellor, such as Adenauer, can largely dictate policy; a weaker chancellor would be more dependent upon the approval and support of at least the most powerful of his ministers.

A relatively recent creation is the Federal Defense Council (*Bundesverteidigungsrat*), a sort of inner cabinet, somewhat similar to the American National Security Council. Its members are selected by the chancellor. In 1956 it included, in addition to the chancellor, the vice-chancellor and the ministers for Atomic Questions (*Atomfragen*),

Defense, Foreign Affairs, Interior (*Bundesministerium des Inneren*), Finance, and Economics. Other ministers and important officials may be invited to attend meetings at the chancellor's discretion.

Two other agencies of the executive branch of the federal government have in recent years played a considerable role in the making of German foreign policy, largely owing to the intimate relationships existing between their respective chiefs and Chancellor Adenauer. The first of these, the Chancellor's Office (*Bundeskanzleramt*), is formally charged with assisting the chancellor in his relations with other branches of the government and important nongovernmental agencies, with keeping him informed on political developments at home and abroad, and with preparing for the decisions that the chancellor may decide to take on the basis of this information. The second, the Press and Information Office of the Federal Government (*Presse und Informationsamt der Bundesregierung*), is supposed to assure close relations between the executive branch and the mass media—both foreign and domestic—, to gather and evaluate data on public opinion, and, generally, to interpret the policies, decisions, and actions of the government to the public at home and abroad. In terms of actual as well as potential influence over the foreign policy-making process, leading officials in both these offices are important members of the decision-making elite within the executive branch, the extent of their influence varying with the prevailing relationship between their incumbents and the chancellor.

C. The powers of the president

The role of the federal president in the foreign policy-making process is normally insignificant. Although he has the right to nominate a candidate for the chancellorship to the lower house of the legislature, he must appoint the choice of the majority of the deputies, whether he approves or not. The incumbent chancellor is supposed to keep the president informed and to consult with him on the policies of his government, but the president for his part is constitutionally bound to cooperate loyally with a man who has the support of a majority of the deputies. He must sign such treaties, bills, and decrees as are submitted to him by the chancellor or his ministers, appoint or dismiss officials on the chancellor's advice, and, in general, exercise his formal powers at the discretion of the chief of government, who bears ultimate responsibility for the actions of the executive branch. Some constitutional commentators would concede the president's limited influence over diplomatic negotiations, but even here a strong chancellor would appear to have the final word as principal decision-maker.

The president's role becomes crucial only if Parliament is so deeply divided that it will neither support the chancellor nor agree on a successor. In this situation—which would resemble the last crisis years of the Weimar Republic before Hitler's rise to power—the Basic Law provides for several contingencies. Thus, should a chancellor fail to receive the vote of confidence that it is his right to demand at any time in the lower house, he has fourteen days within which to exercise his privilege to get the president to dissolve the hostile chamber and order new elections—unless a majority of the deputies can agree on a successor. However, should the incumbent chancellor lose his majority in the lower house, yet prefer not to ask for a vote of confidence or let it come to an electoral contest, his dependence upon the president would increase considerably. Unless or until the lower house agreed on a successor, the president could either grant the chancellor limited powers to govern for a short time without the lower house, or he could compel his resignation. Provided the upper house consented, the president might proclaim a state of legislative emergency (*Gesetznotstand*) under which all but budgetary items might become law without the consent of the lower house. On the other hand, should the president— or the upper house—refuse to support such a step and, in effect, compel the chancellor to resign, he might then recommend a successor of his choice to the lower house and appoint him if his candidate should get at least a plurality in the chamber. He then might support his man in the above-described manner until the latter found a working majority or until the chamber replaced him. Finally, should the president's nominee for the chancellorship fail even to get the support of a plurality of the deputies, the president has the right to dissolve the lower house at his own discretion and order new elections, which may produce a legislature more favorable to the man of his choice. Whenever Parliament and the chancellor become deadlocked, the role of the federal president in the political process and his influence over foreign policy may thus increase a great deal.

D.   The powers of parliament: the *Bundestag*

Of the two chambers of the federal legislature, the lower house (*Bundestag*) has by far the greater power in most matters, including foreign policy. Treaties that regulate the political relations of the Federation or that relate to matters of federal legislation can become the law of the land only with its consent. Similarly, the transfer of sovereign rights of the state to international institutions, such as the European Coal and Steel Community, require legislative action. Finally, all treaties and other legislation that conflict with the Basic Law require constitutional amendments, which must be approved by two-thirds of the membership of the lower house.

Apart from its legislative functions, the lower house is granted certain other powers which are designed to give the members a voice in the foreign policy-making process. A majority elects a chancellor and can dismiss him by choosing a successor. The deputies of the lower house provide half the votes in the Federal Assembly (Bundesversammlung), which every five years chooses a federal president, and which can initiate impeachment proceedings against him before the federal constitutional court.

In the lower house the deputies have the right to investigate and criticize the actions of the executive in plenary sessions or in committees. They may summon and question members of the government when they choose; the latter, for their part, have the right to demand to be heard by the deputies at any time, providing them with potential opportunities to influence important deliberations of the house at decisive moments.

Most of the important contacts between the executive branch and the deputies occur in the sessions of the standing and select committees of the lower house, rather than in plenary sessions. It is here that experts from the various parties examine the actions and requests of the government and question its members thoroughly. The vote in the committee is usually decisive and committee recommendations are usually approved in subsequent plenary sessions. With respect to foreign policy issues, the key committees are Foreign Affairs (Auswärtige Angelegenheiten), Defense (Verteidigung), Budget (Haushalt), Expellees (Heimatsvertriebene), All-German Affairs (Gesamtdeutsche Fragen), and Border Questions (Grenzlandfragen).

The role that the deputies of the lower house may play in the realm of German foreign policy appears to depend primarily on the authority that the chancellor exercises in the chamber. If he commands a stable majority—or better, two-thirds of the votes—his powers are fairly absolute and his position firm. However, if he lacks such strength, his freedom of action would seem to be more limited; he may be forced to rely on the cooperation of uncertain and demanding allies in order to see his program through the legislature and prevent the election of a successor.

In the case of constitutional disputes arising out of foreign policy issues the federal constitutional court may enter the picture. It may be called upon to adjudicate jurisdictional disputes between the federal government and the states or between the executive and the legislative branches of the national government. The court may also be asked to render advisory opinions on the constitutionality of certain pending actions, either upon the joint request of executive and legislature, or upon that of the federal president alone. The latter has the right to refuse to place his signature on treaties, acts of the legislature, or government decrees pending an advisory opinion from the court. Thus, in 1952, President Theodore Heuss tried to withhold his signature from the treaty providing for the arming of the Federal Republic until the constitutional court had advised him that it did not conflict with the Basic Law, but he finally signed the treaty on Chancellor Adenauer's advice.

To summarize what has been said about the formal role of various governmental institutions in making of foreign policy: foreign affairs are a federal matter and, within the federal government, the principal decision-maker is the chancellor, while lesser roles are assigned to the ministers, president, legislature, and constitutional court of the Republic. How this formal arrangement actually functions depends primarily on the prevailing relationship between a chancellor and the lower house of the legislature. A strong chancellor who commands a comfortable majority in the lower house will have a great deal of freedom in the conduct of foreign affairs; a chancellor who lacks such support is likely to be far more dependent on either or both the cooperation of the legislature and that of the president. Experience during the first seven years of the Republic's existence indicates that the chancellor's position vis-à-vis both Parliament and legislature rests largely on his relationship to his party and on that party's strength and cohesion. A future chancellor might not necessarily be a party man at all not even a member of the legislature—nonetheless, his power of making decisions would still depend primarily on his ability to gain the majority party or coalition of parties in the legislature. The formal organization of the foreign policy-making process thus becomes a functioning party system, though it does provide the chancellor with some limited means of governing temporarily without parliamentary support should the parties fail to produce a stable majority behind him.

E.   The role of the political parties

The Basic Law of the Federal Republic is unique in its specific recognition of the decisive role of political parties in the formulation of national policy. Through their representatives in the executive and legislative branches of the national government the parties are supposed to act as the responsible agents of the electorate in the conduct of government. The existing electoral law compels all aspirants for seats in the popularly elected lower house to belong to a party and thus to identify themselves with and bear responsibility for its policies and actions. Referenda, plebiscites, and other devices for "direct democracy," by-passing parties and legislature, have been deliberately omitted from the constitution; its framers were all too aware of the antidemocratic uses to which such devices had been put in the past by demagogues who appealed to the "popular will" against the "selfish" interests of parties.

Anyone may organize a political party in the Republic, as long as its objectives and organization accord with the democratic principles of the constitution and do not aim at the overthrow of the present state. In fact, however, the electoral laws have made it almost impossible for any party receiving less than 5 per cent of the electoral votes to gain representation in the national legislature.

Contrary to the apparent expectations of the framers of the constitution, recent years have seen the gradual elimination of the traditional German multiparty system and the emergence of two major parties as the principal representatives of the electorate. These are the Christian Democratic Union and the Social Democratic Party. Between them, these parties received 60 per cent of the votes and 67 per cent of the seats in the election for the first Bundestag in 1949; 74 per cent of the votes and 83 per cent of the seats in the election of the second Bundestag in 1953; and 82 per cent of the votes and 88 per cent of the seats in the 1957 election of the third Bundestag.

The Christian Democratic Union (*Christlich Demokratische Union*), CDU—operating in Bavaria as the Christian Social Union (*Christlich Soziale Union*), CSU—represents a departure from the traditional German parties. Instead of following the traditional pattern of parties in Germany and becoming closely identified with some particular ideology, religious group, or economic interest, the CDU/CSU has managed to attract the support of rather heterogeneous elements among the voters in the name of its "Christian principles." Moderately conservative in its domestic economic and social program, the party has faithfully followed the lead of its chairman, Konrad Adenauer, in the realm of foreign policy. Its professed aims have been the reunification of Germany "in peace and freedom," the peaceful recovery of the German lands presently "administered" by Poland and the Soviet Union, permanent and intimate collaboration with the Western powers, and the economic, military and—ultimately—political integration of the states of Western Europe.

The Social Democratic Party (*Sozialdemokratische Partei Deutschlands*), SPD, is more strongly rooted in the past than the CDU/CSU

—both in terms of its objectives and its supporters. The SPD is primarily a workers' party, as before the advent of Hitler and the prohibition of the party in 1933, many of whose supporters have been adherents for many decades. Far more homogeneous in both membership and electorate than the CDU/CSU, the SPD reflects in its domestic program the desire of the workers for social and economic betterment through economic planning, "codetermination" in basic industries, and moderate nationalization of key enterprises. In its foreign policy the SPD has strongly opposed the CDU/CSU. Although definitely a pro-Western party, it has maintained that too-close collaboration with the Western powers would prevent both reunification and the recovery of the eastern territories. It has advocated the permanent neutralization of a united Germany in the hope that such an arrangement would induce the Soviet Union to agree to reunification.

None of the minor parties represented in the national legislature has played a very significant role in matters of foreign policy. The largest of them, the Free Democratic Party (*Freie Demokratische Partei*), FDP, aspires to hold the balance of power between the two major parties and has oscillated between opposing and supporting the CDU/CSU. Extremist parties have been conspicuous by their absence; the insignificant Communist party had had no representation in the national legislature even before it was outlawed in 1956; a small neo-Nazi party was also banned by the constitutional court; other extremist parties have been singularly unsuccessful in gaining support among the electorate.

The formulation of German foreign policy has thus been primarily in the hands of the two major parties. As the governing party since the establishment of the Federal Republic in 1949, the CDU/CSU has borne the prime responsibility for initiating and executing foreign policy decisions. The SPD has been compelled to play the role of a permanent opposition, endeavoring with mixed success to influence foreign policy through criticism of the government, through attempts to amend government bills in the national legislature, and through efforts to mobilize public opinion in order to compel the government to modify its position. Both parties have sought between elections to establish a clear distinction in the public mind between their respective policies in order to present the electorate with a decisive choice at election time. However, in foreign affairs the exigencies of the situation in which the Federal Republic has found itself have made it difficult for the Social Democratic opposition to formulate convincing alternative proposals for the conduct of West German foreign policy.

F.   The role of the interest groups

The constitution grants all Germans the right to form organizations to represent their particular political, economic, or religious interests, as long as such groups are not directed against "the principle of international understanding." As in the United States, there exist in the Federal Republic numerous associations that in one way or another seek to influence the conduct of foreign affairs in accordance with their perceived interests. However, German interest groups are more inclusive, more tightly organized, and occupy a more privileged position in public life than do their counterparts in this country. On the other hand, public opinion in Germany tends to be more critical and suspicious of the influence of such interest groups than it is in the United States.

Economic and socio-political interests are organized into large national organizations (*Spitzenverbände*), all of which are ostensibly nonpartisan but by no means nonpolitical. Religious interests are primarily represented by the two major churches, the Roman Catholic and the Protestant, and their affiliated lay organizations. In general, the influence of interest groups in the conduct of foreign affairs has increased in direct proportion to the gradual restoration of German sovereignty and the recovery of independence of action by the government of the Federal Republic. Most of them have endeavored to exercise their influence over national policy through the political parties and, particularly, through party leaders in the executive and legislative branches of the federal government.

Economic interest groups in the Federal Republic fall roughly into two major categories: (1) employers' organizations, and (2) organizations representing employees, independent farmers, independent craftsmen, and the professions. The former groups have the greater financial resources, the latter the greater voting strength to offer to political leaders and parties. Reliable figures on financial support are lacking, but some of the potential voting power of different economic interests may be apparent from the 1955 percentage figures of gainfully occupied persons and their dependents, given earlier in this chapter (p. 89).

German employers are organized both regionally and by economic sectors. Every employer must belong to one of the 81 regional Chambers of Industry and Commerce, which are represented nationally by the Association of German Chambers of Industry and Commerce (*Deutscher Industrie- und Handelstag*), perhaps the most powerful of the employer groups. Next in importance is the Association of German Industry (*Bundesverband der deutschen Industrie*), which represents the interests of the 38 branches of German industry. The Coordinating Committee of German Trade and Industry (*Gemeinschaftsausschuss der deutschen gewerblichen Wirtschaft*) includes all major employer groups and acts as a coordinating agency among the component interest groups. Other important employer interest groups concerned with foreign affairs are the Federal Association of Private Banking (*Bundesverband des privaten Bankgewerbes*), the Association of German Wholesalers and Exporters (*Gesamtverband des deutschen Gross- und Aussenhandels*), the Central Organization of German Retailers (*Hauptgemeinschaft des deutschen Einzelhandels*), the German Shipowners Association (*Verband der deutschen Reeder*), the German Section of the International Chamber of Commerce (*Deutsche Gruppe der internationalen Handelskammer*), and the Committee for Foreign Trade of German Business (*Arbeitsgemeinschaft Aussenhandel der deutschen Wirtschaft*). In addition to these permanent national organizations various business groups frequently will form temporary alliances for special ends, such as export drives or tariff reform.

Among employee groups, by far the largest and most important is the German Confederation of Trade Unions (*Deutscher Gewerkschaftsbund*). With 6.1 million members (1955) it not only includes all wage-earners' unions, but it is also the largest organization of salaried employees and civil servants. About 35 per cent of all wage-earners, 12 per cent of all salaried employees, and 41 per cent of all civil servants in the Federal Republic belong to the Confederation. Eighty-three per cent of its members are wage-earners (11 per cent salaried employees, 6 per cent civil servants), and the large industrial enterprises are the most thoroughly organized and represented within the Confederation. IG Metall, the largest industrial union, contributes 25 per cent of the total membership of the entire Confederation. The German Employees Union (*Deutsche Angestelltengewerkschaft*), with some 420,000 members (1955), includes about 8 per cent of all salaried employees, and the German Federation of Civil Servants (*Deutscher Beamtenbund*) with some 517,000 members (1955) about 43 per cent of all civil servants. Between them, these three groups thus include about 35 per cent of the wage-earners, 20 per cent of the salaried employees, and 84 per cent of the civil servants in the Republic. Individually or collectively, these organizations endeavor to influence the foreign policy-making process whenever they consider their special interests to be involved.[9]

The League of German Farmers (*Deutscher Bauernverband*) with 1.3 million members (1952) represents 77 per cent of all independent farmers. Perhaps its most important objective has been the protection of the high-cost, small German farm units against cheaper agricultural imports.

The League of German Artisans (*Zentralverband des deutschen Handwerks*) with 864,000 members includes practically all the independent craftsmen in the nation. Its interest in foreign affairs appears to be limited primarily to the protection of its members against cheaper imports and the promotion of the export of their products.

Organizations concerned with such matters as migration, trade, investment, tourism, and banking are obviously interested in asserting influence in the foreign policy-making process, but other groups, too, may take a strong interest when their particular economic sector is thought to be affected, as in the case of tariffs, international marketing arrangements, and wage-price agreements. Special issues may lead to temporary alliances between groups that may disagree on other subjects. Farm and industry groups may jointly seek tariff protection; employer and employee organizations in particular industries may temporarily unite to fight for or against proposed international agreements that affect them; or export industries may ally themselves to gain government support for trade expansion.

Only a few of the special socio-political interest groups play any significant role in the Federal Republic. The most important of these are the organizations of expellees—German citizens and ethnic Germans who fled or were expelled from German lands east of the Oder-Neisse line presently "administered" under the Potsdam Agreement of 1945 by Poland and the Soviet Union, and from other parts of Eastern and Southeastern Europe. There are about 8.6 million of these expellees living in the Federal Republic today, constituting about 17 per cent of the total population; about half of them are former residents of Silesia and the Sudetenland. Only a fraction of the expellees are organized into the various groups that claim to defend their common interests. The most important of these are the League of Expelled Germans (*Zentralverband Vertriebener Deutscher*) and the League of Regional Groups (*Verband der Landsmannschaften*), with its major affiliates of Silesians (*Landsmannschaft Schlesien*) and Sudeten Germans (*Sudetendeutsche Landsmannschaft*). There are also about 2.6 million refugees from the Soviet zone of Germany in the Federal Republic (5.2 per cent of the

---

[9] Figures from the *Statistisches Jahrbuch für die Bundesrepublik Deutschland 1956*, pp. 111, 128; and from *Jahrbuch*, pp. 3-4.

population), but although there are numerous organizations that would like to represent their interests, few of the refugees belong to them. Together, expellees and refugees number about 11 million persons or 22 per cent of the population, but most of them appear to have found adequate representation of their interests in the major political parties.

Mention should also be made of close to 1,200 veterans organizations, though few, if any, of them appear at this time to exercise any major influence in German politics. The largest and potentially the most influential is the League of German Soldiers (*Verband deutscher Soldaten*), primarily an organization of present and former professional soldiers. Among its stated objectives are "loyalty to an undivided fatherland," the rehabilitation of all "defamed" former soldiers, and the liberation of still-imprisoned soldiers convicted of war crimes. The pre-Hitler, right-wing veterans organization "Steel Helmet" (*Stahlhelm*) is a much smaller association with apparently little influence. The same is true for the Air Force Circle (*Luftwaffenring*) which is composed of former members of the German air force.

According to the 1950 census, 51.2 per cent of the population of the Federal Republic professed the Protestant and 45.2 per cent the Roman Catholic religion, compared to 60.6 per cent and 33.3 respectively in prewar Germany. In terms of relative strength the potential influence of the Roman Catholic Church in national affairs has thus increased considerably. However, no more than 11 million West Germans—about half of those professing the Roman Catholic faith—are thought to be active members of their church; in the case of the Protestants the proportion is about one-eighth. Of the two major churches the Roman Catholic is probably politically the more active and influential.

The supreme organ of the Roman Catholic Church, the annual meeting of the hierarchy at the town of Fulda (*Fuldaer Bischofskonferenz*), also claims jurisdiction in the Soviet-controlled German Democratic Republic. Nonetheless, the influence of the Church is largely restricted to the Federal Republic, for not only are less than 20 per cent of the Germans living in the Soviet zone Roman Catholics, but the Communist government has greatly restricted contacts between the West German hierarchy and Roman Catholics living in the Democratic Republic. In the Federal Republic the Church maintains a liaison office at the capital to represent its interests. With the encouragement of the hierarchy, the members of numerous lay groups affiliated with the Church endeavor to translate Catholic interests into Catholic action by playing an active role in public life. Thus in a 1952 poll almost two-thirds of the Roman Catholics but only about one-half of the Protestants expressed approval of one of the two major parties: 35 per cent of the Catholics but only 22 per cent of the Protestants endorsed the

CDU, while an equal proportion of 30 per cent in both denominations endorsed the SPD.

The German Evangelical Church (*Evangelische Kirche in Deutschland*), EKD, is a union of German Protestant Churches in both the Federal Republic and the Communist Democratic Republic. Since over 80 per cent of Germans living under Communist rule are Protestants and their church still exercises considerable influence over them, the EKD and its member churches have considerably stronger ties to and interest in the population of the Democratic Republic than the Roman Catholic Church. The Synod, Council, and Conference of the Evangelical Church are the recognized representatives of the Protestants in both parts of the divided country, the annual rally (*Kirchentag*) of the German Evangelical Church is held alternately in the Federal Republic and in the Democratic Republic, and the EKD maintains a liaison office at the seat of each government. Through its Office for Foreign Affairs (*Kirchliches Aussenamt*) the church maintains relations with other churches in both Communist and non-Communist countries.

The orthodox Lutherans among German Protestants have traditionally shunned political action on behalf of their church. Today, too, they exert only indirect influence in political affairs through their tacit support of the dominant liberal leadership of the Evangelical Church. The leaders of this liberal wing, although numerically in the minority, occupy most of the positions in the EKD and in this capacity endeavor to exercise some influence in both the Federal Republic and the Democratic Republic. In the Democratic Republic this has involved the church in many bitter clashes with the Communist rulers; in the Federal Republic its participation in public life is neither as extensive nor as intensive as that of the Roman Catholic Church. Although individual church leaders occasionally speak out on public issues, organized Protestant groups play a comparatively small role in the political process.

III.   The System in Operation: The Substance of Foreign Policy

The actual operation of German foreign policy-making is heavily influenced by three factors: the aims of German policy-makers, the pressure of various interest groups, and the massive involvement of the German economy with the United States, through various forms of United States aid and through private business relations. The intra-

German factors will be discussed below, but the German stake in United States-German political and economic relations is so substantial that we must try to say something about its magnitude at the outset.

A. The economic influence of the United States

To indicate even the order of magnitude of the American dollar flow into the Federal Republic and West Berlin is not an easy task. The aid has been given in a large variety of ways, under a bewildering succession of alphabetical agencies: GARIOA, ECA, MSA, FOA, and others. Although these accounted publicly for their operations, data for other channels of dollar inputs into the German economy have not been so readily available. In the case of Germany, as in that of some other countries, many of these extraordinary dollar receipts, as a report of the U.N. Economic Commission for Europe points out, ". . . belong to the twilight zone of quasi-strategic information: at best, only general orders of magnitude are known. . . ." [10]

What is this general order of magnitude? The German Federal Ministry for Economic Cooperation acknowledged in 1956 that Germany had received almost $10 billion up to June 30, 1956, presumably for a period since early 1948.[11] Of the exact total of $9,935 million, $6,355 million was listed as aid to the Federal Republic in general, and $3,580 million as aid to West Berlin.[12] Even if one assumes that this total includes all dollar aid since 1946, one would arrive at an average of $1 billion per year; or approximately $20 per year for every German man, woman, and child.

The effectiveness of these dollar inputs into the German economy was greatly increased by the manner in which they were employed and by the efficient response of German management and labor. Through counterpart funds and other devices a considerable part of these funds was used to increase capital investment and thus the technological equipment of German industry, without any of the sacrifices that German consumers otherwise would have had to make for an investment program of this magnitude. The result was an increase in both capital equipment and consumer goods. "To use a medical term," says a German government publication, "it was 'dollar therapy'

---

[10] United Nations, Department of Economic Affairs (Economic Commission for Europe), *Economic Survey of Europe in 1953* (Geneva, 1954), pp. 19-20.

[11] Bundesministerium für wirtschaftliche Zusammenarbeit, *Der europäische Wirtschaftsrat—OEEC: Handbuch, 1956* (Godesberg: Verlag für Publizistik), p. 70.

[12] *Ibid.* The latter sum may have included orders placed in West Berlin for work done elsewhere in the Federal Republic.

and the tonic effect of an American blood transfusion. . . . Every Marshall Plan dollar spent in Germany has resulted in $10 to $20 worth of goods produced and services rendered." [13]

The economic influence of the United States is heavily reinforced by psychological, social, and military considerations that make American friendship appear as the most important basis of what security the members of the West German foreign policy elites can hope for in this uncertain world. The results of this relationship have been conspicuous. In every major German foreign policy decision the government of the United States has been an invisible—and sometimes not so invisible—partner. Nevertheless, there has been a growing autonomous component in German foreign policy-making. The interplay of German aims and United States influence, and of the various domestic German interests, can be seen best by glancing briefly at a few actual cases of such policy decisions. The questions of German membership in the European Coal and Steel Community; of German rearmament; of German reparations to Israel; and of negotiations with the Soviet Union about German reunification—these are the cases in which we shall try to watch German foreign policy-making in operation.

B.   Toward the recovery of German influence

A primary objective of German foreign policy since the creation of the Federal Republic in 1949 has been the recovery of German influence in international affairs. There have been differences between various elite groups and among the public at large over the means to be employed, but solid unanimity concerning the general objective. The man primarily responsible for the conduct of German foreign policy from 1949 to 1957, Chancellor Konrad Adenauer, was singularly successful in his efforts to regain for Germany independence of action in the conduct of foreign policy without losing the political, military, and economic support of the Western allies—particularly the United States. Adenauer's policy was to establish Germany as the leading power and the senior partner of the United States on the European continent by means of adroit and subtle moves, which gained for the Federal Republic full sovereignty and a leading position within the Western Alliance system in the course of a few years. In the face of frequently bitter opposition from some foreign policy elites, particularly the Social Democratic leadership, and often without the specific support of public opinion, he gained his ends through close collabora-

---

[13] *Germany Reports*, 1953, pp. 239-243.

tion with the Western powers, particularly the United States. Adenauer gambled successfully that temporary concessions would eventually yield major gains for German foreign policy and that the voters would sustain him at election time. He owed his success to a combination of factors, including his unrivalled position as the leader of the governing political elite, his remarkable prestige inside and outside Germany, his ability to enlist the support of crucial German elites for specific foreign policy moves in spite of public opposition or indifference, his influence among leading policy-makers in Western countries, and last, but not least, the exigencies of the international situation. In general, Adenauer has exploited to the fullest his great formal and informal powers as chancellor and as leader of the largest German party—if necessary in the face of widespread public opposition at home and abroad—in order to gain his ends in foreign affairs.

1. *The European Coal and Steel Community Treaty.* The first step toward the recovery of German sovereignty and Germany's liberation from allied controls after the creation of the Federal Republic was taken with the creation of the European Coal and Steel Community (ECSC), popularly known as the Schuman Plan. Under the Occupation Statute of 1949, the new German state gained only limited independence from control over its affairs by the three Western occupation powers—the United States, Great Britain, and France. A tripartite Allied High Commission was established, endowed with broad powers designed to assure that the Federal Republic would conform to Western plans for a democratic and demilitarized Germany and would honor the political and economic obligations it had undertaken in return for Allied agreement to the establishment of the new state. The Allied High Commission controlled the organization and operation of German business, endeavoring to prevent its reconcentration in cartels and trusts and diverting a considerable share of the production of the Ruhr coal to foreign countries who had been victims of German aggression. It regulated political and economic relations between the new state and foreign countries; and, for all practical purposes, the Commission represented the interests of the Federal Republic and its citizens abroad.

The new German government, a coalition led by Adenauer, immediately sought ways and means to gain freedom from allied supervision. These efforts were helped immeasurably by the rapid economic recovery of the new German state—aided largely by generous financial assistance from the United States government—and by the intensification of the conflict between the Western allies and the Soviet Union.

Failure to achieve agreement with the Soviet Union on the reunification of Germany and the belief that Russia might attack Western Europe through the territory of the Federal Republic led the Western occupation powers to yield to Adenauer's demands for complete sovereignty. Even before the outbreak of the Korean conflict in July, 1950, Western policy had begun to change from treating the Federal Republic as a defeated enemy to seeking its inclusion in the Western Alliance system as a major bulwark against Soviet aggression. These developments played directly into the hands of the leaders of the Federal Republic, who offered intimate collaboration to the Western powers in return for independence and complete German equality in the councils of the Western Alliance. Their first opportunity to move toward their objective came almost as soon as the new state had come into being, in May, 1950, when French Minister Robert Schuman called for the pooling of Franco-German coal and steel production in an economic union which he invited other interested European states to join.

The French foreign minister made his proposal for a variety of political, economic, and military reasons, including the desire to prevent the restoration of an independent German power on the continent that might once more become a threat to French security. Conscious of the rapid recovery of German power, Schuman sought to make a virtue of apparent necessity by proposing a close organic bond between the Federal Republic, France, and other states of Western and Eastern Europe which, he hoped would permit resurgent German power to benefit, rather than threaten, the anti-Communist nations of Europe. Schuman advertised his proposal as the first step toward the economic and political unification of Europe which, he claimed, would put an end to past Franco-German conflicts and prove advantageous to all participating states.

Chancellor Adenauer immediately hailed Schuman's proposal as "epoch-making" and called for its speedy implementation in the form of a treaty. However, the spokesmen of the Federal Republic let it be known that their country would join the proposed community only if all existing restrictions on the Republic's sovereignty, imposed by the occupation powers, were removed. The Occupation Statute of 1949 was gradually revised in the course of the negotiations leading to the signing of the European Coal and Steel Community treaty in April, 1951. The Federal Republic was given partial control over its foreign relations and some of the most severe allied controls over its domestic affairs were gradually dropped. In January, 1952, the Bundestag approved the ECSC treaty by a vote of 232 to 143.

Bundestag approval of the ECSC treaty was not due to overwhelming public support. The "attentive public" in favor of the proposed coal and steel community declined steadily during negotiations, while opposition increased. The largest number of Germans, however, appear to have become increasingly indifferent toward the issue, leaving the final decision to the foreign policy-makers.

2. *West German armament as an instrument of foreign policy.*   On the morning of May 9, 1955, the black, red, and gold flag of the German Federal Republic rose at the Supreme Headquarters, Allied Powers Europe (SHAPE), while the band played the old German national anthem, *Deutschland, Deutschland über alles, über alles in der Welt.* It signified the admission of a free and sovereign German state to the North Atlantic Treaty Organization (NATO)—almost ten years to the day since its new allies had dictated armistice terms to a vanquished Germany. After almost six years of determined efforts to throw off Western allied controls over German affairs, Chancellor Adenauer and his associates appeared at last to have obtained their goal. In exchange for the promise of a German military contribution to the defense of Western Europe they had gained for the Federal Republic "the full authority of a sovereign state over its internal and external affairs," a national military establishment, a major voice in the councils of the Western powers, assurances of Western military and political support against Soviet Russia, and, finally, Western recognition of the Bonn government as "the only German Government . . . entitled to speak . . . as the representative of the [entire] German people in interna tional affairs." [14]

As in the case of ECSC, the negotiations leading to the abolition of Western controls and the recognition of the Federal Republic as a sovereign and equal member of the NATO alliance demonstrated the far-reaching and generally uncontested independence of German foreign policy decision-makers from the influence of domestic public opinion. The price that the Adenauer government agreed to pay for sovereignty and NATO membership was the setting up of a national military establishment, a decision repeatedly opposed during the period of negotiations by more Germans than supported it.

Adenauer and his closest associates sought to achieve their objective

---

[14] See U.S. Congress, Senate, *Protocol on the Termination of the Occupation Regime in the Federal Republic of Germany and Protocol to the North Atlantic Treaty on the Accession of the Federal Republic of Germany*, 83d Congress, 2d Session, Executives L and M, (Washington, D.C.: United States Government Printing Office, 1954).

—as in the case of the European Coal and Steel Community—in the name of European integration. In December of 1949 Adenauer launched a trial balloon by suggesting that Germans should contribute to the defense of Europe in a European Army. Apparently anticipating early Western demands for a German defense contribution, on the basis of formal and informal current suggestions along these lines from Western political and military leaders, he maintained his position in the following months despite violent opposition both in the Federal Republic and abroad. Adenauer sought to impress upon Western leaders the value of the Federal Republic as an ally and the crucial role that it might play in a future· conflict between the Soviet Union the NATO powers. He claimed that the industrial and demographic resources of the Federal Republic might prove decisive in a future war; he stressed the danger of large-scale Soviet troop concentrations in Central Germany and the growing power of the so-called "People's Police" of the Communist-dominated German Democratic Republic, suggesting that short of a military contribution from the Federal Republic the Western powers lacked the forces to repel an attack from the East. For political as well as military reasons, Adenauer maintained, the Western powers needed the loyal support of the people of the German Federal Republic; he offered it in exchange for an end to allied controls and the termination of existing limitations on the sovereignty of the Federal Republic.

To gain his objective Adenauer was willing to risk Soviet threats against the Federal Republic and the possibility that the reunification of Germany might be deferred indefinitely; as in the case of ECSC, he was prepared to sacrifice *potential* sovereign rights in return for the surrender of *actual* sovereign powers by other nations participating in the creation of a European defense community. The same ideological motives that influenced the CDU elite, under Adenauer's leadership, to support the Schuman Plan of May 1950 also led it to support concurrent proposals for the creation of a European army, even though every one of ten opinion polls between 1950 and 1954 showed more opponents than supporters for the plan.

However, political considerations were every bit as important. Membership in a European integration scheme for a German state both wealthier and more populous than any other continental state held out the prospect not only of equality for the Federal Republic in such a union, but of potential leadership of the democratic nations of continental Europe. Instead of remaining merely a rump German state, facing the prospect of indefinite occupation and control by foreign powers, the Federal Republic might at least become "first among equals," playing a leading role in international affairs as the leader of the continental nations, particularly toward the United States and the Soviet Union, the two super-powers of the world. Finally, such a role for Germany in a European military union promised to make it less dependent on foreign powers and to give its leaders a greater voice in matters affecting the defense of the Federal Republic against attack from the East. To gain these ends Adenauer was prepared to defy popular opposition to German rearmament. Sovereignty and equality for the Federal Republic through European integration were to him worth the price of a German military contribution, as Adenauer's official biographer was to note.[15]

Adenauer's arguments for a German military contribution to the defense of Western Europe against Communist attack seemed substantiated by the North Korean attack on South Korea in July of 1950. Particularly in the United States government, military and political leaders—some of whom had favored a German military contribution, at least since 1949—reportedly interpreted the unexpected invasion as a clear warning that either the Soviet Union herself, or her East German satellite, might invade the Federal Republic too. Western allied forces in Germany, never very strong and further weakened by the diversion of military resources to Korea, appeared inadequate to meet the threat. Simultaneously, the French government informed the United States that it was not interested in an allied strategy that depended primarily on U.S. air-atomic power, but wanted Western Europe to be defended by ground forces as far east as possible.

While United States leaders sought desperately to stem the North Korean sweep down the peninsula, Chancellor Adenauer pointed with increasing emphasis to the exposed situation of his country, and of Western Europe in general. In August 1950 he suggested to the Western allies the formation of a "special force of German volunteers" of the same size and strength as the "People's Police" in the Soviet Zone of Germany—estimated to consist of from 50,000 to 80,000 trained soldiers. He coupled this appeal with the renewed suggestion that the Federal Republic might make a sizable contribution to a European army in return for an end to allied controls and complete equality within a defense arrangement. Simultaneously, Adenauer appointed a former general to head a new office in the Federal government that was to lay plans for such a German military contribution.

The United States government, upon the urgings of its military leaders, replied to Adenauer's proposals by calling openly for the use of

---

[15] See Paul Weymar, *Konrad Adenauer: Die autorisierte Biographie* (München: Kindler, 1955), pp. 500, 557. See also Fritz René Allemann, *Bonn ist nicht Weimar* (Köln-Berlin: Kiepenheuer and Witsch, 1956), pp. 187-212.

German productive resources and military manpower for the defense of Western Europe. Secretary of State Dean Acheson asked British and French government leaders to agree to the inclusion of about ten German divisions in the NATO forces in Europe. But, in the face of French opposition to the creation of an independent German army, the three Western governments agreed that the German military contribution demanded "by democratic leaders in Germany" should become part of an integrated European army.

Urged on by United States leaders, the governments of the Federal Republic of Germany, France, Italy, Belgium, the Netherlands, and Luxembourg for over two years hammered out a scheme for a European Defense Community (EDC) that would more or less parallel the pattern agreed upon for the Coal and Steel Community. While French negotiators, led by Adenauer's friend, Foreign Minister Robert Schuman, sought to limit German influence in the proposed military arrangement, the representatives of the Federal Republic demanded complete equality and the termination of allied controls over German affairs. The German spokesmen were aided not only by strong United States support, but, paradoxically, by popular opposition to any rearmament in Germany itself. Pointing to gains for the opposition Social Democrats—strongly opposed to the scheme—in various local elections, Adenauer extracted major allied political concessions for the more "cooperative" German leaders.

When the EDC treaty was finally signed in May 1952, it provided for the creation of 12 German divisions, an air force, and a small navy, which were to become major components of a European military establishment. True, the German Federal Republic was not yet admitted to NATO, but Chancellor Adenauer had no doubts that membership would follow as soon as the German defense contribution had begun to take concrete form. Simultaneously with the signing of the EDC treaty the Federal Republic concluded a Contractual Agreement with the three Western occupation powers which was to replace the Occupation Statute of 1949. In effect, this agreement terminated the occupation and put an end to practically all allied controls. However, Western forces remaining in Germany as "allies" retained the right to intervene in case the democratic order in the Federal Republic should be threatened either from within or without.

In May 1953 the Bundestag approved the two agreements by a majority of 59 votes, a considerably smaller margin of victory for Adenauer's policies than in the case of the ECSC vote only a few months earlier. The treaties became the major issues of the campaign for the election of a new parliament, which followed ratification. The Christian Democratic elite, supported only diffidently by leaders of the smaller parties in the Adenauer coalition, claimed a major political victory for Germany. Opposition came largely from a peculiar alignment of militarists, pacifists, nationalist opponents of European integration, and "neutralists" who feared that military alignment with the West would prevent any Soviet agreement to the reunification of Germany. The Social Democratic and trade union elites, this time united, claimed that rearmament would restore the antidemocratic and bellicose German military leadership of the past and perpetuate the division of Germany. The Protestant elite was divided. Important members—like the Social Democratic leaders particularly sensitive to the needs of their silent "constituents" living under Soviet control in Central and Eastern Germany—claimed that membership in EDC would constitute a "betrayal" of their "oppressed brethren." The old military elite was also divided into proponents and opponents of EDC. Some supported Adenauer's claim that the political and military gains for Germany outweighed whatever disadvantages the agreements might include. Others maintained that the limitations imposed upon a new German military establishment were unacceptable and asked that rearmament be deferred until political conditions and popular opinion had become more favorable.[16] Strenuous Communist efforts, directed from the Soviet Zone, to draw the various opposition groups into a united "patriotic" front proved unsuccessful.

Despite widespread popular opposition to rearmament the promised restoration of German sovereignty and the gains in Germany's international position impressed many voters. Adenauer won a resounding personal victory in the election of 1953. His prestige and reputation as an effective representative of German interests gave the Christian Democrats for the first time an absolute majority in the Bundestag; the ruling coalition now commanded the two-thirds majority required for constitutional changes, which armament might require. Adenauer's policy of German political recovery in international affairs through European integration was dealt a setback in August 1954, when the French Chamber of Deputies rejected the EDC treaty and thus defeated the scheme. However, only 37 per cent of the respondents in a German poll following this defeat expressed regret for the failure of the project.

The German chancellor immediately demanded complete sovereignty for the Federal Republic, maintaining that it had fulfilled its

---

[16] See, for example, excerpts from a memorandum by former Fleet Admiral Heinrich Gerlach, reprinted in *Der Spiegel*, April 3, 1957, p. 16.

part of the bargain and was not to blame for the failure of the armament scheme. However, the British and American governments insisted that a German military contribution agreed to by the French remained the *sine qua non* for political sovereignty. On British initiative, representatives of the United States, Britain, Canada, and the six continental countries that had signed the EDC treaty, formulated a hasty substitute. It provided for the creation of a national German military establishment and the admission of the Federal Republic to the North Atlantic Treaty Organization as a sovereign and equal partner, subject only to certain limitations on its future military power and the retention of a few formal rights on the part of the former occupation powers pertaining to West Berlin and German reunification. By May 1955 all the governments concerned had ratified these "Paris Agreements." A major goal of Adenauer's foreign policy since 1949 had been achieved, though not exactly in the manner the chancellor had intended. The immediate political gains for the Federal Republic were even greater than under the proposed EDC arrangement; however, many of the proponents of European integration among the German leaders paid the price only reluctantly. The immediate gains of sovereignty, NATO membership, and a national military establishment did not appear to them to be worth the sacrifice of the European army scheme and its apparent promise of German leadership of a European political union.

C.   An unresolved foreign policy issue: German reunification and relations with the Soviet Union

The preceding analysis has suggested repeatedly that foreign policy-makers in the Federal Republic have tended to show a great deal of independence from the pressure of public opinion. To this, there has been one conspicuous exception. On the issue of German reunification no important leader has dared suggest that the Federal Republic is more than a provisional arrangement pending the "liberation" of the Soviet zone. During the years that German policy-makers concentrated on gaining sovereignty and freedom of action for the "rump" German state, reunification as a policy objective took second place to these more immediate foreign policy goals, leading many non-German observers to underestimate its potential importance once sovereignty had been achieved. Since 1955, however, it has become increasingly apparent that peaceful reunification through some sort of arrangement with the Soviet Union is one of the most crucial foreign policy issues confronting decision-makers in the Federal Republic, one that is likely to affect significantly the future relationship between the Republic and its Western allies.

Professions by official government spokesmen of support for European integration have tended to obscure the far stronger sentiment for reunification, which has steadily gained strength in the Federal Republic. Not only do deep-rooted loyalties to the idea of a united German nation appear at the present time far stronger than support for the supranational ideal of European unification, but intimate personal bonds link a large number of citizens of the Federal Republic to German lands and peoples presently under Communist domination. Over 27 per cent of the foreign policy elites and 26 per cent of the population are natives of Central and Eastern Germany. In February 1953, 44 per cent of the respondents in a public opinion poll claimed either relatives or friends living in the Soviet zone of Germany; when one adds to these the number of West Germans with personal acquaintances, the share of West Germans with such personal contacts should be well above one-half the population of the Federal Republic. Many of these human contacts have remained active; in February 1953 almost two West Germans out of every five said they were sometimes writing letters to the East zone, and almost one in three had sent Christmas packages there. Every month several thousand refugees from the Soviet zone enter the Federal Republic, serving as a constant reminder that 18 million Germans remain outside the present "rump" German state.

In addition to national and personal sentiments, visions of potential political and economic gains motivate the demand for reunification. With a population of 78 million and the largest area by far of all European states, a united Germany would once more rank among the leading powers of the world—second only to the United States and the Soviet Union. Although presently trade between the Federal Republic and Communist countries is negligible—even trade with the Soviet zone amounted to only about 2 per cent of its total foreign trade—reunification might open up vast new markets.

The magnitude and intensity of popular pressure for German reunification is evidenced by the attitudes of the elites. Opinion leaders in the Federal Republic have sought to outdo each other in denouncing the division of Germany as intolerable and in labeling reunification the most important national duty confronting the government. General agreement exists that reunification must be achieved peacefully and by means of free elections of a national assembly throughout Germany, and not through negotiations with the "puppet" regime of the Soviet zone. Elite views diverge, however, on the strategy that should be employed by the government of the Federal Republic in achieving reunification.

Most German leaders acknowledge—however reluctantly—that the government is not a free agent in the matter of reunification. German unity, they admit, depends in the last analysis upon agreement between the United States and the Soviet Union. Chancellor Adenauer and his supporters have taken the position that the best means of obtaining such an agreement consists in inducing the Western leaders —and United States leaders in particular—to adopt this German national objective as their own, and to treat it as more important than any other United States interest that might conceivably be served by an American-Soviet settlement on other issues. Any general settlement of outstanding East-West differences, it is argued, would then have to include the unification of Germany on terms satisfactory to the government of the Federal Republic. To gain such support, however, the Republic and its leaders must convince Western leaders of their devotion and loyalty to the Western Alliance; above all, they must convince them that a reunified Germany would be no threat to the peace of the world. According to Adenauer, the most effective way to earn such confidence and support is for the Federal Republic to take the leadership in the movement for European Union. Therefore, the Chancellor has claimed, without the unification of Europe there can be no unification of Germany.

The Adenauer course for reunification has been opposed by a conglomeration of neutralist, pacifist, and nationalist elements who have otherwise little in common. It includes leaders of the Protestant Church, right-wing conservatives and nationalists, former officers, Social Democratic and trade union leaders, and businessmen. In general, they hold that the cause of German unity would be better served by loosening the ties that Adenauer has forged between the Federal Republic and the Western powers. Particularly the severance of present military bonds, they hold, would diminish Soviet opposition to German reunification by eliminating the Russian leaders' fears of resurgent German military power allied with the West. These elements dispute Adenauer's claim that German and Western interests regarding reunification are more or less identical and, both overtly and covertly, they seek to influence the decision-makers to adopt a more "independent" course in pursuit of what they conceive to be exclusively German national interest. The task of a dynamic German foreign policy, as they see it, is to create and exploit opportunities that would permit the government of the Federal Republic to avoid binding commitments to either of the two major power blocs, while using its bargaining power to mediate an agreement on German unification between them. Otherwise, it is claimed, the *status quo* will be perpetuated by a tacit understanding between the leaders of the great powers to shelve the issue of German unification indefinitely for the sake of some compromise on other issues, such as an agreement on disarmament.

By 1957 Germany seemed no closer to reunification than in 1949; at best the foreign policy of the Adenauer government appeared to be preserving the *status quo,* at worst it seemed to be aggravating the division of the nation. Adenauer's failure to register any concrete gains by a supposedly dynamic drive for reunification seemed all the greater in contrast with the apparent ease with which the Chancellor had previously managed to obtain concessions from the Western allies in establishing the Federal Republic as the leading power on the European continent. The opposition charges that Adenauer and his associates merely have paid lip-service to the cause of reunification while they have been, actually, anything but enthusiastic about joining the socialized economy and the Protestant population of the Soviet zone with the Federal Republic. The predominantly Roman Catholic, West and South German, and conservative elites supporting Adenauer and influencing his foreign policy decisions are said to fear the political and economic effect that reunification might have upon their present positions of power. Yet, although there might be some truth in these charges, the real reason for the present paralysis of German policy-makers with regard to reunification appears to lie beyond their control.

German foreign policy-makers are faced with a deadlock between Soviet and Western leaders on a formula for German unity. Both sides conceive the potential status of a united Germany as a matter so vital to their respective interests that they have found it impossible to make the concessions that a compromise solution would require. Western leaders see the terms for reunification proposed by the Soviet leaders as designed to give control over this strategic area to the U.S.S.R., while the latter insist that a Germany united according to Western plans would constitute a menace to the Soviet Union and its allies in Eastern Europe. The resulting deadlock has aroused widespread suspicions in the Federal Republic that neither Western nor Soviet leaders are genuinely interested in resolving the issue—protestations by both sides to the contrary—while the German government seems unable to do anything about it. "The German people . . . [are merely] the subjects of negotiations between foreign powers which pursue only their own interests," observed the leading foreign affairs journal in the Federal Republic after ten years of inconclusive four-power negotiations on German unification. This sense of exasperation and frustration has repeatedly led to demands that the leaders of the Federal Republic take matters into their own hands and negotiate directly with the Soviet government. However, attempts in this direction have been singularly unsuccessful. This was illustrated by Adenauer's visit to Moscow in September 1955.

The termination of the occupation regime in May 1955 was taken by many influential leaders of the Federal Republic as the signal for the start of direct negotiations with the Soviet Union on reunification. Such sentiments were strengthened by the failure of the Geneva four-power talks on German unification the following July. Therefore, when Soviet leaders invited Adenauer to come to Moscow in September 1955, he accepted, evidently sharing the widespread German view that his bargaining position was strong enough to extract favorable terms from the Soviet government. It turned out, however, that he had overestimated his own position and underestimated that of the Russian leaders. The latter refused to discuss reunification, but suggested that he negotiate directly with the leaders of the German Democratic Republic—the satellite regime of the Soviet zone—which no political leader in the Federal Republic was then, or is now, willing to do. Adenauer refused, but agreed to the establishment of diplomatic relations between the Federal Republic and the Soviet Union in return for the release of several thousand German prisoners of war still in Soviet captivity. To many opinion-leaders in Germany it seemed that Adenauer had walked into a Soviet trap. By agreeing to the establishment of diplomatic relations he seemed to have accepted the Soviet claim that there were two German states, both represented in Moscow, and that unification could only come about by negotiations between their respective governments. However, Adenauer quickly sought to dispel the impression that he had abandoned the claim of the Federal Government to be the only German government and that he was moving toward recognition of the Soviet-zone regime. In fact, he had obtained the release of some prisoners, which his Western allies had failed to procure. The presence of a Russian ambassador in Bonn, and of a West German ambassador in Moscow, represented a relative increase in German independence and bargaining power vis-à-vis the West; and Adenauer had gained these points without injuring in any way his reputation for rock-solid reliability as an ally of the Western powers. However, it was evident that the Federal Republic could ill afford to go much further in the way of independent negotiations with the Soviet Union, and that it still depended upon the Western powers—and particularly upon the United States—to achieve the professed major foreign policy objective of its leaders: German unity.

Between 1949 and 1956 Germany foreign policy-makers were highly successful in obtaining their objectives in negotiations with the Western occupation powers primarily because the latter were willing and able to pay the price demanded. To obtain the political, military, and economic participation of the Federal Republic in the Western Alliance against the Soviet Union, they agreed to Adenauer's demands for sovereignty and equality. Reunification is another matter. So long as international tensions remain acute, a united Germany may seem too dangerous to either side in the East-West contest. Small or unarmed countries can be neutral in the sense that neither side is forced to count them as enemies or allies, but a large, armed country would be not so much neutral as just uncommitted; it might keep everyone in fear as to what it might decide to do at any time with its concentrated power. In the case of Germany, now still divided, neither Eastern nor Western leaders seem overly eager to hasten the day when such fears might become real. Although German reunification often has been described—particularly by German leaders—as a major means to lessen tensions between East and West, it seems possible that a reduction of international tensions through compromises on some other issues might make German reunification more acceptable to the other powers.

Thus, the great threat confronting the German objective of a reunited nation is the possibility of a tacit agreement between the great power leaders to leave the issue indefinitely in abeyance—as in the case of divided Korea and Indochina. This possibility has become particularly acute with recent attempts to halt the armament race between the Soviet Union and the United States. Prodded by Chancellor Adenauer, Western leaders formerly insisted that agreement on German reunification must precede agreement on disarmament, but indications have been abundant that their position need not remain rigid: German unification, unlike disarmament, has little appeal among either foreign-policy elites or publics outside Germany.

German leaders could render the achievement of such East-West compromises on other issues more difficult. If they chose, they could exercise their influence to hamper or even block agreement on disarmament; they probably could intensify and dramatize the daily East-West frictions in divided Germany. But it is difficult to see how any such action would bring reunification closer. At most they could use their insistence on the priority of reunification as a bargaining technique, in order to exact concessions from both East and West to German interests on other and more manageable matters.

IV.   Prospects for German Foreign Policy

The study of the background of foreign policy-making in the German Federal Republic among the various policy-making institutions, interest groups, and sectors of public opinion, reveals a limited area of agreement, surrounded by substantial cleavages of attitudes and interests and by the possibility of stubborn deadlocks.

Government, interest groups, and the general public all desire, by and large, a peaceful return of Germany to leadership and power in Europe—and through Europe, perhaps in a larger area of the world. A substantial majority want peace, freedom from Communist control, and economic and political links to the United States—and they do not want to have to choose between these aims. Second to these primary goals comes German reunification as a long-range aim.

A.   "The First Servant of Europe"

European integration comes only in third place; it is often seen as a road to German leadership or to the attainment of other German goals, rather than as an end in itself. Among German elite members, as well as among the electorate, there are many who are likely to show little enthusiasms for remaining in any close European community that would prove unresponsive to German leadership or major influence. Other groups—though perhaps less strong—might be willing to accept a more modest role for Germany in a united Europe. The cleavage between those who want Germany to lead a Western European community and those who want her merely to join it has been adroitly bridged for the time being by the formulation of a prominent CDU leader and former diplomat, the President of the Bundesrat, Kurt Sieveking:

> England and France . . . will always . . . be preoccupied by extra-European tasks. . . . Italy is . . . not yet developed to its full strength. From this it is evident that Germany will become ever more the natural nucleus of crystallization for Europe. . . . Above all it must be made absolutely clear that this German foreign policy is far from any thought of any hegemony over Europe and that Germany, as one put it in a well-known saying, is "the first servant of Europe."

The "well-known saying," so aptly recalled by Herr Sieveking, is indeed well known to almost every educated German: it is the classic eighteenth-century phrase in which the absolute ruler of Prussia, King Frederick the Great, called himself "the first servant" of the State, and thus pictured his enlightened despotism as a matter not only of right but of duty. Nationalists may take heart from what they may well read as a broad hint of future aspirations, whereas more liberal-minded "Europeans" may take comfort from the explicit rejection of any thought of German hegemony, which prefaces it in the same sentence. Like many a present-day political leader, Herr Sieveking is raising here two sets of overtones and expectations in the same statement, and thus appealing at the one and same time to different sections of his variegated audience.

B. How much stress on military power?

In practice, this policy of cautious advance toward greater power within the Western Alliance system may mean that German reunification will remain largely in the realm of rhetoric. The Soviet government has no motive, for the time being, to concede German reunion on Western terms, and the Western powers have no effective means of pressure to make the Soviets change their minds. Faced with a deadlocked international situation and a divided public opinion at home, some German statesmen in early 1957 again sought unity through ambiguity, by promising greater German power that would force concessions from other countries, yet not endanger peace beyond the limits of tolerable risk. The implications for foreign policy have been put illuminatingly in an article by the Federal Minister of Defense, Franz-Josef Strauss:

> In the age of the *pax atomica* there are no military solutions. . . . The problem of reunification, too, must and can only be solved politically. . . . However one may regret it . . . the fact remains that the position and influence of a people depend as well upon the strength and dependability of its allies as upon its own military power. . . . Those who ask us—quite rightly—to accept Soviet power as a reality, should after all not deny their own people the right and the opportunity to become likewise a reality. In all negotiations about reunification, risks and chances must be weighed against each other. The risks will diminish, the chances will improve, the more Germany herself has to throw into the scales. . . . A policy of strength in the age of the hydrogen bomb means in no case that one wants to use military pressure, with the risk of a third world war, in order to bring about some territorial changes, if necessary even by force. A policy of strength means rather that one's own freedom of decision cannot be influenced by pressure from hostile or unfriendly quarters . . . Germany . . . must become so

indispensable to her Western friends, and so respectable for her potential adversary, that both will value her presence in the negotiations.

In another formulation of his views, Herr Strauss was quoted as adding:

> . . . although there exists a preference . . . for a reunited Germany to belong to a military alliance with the West, the hard political requirements of the German people might cause them to make a decision according to the Austrian pattern (of neutralization between East and West). . . . Such a decision would have to rest on very sober political and military considerations. . . . Without possessing potential power, Germany will never have a chance to be heard.

C.   The game with two balls— and its limits

Some journalists took an exuberant view of German opportunities in the near future; thus a popular weekly wrote in April 1957:

> If all goes according to plan, German foreign policy . . . will at last be able to play the diplomatic game with two balls: On the one hand, one will be able to negotiate with the Western powers about an initiative in the German question, and on the other hand with the Soviets about an improvement in relations, which is—according to the concurrent views of Konrad Adenauer and Nikolai Bulganin—the precondition for reunification.

A respected review gave a more sober estimate:

> We have more of a bipartisan foreign policy than both (major) parties care to admit. . . . In foreign policy matters we are not independent, and it often smacks of phrase-making to call here for German initiatives. It is rather in regard to our internal affairs that we are really sovereign.

The four views just cited—the hopes for German leadership in Europe, for German military power as a counter in diplomatic bargaining, the play with the "two balls" of possible negotiations with East and West, and the resigned acceptance of Germany's lack of real independence in international affairs—indicate some of the limits of the narrow space within which German policy-makers are confined for the decisions left to them. Thus confined and limited in its possibilities, German foreign policy might well promise stability for some years to come.

Much of this prospective stability, however, depends on outside limits and on outside props. If economic prosperity in the Western world should give way to a serious depression; or if American interest and aid should be withdrawn; or if a sharply increased risk of war should put much greater short-term strains and burdens upon Germany; or if the Soviet Union should make some substantially more favorable offer on matters of German reunification; or if a further deterioration of the French position at home or in her overseas territories should bring about a changed situation in Western Europe; or if some drastic change in some of the countries of the Soviet bloc should create new conditions among Germany's Eastern neighbors—in any of these events German foreign policy-makers might find themselves quickly face-to-face with the need for major new decisions.

Such decisions in response to major international changes might easily entail a broad revision of German foreign policy. What their outcome would be is hard to foresee. Here we encounter some of the limits of any political analysis based on the past and on the background conditions of the policy-making process. The past suggests that some German responses could be dramatic; but it does not tell us what they would be.

We can, however, look to some German policy choices that are currently being made—sometimes as specific moves, sometimes as mere shifts of emphasis—which may be tell-tale indicators of the possible ways in which larger decisions might be made if circumstances should demand them. Comprising one such tell-tale indication are current German attitudes toward any efforts at reducing East-West tensions or at limiting the arms race, particularly in nuclear weapons. Will German policy leaders welcome such efforts as favoring the chances of later German reunification, or will they insist that reunification must come first? Related to this are changes in the emphasis on the theme of Germany's need for greater military power, in order to make the U.S.S.R. and other countries more receptive to the German point of view. Will such themes and hints diminish or increase as time goes on? What will happen in this respect when the German army becomes stronger, and when the question of nuclear weapons for Germany becomes acute?

What will be the next developments in German-Soviet relations? Some members of the German foreign policy elite are urging "genuine and fruitful" diplomatic relations with the U.S.S.R. "It makes no sense," wrote an SPD leader, Carlo Schmid, "to act as if the Soviet Union did not exist as a genuine business partner. For that our direct and indirect business dealings with them are too large." In the same connection the question of German diplomatic relations to other Soviet-bloc countries has been raised, with both Social Democrats like Carlo Schmid and CDU leaders like Kurt Sieveking coming out publicly in favor of the opening of formal diplomatic relations with Poland.

Other indications of possible trends are found in German policies toward Western European integration, and in the development of German elite and popular attitudes toward the conflicts of West European powers with native independence movements in their colonies. A poll in November 1956 showed the complexity of some of these attitudes: 86 per cent of respondents expresed sympathy for the Hungarian rebels, as against only 1 per cent who sympathized with the Russians, who had just intervened against them, and 13 per cent who were uninformed or undecided; but at the same time, a majority of 56 per cent declared themselves on the side of Egypt in the Suez crisis, while only 10 per cent expressed sympathy for France and England, and 34 per cent were uninformed or undecided.[17] This large outpouring of popular sympathy for Egypt at a time when she defied the West and was in open conflict with France, Germany's major partner in European integration, showed little of the "European" solidarity that has often been a general theme in official German foreign policy pronouncements. German press opinion has tended to stress the inevitability and strength of Asian and African independence movements, and to rejoice in the favorable reception that German products and German businessmen have found in many of the newly independent countries. No European economic or political union, it is held, could possibly reverse this trend: "Also the sum total of West European national states," writes a recent contributor to *Aussenpolitik*, "will not be able to avoid the positive answer to the claim of colonial peoples for independence. . . ."

D.   What kind of Germany?

Perhaps the most important of all current tell-tale decisions that may indicate possible German behavior in the event of a drastic international change or major crisis are those decisions which bear on the official and unofficial attitudes toward the remnants of Nazism and old-line militarism inside Germany. Any major crisis in foreign policy is likely to strain the limited consensus of the different ideological and interest groups that have been held together by the conditions of the Adenauer era. Under such strains, any major decision about German foreign policy may well become involved in a decision as to what kind of country Germany is to become and what groups and ideas are to lead her. Some decisions of this kind—on the attitudes to the Nazi past, to the war criminals, to authoritarianism—have been made,

---

[17] Erich Peter Neumann, "Nützt Ungarn der CDU?" *Der Spiegel*, 11:2, January 4, 1957, p. 13.

while others have been largely or partly shelved thus far. If the rest of the world remains stable for the next ten years, Germany's moderate foreign policy and constitutional domestic evolution may well remain secure. The small current decisions about Germany's foreign policies, however, and even more those about her internal democracy and her domestic prestige and power structure, may give us some inkling of the conflicts that might erupt among different German foreign policy elites, and among different opinion groups, if times should become acutely critical or dangerous again.

On the surface, the German Federal Republic looks like a stable political community, whose leaders are pursuing a steadfast policy of national recovery within a Western Alliance, and who are backed in this enterprise by a wide measure of solid political consensus among their people. More closely considered, the same Republic resembles rather a political and psychological convalescent. The political unity of her population still is precarious, and it could easily break under strain. Any policy by other Western powers designed to make Germany bear the major burdens of maintaining Western power in Europe in a period of major stress might well prove hazardous in the extreme.

Under these conditions, time wisely used might well work for the West. Each additional year of peace, prosperity, and confidence might aid in the consolidation of German democracy and help Germany to become a full member of the Western community of nations by inner conviction and tradition, rather than only by strategic association and expediency. The great humanitarian and democratic traditions are alive in Germany today, and a constitutional system of government has had a few years to take root. Very much may depend on giving these traditions a chance to become stronger in the next few years in an international environment that is sufficiently peaceful to permit them to become more firmly and deeply established in the social fabric and the living memories of the German people.

Selected Bibliography

Almond, Gabriel A., ed., *The Struggle for Democracy in Germany* (Chapel Hill: University of North Carolina Press, 1949).

Bathurst, M. E., and J. L. Simpson, *Germany and the North Atlantic Community: A Legal Survey* (London: Stevens and Sons, 1956).

Buchanan, William, and Hadley Cantril, *How Nations See Each Other: A Study in Public Opinion* (Urbana: University of Illinois Press, 1953).

Craig, Gordon A., *NATO and the New German Army* (Princeton: Center of International Studies, Memo No. 8, 1955).

Deutsch, Karl W., S. A. Burrell, R. A. Kann, M. Lee, Jr., M. Lichterman, R. E. Lindgren, F. L. Loewenheim, and R. W. Van Wagenen, *Political Community and the North Atlantic Area* (Princeton: Princeton University Press, 1957).

Deutsch, Karl W., and Lewis J. Edinger, *Influences in Contemporary German Foreign Policy: Mass Opinion, Interest Groups and Elites.* (Forthcoming).

Deutsch, Karl W., *Nationalism and Social Communication* (Cambridge: M.I.T. Press; New York: Wiley, 1953).

Dicks, Henry V., "Some Psychological Studies of the German Character," in T. H. Pear, *Psychological Factors of Peace and War* (New York: Philosophical Library, 1950).

Edinger, Lewis J., *German Exile Politics* (Berkeley: University of California Press, 1956).

————, *West German Armament* (Research Studies Institute, Air University, Maxwell Air Force Base, Ala., October, 1955).

Eyck, Franz, "Tensions in Western Germany," *Contemporary Review,* No. 1098 (June 1957), pp. 325-328.

Grossman, Kurt R., *Germany's Moral Debt; The German-Israel Agreement* (Washington, D.C.: Public Affairs Press, 1954).

Haas, Ernst B., *The Schuman Plan and European Integration 1950-1956: Process of Community Formation* (Stanford: Stanford University Press, 1958).

Kecskemeti, Paul, and Nathan Leites, *Some Psychological Hypotheses on Nazi Germany* (Washington, D.C.: Experimental Division for the Study of Wartime Communications, Library of Congress, 1945). (Also in *Journal of Social Psychology,* November 1947–August 1948.)

Kirchheimer, Otto, "The Political Scene in West Germany," *World Politics,* April 1957, 433-445.

Kliemann, Horst G., and Stephen S. Taylor, eds., *Who's Who In Germany* (Munich: Intercontinental Book and Publishing Company, 1956).

Knight, Max E., *The German Executive 1890-1933* (Stanford: Stanford University Press, 1952).

Mason, Henry L., *The European Coal and Steel Community: Experiment in Supranationalism* (The Hague: Nijhoff, 1955).

Parsons, Talcott, "Democracy and Social Structure in Pre-Nazi Germany," in *Essays in Sociological Theory* (rev. ed.; Glencoe, Ill.: Free Press, 1954), pp. 104-123.

————, "The Problem of Controlled Institutional Change," *ibid.,* pp. 238-274.

Pollock, James Kerr, and Homer Thomas, *Germany in Power and Eclipse* (New York: Van Nostrand, 1952).

Press Office, German Diplomatic Mission, Washington, *Handbook of German Affairs* (Washington, 1954).

Price, Hoyt, and Carl E. Schorske, *The Problem of Germany* (New York: Council on Foreign Relations, 1947).

Schaffner, Bertram, *Father Land: A Study of Authoritarianism in the German Family* (New York: Columbia University Press, 1948).

Speier, Hans, *German Rearmament and Atomic War: The Views of German Military and Political Leaders* (Evanston, Ill.: Row, Peterson and Co., 1957).

————, and W. P. Davison, eds., *West German Leadership and Foreign Policy* (Evanston, Ill.: Row, Peterson and Co., 1957).

Strange, Susan, "The Schuman Plan," *The Yearbook of World Affairs* (London: Stevens, 1951).

United Nations, Department of Economic Affairs (Economic Commission for Europe), *Economic Survey of Europe in 1953* (Geneva, 1954).

United Nations, Statistical Office, *National and Per Capita Incomes of 70 Countries in 1949*, Statistical Papers, Series E, No. 1 (New York, 1950).

United Nations, Statistical Office, *Per Capita National Product of 55 Countries, 1952-54*, Statistical Papers, Series E, No. 4 (Sales No. 1957 XVII. 2) (New York, 1954).

United States, International Cooperation Administration, *Operations Report, Data as of March 31, 1956* (Washington, D.C., 1956).

United States Congress, Senate, *Protocol on the Termination of the Occupation Regime in the Federal Republic of Germany and Protocol to the North Atlantic Treaty on the Accession of the Federal Republic of Germany*, 83rd Congress, 2d Session, Executives L and M (Washington, D.C.: United States Government Printing Office, 1954).

United States, Department of Commerce, *Foreign Grants and Credits by the United States Government*, December 1955 Quarter (Washington, D.C.: U.S. Dept. of Commerce, Office of Business Economics, 1956).

United States, Office of the High Commissioner for Germany (HICOG), *Reports;* listed in Smith, Bruce Lannes, and Chitra M. Smith, *International Communication and Political Opinion* (Princeton: Princeton University Press, 1957); pp. 205-212.

Wallenberg, Hans, *Report on Democratic Institutions in Germany* (New York: American Council on Germany, 1956).

Wallich, Henry C., *Mainsprings of the German Revival* (New Haven: Yale University Press, 1955).

Weymar, Paul, *Konrad Adenauer: Die autorisierte Biographie* (München: Kindler, 1955).

Wildenmann, Rudolf, *Partei und Fraktion. Ein Beitrag zur Analyse der Politischen Willensbildung und des Parteisystems in der Bundesrepublik* (Meisenheim: Westkulturverlag Anton Hain, 1954).

Wiskemann, Elisabeth, *Germany's Eastern Neighbors* (Oxford-London-New York: Oxford University Press, 1956).

5 . . .

SOVIET FOREIGN POLICY

. . . Vernon V. Aspaturian

I.   Continuity and Change in Russian Foreign Policy

ONE OF THE MOST baffling aspects of Soviet foreign policy is its
remarkable capacity for evoking the most variegated and contradictory
responses to its diplomacy. "In its distant objectives," writes Edward
Crankshaw, "the foreign policy of the Soviet Union is less obscure and
more coherent than that of any other country," yet its immediate intentions and the motivations behind its day-to-day diplomacy often
appear incoherent, capricious, and almost always enigmatic.[1]

The foreign policy of any country, the Soviet Union included, is not,
however, simply the sum total of its avowed intentions, no matter how
sincerely and devotedly they are adhered to, but must depend upon
the capacity, in the present or in the future, to carry out its intentions.
"In order to transform the world," Stalin told H. G. Wells in 1934, "it
is necessary to have political power . . . as a lever of change."[2]
Marxist ideology, reinforced by the early experiences of the Soviet
regime, thus has persuaded the Kremlin that the capacity to transform intentions into reality is indistinguishable from power, a power
which is objectively determined by the economic and social founda-

---

[1] *New York Times Book Review,* July 3, 1949, p. 4.

[2] J. V. Stalin and H. G. Wells, *Marxism vs. Liberalism* (New York, 1934),
p. 14.

tions of society, but which, in turn, can dictate the evolution of society towards particular ethical and political goals.

In order to draw a proper appraisal of Soviet diplomacy at any given time, the voluntaristic aspects of Soviet foreign policy must always be measured against its power to overcome the deterministic impediments of international reality. Thus, although the Soviet Union can plan the calculated growth of the economic and military foundations of its power, it cannot "plan" foreign policy. This fact was eloquently stated by Maxim Litvinov to the Central Committee of the Party in 1929:

> Unlike other Commissariats, the Commissariat for Foreign Affairs cannot, unfortunately, put forward a five-year plan of work, a plan for the development of foreign policy. . . In . . . drawing up the plan of economic development we start from our own aspirations and wishes, from a calculation of our own potentialities, and from the firm principles of our entire policy, but in examining the development of foreign policy we have to deal with a number of factors that are scarcely subject to calculation, with a number of elements outside our control and the scope of our action. International affairs are composed not only of our own aspirations and actions, but of those of a large number of countries . . . pursuing other aims than ours, and using other means to achieve those aims than we allow.[3]

The balance between the voluntaristic and deterministic components of Soviet foreign policy is neither fixed nor stable but is in a state of continual and deliberate flux. In the initial stages of the Bolshevik Republic, its foreign policy was virtually at the mercy of external forces over which it could exercise little control, and Soviet diplomacy assumed the characteristic contours of a weak power struggling for survival under onerous conditions. As its economic and military position enhanced, it gradually assumed the characteristics of a Great Power, and given its geographical and cultural context, it took on the distinctive features of its Tsarist predecessors and the impulse to subjugate its immediate neighbors.

A.   The geographic and historical
inheritance

"Marxism," writes a contemporary Soviet specialist on diplomacy, "teaches that economic factors determine the foreign policy and diplomacy of a state only in the long run, and that politics and diplomacy are, in a certain sense, conditioned by the concrete historical period

---

[3] *Protokoly Zasedani Tsentralnovo Ispolnitelnovo Komiteta Sovetov*, Bulletin 14, (Moscow, 1930), p. 1.

and by many other elements (not excluding even, for instance, the geographical situation of a given country)." [4] Although Soviet writers may still tend to agree with the observation of the hapless Karl Radek, that "it is silly to say that geography plays the part of fate, that it determines the foreign policy of a state," geography is nonetheless the most permanent conditioning factor in a country's foreign policy; for location, topography, and natural resources are significant—and often decisive—determinants of a country's economic and military power.[5] Geography's effects, however, are relative, rarely absolute, always dependent upon the more variable factors in a country's character, such as its cultural traditions, political institutions, size and diversity of its population, the exploitation of its natural resources, and the skill of its statesmen. A country's geography, with rare exceptions, cannot be remade; it can only be utilized more effectively. Thus, although Radek's contention that "the questions raised by geography are dealt with by each social formation in its own way . . . determined by its peculiar economic and political aims," remains incontestable, it was the blessing of Providence that this vast empire secreted all the basic ingredients for the erection of a powerful industrial and military state, given the necessary will and determination of its leadership. Had Russia been a wasteland with limited raw materials, she would have been doomed as a permanent pre-industrial society, and the character of her foreign policy, to say nothing of her very existence, would have been vastly different, and her vaunted ideology would have long been relegated to the ash cans of history.

The Soviet Union, like Tsarist Russia before it, is the largest single continuous intercontinental empire in the world. Embracing fully one-half of two continents, the Soviet Union has the world's longest and most exposed frontier, which is both its greatest potential hazard and one of its prime assets in international politics. As a part of both Europe and Asia, and embracing more than 150 ethnic and linguistic groups ranging from the most sophisticated nations to the most primitive, the U.S.S.R. achieves a unique microcosmic character denied any other country, including the United States with its ethnically variegated but linguistically assimilated population. Russia's serpentine frontier is both a consequence of the indefensible character of the central Russian plain and at the same time an important conditioning factor in the further evolution and execution of its foreign policy. For

---

[4] F. I. Kozhevnikov, "Engels on 19th Century Russian Diplomacy," *Sovetskoye Gosudarstvo i Pravo* (No. 12), December 1950, pp. 18-34.

[5] Karl Radek, "The Bases of Soviet Foreign Policy," in H. F. Armstrong, ed., *The Foreign Affairs Reader* (New York, 1947), p. 173.

a weak Russia, such a frontier affords maximum exposure to attack, but for a powerful Russian state, this extended frontier, bordering on nearly a dozen states, offers an enviable and limitless choice for the exertion of diplomatic pressure. Since 1939 the Soviet Union has annexed four of its former neighbors, seized territory from seven more, and has made territorial demands upon two others; most of this territory was previously lost by a weakened Russia. Of all her bordering states, only Afghanistan has not been imposed upon to cede territory to the Soviet Union.

In the past, Russia's geographical position has exposed her to continuous depredations and subjugation from all directions—an inevitable consequence of political disunity in a geographically indefensible community. If geography simplified the conquest of a divided Russia, it also facilitated the expansion of a united and powerful Russian state, which pushed out in all directions, until it was arrested by superior force.

In the absence of more obvious geographical obstacles to her enemies, Russia's physical security became irrevocably attached to landspace, while her psychological security became inseparable from political centralization. This conviction was confirmed by Stalin, himself, on the occasion of Moscow's 800th anniversary in 1947:

> Moscow's service consists first and foremost in the fact that it became the foundation for the unification of a disunited Russia into a single state with a single government, a single leadership. No country in the world that has not been able to free itself of feudal disunity and wrangling among princes can hope to preserve its independence or score substantial economic and cultural progress. Only a country united in a single centralized state can count on being able to make substantial cultural-economic progress and assert its independence.[6]

It is a persisting fact of Russian history that this dual quest for physical and psychological security has produced a unique dynamic in Russian foreign policy: A divided Russia invites attack, but a united Russia stimulates expansion in all directions. The Revolutions in 1917 and the terrible purges of the 'thirties—which Stalin undertook to enforce unity at home under his monolithic leadership—exposed Russia's internal schisms to the world and stimulated foreign intervention. In each crisis, after surviving the initial assault from without, she embarked on a campaign designed to carry her beyond her self-declared national frontiers. The campaign failed in 1921 but succeeded after World War II in bringing all of Eastern Europe under her hegemony.

---

[6] *Pravda,* September 11, 1947.

The Bolsheviks fell heir not only to Russia's geography and natural resources but also to the bulk of her population, her language, and the Russian historical and cultural legacy. Marxism gave Russia new goals and aspirations, but once the decision was taken to survive as a national state, even on a temporary and instrumental basis, the Soviet Union could not evade assuming the contours of a Russian State and falling heir to the assets and liabilities of its predecessors. Although Lenin thought that he had irrevocably severed the umbilical cord with Russia's past, the choice to unburden the new Soviet Republic of the disadvantages of Tsarist diplomacy was not exclusively his. Foreign attitudes remained remarkably constant; fears and suspicions, sympathies and attachments, wherever they existed, were reinforced more than erased. Designs on Soviet territory still came from the same quarter, exposure to attack remained in the same places, and the economic and commercial life-lines of the Tsars became no less indispensable to the new regime. In short, even if the Soviet Union refused to remain Russia, Japan remained Japan, Poland remained Poland, and the Straits remained the Straits.

The Russian language, permanently encrusted in its Cyrillic shell, became the official speech of Soviet diplomacy, and, as the vehicle of the Marxist dogma, it was pompously proclaimed the "language of the future." Russian cultural and scientific achievement became the basis for Soviet claims to cultural supremacy, of which Soviet science and culture were pronounced a continuation; the symbolism of Holy Russia was revived. Although Moscow eagerly laid claim to all the advantages of historic Russia, the outside world just as assiduously refused to permit her to evade the liabilities and vulnerabilities of the Russian past. Thus, partly by choice and partly by necessity, the foreign policy of the Soviet Union could not but assume the contours of its predecessors.

The impact of a voluntaristic doctrine like Marxism on the geographical facts of Russia and her messianic traditions not only reinforced the psychological obsession for security, but provided an ideological rationale for assuming the implacable hostility of the outside world and sanctified Russian expansion with the ethical mission of liberating the downtrodden masses of the world from their oppressors. The hostile "West" of the Slavophils was transformed into the hostility of capitalism and imperialism; instead of the parochial messianism of the pan-Slav enthusiasts, Marxism provided Russia with a mission of universal transcendence—transforming the outside world into her own image in fulfillment of her historic destiny and as the only permanent guarantee of absolute security. Up until the 20th Party

Congress in 1956, the Leninist-Stalinist thesis that "the destruction of capitalist encirclement and the destruction of the danger of capitalist intervention are possible only as a result of the victory of the proletarian revolution, at least in several large countries," [7] continued to be in force. Although "capitalist encirclement" was declared ended by Stalin's successors, the recent events in Poland and Hungary may have convinced the Kremlin that this proclamation was premature.

To assume, however, that Soviet foreign policy is merely Russian imperialism in new garb would be a catastrophic mistake on both sides. Soviet foreign policy was bound to assume "Russian" characteristics during one phase of its metamorphosis, but now that the maximum, but still limited, aims of Tsarist imperialism have been virtually consummated, the aggressive (no longer necessarily expansionist) aspects of its foreign policy will assume a purely Marxist character, while only the defensive aspects (*i.e.*, the preservation of its present power position) of its diplomacy will retain distinctively "Russian" features. That these two aspects of current Soviet foreign policy are in flagrant contradiction is self-evident, even to the Kremlin and other Communist leaders. Chinese accusations of "Great Power chauvinism," the de-Stalinization campaign, and the uprisings in Poland and Hungary, are all manifestations of this fundamental schism in Soviet foreign policy. Whereas in the past, when the Soviet Union was weak, indiscriminate emphasis on the revolutionary aspects of its foreign policy tended to undermine its basic instinct to survive, now, its "defensive" reflexes tend to subvert not only its continuing leadership of world Communism, but the eventual success of the movement itself.

B.   World revolution and national interest in Soviet diplomacy

Deciphering Soviet motives is an elusive and hazardous undertaking, yet it must be done systematically and with calculation, otherwise *ad hoc* and unconscious assumptions acquire priority by default. Miscalculation of motives can often be catastrophic since foreign policy expectations are built upon assumptions concerning the motives and capabilities of other powers, and diplomatic success or failure often depend on the degree of accuracy with which these assumptions approach actuality. Much of the agony of postwar Western diplomacy can be traced directly to illusory expectations resulting from false calculations of Soviet motives by Western leaders. Diplomacy, however, is not an intellectual exercise, and motives are not always sus-

---

[7] *Kommunist* (No. 2), January 1953, p. 15.

ceptible to rational and logical analysis. Assessment of motives, in any event, is rarely certain and in most cases calls not only for acute analytical intelligence, but for espionage, and above all for the intuitive wisdom of long experience in statecraft.   •

Information concerning Soviet motives is derived from three principal sources: (1) word, (2) conduct, and (3) personal contact with the Soviet leadership. In general, whenever there exists a discrepancy between publicly stated intention and conduct, the latter is a more reliable indicator of motives on a short-run basis. Actually there are three possible relations between speech and practice in Soviet diplomacy: (1) *identity;* (2) *approximation,* usually implying a temporary accommodation or modification of a preconceived intention, unless the latter itself receives explicit reformulation; and (3) *divergence.* Cleavages between word and conduct may, in turn, result from faulty execution, misinformation, miscalculation, or deliberate confusion.

Analyzing Soviet diplomacy purely from documents, speeches, and ideological statements, gives undue weight to "rational" factors, since the irrational and accidental aspects of diplomacy can hardly be culled from documentary sources, and, although such a study may give a fairly lucid picture of the long-range outlines of Soviet policy, it is of limited validity as an investigation of Soviet diplomacy. On the other hand, calculating Soviet motives purely on the basis of day-to-day conduct and responses to particular situations can easily produce a distorted conception of Soviet foreign policy and lead to the erroneous conclusion that it is only slightly distinguishable from traditional Great Power diplomacy.

Diplomacy is neither impersonal nor automatic in its execution—although its working executors may often be both—but it is a human enterprise. Soviet motives cannot be separated from the character and personality traits of the principal decision-makers in the Kremlin. Any evaluation of the foreign policy of the Soviet Union, whose principal decision-makers are a well-defined oligarchy, without a prudent and careful examination and consideration of the various estimates and observations of the "human equations" in Soviet diplomacy is bound to be defective. The personal factor, particularly in the last fifteen years of Stalin's life, was of crucial significance in any evaluation of Soviet foreign policy. Personal observations of the Soviet leadership, however, are essentially subjective; they originate with observers who are free from neither ignorance, prejudice, nor gullibility, and the observations are apt to vary accordingly. Any attempt to distill the essence of Soviet diplomacy solely from personality considerations is in fact doomed to hopeless confusion and sterility. A sound analysis of

Soviet motives must take into consideration ideology, conduct, and personalities, not as separate and independent entities, but as basic variables whose relative and relational significance is in a constant state of flux.

One question that inevitably arises is whether Soviet policy is actually motivated by ideological ends, such as world revolution, or by some other more mundane consideration, such as "power" or "national interest." Soviet ideology itself defines "national interest," "power," and "world revolution" in such a way as to make them virtually as indistinguishable and inseparable as the three sides of an equilateral triangle. The transcendental goal of Soviet foreign policy, world revolution, was defined by Lenin even before the existence of the Soviet state, when he declared in 1915 that "the victorious proletariat of [one] country . . . would stand up against . . . the capitalist world . . . raising revolts in those countries against the capitalists, and in the event of necessity coming out even with armed force against the exploiting classes and their states." [8] " 'The fundamental question of revolution is the question of power,' " wrote Stalin quoting Lenin, and he went on to say that as the effectiveness of the Soviet Union as an instrument of world revolution is measured in terms of power, "the whole point is to retain power, to consolidate it, to make it invincible." [9] As a contrived and temporary nation-state, the Soviet Union assumed particular interests, but "the U.S.S.R. has no interests at variance with the interests of the world revolution, and the international proletariat naturally has no interests that are at variance with the Soviet Union." [10] Stalin's final fusion was to identify the consolidation and extension of his own power with the interests of the world revolution.

The abstraction of a Soviet national interest outside the context of Soviet ideology, no matter how superficially attractive it may appear to be as a useful analytical tool, ruptures the image of Soviet reality and results in the calculation of Soviet foreign policy on the basis of false assumptions. Soviet foreign policy is based upon the image of reality provided by the Marxist-Leninist ideological prism, and whether this image be faulty or not is totally irrelevant in the calculation of Soviet motives, although such a foreign policy will eventually reap its toll in diplomatic failure. The Soviet conception of "interest" cannot be separated from class categories, and its determination is essentially horizontal rather than vertical. Although the legal expression of class

---

[8] V. I. Lenin, *Selected Works* (New York, n.d.), Vol. V, p. 141.
[9] J. V. Stalin, *Problems of Leninism* (Moscow, 1947), p. 39.
[10] W. K. Knorin, *Fascism, Social-Democracy and the Communists* (Moscow, 1933).

interests is temporarily articulated through the nation-state, and assumes the character of a "national interest," nonetheless in the Soviet view there exist within each state not one but several parallel "national interests," corresponding to its socio-economic development. The "national interest" reflected by the state in its diplomacy, however, can only represent the interests of the "ruling class," and no other, regardless of its pretensions.

Soviet ideology recognizes the co-existence of three qualitatively distinct national interests in the modern world, owing to the uneven development of society: (1) the national interest of the feudal aristocracy, surviving only in extremely backward societies; (2) the national interest of the bourgeoisie, which allegedly is the dominant expression of most non-Communist states; and (3) the national interest of the proletariat, receiving diplomatic expression only in Communist states, which is presumed by the dialectic to be coterminous with that of society as a whole.

Marxism tenaciously holds to the view that the community of interests that binds identical classes of different nations is more fundamental and decisive than that which binds different classes within the same nation-state. Although division and disunity are inherently characteristic of the bourgeois classes of different states, whose conflicts of interest are periodically expressed in war, the interests of all proletarians (together with their peasant and colonial allies) are considered to be in total harmony, their basic identity being temporarily obscured by artificially stimulated national distinctions.

Given the premise of the total identity of interests on a class basis, the Soviet Union, as the only avowed proletarian state in existence and the self-proclaimed embryo of a universal proletarian state, pronounced its interests to be identical with those of the world proletariat:

> The Communist Party of the Soviet Union has always proceeded from the fact that "national" and international problems of the proletariat of the U.S.S.R. amalgamate into one general problem of liberating the proletarians of all countries from capitalism, and the interests . . . in our country wholly and fully amalgamate with the interests of the revolutionary movement of all countries into one general interest of the victory of socialist revolution in all countries.[11]

Although this view is vigorously contested, is far from universally recognized, and does not correspond to actual facts, it is not thereby invalidated as a basis for diplomatic action or analysis.

---

[11] *Kommunist* (No. 2), January 1953, p. 15.

The presence of one of two factors, both capable of objective verification, is sufficient to impart to the national interests of a particular state an authentic international quality. These factors are: (1) the creation of appropriate forms of political organization designed to articulate the national interests of one state as those of the world at large; and (2) mass recognition in other countries that the national interests of a foreign state are identical with a higher transcendental interest. Not one, but both of these desiderata characterize Soviet foreign policy. It is a cardinal aim of Soviet policy to replace the nation-state system with a world Communist state by shifting allegiance and loyalty from the nation-state to class, and this policy not only invites the nationals of other countries to recognize a higher class loyalty to the Soviet Union, but actively engages in fostering the appropriate political institutions, such as the Comintern, foreign Communist parties, front organizations, and the like, to implement this fusion.

The Soviet invitation to commit mass disloyalty has elicited wide response, and the formula identifying Soviet interests with the interests of the world proletariat has been accepted by millions of Communists throughout the world as a basis for political action. This gives to Soviet national interests an undeniable transcendental quality, denied to the national interests of any other state, no matter how persistently it may claim to be motivated by the interests of all mankind, for if such a claim neither is accompanied by a serious effort at implementation nor evokes a response in other countries, it remains an empty and pious pretension. Transcendental ethical ends in foreign policy, irrespective of their substantive nature, have relevance only if they function as effective instruments or stimulants for the limitation, preservation, or further accumulation of power, or as instruments for its focalization. Otherwise, they are meaningless slogans and utopias, devoid of anything but peripheral significance in the calculation of a country's foreign policy.

Expansionism is thus inherent in the Leninist-Stalinist ideology, since the Soviet state was conceived as an ideological state without fixed geographical frontiers. Not only did this idea of the Soviet Union as the nucleus of a universal Communist state receive expression in the basic documents of the Comintern,[12] but the Soviet Constitution of 1924 itself, proclaimed the new Union to be open to all future Soviet republics and a "decisive step towards the union of workers of all countries into one World Socialist Soviet Republic." [13] And at Lenin's

---

[12] *Cf.* W. H. Chamberlin, ed., *Blueprint for World Conquest* (Chicago, 1946).
[13] Full text in M. W. Graham, *New Governments of Eastern Europe* (New York, 1927), p. 608.

bier Stalin personally vowed "to consolidate and extend the Union of Republics." [14] As the indispensable instrument and base of the World Revolution, the extension of Soviet power and territory, by any means, was equated with the exfoliation of the Revolution.

Stalin's attempt to preserve the dominant and privileged status of the Soviet proletariat in the postwar Communist fraternity of nations resulted in a specific form of Soviet imperialism that brought about Tito's defection and unleashed corrosive forces within the orbit as a whole. The failure of Stalin and his successors to calculate accurately the persistence and vitality of the community of interests based on national peculiarities is actually a reflection of the inadequacy of Marxist categories to deal with the conflicting interests of national communities, whether they be Communist or bourgeois.

Paradoxically, as long as the Soviet Union was the only Communist state, its universalistic pretensions were unchallenged by foreign Communist parties, but with the eclipse of the Soviet monopoly on the interests of the world proletariat, occasioned by the emergence of a Communist China and national Communism in Eastern Europe, the universalistic pretensions of the Leninist doctrine have been blunted, while, at the same time, stimulating a more limited "regional interest" aimed at synthetizing the various national interests of the Communist orbit. The transmutation of several national interests into a single supranational interest remains an insuperable difficulty in the Communist world, so long as the incompatibility of individual Communist national interests, which the Marxist dogma fails to perceive accurately, prevails:

> Marxism-Leninism has always strongly advocated that proletarian internationalism be combined with patriotism. . . . The Communist Parties of all countries must . . . become the spokesmen of the legitimate national interests and sentiments of their people [and] . . . effectively educate the masses in the spirit of internationalism and harmonize the national sentiments and interests of these countries.[15]

II.   Soviet Ideology and Foreign Policy

The exact relationship between Soviet ideology and foreign policy has been subject to great controversy, ranging from the view that it is

---

[14] *History of the Communist Party of the Soviet Union* (New York, 1939), p. 269.

[15] *Pravda*, December 31, 1956. Full text of the statement by the Chinese Communist Party, "Once More on the Historical Experience of the Dictatorship of the Proletariat."

substantially irrelevant to the conviction that foreign policy is rigidly dictated by ideology. Actually, aside from providing the transcendental objectives of Soviet diplomacy, Soviet ideology performs five additional and distinct functions in foreign policy: (1) As a system of knowledge and as an analytical prism it reflects an image of the existing social order and the distinctive analytical instruments (dialectical laws, and categories like the "class struggle," "historical stages," and so on) for its diagnosis and prognosis. (2) It provides an action strategy whereby to accelerate the transformation of the existing social order into the Communist millenium. (3) It serves as a system of communication unifying and coordinating the activities of its adherents. (4) It functions as a system of higher rationalization to justify, obscure, or conceal the chasms that may develop between theory and practice. (5) It stands as a symbol of continuity and legitimacy.

This compartmentalization of Soviet ideology is frankly arbitrary and actually ruptures its basic unity, which is not necessarily to be found in its logic or reason but in the intuitive faith and active experience of its partisans—factors which often elude rational analysis. Elements of Soviet ideology that appear logically incompatible, in fact, are, but these rational contradictions can be unified only in the cruci-. bles of revolutionary action, not in the intellectual processes of the mind. The true meaning of the Marxist-Leninist insistence on the "unity of theory and practice" is that contradictions cannot be resolved by logic, but by action, which is the final judge of "truth." Communist "truth" cannot be perceived without intuitive involvement, *i.e.*, revolutionary action and experience, and to the outsider it remains as enigmatic as the mysteries of Zen.

A. The Soviet image of the world

The Soviet ideological prism reflects an image of the world that is virtually unrecognizable to a non-Communist, yet it is upon this image that Soviet foreign policy is based. It reflects a world of incessant conflict and change, in which institutions, loyalties, and philosophies arise and decay in accordance with the convulsive rhythm of the dialectic, which implacably propels it upon a predetermined arc to a foreordained future—world Communism. This image is accepted as the real world by Soviet leaders. Their foreign policy rests upon the conviction that Marxism-Leninism is a scientific system that has uncovered and revealed the fundamental and implacable laws of social evolution and hence affords its adherents the unique advantage of prediction and partial control of events. This conviction imparts to Soviet diplomacy an air of supreme confidence and dogmatic self-righteousness:

Soviet diplomacy . . . wields a weapon possessed by none of its rivals or opponents. Soviet diplomacy is fortified by a scientific theory of Marxism-Leninism. This doctrine lays down the unshakeable laws of social development. By revealing these norms, it gives the possibility not only of understanding the current tendencies of international life, but also of permitting the desirable collaboration with the march of events. Such are the special advantages held by Soviet diplomacy. They give it a special position in international life and explain its outstanding successes.[16]

The history of Soviet diplomacy, however, is by no means a uniform record of successes, though "errors" in foreign policy are ascribed not to the doctrine but to the improper apprehension and application of these infallible laws. Failure to apply these laws, according to the Soviet view, divorces foreign policy from international realities, and although it is true that "the record of Soviet diplomacy shows an inability to distinguish between the real and the imaginary, a series of false calculations about the capabilities and intentions of foreign countries, and a record of clumsy coordination between diplomacy and propaganda," [17] it is fatuous to deny that Marxism-Leninism, on the whole, has furnished Soviet leadership with a system of analysis that, while frequently out of focus with reality, gives a sufficiently accurate comprehension of power, its calculation and distribution in the world, and the opportunities and limitations such calculations afford for Soviet foreign policy. The dogmatic reliance on techniques and methods that have proven successful under other conditions, the frequent refusal to jettison concepts that either have outlived their usefulness or consistently produce dismal results in terms of foreign policy aims, and the concentration of all decision-making authority in one man or in a tight oligarchy—these practices at times tend to convert Marxism-Leninism from a unique asset for Soviet diplomacy into a strait jacket.

1. *The dialectical image of history.* Soviet ideology exposes the forces and tendencies operating in international politics, but it is up to the leadership to calculate these forces properly, seek out the most decisive trends, and coordinate Soviet diplomacy with the inexorable march of history. The success of Soviet diplomacy, according to the Soviet view, is maximized as it is attuned to the rhythm of the historical dialectic, and its failures are multiplied as it falls out of har-

---

[16] V. P. Potemkin, ed., *Istoriya Diplomatii* (Moscow, 1945), Vol. III, pp. 763-764.

[17] Max Beloff, *Foreign Policy and the Democratic Process* (Baltimore, 1955), p. 98.

mony. Conversely, the occasional successes of bourgeois diplomacy are due to fortuitous and haphazard coordination with historical development, or to the equally accidental deviation of Soviet foreign policy from the implacable dictates of history. These accidental deviations are attributed to faulty application of historical laws by individual leaders.

Without attempting any extended discussion of Soviet dialectics, it can be said that in the Communist view, history progressively exfoliates as a series of qualitative stages, each with its own peculiar economic organization of society giving rise to corresponding social, political, and religious institutions. This inexorable movement from lower to higher forms of economic and social organization is propelled by means of a dialectical duel between perpetually developing economic forces of society and the social and political institutions that attempt to preserve the economic order in the interests of a particular ruling class, whose servants they are. As long as the institution of private property survives, class distinctions between property-holders and the propertyless, whose interests are irreconcilable, are perpetuated and eventuate in conflict, war, and revolution, only to be replaced by a new economic system that perpetuates class divisions and conflicts in new form. The class struggle, which is the principal motivating force of historical revolution, comes to an end only with the overthrow of the capitalist system by the proletariat, after which class distinctions, conflict, and war are finally eliminated. Once Communism achieves victory on a world scale, the state itself and its coercive institutions are supposed to "wither away." [18]

The Communists recognize five qualitative historical stages: primitive communism, slave-system, feudalism, capitalism, and socialism-communism, all of which, except for the first and last, are characterized by the institution of private property, two main contending classes (owners of the means of production and workers), and a state that represents the interests of the ruling class. Although the movement of history is from lower to higher stages, this movement is neither uniform nor without complications, and it does not pursue a uniform and rigid chronological evolution. This has been particularly true of the twentieth century. At the present time, Communists acknowledge the co-existence of all historical stages; and this recognition has had a profound influence on Soviet foreign policy. Furthermore, each his-

---

[18] For a more elaborate statement of the author's views on the nature of Soviet ideology, cf. Vernon V. Aspaturian, "The Contemporary Doctrine of the Soviet State and Its Philosophical Foundations," *American Political Science Review*, Vol. XLVIII, December 1954.

torical stage is characterized by manifold substages or "transitional forms."

The recognition of new or unforeseen historical stages or transitional forms in the dialectical movement of history is the most delicate and crucial problem of "creative Marxism," since Soviet policy must be based on a constantly changing historical reality and its strategy is subordinated to the dictates of each stage and varies geographically in accordance with different co-existing stages. Major doctrinal schisms arise whenever serious differences about the existence or nature of historical stages and their transitional forms cannot be reconciled. According to Stalin, Marxism is not

> . . . a collection of dogmas that "never" change despite changes in the conditions of the development of society. . . . Marxism as a science cannot stand still, it develops and improves. In its development Marxism cannot but be enriched by new experience, new knowledge—consequently some of its formulae and conclusions cannot but change with the passage of time, cannot but be replaced by new formulae and conclusions, corresponding to new historical tasks. Marxism does not recognize invariable conclusions and formulae obligatory for all epochs and periods.[19]

Even seemingly unambiguous concepts like "inevitability" are neither absolute nor fatally deterministic, but must be understood within the context of a particular historical stage and under given conditions. Thus what may appear inevitable, *viz.*, war, in one stage and under one set of conditions may no longer be inevitable if the conditions change or a new historical stage manifests itself. The single absolute is the abstraction of the dialectical movement itself; its content varies and hence is relativistic. Consequently, interpretation of Soviet dogma often assumes the character of tortured scholastic wrangling and frequently leads to tautological absurdities like "fatal inevitability," which presumably means inevitability in the absolute sense as differentiated from inevitability in the relative sense.

Soviet ideology is not self-executing; that is, it does not interpret itself automatically and does not reflect images of reality that can be unambiguously perceived, but rather it is based upon an authoritative interpretation of changing events by the Soviet leaders, who must choose from among a variety of possible interpretations, only one of which can be tested at a time for truth in the crucible of action. As long as Stalin was alive, interpretation of doctrine was a monopoly reserved for him alone, and it was his interpretation, whether it was concerned with the materialistic basis of the thought processes of the deaf and

---

[19] J. V. Stalin, *Concerning Marxism in Linguistics* (London, 1950), pp. 39-40.

dumb or with the nature of the state, that became the basis for official policy. All other possible interpretations were consigned to heretical oblivion, to be resurrected later by him or by his successors who silently disputed his conception of reality.

2. *The two-camp image.*   Stalin's image of the world after the Russian Revolution was one of forced "co-existence" between a single socialist state and a hostile capitalist world surrounding it—a co-existence imposed upon both antagonists by objective historical conditions. Neither side being sufficiently powerful to end the existence of the other, they were fated to exist together temporarily on the basis of an unstable and constantly shifting balance of power:

> The fundamental and new, the decisive feature, which has affected all the events in the sphere of foreign relations during this period, is the fact that a certain temporary equilibrium of forces has been established between our country . . . and the countries of the capitalist world; an equilibrium which has determined the present period of "peaceful co-existence." [20]

The establishment in a capitalist world of a socialist bridgehead, which was inevitably destined to envelop the entire globe was, for Stalin, the supreme and ineluctable contradiction in the international scene. Although the capitalist world was infinitely stronger and could overwhelm the Soviet Republic if it could embark on a common enterprise, it was viewed as torn by internal divisions and conflicts that prevented the organization of an anti-Soviet crusade. Beside the overriding contradiction between the Socialist camp and the capitalist camp, the bourgeois world was plagued with four additional inescapable contradictions: (1) the contradiction between the proletariat and the bourgeoisie in each country; (2) the contradiction between the revisionist and *status quo* powers (Stalin referred to them as "victor" and "vanquished" capitalist states); (3) the contradiction between the victorious powers over the spoils of war; (4) the contradiction between the imperialist states and their colonial subjects.

The contradiction between the socialist and capitalist camps was considered by Stalin the most fundamental and decisive, but it was not to be aggravated so long as the Soviet Union was in a weakened condition. War between the two camps was viewed as inevitable; however, it could be temporarily avoided and delayed by astute maneuvering within the conflicts raging in the capitalist world:

---

[20] J. V. Stalin, *Political Report of the Central Committee to the 14th Congress of the C.P.S.U. (B)* (Moscow, 1950), p. 8.

England's attempts to form a united front against the U.S.S.R. have failed so far. The reasons for this failure are: the antagonisms of interests in the camp of the imperialists. . . . Hence the task of taking into account the antagonisms in the camp of the imperialists, of postponing war by "buying off" the capitalists. . . . We must not forget what Lenin said about very much in our work of construction depending upon whether we succeed in postponing war with the capitalist world, which is inevitable, but which can be postponed either until the moment when the proletarian revolution in Europe matures, or until the moment when the colonial revolutions have fully matured, or, lastly, until the moment when the capitalists fight among themselves over the division of the colonies.[21]

During Stalin's lifetime, despite his periodic strictures against "dogmatism," his image of the two-camp world remained remarkably fixed, although the center of the developing anti-Soviet crusade passed first from England to Nazi Germany and finally to the United States, which he had predicted as early as 1925 would become the final bastion of world capitalism. Although this image of reality failed to apprise correctly the nature and motivations of Nazi Germany and incorrectly assumed the impossibility of a Soviet alliance with the Western Powers, Stalin's fixed vision of "two camps" poised in uneasy co-existence dominated Soviet diplomacy in the postwar period, becoming even more indelibly etched in Soviet ideology.

Stalin's postwar policy was predicated upon an inevitable conflict with the West, organized by the United States. The organization of the Cominform and the forced unity of the Communist orbit, the expulsion of Tito from the Communist fraternity, the extraction of public statements of loyalty from Communist leaders in all countries, the urgency with which Stalin sought to eliminate all possible power vacuums between the two blocs along the periphery of the Communist world, all were preparatory measures based on the false assumption that the American ruling class was betraying anxiety at the growth of Soviet power and was preparing the final Armageddon. At the founding convention of the Cominform the late Andrei Zhdanov revealed the authoritative Soviet interpretation of the emerging bipolarization of power:

The fundamental changes caused by the war on the international scene and in the position of individual countries have entirely changed the political landscape of the world. A new alignment of political forces has arisen. The more the war recedes into the past, the more distinct become two major trends in postwar international

---

[21] J. V. Stalin, *Political Report . . . to the 15th Congress* (Moscow, 1950), pp. 29-30.

policy, corresponding to the division of the political forces operating on the international arena into two major camps; the imperialist and antidemocratic camp, on the one hand, and the anti-imperialist and democratic camp, on the other. The principal driving force of the imperialist camp is the U.S.A. . . . The cardinal purpose of the imperialist camp is to strengthen imperialism, to hatch a new imperialist war, to combat Socialism.[22]

Based on this grim image of the imminent expectation of violence, Soviet foreign policy assumed increasingly bellicose tendencies, which, in turn, evoked the natural response in the West that the Soviet Union, itself, was preparing to overrun Western Europe and all of Asia. Friction all along the periphery dividing the two worlds was frequent and finally erupted in the Korean war, when Stalin sanctioned the move into South Korea on the assumption that it had become a vacuum between the two blocs. This action accelerated defensive preparations in the West, and Stalin's policies, by predicting the increasing hostility of the West, actually forced its materialization.

During the Korean war and just prior to the 19th Party Congress in 1952, a "great debate" had apparently taken place in the Politburo concerning the validity of the expectation of imminent war between the two camps. Two essentially divergent views were petulantly discussed by Stalin in his *Economic Problems of Socialism:* (1) that wars between capitalist countries had ceased to be inevitable and hence war between the two camps was imminent, the view that was then current; and (2) that wars between capitalist states remained inevitable, but that war between the two camps was unlikely. Although the first view was the basis of Soviet postwar policy, Stalin ascribed it to "mistaken comrades," and elevated the second to doctrinal significance:

> Some comrades hold that, owing to the development of new international conditions since the Second World War, wars between the capitalist countries have ceased to be inevitable. They consider . . . that the U.S.A. has brought the other capitalist countries sufficiently under its sway to be able to prevent them going to war among themselves and . . . that the foremost capitalist minds have been sufficiently taught by the two world wars . . . not to involve the capitalist countries in war with one another again. . . . It is said that the contradictions between capitalism and socialism are stronger than the contradictions among the capitalist countries. Theoretically, of course that is true. It is not only true now, today; it was true before the Second World War. . . . Yet the Second World War began not as a war with the U.S.S.R., but

---

[22] Full text reprinted in *Strategy and Tactics of World Communism* (Washington, D.C.: G.P.O., 1948), pp. 216-217.

as a war between capitalist countries. Why? . . . because war with the U.S.S.R., as a socialist land, is more dangerous to capitalism than war between capitalist countries; for whereas war between capitalist countries puts in question only the supremacy of certain capitalist countries over others, war with the U.S.S.R. must certainly put in question the existence of capitalism itself. . . . It is said that Lenin's thesis that imperialism inevitably generates war must now be regarded as obsolete. . . . That is not true. . . . To eliminate the inevitability of war, it is necessary to abolish imperialism.[23]

Stalin's only modification of his two-camp image was thus to concede that imminent war between the two blocs was no longer inevitable, but would first be preceded by a series of inevitable wars among the capitalist powers themselves—between the United States and its satellite allies, France and Britain, and its temporary vassals, Germany and Japan, whose ruling classes' resentment at American domination would provoke "national revolutions" and a renewed war over the ever-shrinking capitalist market, occasioned by the emergence of a "parallel" Communist market, which would remain outside the arena of capitalist exploitation. The Soviet Union would remain outside the conflict, which would automatically seal the doom of world capitalism. Stalin's policies actually accentuated the very conflict—that between the two camps—he wished to temporarily deemphasize, while submerging those—among the capitalist states—which he wished to exacerbate. Soviet policy, by predicting war, was threatening to make a nuclear holocaust, which would destroy both worlds, inevitable.

3. *The post-Stalin image.* Stalin's image of reality was first challenged by Tito in 1948 and apparently later by his own colleagues on the Politburo. Khrushchev admitted that these differences were so serious that Stalin was plotting to liquidate all of his old associates for daring to question his ideological infallibility. Stalin's obstinate refusal to keep in step with changing conditions resulted in converting Soviet ideology from a prism that reflected reality into a prison that concealed it, resulting not only in a series of diplomatic blunders, but also in blinding Moscow to new diplomatic opportunities. As the man, next to Stalin, most closely associated with Soviet foreign policy, Molotov confessed on behalf of his departed chief:

We do not infrequently still remain prisoners of habits and patterns formed in the past, before World War II, and which now hinder the deployment of new, wider, and more active forms of

---

[23] J. V. Stalin, *Economic Problems of Socialism* (New York, 1952), pp. 27-30.

struggle. . . . We not infrequently still suffer from underestimation of the new possibilities which have opened before us in the post-war period. . . . We must stop underestimating the immense pos-sibilities which we have. . . . In the field of foreign policy our Party proceeds from the need for the most serious consideration of concrete conditions and from the need for understanding the given situation and the prospects of historic development. The Leninist combination of adherence to principle and elasticity in pursuance of the foreign policy line is the factor which insures success for our Party in the solution of internal tasks.[24]

At the 20th Party Congress, Stalin's image of the world was con-siderably modified in an attempt to bring it into closer focus with the realities of international politics. These modifications were made to eliminate the threatening schisms in the Communist camp, to break up the unity of the non-Soviet world and dismantle anti-Soviet instru-ments like NATO, to head off the impending nuclear war that Stalin's doctrines and policies were unwittingly encouraging, and to enhance the flexibility of Soviet diplomacy in exploiting the contradictions of the capitalist world.

In place of Stalin's fatalistic image of a bipolarized world, the 20th Party Congress drew a more optimistic, and, in many respects, a mel-lower picture:

1. "Capitalist encirclement" was officially declared terminated as major speakers like Molotov echoed the Titoist doctrine that "the period when the Soviet Union was . . . encircled by hostile capi-talism now belongs to the past." [25] The permanent insecurity of the Soviet Union, pending the world-wide victory of Communism, as visualized by Stalin, was replaced with the image of a permanently secured Soviet Union, surrounded by friendly Communist states in Europe and Asia, embracing nearly one-third of the world, with imperialism in an irrevocable state of advanced decay.

2. In place of Stalin's fixed vision of "co-existence" between two irreconcilable camps poised in temporary balance, which was de-clared obsolete and inapplicable to the postwar world, his succes-sors recognized a third "anti-imperialist" but nonsocialist group of powers carved out of decaying colonial empires, which had sepa-rated from the capitalist camp but had not yet joined the Communist. Stalin's inflexible two-camp image needlessly alienated these new states and tended to force them into the capitalist orbit. This belt of neutralist states—a concept which Stalin refused to recognize—in-sulated the entire Communist orbit from the capitalist world and, together with the socialist states, was viewed as constituting "an extensive 'zone of peace,' including both socialist and nonsocialist

[24] Full text as broadcast by the Moscow Radio, February 20, 1956; cf. also New York Times, February 21, 1956.
[25] Ibid.

peace-loving states of Europe and Asia inhabited by nearly 1,500,-000,000 people, or the majority of the population of our planet." [26]

3. Stalin's doctrine of the "fatal inevitability" of wars was pronounced antiquated, since its emphasis on coercive and violent instruments of diplomacy tended to render the Soviet peace campaign hypocritical, accelerated the formation of anti-Soviet coalitions, and, in an era of nuclear weapons, appeared to doom both worlds to a war of mutual annihilation. Soviet leaders, however, continue to go through the motions of insisting that war would result only in the unilateral extinction of capitalism, although it is unlikely that they really believe this.

4. Stalin's five main contradictions were retained as valid and persistent, but the radical shift in the equilibrium of class forces in the world dictated a change of emphasis and the reordering of priorities. Stalin stressed the conflicts among the major capitalist countries as the main object of Soviet diplomacy, relegating other contradictions to minor roles, but his successors see the main contradiction of the current historical stage to be that between the anticolonial and the imperialist forces. Just as "antifascism" was the key to the weakening of the prewar capitalist world, in the current phase, "anticolonialism" is viewed as promising the most successful possibilities for Soviet diplomacy. The sudden Soviet solicitude for Arab aspirations, the spectacular gestures to the countries of Southeast Asia, the conspicuous and indiscriminate support given to the anticolonial bloc in the United Nations, all are manifestations of the conviction that by harnessing the energies of the nationalistic anticolonial countries to the Soviet chariot, the capitalist world will be effectively isolated and more easily liquidated. In short, the world has moved out of the stage of the "capitalist encirclement" of the Soviet Union and during the current phase of "co-existence" is moving into the stage of the "socialist encirclement" of the United States as a prelude to the final victory of Communism.

The new image of the world drawn by Khrushchev at the 20th Party Congress was by no means the consequence of a unanimous decision, but was opposed by at least four and possibly five full members of the eleven-man Presidium. Aside from his vigorous opposition to Khrushchev's adventurist innovations in industry and agriculture, Foreign Minister Molotov and the so-called Stalinist faction bitterly resisted the demolition of the Stalin myth and the entire de-Stalinization program; and they systematically sabotaged the foreign policy decisions of the 20th Party Congress, which they publicly accepted.

Molotov's disagreement with the Khrushchev faction was not merely over the execution of foreign policy but over fundamental doctrinal

---

[26] Full text as broadcast by Moscow Radio, February 18, 1956; *cf.* also *New York Times*, February 19, 1956 (Mikoyan Report).

propositions as well. Thus he disputed the thesis on the "fatal inevitability of wars" that was one of the key decisions of the Party Congress. "Comrade Molotov," according to the resolution of the Central Committee which expelled him from the Presidium on June 29, 1957, "opposed the fundamental proposition worked out by the party on the possibility of preventing wars in the present condition." Furthermore, he controverted the Titoist doctrine "on the possibility of different ways of transition to socialism in different countries," and resisted the decision "on the necessity of strengthening contacts between the CPSU and the progressive parties abroad [*i.e.* non-Communist socialist parties]." [27]

Molotov's doctrinal differences had practical consequences in the actual formulation and execution of foreign policy. His constant carping criticism of existing policies, together with the precarious nature of Khrushchev's majority in the Presidium, introduced an uncharacteristic hesitancy into Soviet diplomacy. The vacillations, abrupt reversals, hesitations, discrepancies between policy and administration, and other eccentricities of Soviet diplomacy after Stalin's death were due not only to the incapacitating incompatibilities in the Presidium, but also to Molotov's use of the Foreign Ministry and Soviet missions abroad as instruments to subvert the Government's policy in favor of his own.

Molotov strenuously objected to the decisions to seek a reconciliation with Marshal Tito and to meet President Eisenhower at Geneva. When Khrushchev and Bulganin returned from Geneva, Molotov was waiting with sarcastic and biting comments on their personal diplomacy. As a result of his persistent criticism and obstructionism, he was disciplined by the Central Committee in July 1955 and his "erroneous stand on the Yugoslav issue was unanimously condemned." This was followed shortly by his forced and pained confession of doctrinal error, which superficially appeared to have no connection with foreign policy but appeared designed to tarnish his ideological orthodoxy and was an unmistakeable sign that he was on his way out. His unrelenting sabotage through the Foreign Ministry, in particular his determination to poison relations with Tito, finally led to his ouster as Foreign Minister in favor of Shepilov on the eve of Tito's visit to Moscow in June 1956. Apparently Shepilov also fell out of sympathy with the foreign policy he was supposed to execute and for opportunistic reasons (Khrushchev scathingly characterized him as "the careerist Shepilov

---

[27] Full text of the resolution reprinted in the *New York Times*, July 4, 1957. These and all subsequent references to this resolution are taken from this version.

who . . . showed himself to be a most shameless double-dealer")
cast his lot with the Stalinist faction. The Molotov group suddenly
contrived a majority in the December 1956 Plenum of the Central
Committee, but when Khrushchev regained it at the February 1957
Plenum, Shepilov was summarily dismissed as Foreign Minister in
favor of Andrei Gromyko, who, as a professional diplomat, was neither
able nor equipped to join the Kremlin power intrigues, and thus could
be counted upon not to pursue a personal foreign policy.

In the bill of particulars against Molotov, who was supported most
consistently by Kaganovich and sometimes by Malenkov, there was revealed an almost complete alternative foreign policy to the one currently adopted by the Soviet Government, one that in effect unwittingly
constitutes the platform of a "disloyal opposition." "In the sphere of
foreign policy," according to the indictment, "the group, in particular
Comrade Molotov, showed narrow-mindedness and hampered in every
way the implementation of the new pressing measures intended to ease
international tension and promote universal peace." It was charged:

1. "For a long time, Comrade Molotov, in his capacity as Foreign Minister, far from taking through the Ministry of Foreign
Affairs measures to improve relations between the U.S.S.R. and
Yugoslavia, repeatedly came out against the measures that the Presidium . . . was carrying out to improve relations wtih Yugoslavia."
2. "Comrade Molotov raised obstacles to the conclusion of the
state Treaty with Austria and the improvement of relations with
that country, which lies in the center of Europe. The conclusion of
the Austrian Treaty was largely instrumental in lessening international tension in general."
3. "He was also against normalization of relations with Japan,
while that normalization has played an important part in relaxing
international tension in the Far East."
4. "Comrade Molotov repeatedly opposed the Soviet Government's indispensable new steps in defence of peace and security
of nations. In particular he denied the advisability of establishing
personal contacts between the Soviet leaders and the statesmen of
other countries, which is essential for the achievement of mutual
understanding and better international relations [probably a reference not only to the Geneva Conference but also to the various
junkets of Bulganin and Khrushchev throughout Asia and Europe,
none of which included Foreign Minister Molotov]."

Beside these publicly stated charges against Molotov, it was reported from Warsaw that Khrushchev admitted in the Central Committee that Dulles was "practically right" when he accused Moscow of
"trying for months to torpedo the disarmament talks," but he qualified
this by saying that "it was not the Soviet Union that tried to torpedo

the talks but Molotov, Kaganovich, and Shepilov." [28] He also accused Molotov of enflaming relations with other Communist Parties, probably those of China, Poland, Japan, Italy, and the United States.

"Molotov," Khrushchev bluntly stated in a later speech, "found more convenient a policy of tightening all screws, which contradicts the wise Leninist policy of peaceful co-existence." [29] Thus, it can be assumed that Molotov advocated a continuation of the basic foreign policies of the Stalinist era, as modified during the Malenkov regime, based on a perpetuation of the two-camp image. It was Molotov's contention that Soviet policy could reap its greatest dividends by maintaining international tensions at a high pitch and running the risks of nuclear war on the assumption that an uncompromising, cold-blooded policy would force Western statesmen, through lack of nerve and under pressure of public opinion, to continually retreat in the face of Soviet provocation for fear of triggering a war of mutual extinction. It appears that he considered as un-Marxist the idea that the ex-colonial countries could be regarded as having deserted the capitalist camp and as constituting an "extensive zone of peace" together with the Soviet bloc, but rather he considered their behavior in international politics to be motivated purely by considerations of opportunism and expediency. The main arena of rivalry for Molotov remained in Western Europe and the Atlantic area—the bastions of capitalism—and not in Asia or Africa, and he continued to view the new countries of Asia and Africa with hostility and suspicion as appendages to the capitalist camp.

Molotov's policy of "tightening all screws" was opposed by the Soviet Army and also by Peking, which seems to have played an influential role in reorienting Soviet policy eastwards. Speaking in Peking, Anastas Mikoyan, reputedly the principal Kremlin architect of the new Soviet diplomatic strategy, invoked Lenin in support of the current policy. Quoting Lenin's famous formula that "in the last analysis, the outcome of the struggle will be determined by the fact that Russia, India, China, etc. constitute the overwhelming majority of the world's population," he roundly condemned the Stalinist two-camp image to which Molotov still subscribed:

> We must consider it harmful that all countries not belonging to the socialist system are sometimes put in the same category and then are mechanically included in the capitalist camp. . . . The paths which are now being followed and blazed by India, Burma,

---

[28] *New York Times*, July 6, 1957.
[29] *New York Times*, July 7, 1957.

Indonesia, Egypt and other countries which have won their independence have a general international significance. . . . The development of these countries and their policies weaken imperialism,
deepen the crises in the capitalist system, destroy colonialism as one
of the mainstays of this system and hasten the end of capitalism.[30]

III.   The Formulation of Soviet Foreign Policy

A.   Introduction

Any attempt to describe the formulation of Soviet foreign policy in
the crucibles of its decision-making organs is bound to be a hazardous
and frustrating enterprise. The absence of periodic or systematic publication of documents, the inaccessibility of archives and officials, the
virtual nonexistence of memoirs or diaries of retiring statesmen, the
puzzling duplication of state and party institutions, the perplexing
fluctuations in their relationships, the ambiguity of Soviet ideology
and the wide discrepancy between theory and practice, the bewildering profusion of constitutional and institutional changes, the arbitrary
tendency to ignore or short-circuit elaborately detailed institutional
channels, and, finally, the capricious and convulsive turnover of personalities, are the more familiar impediments that must be contended
with.

The decision-making process itself is a dynamic interaction between
institutions and personalities, whose character varies with the effectiveness of institutions to impose limits on the acts of individuals. In constitutional states, characterized by relatively permanent institutions,
the restraints upon officials are carefully defined, imposing ineluctable
limits not only on the range of policy formulation but upon the choice
of means as well. In a totalitarian system like the Soviet Union, where
the impermanently rooted institutions are subordinated to relatively
permanent personalities, the institutional aspects of the decision-making process are little more than ceremonial, in which case decision-
making is essentially personal and bound to vary with the evolution of
the ideological convictions, character, and judgment of the personalities in control of the levers of power, the nature of the rivalries between them, and, finally, their reaction to the internal and external
political and social pressures that bear upon them.

The Soviet political superstructure, during most of its existence, was
a complicated mosaic of shifting and interlocking institutions resting
upon an entrenched foundation of one-man dictatorship, in which all

---

[30] *Pravda*, September 18, 1956.

powers were delegated from above. The institutions of both Party and State, as well as their relationship to one another, were essentially creatures of the late Joseph Stalin and were designed, not to limit his own power, but to limit that of his subordinates and rivals, and to facilitate the solidification of his own authority. As the instruments of his creation and manipulation, they could not, and did not, function as restraints upon his latitude of decision. Both institutions and subordinates were liquidated with remarkable dispatch when the occasion demanded.

The system of duplicating and overlapping political organs between the Party and State allegedly reflects a division of functions between the formulation and execution of policy, with policy formulation a monopoly reserved exclusively for the Party, while the function of the government was to be restricted to formalizing and legalizing the decisions of the Party into official acts of state. This dichotomy was never either rigid or absolute, but constantly varied in accordance with the degree of interlocking of personnel at the summits of the Party and State hierarchy.

B.   The Party Congress

In theory the most exalted, but in practice the most degraded of the central Party institutions in the formulation of policy is the Party Congress. Traditionally the most important fundamental pronouncements on foreign policy have been made before the Party Congress, which is empowered to set the basic "line" of the Party and State, but in actual fact merely hears and rubber-stamps the decisions made elsewhere. All higher organs of the Party, including the Presidium and Secretariat, are responsible and accountable to the Party Congress which theoretically can remove and replace their membership.

The role of the Congress in foreign policy has actually varied throughout its existence. Under Lenin, and, in fact, as late as the 16th Party Congress (1930), serious debate on foreign policy and international revolutionary strategy frequently ensued, although never with the same intensity or wide range of diversity as on domestic policy. Because of its massive size (nearly 2,000 delegates), the Congress became increasingly unwieldy as an organ of debate and discussion, and it gradually was converted into a forum which heard various sides and finally into a subdued sounding board for Stalin's deadly rhetoric. Discussion and debate first slipped behind the doors of the Central Committee and eventually vanished into the Politburo. All decisions were made in the Politburo, then reported to the Central Committee and, with increasing infrequency, to the Party Congress. The principal function of the Party Congress was reduced to the hearing of reports by the prominent figures of the Party.

The two most important reports to Party Congresses relating to foreign policy are the Main Political Report of the Central Committee, delivered in the past by Stalin (except at the 19th Congress), and a report on the activities of the World Communist movement. At the 19th Congress, Malenkov delivered the Main Report, while Stalin restricted himself to a few enigmatic remarks to foreign Communist representatives at the close of the session. However, Stalin had ordered published his *Economic Problems of Socialism* on the eve of the Congress and this set the tone and dominated the entire proceedings of the Congress. At the 20th Congress, Khrushchev delivered the Main Report, incorporating radical doctrinal innovations affecting foreign policy, while Molotov confined himself to reluctantly praising the new policy and resentfully subjecting his own past conduct of foreign policy to self-criticism. The activities of foreign Communist parties were reported by their own representatives.

A close examination of the Main Political Reports betrays an almost rigid uniformity in organization. The entire first section is devoted to international affairs; an authoritative interpretation of the world situation; an appraisal of the Soviet position; trends, developments, and opportunities to watch for; warnings, threats, boasts, and invitations to bourgeois powers; congratulations and words of praise for friendly countries; and, finally, a summary of the immediate and long-range objectives of Soviet foreign policy. This report sets the line to guide Communists everywhere in their activities, and, thus, the Congress becomes not a forum for debate, but a unique medium of communication.

Debate and discussion vanished after 1930 and meetings of the Congress became less frequent until they threatened to vanish altogether. In his secret speech to the 20th Congress, Khrushchev gave this vivid description of the deterioration of the Party Congress:

> During Lenin's life, party congresses were convened regularly; always when a radical turn in the development of the party and country took place, Lenin considered it absolutely necessary that the party discuss at length all basic matters pertaining to . . . foreign policy. . . . Whereas during the first years after Lenin's death, party congresses . . . took place more or less regularly, later . . . these principles were brutally violated. . . . Was it a normal situation when over 13 years [1939-1952] elapsed between the Eighteenth and Nineteenth Congresses? . . . Of 1,966 delegates [to the

17th Congress in 1934] with either voting or advisory rights, 1,108 persons were arrested on charges of revolutionary crimes.[31]

C. The Central Committee

As the body that "guides the entire work of the Party in the interval between Congresses . . . and . . . directs the work of the Central and Soviet public organizations [*i.e.*, the government]," [32] the Central Committee became the principal arena of debate and discussion of foreign policy during the period preceding 1934. According to the Party rules at that time, the Politburo was obliged to report to this body at least three times a year, so that its decisions might be examined, criticized, and judged. The Central Committee elected the members of the Politburo, the Orgburo, and the Secretariat, and theoretically was empowered to appoint, remove, or replace its members. The Central Committee itself was elected by the Party Congress and was empowered to replace its members by a two-thirds vote, but this rule was rudely violated by Stalin who removed and appointed members of the Central Committee virtually at will.

On some occasions the Foreign Commissar—who invariably is at least a full member of the Central Committee—as well as high Soviet functionaries of the Comintern reported to the Central Committee on foreign policy and international Communist activities. More often, the Secretary-General (Stalin) would deliver a report on the nature and scope of the Politburo's work and explain the precise application of the "line" under changing international conditions. A fairly large body, composed of full members and alternate members (about equally divided), it was empowered to alter the policies of the Politburo and support the views of the minority. Only full members exercised the right of vote, while candidates had the right to participate in debate. Some of these reports, but not all, were made public, particularly if important modifications of the policies announced at the previous Party Congress were made. The records of the Committee's proceedings remain generally unpublished and inaccessible for examination.

The Central Committee too, in time, was reduced to little more than a sounding board; its meetings became increasingly infrequent, and there is little reason to believe that after 1934 its decisions were anything less than unanimous. According to Khrushchev:

---

[31] This extract and all subsequent references to Khrushchev's secret report to the 20th Congress are taken from the full text published in the *New York Times*, June 5, 1956. The speech has been widely reprinted elsewhere.

[32] *The Land of Socialism Today and Tomorrow* (Moscow, 1939), p. 473.

Even after the end of the war . . . Central Committee plenums were hardly ever called. It should be sufficient to mention that during the years of the Patriotic War [World War II] not a single Central Committee plenum took place. . . . Stalin did not even want to meet and talk with Central Committee members. . . . Of the 139 members and candidates of the Party's Central Committee who were elected at the Seventeenth Party Congress [1934], 98 persons, *i.e.* 70 per cent, were arrested and shot.

D.   The Party Presidium (formerly the Politburo)

There is no question but that the most important organ of decision-making in the Soviet Union has been, and continues to be, the Presidium of the Party. In accordance with the principle of "democratic centralism," the ultimate power of the Party is entrusted to this organ. Its internal organization and recruiting procedures, the composition and convictions of its factions, and its voting practices remain essentially a mystery. No proceedings of its deliberations have been made public in decades, and, in the absence of any recent defections from this body, information concerning its procedures and activities can be derived only from the following sources: (1) fragmentary records of very early meetings; (2) public exposure of its deliberations by Leon Trotsky and other rivals of Stalin during the period before 1930; (3) accounts by high-ranking diplomats or government and Party officials, whose activities brought them into close range of the Politburo, and who have defected from the Soviet Union; (4) personal accounts and memoirs of foreign statesmen who negotiated with members of the Politburo or with Stalin; (5) accounts of renegade officials of the Comintern and foreign Communist parties; (6) secrets spilled as a result of the Stalin-Tito feud; (7) Khrushchev's secret speech at the 20th Party Congress and its aftermath; (8) calculated leaks by the Polish Party and government since the rise of Gomulka; (9) examination of the decisions already taken; (10) rare public disputes between leading press organs of the Party and government; (11) shifts in Party and governmental officials; and (12) rare Central Committee Resolutions like that of June 29, 1957.

Under Stalin, all decisions of the Politburo on questions of foreign policy were in essence his, in one form or another. All rival and dissident views were quashed and their adherents liquidated. The membership of the body was hand-picked by him. In his relations with the Politburo, Stalin could either announce his decisions and expect unanimous approval, submit them for examination and ask for discussion with or without a vote, simply act without consulting his colleagues, or consult with various members on certain questions to the exclusion of others. According to a former Soviet diplomat, who was an eye-witness to some Politburo meetings in 1933:

> A thin appearance of collective work is still kept up at Politburo meetings. Stalin does not "command." He merely "suggests" or "proposes." The fiction of voting is retained. But the vote never fails to uphold his "suggestions." The decision is signed by all ten members of the Politburo, with Stalin's signature among the rest. . . . The other members of the Politburo mumble their approval of Stalin's "proposal." . . . Stalin not only is generally called "the Boss" by the whole bureaucracy, but *is* the one and only boss.[33]

This general description of Stalin's style of work has been confirmed many times by diplomats and statesmen of many countries who observed that Stalin often made important decisions without consulting anyone, while Molotov and others would request time to consult with their "government." In the realm of decision-making, the role of the other members of the Politburo could best be described as consultative, although within the area of their own administrative responsibility they exercised the power of decision. Testimony concerning Stalin's intolerance of dissent is uniformly consistent. "Whoever opposed . . . his viewpoint," complained Khrushchev, "was doomed to be removed."

The relationship between the Foreign Ministry and the Presidium has always been unique. Since relations with other states are viewed in terms of a struggle for power among various "ruling classes," and thus directly involve the security and the very existence of the Soviet state, the Party center has always retained a tight supervision over the Foreign Ministry. This supervision assumes different forms, depending upon the Party rank of the individuals who hold the posts of Foreign Minister and of Premier. The Premier has always been a Party figure of the highest rank, while the Foreign Minister may or may not be a member of the Party Presidium.

During the period when Maxim Litvinov was Foreign Commissar, his work was supervised by Molotov, the Premier of the government and his formal superior. Matters of routine interest, not involving questions of policy or fundamental maneuver, were decided by Litvinov

---

[33] Alexander Barmine, *One Who Survived* (New York, 1946), p. 213. "Thousands of relatively unimportant, as well as all-important, problems," writes Barmine, "must pass through Stalin's hand for final decision. . . . Weeks are spent in waiting; Commissars wait in Stalin's office."

himself in consultation with his collegium. More substantial questions were taken to Molotov, who, depending upon the nature of the question, would make a decision, or take it to the Politburo.[34]

The Politburo itself was broken down into various Commissions dealing with different aspects of policy. Questions of foreign policy were first considered by the Politburo Commission on Foreign Affairs, which included the Politburo specialists on the Comintern, Foreign Trade, and Defense. In matters involving exceptional or immediate importance, Molotov would deal directly with Stalin and get a decision.

The procedures of the Politburo were neither systematic nor rigid. Often Stalin would personally consult with the Foreign Commissar and his chief advisers; and Litvinov, on a few occasions, would be asked to make a report to the Politburo. The principal function of the Commission on Foreign Affairs was to act as a coordinating agency of all the departments concerned with foreign relations, to assemble and evaluate intelligence information flowing from different channels, to devise strategy and policy, examine analyses, projects, and reports drawn up by specialists in the Foreign Commissariat, study reports of diplomats abroad, and then make a comprehensive report either to Stalin or to the Politburo as a whole.

Once the decisions were made, they would be transmitted in writing or verbally by Molotov to Litvinov for execution. These bureaucratic channels were often ignored and Stalin would act directly with Molotov, his principal agent, and they would personally give instructions to Litvinov. Deviation or improvisation from instructions by the Foreign Commissar or his subordinates in the Commissariat was neither permitted nor tolerated. According to Khrushchev, the system of Politburo Commissions was not primarily for organizational efficiency, but was a sinister device whereby Stalin weakened the authority of the collective body:

> The importance of the . . . Political Bureau was reduced and its work disorganized by the creation within the Political Bureau of various commissions—the so-called "quintets," "sextets," "septets" and "novenaries."

When Molotov replaced Litvinov in May, 1939, this cumbersome procedure was simplified. The Nazi-Soviet Pact was worked out principally by Stalin and Molotov, with Zhdanov and Mikoyan the only other members of the Politburo apparently apprised of the crucial decisions contemplated. The Politburo Commission on Foreign Affairs

---

[34] Cf. Merle Fainsod, How Russia Is Ruled (Cambridge, Mass., 1953), p. 282.

gradually increased in size until, by 1945, it was large enough to be converted by Stalin from a "sextet" into a "septet." As it grew in size, so its importance diminished. During the war, Stalin appeared to consult only Molotov on questions of foreign policy and frequently made decisions on the spot at the Big Three conferences.

Although Khrushchev reported that "during Stalin's leadership our peaceful relations with other nations were often threatened, because one-man decisions could cause and often did cause great complications," he failed to elaborate. He specifically accused Stalin of personally making the decision to break with Marshal Tito, while Walter Ulbricht, the German Communist leader, reported that Stalin's arbitrary policies, almost drove Mao Tse-tung out of the Soviet orbit. After Stalin's death the Korean war was halted, the demands on Turkey withdrawn with appropriate apologies, Soviet interference in Manchuria arrested, the rift with Tito ended, the bases in Finland evacuated, and a number of other reversals of Stalinist policies undertaken. Molotov's complicity in these decisions remains obscure, but since he was in charge of foreign affairs during most of the period concerned, and in view of his expulsion from the Presidium, he probably played an important consultative role.

Khrushchev's description of how decisions were made by Stalin and the Politburo is probably exaggerated and self-serving, but accurate in its general outline:

> After the war, Stalin became even more capricious, irritable, and brutal; in particular his suspicion grew. His persecution mania reached unbelievable dimensions. Everything was decided by him alone without any consideration for anyone or anything. . . . Sessions of the Political Bureau occurred only occasionally . . . many decisions were taken by one person or in a roundabout way, without collective discussion. . . . The importance of the Political Bureau was reduced and its work disorganized by the creation within the Political Bureau of various commissions. . . . The result of this was that some members of the Political Bureau were in this way kept away from participation in the decisions of the most important state matters.

E. Decision-making in the post-Stalin period: the agonies of collective leadership

The death of Stalin stimulated the expression of various opinions and unleashed a struggle for power among his successors. Six months before his death, at the 19th Party Congress, Stalin radically reorganized the Party summit, abolishing the Orgburo and replacing the

11-man Politburo with a Presidium of 25 full members and 11 candidate members as the key decision-making organ of the Soviet system.
Since many of the new members of the Presidium were burdened with
permanent administrative responsibilities far from Moscow, and since
it was much too large to function as a decision-making body, there was
secretly organized, in violation of the new Party charter, a smaller
Bureau of the Presidium, whose membership has never been revealed.
Whether expansion of the Presidium was designed by Stalin to widen
the area of decision-making and prevent a struggle for power after his
death—thus preparing the conditions for orderly transition from personal to institutional dictatorship—or whether it was a sinister device
for liquidating his old associates in favor of a generation ignorant of
his crimes, remains an intriguing enigma. According to Khrushchev:

> Stalin evidently had plans to finish off the old members of the
> Political Bureau. . . . His proposal after the 19th Congress, con-
> cerning the selection of 25 persons to the Central Committee's
> Presidium, was aimed at the removal of the old Political Bureau
> members and the bringing in of less experienced persons so that
> they would extol him. . . . We can assume that this was a design
> for the future annihilation of the old Political Bureau members,
> and in this way, a cover for all the shameful acts of Stalin.

Immediately after Stalin's death, with utter contempt for the elaborate institutional rituals devised at the 19th Congress, the old members of Stalin's entourage repudiated his handiwork. The Presidium
was summarily reduced to its former size, as the principal aspirants to
Stalin's power maneuvered against one another under the ideological
umbrella of "collective leadership." The removal of Beria and the dismantling of his secret police apparatus introduced an uneasy equilibrium among the various factions in the Presidium, none of which
was powerful enough to overwhelm the others.

In the post-Stalin Presidium, decisions have been taken only after
stormy controversies and agile maneuvering among the various factions, which have been posed in uneasy and rapidly fluctuating equilibrium. As a consequence, necessity was converted into ideology and
conflicting opinions, within carefully circumscribed limits, were given
official sanction:

> Clash of opinions, on a foundation of Marxist-Leninist principles,
> must be thoroughly encouraged and developed . . . [but] within
> the framework of allegiance to the Party and Marxism—a clash in
> the course of which incorrect tenets and conclusions are rejected
> and a common viewpoint worked out.[35]

---

[35] *Kommunist* (No. 10), August 1956, pp. 3-13.

At the same time, the authoritative theoretical journal, *Kommunist*, warned that "views that are objectively directed toward dethroning the leadership elected by the Party masses," would not be tolerated. This danger is clearly adumbrated in the Party Statutes, Article 28 of which reads:

> A broad discussion, in particular on an all-Union scale concerning the Party policy, should be so organized that it would not result in the attempts of an insignificant minority to impose its will on the majority of the Party or in attempts to organize fractional groupings which would break down Party unity, or in attempts to create a schism that would undermine the strength and the firmness of the socialist regime.[36]

Diversity and clash of opinion have not been permitted to filter down below the level of the Central Committee (and even in this body they are carefully manipulated), for if the factional divisions in the Presidium should crack the Party pyramid down to its base, it would be impossible short of reestablishing one-man rule to prevent an eventual evolution towards a two or more party system operating within the framework of the Marxist-Leninist ideology. Already such an evolution has approached a crucial stage in the Polish Communist Party.

Decisions in the Presidium, whose proceedings remain unpublished, are reached by simple majority, with only full members entitled to vote, although alternate members participate in the debate and discussion. Meetings of the Presidium are regularly held at least once a week, and according to both Khrushchev and Mikoyan most decisions are unanimous. Mikoyan has further elaborated by stating that if a consensus were unobtainable, the Presidium would adjourn, sleep on the matter, and return for further discussion until unanimity was achieved. Since 5 full members out of 11 were expelled on June 29, 1957, for persistent opposition and obstruction to the Party line, the unanimity of the Presidium's deliberations appears to have been exaggerated.

In view of Khrushchev's bitter attack on the organization of Politburo Commissions under Stalin, the Presidium's internal compartmentalization may not be as rigidly demarcated as before, and foreign policy decisions, instead of being merely the concern of the Commission on Foreign Affairs, are discussed and made by the body as a whole. "Never in the past," Molotov sputtered regretfully at the 20th Party Congress, "has our Party Central Committee and its Presidium been engaged as actively with questions of foreign policy as during

---

[36] *Pravda*, October 14, 1952.

the present period." [37] The vitiating effects of Stalin's Commission system, however, have been more than matched by the crystallization of factional groupings and cliques within the Party's highest body.

Under the Soviet one-party system, which does not permit the organization of an opposition with an alternative slate of leaders and policies, factional rivalry within the Party summit becomes a crude and primitive substitute for a two-party contest, while the relationship between the Central Committee and its Presidium constitutes the nearest approximation to a system of institutional responsibility and accountability.

The sharp and close divisions in the Presidium have revived the prominence and activity of the moribund Central Committee. Factional differences have been displayed before Plenums of the Central Committee (at least twice a year) where the actions of the Presidium have been appealed by the opposition for reversal or revision. In this relatively large body of 133 full members and 122 alternates, discussion of the various views current in the Presidium is still more ritualized than free, with each faction in the Presidium supported by its own retinue of retainers in the Central Committee. Voting is conditioned not only by divisions in the Presidium but also by considerations of political survival and opportunism, with members being extremely sensitive to the course that the struggle assumes in the higher body. "At Plenums of the Central Committee," according to the revealing statement of one low-ranking member, "Comrade Khrushchev and other members of the Presidium . . . corrected errors in a fatherly way . . . regardless of post occupied or of record." [38]

It was in the Central Committee that Malenkov reputedly indicted Beria and where, in turn, he and Molotov were disciplined and attacked by the Khrushchev faction. Shifts in the balance of factions in the Presidium are almost always immediately registered in the Central Committee, whose proceedings inevitably sway with those of the higher body. The Central Committee, whose decisions are invariably reported as unanimous, is empowered to alter its own membership and that of its higher bodies by a two-thirds vote; and in the June 1957 Plenum it expelled three full members and one alternate from the Presidium and the Central Committee, demoted one to alternate status, and cut off still another at full membership in the Central Committee. Correspondingly, the Presidium was expanded to 15 full members and 9 alternates.

[37] Molotov's speech at the 20th Congress; cf. footnote 24, above.
[38] Moscow Radio broadcast, February 21, 1956. Speech of Z. I. Muratov, First Secretary of the Tatar Oblast Committee.

1. *Factional rivalry and foreign policy.* Differences in the Presidium arise as a result of both personal ambitions for power and fundamental conflict over doctrine and policy. Both factors are so intricately interwoven that attempts to draw fine distinctions between personal and policy conflicts are apt to be an idle exercise. Although Soviet ideology neither recognizes the legitimacy of factional groupings in the Party nor tolerates the doctrinal schisms that are their ideological expression, the Party throughout its history has been constantly threatened with the eruption of both. After Stalin's death the rival cliques he permitted—and may even have encouraged—to form among his subordinates developed into factions, each with its own aspirations and opinions. Since no single faction was sufficiently powerful to annihilate the others, necessity was converted into virtue and the balance of terror in the Presidium was ideologically sanctified as "collective leadership."

Even before the revelations of the resolution that hurled Molotov and his associates from their places of eminence, it was unmistakeable that serious factional quarrels kept the Presidium in a continual state of turmoil. At least three factions appear to have existed in the Presidium before June 1957, although the members of each faction were not permanently committed to issues; and personality and tactical shifts, though not frivolous, were also not unusual. The Presidium was divided against itself on four major issues that had important foreign policy repercussions: the Stalinist issue; the relations between the Soviet Union and other Communist states and parties; economic policy and reorganization; and relations with the ex-colonial states.

The so-called Stalinist faction had at its core the veteran Politburo members, Molotov and Kaganovich, and was frequently supported by Malenkov and possibly also Suslov. The anti-Stalinist group was made up of Khrushchev, Mikoyan, Bulganin, Voroshilov, and Kirichenko (as well as all the alternate members). This faction had decisive control of the Party apparatus and the Central Committee, and it found crucial support in the Army, Peking, Warsaw, and Belgrade. Pervukhin and Saburov made up the so-called "Managerial-Technical" faction, which appeared to have had close connections with Malenkov in the past, but cast its vote with the Khrushchev group on questions of Stalinism and deserted Malenkov when the latter appeared to be the apostle for increased consumer-goods production and when Khrushchev adopted a decisive stand in favor of continued stress on heavy industry.

The events in Poland and Hungary and the uncompromising attitude of Marshal Tito encouraged the Stalinists, while Khrushchev's schemes for decentralizing the economic system stampeded the Managerial group into forming an anti-Khrushchev coalition with the Stalinist opposition in a desperate effort to thwart Khrushchev's proposed dismantling of the centralized structure of Soviet heavy industry. This combination forged a majority at the December 1956 Plenum and Pervukhin was installed as virtual economic dictator. Foreign Minister Shepilov deserted to the Molotov faction, a virtual halt was put on the de-Stalinization program, relations with Tito were deliberately enflamed, and satellite policies appeared to harden once again. During this period Malenkov, as representative of the new majority, accompanied Khrushchev to the Communist gathering held in Budapest and from which both Warsaw and Belgrade were deliberately excluded.

Peking intervened, however, by sending Chou En-lai on an emergency trip to Moscow and Eastern Europe to shore up the Khrushchev faction and to let the Kremlin know that Red China would find extremely distasteful any return of Molotov to the helm of Moscow's foreign policy. Because of the unnatural and unstable amalgamation that made up the new majority, Khrushchev's ouster was deferred. Once the crisis had subsided and it was clear that the Armed Forces and Peking clearly prefered the Khrushchev policies, a re-alignment of forces in the Presidium took place. At the February 1957 Plenum of the Central Committee the First Secretary was able once again to reconstitute his majority, when a member of the Stalinist faction with a strong instinct for survival (probably Suslov) switched sides. Pervukhin was toppled from his new post, the levers of economic power wrenched from his hands, while Shepilov was ousted from the Foreign Ministry.

With the Presidium so sharply and evenly divided, "collective leadership" threatened to abandon Soviet foreign policies to the mercies of an inconclusive see-saw struggle plunging the Kremlin into a perpetual condition of indecision. The Stalinist faction resolved to unseat Khrushchev through a parliamentary ruse by engineering a rump meeting of the Presidium, ostensibly to discuss minor matters, while key Khrushchev supporters were out of town. When the meeting took place on June 17-18, 1957, the First Secretary found himself outmaneuvered and outvoted. Refusing to resign as First Secretary, he replied in kind by conducting a filibuster while his supporters collected the required number of signatures to petition a special meeting of the Central Committee.

The special Plenum of the Central Committee and its Central Auditing Commission (a total of 319 members) sat from June 22-29. After bitter ventilation of all the contentious issues of doctrine and policy, during which 60 members reportedly took part in the debate and 115 filed statements, the Molotov-Managerial coalition was overwhelmed by a unanimous vote tarnished only by a single obstinate abstention by Molotov—the first such publicly admitted dissonance in a Central Committee vote in almost thirty years. The Molotov group, but not the Managerial part of the coalition, was charged in the resolution that expelled them with engaging in illegal factional activity and cabalistic intrigue:

> Entering into collusion on an anti-Party basis, they set out to change the policy of the Party, to drag the Party back to the erroneous methods of leadership condemned by the 20th Party Congress [i.e. Stalinism]. They resorted to methods of intrigue and formed a collusion against the Central Committee.

2. *Interest groups and foreign policy.* It is at once obvious that factions could neither arise nor flourish unless they received constant sustenance from powerful social forces in Soviet society. Just as Party factions do not organize into separate political organizations competing with the Party for political power, so interest groups in Soviet society do not constitute separate organizations, but rather seek to make their influence felt as formless clusters of vested interests. Within the context of Marxist-Soviet ideology an interest group can only be a social class with economic interests that conflict with the interests of other classes. After the Revolution only the interests of the working class, as distorted by the Marxist prism, were given legitimate recognition—although the concrete political articulation of these interests was usurped by the Communist Party—and all other interests and parties were condemned to oblivion. In 1936 Stalin declared the eradication of class conflict in Soviet society, but he continued to recognize the existence of separate social classes, whose interests had merged into a single identity. The Communist Party was transformed from a party representing only the interests of the working class into one representing the transcendental interests of all Soviet social classes. Consequently, Soviet ideology neither recognizes the legitimacy of competing interest groups nor tolerates their autonomous existence. In Soviet jargon, an interest group that develops interests that deviate from the Party line is a hostile class; the faction that represents it in the Party is an attempt to form a party within a party; and its articulated views on policy and doctrine constitute an ideological deviation.

Separate interest groups, however, continue to flourish in Soviet society, but not in conformity with the doctrinaire and contrived premises of nineteenth-century Marxism, nor within the synthetic social divisions given official sanction. The collective-farm peasantry and the working class constitute the numerically preponderant classes in Soviet society, but the major interest groups with sufficient power and influence to apply political pressure do not follow the artificial constructions of Soviet ideology; in accordance with the unique dynamic of Soviet society the privileged elites find their social differentiation within a single recognized group, the intelligentsia, which is not recognized as a social class but is euphemistically called a *stratum*.

Although the Soviet intelligentsia (roughly identical with what Milovan Djilas labels the "New Class") is a variegated congeries of differentiated elites, they all have in common a desire to perpetuate the Soviet system from which they have sprung and from which they benefit as privileged groups. But each group is immediately concerned with its own vested stake in Soviet society and seeks to force doctrine and policy to assume the contours of its own special interests. Since these groups do not enjoy official recognition, they all seek to exert their influence through the Communist Party, not outside it, and political rivalry assumes the form of competing for control of the Party's decision-making organs and its symbols of legitimacy. Because Soviet ideology rigidly and inaccurately insists upon the existence of a single monolithic interest, representing that of society in its collective entity, conflicts between major groups are resolved not by political accommodation but by mutual elimination and by the attempt of one interest group to establish its supremacy and to impose its views as those of society as a whole. Thus the Comunist Party, under the pressures of diverse groups seeking political articulation and accommodation, has become a conglomeration of interests whose basic incompatibilities are only partially obscured by a veneer of monolithic unity.

Not all interest groups in the Soviet Union are sufficiently powerful to exact representation for their views by factions in the Party hierarchy. There are six principal groups within Soviet society that have accumulated sufficient leverage, either through the acquisition of indispensable skills and talents or through the control of instruments of persuasion, terror, or destruction, to exert pressure upon the Party. These are: (1) the Party apparatus, consisting of those who have made a career in the Party bureaucracy; (2) the government bureaucracy; (3) the economic managers and technicians; (4) the cultural, professional, and scientific intelligentsia; (5) the Police; (6) the Armed Forces.

These major groups are by no means organized as cohesively united bodies, speaking with a single authoritative voice, but rather themselves are made up of rival personal and policy cliques, gripped by internal jealousies, and often in constant collision and friction with one another in combination or alliance with similarly oriented cliques in other social groups.

The Party apparatus itself was thus divided into rival cliques, the two main contending groups being those led by Khrushchev and Malenkov. Since the denouement of Malenkov, his supporters in the Party apparatus have been systematically rooted out and replaced with followers of Khrushchev. Although the function of the Party bureaucracy is essentially administrative rather than policy-making, it has a tendency to feel that it "owns" the Party and thus seeks first to subordinate the Party to its control and then to force the other major groups to submit to the domination of the Party. After Stalin's death, the serious and imminent threat posed to the Party by Beria and his Secret Police caused Khrushchev and Malenkov to temporarily bury their rivalry in the apparatus of the Party in order to crush the Secret Police, which under Beria had developed into an independent center of power and threatened to subjugate the Party to its will. The Secret Police was dismembered with the aid of the Army, which then displaced the Police as the most important instrument of violence in the Soviet system.

After Beria was dispatched, the rivalry in the Party apparatus entered its crucial phase. Malenkov was at a distinct disadvantage because he had given up his post in the Party Secretariat in favor of the Premiership, and although he had built up a substantial following in the Government bureaucracy, principally among the energetic and ambitious young corps of managers and technicians in Soviet society, he was outmaneuvered in the Party Secretariat as Khrushchev systematically replaced Malenkov's Party bureaucrats with his own. A close scrutiny of the convulsions that have taken place in the Party summit since Stalin's death reveals that Malenkov's followers in the Party bureaucracy were essentially in the Central Apparatus, while Khrushchev's supporters were principally provincial Party leaders, most of whom had had some experience in the Ukrainian Party organization. By ousting Malenkov from the Secretariat, Khrushchev was able to destroy his organization in the Party Apparatus, and then by forcing his resignation as Premier, the groundwork was prepared for dispersing his adherents in the Government bureaucracy, particularly in the economic sector.

The lines of rivalry and clique formation in the other major groups tend to follow the contours of those which develop within the Party Secretariat, with various cliques uniting their fortunes with contending forces in the Party Secretariat. Their representation in the Party is thus not functional, but fortuitous and opportunistic, and the views of their representatives in the Party's leading bodies often reflect only the views of the prevailing clique within each group. The fall from grace of a leading member of the Secretariat (Andrei Zhdanov, G. M. Malenkov) is registered throughout all the major social and functional forces in Soviet society and is accompanied by purges in the Party Apparatus, the Government, the Armed Forces, the Arts, Sciences, and Professions.

There appears to be no systematic attempt to select members of the Central Committee and its Presidium from among the major forces in Soviet society; and the composition of these bodies appears to depend upon the balance of forces at any given time. Ample evidence exists, however, that their composition reflects deliberate recognition of these major interest groups. Traditionally the Party Apparatus accounts for slightly less than half the total membership of the Central Committee, with the Government bureaucracy (including the economic administrators) following close behind. The representation of the other groups is substantially less, although, because virtually all members of the Party's two highest bodies who are not career Party bureaucrats are employed by the State, it is often difficult to distinguish the main line of work pursued by a particular member of the Central Committee. This is especially true in cases where an individual moves from one group to another. Consequently all distinctions are provisional and in some cases arbitrary because of the ambiguous careers of many members of the Party's highest bodies. With respect to the composition of the Presidium, differentiation is more precise and accurate, although even here, because of the interlocking nature of the top organs of State and Party, some ambiguity prevails.

Major Groups Represented in the Central Committee

	1952	1956
Party Apparatus	103	117
Government Bureaucracy	79	98
Professional Military	26	18
Police	9	3
Others	18	19
Totals	235	255

Major Groups Represented on the Presidium

	1952	1953	1956	July 1957
Party Apparatus	13(5)	2(2)	4(3)	10(6)
Government Bureaucracy				
Economic Sector	5(3)	4	4	1(2)
Noneconomic	4(2)	3(1)	3(1)	3
Professional Military	0	0	0(1)	1
Police	2	1(1)	0	0
Cultural Intelligentsia	1(1)	0	0(1)	0(1)
Totals	25(11)	10(4)	11(6)	15(9)

Today (1958), as in 1952, the Party Apparatus dominates the composition of the Party's highest body, but whereas at the 19th Party Congress the Party bureaucrats in the Presidum represented two rival cliques led by Party Secretariat Malenkov and Khrushchev, in the current Presidium all the career Party officials, with the exception of Suslov and Kuusinen, are part of the Khrushchev machine. The Government Bureaucracy correspondingly has suffered a drastic decrease in representation, with the economic sector being in a state of virtual eclipse. Pervukhin, disgraced and demoted to lowest-ranking alternate, is the only representative of the hitherto powerful managers of heavy industry. Since the execution of Beria, the Police, Stalin's favorite instrument of terror, has been deprived of its traditional seat on the Party's highest body, the seat being temporarily given to its principal competitor, the Army. The representatives of the Cultural intelligentsia in the Presidium appear barely distinguishable from those of the Party Apparatus, since they are normally professional ideologists and propagandists.

The informal recognition of groups with distinctive special interests of their own and the admission of their representatives to the decision-making bodies of the Party cannot but exercise fundamental influence on the country's foreign policy, although how this influence is exerted and in what direction is difficult to determine. Although it is true that none of the major groups has publicly thwarted the decisions of the Party in foreign policy, it has been officially admitted that Party decisions have been administratively distorted by both a Minister of Internal Affairs and two Foreign Ministers. The removal of the Managerial bureaucrats from both the Presidium and high government posts was motivated at least in part by the fear that their control of the key economic levers of society could be used to frustrate the decisions of the Party.

Marshal Zhukov's leadership of the Army posed an even grimmer potential threat to the supremacy of the Party Apparatus, had he been permitted to remain in the Presidium and the Defense Ministry where he could seriously question the basic decisions of the Party concerning military and foreign policy and frustrate their implementation. His removal in October 1957 from both strategic positions over the relatively trivial controversy concerning the political indoctrination of the military was essentially a preventative measure designed to remove a popular and commanding personality who might at some future date challenge even more crucial decisions of the Party and thus produce an internal crisis of incalculable magnitude. Zhukov's dénouement was painlessly engineered by skillful exploitation of his own vanity and the intense personal jealousies and factional cleavages within the Army leadership itself as well as by adroit manipulation of the Middle-Eastern crisis. His replacement on the Presidium was not another representative from the military, but yet another worker in the Party Apparatus, promoted up from alternate membership.

As of 1958, the Party Apparatus under Khrushchev's direction had dismembered the Police, domesticated the Managerial Bureaucrats and decentralized their empire, exiled the leaders of factional groupings in the Party to Siberia, and subordinated the military to its will. As the chart indicates, neither major instrument of coercion in the Soviet system now has a representative in the Party Presidium, which is now overwhelmingly dominated by career Party *apparatchiki.*

As the Soviet system matures and becomes inextricably identified with the interests of its various privileged elites, the decision-makers must give greater consideration in the calculation of foreign policy to factors affecting the internal stability of the regime; and they will show greater sensitivity to the effects of decisions on the vested interests of the various elites in Soviet society. The rise of powerful social and economic classes in the Soviet Union and their insistent pressures for participation in the exercise of political power could not but introduce stresses, strains, conflicts, and hence new restraints into Soviet diplomacy.

Within the context of an ideology that imposes a single interest representing society as a whole, each interest group will tend to distort ideology and policy in an endeavor to give it the contours of its own interests; the next step is to elevate these to transcendental significance. Under these conditions, Soviet ideology may be constantly threatened with a series of fundamental convulsions if one interest group displaces another in the struggle for the control of the Party machinery, unless a rational system of accommodating conflicting interests evolves to replace the custom of mutual obliteration. As the vested stake of each major group becomes rooted in the Soviet system, the contours of Soviet diplomacy and national interest will inexorably tend to be shaped more by the rapidly moving equilibrium or accommodation of

interests that develop internally than by abstract ideological imperatives, which may conflict with the concrete interests of specific major
elites in Soviet society.

Only as long as a major Soviet elite whose vested stake is the
function of maintaining the purity of ideological objectives (the Party
Apparatus) remains in undisputed control of the Party machinery and
can subordinate the other elites to its direction can the transcendental
revolutionary objectives of the Marxist doctrine remain fully compatible with Soviet national interests. On the other hand, any foreign
policy that threatens to upset the equilibrium of interests in Soviet
society or that strikes at the vested position of any powerful social
group may encounter resistance, and the group may take desperate
measures to preserve its status, regardless of ideological considerations. In a real sense, Soviet ideology and national interests will be
increasingly shaped by the internal interests of the Soviet elite—or
combination of elites—that succeeds in establishing control over the
machinery of the Party; thus ideology and interests are bound to
undergo periodic transmutations.

IV. The Administration and Execution of Soviet Foreign Policy

A. Party policy and state administration: conflict and harmony

Responsibility for the actual *execution* of foreign policy as distinct
from its *formulation* rests with the Council of Ministers and its Presidium, which is nominally accountable to the Supreme Soviet and its
Presidium but in fact is subordinate to the Party Presidium, with which
it normally shares key personnel. The relationship between the Party's
highest body and the Council of Ministers and its Presidium in the
decision-making process, which is often ambiguous and is currently
in a state of transition, depends more upon the degree of interlocking
membership between the two organs than upon constitutional forms.
Under Stalin, particularly after he became Premier in 1941, interlocking membership was virtually complete and was designed to ensure
maximum harmony between Party policy and state administration.
Distinctions between formulation and execution of policy were ambiguous to the point of complete irrelevance under these conditions.
Before Stalin held any formal executive position in the Government,
the institutions of the Party were the chief decision-making bodies of
the regime, but with Stalin's assumption of the Premiership, Stalin
the Secretary-General of the Party made policy, and in his capacity
as Premier he was also in charge of its execution and administration.

As head of both Party and Government he did not need to employ all the institutions of decision-making; and those of the Party virtually withered away. Since all diplomatic relations with the outside world are carried on through State institutions, the organs of the State had to retain sufficient vitality to legalize Stalin's decisions into formal acts of government.

The apparent rise of the State to a position superior to that of the Party was undoubtedly a major factor in Malenkov's decision to succeed Stalin as Premier rather than as First Secretary of the Party. Legally, as Premier, he had under his control the two principal instruments of violence, the Police and the Armed Forces; and thus he chose the State in preference to the Party Secretariat as his instrument with which to subdue his rivals in the Presidium. The Police and the Army, however, turned out to be virtually separate entities with their own informal lines of organization and loyalty which radically departed from constitutional and legal patterns. By relinquishing control of the Party Secretariat to Khrushchev in favor of the Premiership, Malenkov abdicated the symbols of legitimacy in favor of the shell of power, since within the context of the Party rules and institutional controls bequeathed by Stalin, the Premier and the Government were mere creatures of the Party's will. As long as the Secretariat and the Premiership are united in a single personality, relationships of control and subordination are irrelevant, but once they are separated, custom and precedent, as well as ideology, favor the Secretariat in any rivalry for supremacy.

With the eruption of factional rivalry in the Presidium and the separation of the Party Secretariat from the Government, interlocking membership between the Council of Ministers and the Party's highest body, instead of ensuring harmony between policy and administration, in fact guaranteed conflict and friction, as the Party Presidium came under the control of one faction while key administrative organs of State were in the hands of members of rival factions.

The first overt instance of conflict between Party policy and state administration was Beria's attempt to thwart the decisions of the Party through his control of the Ministry and Internal Affairs. Since then, both major and minor discrepancies between policy and administration have taken place. Thus, while Khrushchev could muster narrow majorities in the Presidium, members of the opposition were in strategic administrative positions where they could subvert the implementation of Party decisions. One of the major accusations against Foreign Minister Molotov, and also against Shepilov, was that he was using the Foreign Ministry and Soviet missions abroad to subvert and sabotage, rather than to carry out, the policies formulated by the

Party. Similarly, Khrushchev's plan for breaking up the concentration of economic power in Moscow was probably opposed by the Managerial bureaucrats like Kaganovich, Pervukhin, and Saburov, who controlled key economic levers in the nation's industrial system and could effectively frustrate the dismantling of their own source of power and influence. Thus, before the reorganization of the Presidium in June 1957, of the nine members of the Presidium of the Council of Ministers, four First Deputy Chairmen and one Deputy Chairman were members of the opposition minority in the Party Presidium. It was untenable that the minority faction in the Party Presidium should enjoy a majority in the Presidium of the Council of Ministers, whose function it was to implement the very policies rejected by a majority of its members.

With the reorganization of both Presidia, the interlocking of the two organs has been abandoned, and the Council of Ministers has been virtually rendered impotent as a consequence of the decentralization of the economic system. Whereas before June 29, 1957, there existed a Presidium of nine for the Council of Ministers, of which seven were full members of the Party Presidium, thereafter only Bulganin and Mikoyan of the Presidium of the Party were members of the four-man Presidium of the Council of Ministers. Of course, the situation remains in flux, but it appears likely that interlocking membership between the two organs will be kept at a minimum, until a single group has assumed effective control.

B. The constitutional basis of Soviet foreign relations

Under the Soviet Constitution of 1936, as amended, foreign policy is administered and executed at four different institutional levels: (1) the Presidium of the Supreme Soviet; (2) the Supreme Soviet; (3) the Council of Ministers; and (4) the Union Republics, of which there are now 15. Although the Soviet constitutional system is based on the principle of complete fusion of executive, legislative, and administrative powers, each institutional level is invested with certain foreign policy functions, which may be permissive, exclusive, or concurrent. These legal relationships, however, do not function in any way as limitations on Soviet diplomacy.

1. *The Presidium of the Supreme Soviet.* The Presidium of the Supreme Soviet is vested under the Constitution with a wide range of ceremonial, executive, and legislative functions. Juridically a creature of the Supreme Soviet, for which it acts as legal agent, it is, in fact, its institutional superior and surrogate, since it is empowered

with virtually the entire spectrum of authority granted to the Supreme Soviet during the long and frequent intervals between sessions of the Soviet legislature. Technically, all of its actions are subject to later confirmation by the Supreme Soviet, but, in practice, this is an empty ritual.

According to *Istoriya Diplomatii*, in the area of foreign affairs, the Presidium, in the person of its chairman, functions as the ceremonial chief of state, much like the American President and the British monarch:

> In accordance with the universally recognized doctrine of international law, the supreme representation of the modern state is vested in the chief of state, whether he be an actual person (monarch, president of the republic) or a collective body (Presidium of the Supreme Soviet of the U.S.S.R., Federal Council of Switzerland). . . . As a general rule, the competence of the chief of state includes the declaration of war and conclusion of peace, nomination and reception of diplomatic agents, granting powers for the conclusion of international treaties and agreements of special significance, and the ratification and denunciation of these treaties and accords.[39]

In its ceremonial capacity, the Presidium confers all diplomatic ranks and titles of a plenipotentiary character, formally appoints and recalls diplomatic representatives of the U.S.S.R., and receives the letters of credence and recall from foreign envoys. Although foreign representatives almost always present their credentials to the Chairman of the Presidium, they are, in fact, accredited to the Presidium as a collective entity.

The Presidium's substantive powers are considerable. Article 49 of the Constitution authorizes it to interpret all Soviet laws, convene and dissolve the Supreme Soviet, annul decisions and orders of the Council of Ministers, appoint and remove the higher commands of the armed forces, and issue decrees in its own right, virtually without limits. Furthermore, the Presidium, during intervals between sessions of the Supreme Soviet, "proclaims a state of war in the event of armed attack . . . or whenever necessary to fulfill international treaty obligations concerning mutual defence against aggression," can order general or partial mobilization, and can proclaim martial law in separate localities or throughout the country. The exercise of many of these powers is not subject to later confirmation by the Supreme Soviet, although the Presidium remains technically accountable for all its activities to the Soviet legislature, which theoretically can replace its personnel.

---

[39] *Istoriya Diplomatii*, Vol. III, p. 765.

Certain important powers vested in the Presidium are provisional and delegated. Thus, the Presidium, during periods when the Supreme Soviet is not in session, can appoint and dismiss ministers upon the recommendation of the chairman of the Council of Ministers, but this is subject to later confirmation. Similarly, if the Presidium promulgates decrees of a fundamental nature, outside its formal constitutional competence, they also are subject to confirmation, although this may be several years later.

Although the Constitution appears to give the Presidium a monopoly on the ratification and denunciation of treaties, a law of the Supreme Soviet, "On the Procedure for Ratification and Denunciation of International Treaties," passed on August 19, 1938, defines as treaties requiring its ratification: (1) treaties of peace; (2) mutual defense treaties; (3) treaties of nonaggression; and (4) treaties requiring mutual ratification for their implementation.[40] By implication, and in accordance with past practice, all treaties not specifically enumerated as requiring ratification by the Presidium are left to the discretion of the Council of Ministers. On the other hand, on rare occasions the Supreme Soviet has been asked to ratify or give preliminary approval to particularly important treaties, although there exists no constitutional imperative.

2. *The Supreme Soviet.* As the "highest organ of state authority in the U.S.S.R.," the power of the Supreme Soviet under the Constitution is coterminous with that of the Union.

Composed of two coordinate chambers—the Council of the Union and the Council of Nationalities—of approximately equal size, the constitutional competence of the Soviet legislature in foreign affairs surpasses that of any other organ. In practice, it has abdicated most of its powers to the Presidium and has been left only with the empty shell of ceremony, which may sometimes border on consultation. Both chambers are equally impotent, singly or together, and neither has specific functions or powers denied the other.

The formal authority of the Supreme Soviet in foreign policy falls into seven categories: (1) the enactment of basic legislation and constitutional amendments; (2) the confirmation of the decisions and decrees of the Presidium and the Council of Ministers; (3) ratification of selected treaties; (4) declaration of war and peace; (5) confirmation and authorization of territorial changes and of the creation, admission, promotion, demotion, and abolition of new republics; (6) hearing and approving of foreign policy reports delivered by the

---

[40] *Second Session of the Supreme Soviet of the U.S.S.R.,* verbatim report (New York, 1938), p. 678.

Premier or the Foreign Minister; and (7) the preliminary examination of treaties prior to ratification by the Presidium. Since Stalin's death, all of these activities have been accorded greater publicity.

All proposed laws, treaties, significant statements of policy, results of important conferences, or simply reviews of the international situation—with one or two alleged exceptions, however—were taken on the initiative of the government, under instructions from the Party.

The sessions of the Supreme Soviet are short. Between 1946 and 1954 the Supreme Soviet sat for a total of only 45 days, with the longest session lasting seven days (June 1950) and the shortest, 67 minutes (March 1953); its performance before and during the war was even less auspicious. By far the most significant function of the Supreme Soviet is to hear reports on the foreign policy of the government. It is customary, but by no means the invariable rule, that the Foreign Minister review the government's foreign policy before this body, usually to joint sessions. It listens attentively, with conditioned enthusiasm; if requested, it enacts legislation with rare precision and extraordinary dispatch, unencumbered with either debate or criticism. Fulsome panegyrics delivered by a dozen or more carefully selected deputies on the wisdom and correctness of the government's policies are euphemistically described as "discussion" in the official records, a close examination of which has failed to produce a single note of criticism, to say nothing of a negative vote, in all the deliberations of the Supreme Soviet.

In the words of *Kommunist,* "until recently its [*i.e.* the Supreme Soviet's] sessions concerned for the most part consideration of budget questions and approval of the decrees of the Presidium," [41] but with the replacement of Malenkov by Bulganin in February, 1955, a calculated effort has been made to give it a more conspicuous role in foreign affairs. These changes have, so far, been more ornamental than substantive.

With the installation of Bulganin as Premier in February, 1955, the Supreme Soviet, with much fanfare, issued an appeal to other parliaments for a program of parliamentary exchanges in the form of visiting delegations addressing each other's legislatures; more than a dozen such exchanges have taken place. In July of the same year the Supreme Soviet adhered to the Inter-Parliamentary Union (ITU) and sent a delegation to its 44th annual conference in Helsinki.

Although the two Foreign Affairs Commissions of the two chambers of the Supreme Soviet are supposed to make "a preliminary examination of all matters connected with foreign affairs to be considered by

---

[41] *Kommunist* (No. 10), August 1956, pp. 3-15.

the Supreme Soviet (and its Presidium)," this function had all but withered away and the existence of these bodies was virtually rendered superfluous; they were suddenly brought back to life when the Soviet-Iranian Agreement of 1954, the denunciation of the Anglo-Soviet and Anglo-French Treaties of Alliance, the Warsaw Pact, and the agreement to establish diplomatic relations with West Germany were all submitted, with considerable publicity, to joint sessions of the two Commissions (the Supreme Soviet was not in session) for their solemn consideration. After hearing reports by Molotov and his deputies, they dutifully recommended approval to the Soviet Presidium. At about the same time the two chairmen of the chambers, together with allegedly prominent members of the two Commissions, suddenly appeared at diplomatic receptions, received foreign dignitaries, and pompously pontificated on foreign policy in patent, but bogus, imitation of their counterparts in the American Congress.

The Supreme Soviet was awarded the honor of proclaiming an end to the state of war with Germany on January 25, 1955, and on August 4, 1955, it was called into special session to hear Bulganin's report on the Summit Conference at Geneva, a procedure not used since Molotov addressed a special session on the Nazi-Soviet Pact of 1939. On this same occasion the Supreme Soviet, after "debating" the policy of the government and "interpellating" the Foreign Minister, issued an appeal to the parliaments and governments of the world to "put an end to the arms race." The regular session of the Supreme Soviet was aranged to coincide with the return of Bulganin and Khrushchev from their tour of Southeast Asia, so that both might address the Supreme Soviet on the results of their trip.

Although the activities of the Supreme Court have been stepped up, there is little reason to believe that there has been a corresponding enhancement of its influence and power. It hears more reports on foreign policy, but it has also retained intact its undeviating characteristic of absolute unanimity, whether convened on the spur of the moment or after contrived deliberation. The invocation of the formal prerogatives of the Supreme Soviet, however, is no idle exercise, since it creates certain advantages for Soviet diplomacy. (1) It serves to infuse Soviet citizens with the notion that their representatives participate in the formulation of foreign policy decisions. (2) As a propagandistic maneuver it strives to create the illusion of evolving constitutionalism in the Soviet system. (3) As a purely diplomatic device, it permits the Kremlin to invoke constitutional procedures as a stumbling or delaying mechanism in negotiations and affords a basis for demanding reciprocal action in the ratification of treaties and other diplomatic instruments.

The possibility, no matter how slight, that ceremony may some day be replaced with substance cannot be ignored, but this expectation must yield to the realization that the flurry of activity we have noted can be arrested as abruptly as it began.

3. *The Council of Ministers* (Formerly the Council of People's Commissars, or *Sovnarkom*). As the "highest executive and administrative organ" of the government, the Council of Ministers "exercises general supervision" over the execution and administration of the country's foreign policy, and also directs the state's foreign trade monopoly. Constitutionally, since 1944 the central government no longer exercises a monopoly over foreign affairs but merely represents the Federal Union as a whole and establishes the "general procedure in mutual relations between the Union Republics and foreign states," and thus shares the conduct of diplomacy with its 15 constituent republics.

In actual practice, however, foreign policy in the Soviet Union is the most tightly centralized activity of the Soviet government.

The Council of Ministers has the following powers: (1) grant or withdraw recognition of new states or governments; (2) sever and restore diplomatic relations; (3) order acts of reprisal against other states; (4) appoint negotiators and supervise the negotiation of international treaties and agreements; (5) declare the adherence of the Soviet Union to international conventions not requiring formal ratification; (6) conclude agreements with other heads of governments not requiring ratification (similar to American executive and administrative agreements); (7) ratify all treaties and agreements not requiring ratification of the Presidium; (8) give preliminary examination of all treaties submitted to the Presidium for its ratification; (9) oversee "the current work of the diplomatic organs, effectually direct that work and take the necessary measures in that field;" and (10) appoint and accredit all diplomats below plenipotentiary rank and foreign trade representatives.[42]

Actually there appears to be a great area of overlapping activity between the Presidium and the Council of Ministers in the conduct of diplomacy, and were it not that the one-party system makes all basic decisions, rivalries and jealousies would almost certainly develop between these two organs, rendering coordination of diplomatic activity virtually impossible.

a. *The Chairman and his Cabinet.* The most influential member of the Council of Ministers is its Chairman, referred to in the West as

---

[42] *Cf.* A. Y. Vyshinsky, *The Law of the Soviet State* (New York, 1948), p. 376; *Istoriya Diplomatii*, Vol. III, pp. 767-768, 806-807; Towster, *op. cit.*, p. 279.

the Premier, who is always an important figure of the highest rank in the Party hierarchy. This office, including its predecessors under previous constitutions, has been filled by only six men since the establishment of the Soviet state: Lenin (1917-1924); Rykov (1924-1930); Molotov (1930-1941); Stalin (1941-1953); Malenkov (1953-1955); and Bulganin (1955-   ). After Lenin's death, when Stalin refused to hold formal office, this post was reduced to a mere shadow of the Secretary-General of the Party, but after Stalin assumed formal responsibility for the policies of the government in April, 1941, and held it until his death in March, 1953, the post retrieved its former prestige and power. Stalin's death, and the resultant power rivalries that were unleashed, revived the division of power between the Premier and First Secretary of the Party, since the two positions have once again been separated. Although it has recently lost prestige, it is unlikely that this office, which achieved such internal and external symbolic significance during Stalin's long tenure, will again be easily reduced to the empty shell it was before 1941.

The Chairman has primary responsibility for the conduct of the country's foreign policy and, presumably, has the authority to appoint and remove the ministers concerned with its day-to-day execution. Immediately below the Chairman are his First Deputy Chairmen and Deputy Chairmen, who normally are in charge of a specific ministry, or may be without portfolio. The Chairman, his First Deputies, and his Deputies constitute the Presidium (cabinet) of the Council of Ministers.

The size and composition of the Presidium have undergone serious transformations in recent years. Under Stalin, the Presidium became so large that a Bureau or inner cabinet of the Presidium was secretly organized, whose composition and membership have never been made public. After his death, the number of First Deputies was reduced to four and of Deputies to one, with only the Chairman and the First Deputies admitted into the Presidium. The Bureau of the Presidium was technically abolished, but in fact the Presidium was reduced to the smaller size of the Bureau. The execution of First Deputy Beria and the replacement of Malenkov as Premier resulted in enlargement of the Presidium until it reached its maximum post-Stalinist number of five First Deputies and eight Deputies. As a result of the reorganization of the economic ministries and the expulsion of Molotov, Kaganovich, Malenkov, Pervukhin, and Saburov from the Presidium, it has been reduced to four members. The composition of the Presidium in 1957 must be viewed therefore as strictly transitional.

The Council of Ministers and its Presidium are subordinate in fact to the Party Presidium and in theory to the Supreme Soviet and its

Presidium. If the current Premier of the Government loses a vote of confidence in the Party organ, the decision is reviewed by the Central Committee, whereupon, if it is upheld, he submits his resignation to the Presidium of the Supreme Soviet. The Central Committee, through its First Secretary, nominates the next Premier to the appropriate State organs and a new Government is thus formed.

Since the formation of the Bulganin Government, the Premier and other key members of the Presidium of the Council of Ministers have played an increasingly personal and active role in the country's diplomacy. Not only Bulganin, but important ministers and Marshal Voroshilov, Chairman of the Presidium of the Supreme Soviet, have made state visits to many countries as a part of the Kremlin's new diplomatic offensive. While he was Foreign Minister, Molotov played an active personal role in the country's diplomacy, but he apparently objected to the interference of the other members of the Government in Soviet diplomatic activity. In particular he objected to the travels of Bulganin and Khrushchev and their meetings with the heads of various governments.

b. *The Foreign Minister.*   In forty years of Soviet diplomacy there have been only seven Foreign Ministers: Leon Trotsky (November 1917-April 1918); Georgi Chicherin (1918-1929); Maxim Litvinov (1929-1939); Vyacheslav Molotov (1939-1949; 1953-1956); Andrei Vyshinsky (1949-1953); Dimitri Shepilov (during 1956); Andrei Gromyko (1957-   ). Down to 1949, the typical tenure of a Soviet Foreign Minister was 10 years, and nearly 35 years of Soviet diplomacy have been directed by only three individuals, thus giving Soviet diplomacy a measure of enviable continuity. Since Stalin's death the foreign ministry has changed hands almost as many times as it had up to the time of his passing, reflecting the bitter conflicts that have raged over foreign policy in the past few years.

The Foreign Minister's role and influence in Soviet diplomacy depend almost entirely upon his Party rank. When the Minister is of relatively low rank in the Party, he constitutes little more than a caretaker of the department. If he is of top Party rank, as Trotsky and Molotov were, he participates in the decisions he is asked to execute, and in at least two cases (Molotov and Shepilov), has actually flouted the will of the decision-makers in favor of executing a foreign policy of his own choosing. Even though Chicherin and Litvinov, like Gromyko, were relatively low-ranking members in the Party hierarchy, this by no means indicates that they were less effective as diplomats. There is ample evidence to suggest that the Party leaders would prefer a low-ranking Party member as Foreign Minister rather than one of first rank, except under critical circumstances, since it enhances the flexibility of Soviet diplomacy while hampering that of other countries, who are forced to accommodate their diplomacy to the bureaucratic channels of the Soviet Foreign Office. Normally the Foreign Minister is at least a full member of the Central Committee, although both Chicherin and Litvinov achieved that status some time after they had become Foreign Commissars. Gromyko was elevated to full membership only at the 20th Party Congress. Trotsky and Molotov were the only Foreign Ministers who were full members of the Party's highest body; Vyshinsky and Shepilov were alternate members of the Presidium during their incumbency.

C. The Ministry of Foreign Affairs (formerly the People's Commissariat for Foreign Affairs, or *Narkomindel*)

1. *Evolution of the Ministry.* The government department directly charged with the day-to-day administration of Soviet diplomacy does not materially differ in its structure and organization from its counterparts in other Great Powers, although it betrays a pattern of historical evolution that is unique among foreign ministries. Since its establishment it has undergone a triple metamorphosis.

In the beginning, its primary purpose was to trigger a world revolution and thus create the conditions for its own extinction. It was thought that if the world revolution failed, a Soviet diplomacy would be impossible, and, if it succeeded, unnecessary. "I will issue a few revolutionary proclamations to the people of the world," it was Leon Trotsky's boast, "and then close up shop." [43] On November 26, 1917, a decree from Trotsky's Foreign Affairs Commissariat virtually disestablished the diplomatic apparatus of the Russian state: all members of the Russian foreign service abroad were summarily dismissed unless they expressed loyalty to the Bolshevik regime. In their place, Bolshevik émigrés abroad were appointed as "unofficial" agents of the new government (Litvinov was such an appointee to Great Britain). Trotsky even neglected to establish a permanent home office; he appeared at his office only once—to dismiss all employees reluctant to pledge loyalty to the new regime and to set up a committee to publish the secret treaties in the archives of the Russian foreign office.

The Treaty of Brest-Litovsk imposed upon the new regime diplomatic relations with Germany and its allies, so the Council of People's Commissars was forced to recreate a provisional diplomatic service.

---

[43] Cited in E. H. Carr, *The Bolshevik Revolution, 1917-1923* (London, 1953), Vol. III, p. 16.

A decree of June 4, 1918, with obvious petulance, attempted to rewrite unilaterally the principle of diplomatic ranks adopted by the Congress of Vienna in 1815, by abolishing all Soviet diplomatic titles in favor of a single designation, "plenipotentiary representative" (*Polpred*). In a naive attempt to impose Soviet egalitarian principles upon foreign envoys, the decree peremptorily announced that "all diplomatic agents of foreign states . . . shall be considered equal plenipotentiary representatives regardless of their rank." [44]

Pending the eventual liquidation of the Foreign Affairs Commissariat, the functions of Soviet diplomacy during this initial period fell into three principal categories: (1) the publication of "secret treaties" in order to expose the duplicity and hypocrisy of the Allies and compromise them in the eyes of their own people; (2) the conduct of necessary negotiations and diplomatic relations, on a temporary basis, with capitalist states in a position to impose them; and (3) the utilization of Soviet embassies and legations abroad as centers of revolutionary propaganda, conspiracy, and activity, in clear violation of treaty obligations. In this connection, the Soviet government announced that "The Council of People's Commissars considers it necessary to offer assistance by all possible means . . . to the left internationalist wing of the labor movement of all countries [and] . . . for this purpose . . . decides to allocate two million rubles for the needs of the revolutionary international movement and to put this sum at the disposal of the foreign representatives of the Commissariat for Foreign Affairs." [45]

The failure of the revolution to spread beyond Russia, the success of the seceding border states in maintaining their independence, and the failure of foreign intervention to subdue the Bolshevik regime, forced the expansion of diplomatic contact with the bourgeois world. By 1921 the Soviet foreign office was prepared to pass out of its initial phase into its second, as a quasi-permanent agency for "normalizing" relations with the capitalist powers on the basis of "mutual interests" during the prolonged period of "co-existence" which Lenin now recognized as the inevitable interval between the first and final stages of the world revolution. From an instrument of world revolution the foreign office was converted into an instrument for furthering the interests of the Soviet state.

Since the revolutionary and conspiratorial activities of Soviet diplo-

---

[44] Full text in T. A. Taracouzio, *The Soviet Union and International Law* (New York, 1935), p. 383.

[45] Jane Degras, ed., *Soviet Documents on Foreign Policy* (London, 1951), Vol. I, p. 22.

mats complicated the establishment of desirable trade and political connections with the bourgeois world, the new Commissar of Foreign Affairs, Georgi Chicherin (who succeeded Trotsky in April, 1918), was instrumental in shifting the function of revolutionary agitation from the Foreign Office to the Party. A new diplomatic service was organized from scratch by Chicherin, and shortly after he assumed office the Foreign Commissariat was organized into more than a dozen departments. The first Statute on the Commissariat for Foreign Affairs was issued by the Council of Ministers on July 6, 1921; it defined the sphere of competence of each of the departments. After the formation of the Union and the centralization of diplomacy in Moscow, the Commissariat received on November 12, 1923, its definitive statute, which still constitutes the juridical basis for the organization and structure of the Foreign Ministry. However, it was not until 1924 that Soviet diplomacy was juridically relieved of its revolutionary mission and it entered into its current phase. According to a decree issued on November 21, 1924, and still effective:

> It goes without saying that diplomatic missions abroad are appointed by each of the parties establishing diplomatic relations for purposes which exclude propaganda in the country to which they are accredited. The Soviet diplomatic missions follow and are to follow this principle with absolute strictness.[46]

Although technically the Soviet Foreign Office is supervised by the Council of Ministers, it has always enjoyed a unique, direct relationship with the Party Presidium never approached by other ministries. Unlike the other departments of government in the new Bolshevik regime, the Foreign Commissariat was unencumbered with holdovers from the old bureaucracy, Chicherin being the only prominent figure who had previous diplomatic experience. Consequently, from the very beginning, it was cherished by Lenin:

> The diplomatic apparatus . . . is quite exceptional in the governmental apparatus. We excluded everyone from the old Tsarist apparatus who formerly had even the slightest influence. Here, the whole apparatus, insofar as it possesses the slightest influence, has been made up of Communists. For this reason this apparatus has acquired for itself . . . the reputation of a Communist apparatus which has been tested and cleansed of the old Tsarist bourgeois and petty bourgeois apparatus to a degree incomparably higher than that attained in the apparatus with which we have to be satisfied in the other people's commissariats.[47]

---

[46] Full text in Taracouzio, *op. cit.*, pp. 389-390.
[47] *New York Times*, July 1, 1956. Extract is from suppressed Lenin documents distributed at the 20th Party Congress and later made public.

This quality, in the words of a Soviet diplomat, "helped make it a peculiarly well-fitted apparatus for the expression of new policies." [48]

The Statute governing the Foreign Affairs Commissariat, decreed on November 12, 1923, which has been frequently amended, but never superseded, defined its principal duties as:

> (a) The defence of the political and economic interests of the U.S.S.R. . . . (b) The conclusion of treaties and agreements with foreign countries in accordance with the decisions of the government. (c) Supervision over the proper execution of treaties and agreements concluded with foreign states, and enabling the corresponding organs of the U.S.S.R. and the Union Republics to exercise rights conferred by these treaties. (d) Supervision over the execution by the competent organs of treaties, agreements, and accords concluded with foreign states. [49]

2. *The Foreign Minister and his Collegium.* The administration of the Foreign Commissariat was initially entrusted to a collegium in accordance with the Bolshevik principle of collective responsibility. The Foreign Commissar was forced to share authority and responsibility with a board of three or four other senior officials of the Commissariat.

With the promulgation of the first Constitution in March, 1918, the germ of one-man management was implanted, when the Commissar was invested with the personal power of decision relating to matters within the competence of his department, but if this decision conflicted with the views of the collegium, the latter, without the power of stopping execution of the decision, could appeal its differences to the Council or to the Presidium. As a consequence, collective responsibility became a convenient evasion of concrete responsibility and the collegium frequently abused its powers by issuing orders in its own name, thus lowering the prestige and personal responsibility of the Foreign Commissar.

By 1934, defects of collective responsibility became so serious that Stalin condemned the collective principle as obsolete and subversive of efficient administration; the collegium was abolished and the Foreign Minister installed in complete charge of his department and, in turn, he assumed full personal responsibility for its work.

Four years later, in March, 1938, the collegium was restored in modi-

---

[48] Alexei F. Neymann, in S. N. Harper, ed., *The Soviet Union and World Problems* (Chicago, 1935), p. 229.

[49] The full text of this statute, with amendments through 1927, is reprinted in *Yezhegodnik Narodnovo Komissariata Po Inostrannim Delam Na 1928 God* (Moscow, 1928), pp. 182-193. All subsequent references and extracts refer to this text. *Cf.* also *Istoriya Diplomatii*, Vol. III, pp. 770-771.

fied form, but was clearly divested of its former tyrannical power over the Commissar. The Council, which was too large and unwieldy as a decision-making or even advisory body, was retained as a convenient institution for the diffusion of policy and administrative decision, and the collegium retained its character as the executive committee of the Commissariat. The Commissar retained his plenary authority and responsibility, but the formal prerogatives of the collegium remained considerable.[50]

The institutional relationship established in 1938 between the Foreign Minister and his collegium has survived, substantially unaltered, down to the present. Its size and composition appear to vary, depending upon the discretion of the Foreign Minister, except in unusual circumstances, although appointments to the collegium continue to be made by the Council of Ministers. The collegium is presided over by the Minister or one of his First Deputies. It includes not only the First Deputy and Deputy Ministers, but also about four to six senior officials in the department, one of whom invariably is the Chief of the Press and Information Division. The number of First Deputies has varied from one to three; their rank roughly corresponds to that of the Undersecretary in the American State Department. Immediately below the First Deputies are the Deputies, whose rank corresponds to that of Assistant Secretaries in the American hierarchy; there may be up to six Deputies (in 1958 there were four). The other members of the collegium are normally department heads. Thus the size of the collegium may vary up to a dozen members.

The institutional prerogatives of the collegium fall just short of the power of actual decision, but without weakening in any way the full responsibility of the Minister. It cannot overrule the Minister's decisions, nor issue orders in its own name, but it is mandatory for the Minister to report any disagreement with his collegium to the Council for disposition. The collegium retains the right, individually or collectively, to appeal to the Council and the Central Committee of the party.[51]

3. *The organization and structure of the Foreign Ministry.* The basic organization and structure of the Soviet Foreign Ministry remain governed by the Statute of 1923, which established a flexible system of administration, permitting a wide latitude for internal reorganization at the discretion of the Minister. The Ministry is organ-

---

[50] *Cf. Vyshinsky, op. cit.,* pp. 387-389.
[51] *Ibid.*

ized into "divisions according to the main geographical divisions of the world and the main functions of the department and . . . this apparatus both in its offices in Moscow and its missions in foreign countries does not present any striking differences in structure compared with similar departments in other countries," as one former Soviet diplomat informs us.[52]

At the apex of the Ministry stands the Minister with his collegium, which is provided with a Central Secretariat—headed by a Secretary-General—performing routine secretarial and staff administrative work for the Minister, his deputies, and members of the collegium. The functional divisions, which have become increasingly differentiated with the expansion of Soviet diplomatic activity, are conventional: Protocol, Political Archives, Courier and Liaison, Passport and Visa, Treaty and Legal, Economic, Consular Affairs, Administration, Personnel, Finance, Supplies, and Press and Information.[53] Several related functional divisions are grouped together and supervised by Deputy Ministers, and perhaps also by collegium members.

Since the 1923 Statute does not stipulate the precise number of geographical divisions, the number and composition of these departments vary considerably, and currently are in a phase of expansive reorganization. The Statute merely states that "the divisions of Western Affairs . . . are charged with securing diplomatic relations with the states of Europe and America, the observation and study of the political and economic and other relations between these states and other institutions of the U.S.S.R. which may also have relations with missions in the U.S.S.R." The divisions for "Eastern Affairs" assume identical responsibilities for the states of Asia and Africa.

The cataclysmic political changes of the past twenty years, the massive expansion of Soviet diplomatic relations, and the creation of many new states in Asia and Africa, have affected profoundly the internal organization of the Foreign Office. In the past few years the number of geographical divisions has been increased, while the number of functional divisions has remained fairly constant. As compiled from Soviet press accounts, there are now seven "Western" divisions and four "Eastern" divisions, plus two separate departments for International Organizations and International Economic Organizations. The geographical divisions, which closely approximate those of 1925, are as follows:

---

52 Neymann, *op. cit.*, pp. 226-227.
53 *Cf. Yezhegodnik*, 1925, 1926, 1928, 1929.

1. Division for American Countries (North and South).
2. First European (France, Benelux, and Italy).
3. Second European (United Kingdom and white Commonwealth countries).
4. Third European (the two Germanies, Austria, Switzerland).
5. Fourth European (Czechoslovakia, Poland, Hungary).
6. Fifth European (Balkan states).
7. Sixth European (Scandinavian countries and Finland).
8. Division for Near Eastern and African Affairs.
9. Division for Middle Eastern Affairs.
10. Division for Southeast Asian Affairs (Pakistan, India, Burma, Northern Vietnam, Cambodia, Laos, Thailand, Ceylon, and Indonesia).
11. Division for Far Eastern Affairs (China, Outer Mongolia, North Korea, and Japan).

Before October, 1956, there existed a single division for Near and Middle Eastern Affairs; its separation into two divisions reflects the significance attached to these countries in Soviet diplomacy.

Normally, a Deputy Minister exercises general administrative supervision over the work of several contiguous geographical divisions, and usually he is a former ambassador with diplomatic experience in the geographical area in question.

The appearance of kindred Communist states in Eastern Europe and in the Far East has not modified the geographical divisions of the Ministry. Relations with Communist countries through the Foreign Ministry, however, have been reduced to the bare minimum required by international law and protocol, since substantive and policy questions are handled through corresponding Party organizations. Soviet envoys to important Communist countries are considered primarily as functionaries and emissaries from the Party and secondarily as government agents. Thus, when Tito complained that the Soviet Ambassador was meddling in the affairs of the Yugoslav Party, Stalin replied:

> Tito and Kardelj . . . identify the Soviet Ambassador, a responsible Communist . . . with an ordinary bourgeois ambassador, a simple official of a bourgeois state. . . . The Soviet Ambassador, a responsible Communist . . . not only has the right but is obliged, from time to time, to discuss with Communists in Yugoslavia all questions which interest them.[54]

---

[54] *The Soviet-Yugoslav Dispute* (London: Royal Institute of International Affairs, 1948), pp. 34-35.

This relationship has been confirmed and emphasized since Stalin's death with the adoption of the practice of dispatching high Party functionaries as ambassadors to important Communist states.

4. *The Soviet diplomatic service.* The decree of 1918 reducing all diplomatic ranks to the single and equal rank of plenipotentiary representative remained technically in force until 1941, although it was neither possible nor desirable to honor it in practice. The principle of diplomatic equality was based on the discarded theory that "the representatives of . . . the U.S.S.R. do not personify a quasi-mythical Leviathan state, but only . . . the plenipotentiary of the ruling class," and that diplomats from bourgeois countries were likewise emissaries of their ruling classes.[55] This view was condemned as unduly doctrinaire and subversive of Soviet prestige and diplomacy, since, in practice, it amounted to unilateral renunciation of all the privileges and prerogatives of seniority and rank under traditional norms of diplomatic intercourse.

Soviet diplomacy gradually accommodated itself to existing international practice through the extralegal exchange of supplementary protocols granting informal recognition of rank so that Soviet diplomats might avoid forfeiting recognized privileges accorded to rank and seniority. By 1941, the discrepancy between the law and practice of Soviet diplomatic ranks had reached the point of absurdity, so on May 9, the Presidium issued a decree establishing three diplomatic categories: (1) Ambassador Extraordinary and Plenipotentiary; (2) Minister Extraordinary and Plenipotentiary; and (3) *Chargé d'Affaires.* This decree gave legal sanction to existing *de facto* distinctions. Two years later, on May 28, 1943, the Presidium decreed the establishment of eleven grades in the diplomatic service and thus brought Soviet diplomatic ranking into complete focus with general diplomatic practice: (1) Ambassador Extraordinary and Plenipotentiary; (2) Minister Extraordinary and Plenipotentiary of the First Class; (3) Minister Extraordinary and Plenipotentiary of the Second Class; (4) Counselor, First Class; (5) Counselor, Second Class; (6) First Secretary, First Class; (7) First Secretary, Second Class; (8) Second Secretary, First Class; (9) Second Secretary, Second Class; (10) Third Secretary; and (11) Attaché.[56]

Until Stalin's death, one of the chief peculiarities of the Soviet diplo-

---

[55] E. Korovin, *Mezhdunarodnoye Pravo Perekhodnovo Vremeni* (Moscow, 1924), p. 63.

[56] *Cf. Istoriya Diplomatii,* Vol. III, pp. 778-780. Date of the decree is mistakenly given as June 14, 1943, in this work.

matic service was the relative permanence of the Foreign Minister as contrasted with the turnover of all ranks below. This is almost precisely the reverse of the situation found in other countries where kaleidoscopic changes occur at the ministerial level in contrast to the relative permanence of the diplomatic bureaucracy as a whole. This frequent turnover of personnel has arrested more than once the orderly development of a career diplomatic service, if that is desirable, or even possible, in a one-party state. While scores of ambassadors and high Foreign Ministry officials have been arrested or executed on charges of treason, not a single Foreign Minister (Trotsky excepted) has ever been liquidated or charged with high treason. Ministers appointed to other departments have not been so lucky. The disgrace suffered by Molotov and Shepilov recently while the career service survived virtually unscathed indicates the possible existence of a career service that scrupulously avoids involvement in power intrigues and thus may gain immunity from the effects of factional rivalry.

Although it appears that a professional diplomatic service has been assuming shape during the past decade and a half, it is still fundamentally distinguishable from what is generally understood to be a career service. In Western countries, career officials are insulated from political partisanship (except under unusual circumstances) and manage to survive the changing fortunes of political parties or movements, serving as impersonal instruments of the party that happens to exercise political power. This was true even of Fascist totalitarian states. In contrast, since the Communist Party has a permanent monopoly on political power, all Soviet diplomats must be members of the Communist Party, and senior officials of the Ministry frequently are members of Party organs corresponding to their diplomatic importance.

As a rule, career Soviet diplomats do not rank very high in the Party hierarchy. The Foreign Minister is at least a full member of the Central Committee and frequently a member or alternate member of the Presidium. First Deputies are usually full members of the Central Committee (in 1958 both First Deputies were non-career officials), while career diplomats rarely achieve higher status than candidate membership in the Central Committee. Foreign Minister Gromyko is the only career official with full membership in the Central Committee; only three other career officials (G. N. Zarubin, V. A. Zorin, and Y. A. Malik) are candidate members.

Since Stalin's death, the Soviet diplomatic service has been subjected to a unique infusion of new personnel. Alongside members of the career service, who serve as diplomatic technicians, there now exist numerous high-ranking Ministry officials and diplomats who are primarily State administrators and Party functionaries appear to correspond to the political appointee in the American diplomatic hierarchy. The significance of the transfer of high Party officials into the diplomatic service can not yet be fully assessed, but it cannot be denied. Many actually enjoy higher Party rank than their technical superior, Foreign Minister Gromyko. Here is a partial list of high-placed Party officials in the Foreign Ministry as of 1958:

First Deputy V. V. Kuznetsov: Full member of the Central Committee, former full member of Stalin's expanded Party Presidium (1952-1953), and long-time Chairman of the Central Council of Trade Unions. Also heads Soviet delegation to the U.N.

First Deputy N. S. Patolichev: Full and alternate member of the Central Committee since 1939; former First Secretary of the Byelorussian Party; former alternate member of Stalin's expanded Presidium.

P. K. Ponomarenko, Ambassador to India: Full member of the Central Committee since 1939; full member of Stalin's expanded Presidium and former alternate member of post-Stalin Presidium; former overlord of Soviet cultural affairs; former First Secretary of the Byelorussian and Kazakhistan Parties; recently Ambassador to Poland.

P. F. Yudin, Ambassador to China: Full member of the Central Committee; former alternate member of Stalin's expanded Presidium; former director of the Cominform and a prominent Party ideologist.

N. M. Pegov, Ambassador to Iran: Full member of the Central Committee since 1939; alternate member of Stalin's expanded Presidium; former Secretary of the Party Central Committee and, until recently, Secretary of the Presidium of the Supreme Soviet.

I. F. Tevosyan, Ambassador to Japan: Full member of the Central Committee since 1939; former alternate member of Stalin's expanded Presidium; Deputy Premier in charge of metallurgical industries under Malenkov and Bulganin up to the time of his diplomatic appointment.

A. M. Puzanov, Ambassador to North Korea: Ex-full member of the Central Committee, now candidate member; former Premier of the Russian Republic, then Deputy Premier of the Russian Republic, and former alternate member of Stalin's expanded Presidium.

5. *The channels of Soviet diplomacy.* It is general practice for Soviet envoys to report to the Ministry through routine bureaucratic channels, that is, through the appropriate geographical divisions in the Ministry, but ambassadors in important posts frequently report directly to the Foreign Minister. Reports of an exceptionally important character are also sent directly to the Foreign Minister or his First

Deputies, rather than through normal channels. The close supervision of the diplomatic service by the Party center cannot be overemphasized; and diplomatic channels remain deliberately flexible.

Not all Soviet representatives abroad report to the Foreign Ministry. Envoys to Communist states, particularly those holding high Party rank, probably report to the Central Committee or the Presidium, except for reports of essentially protocol or legalistic significance, which are funneled through normal channels. The jurisdiction of the Foreign Ministry over envoys to Communist countries appears marginal at best.

Although the Ambassador, as the chief legal representative of the Soviet Union in foreign countries, is charged with general supervision over the activities of Soviet representatives and missions abroad to ensure that they are in accord with the general policy of the government, this responsibility is often of little more than formal or legal significance. According to defectors like Igor Gouzenko and Vladimir Petrov, Soviet missions abroad are organized into five separate divisions, each with separate and independent channels of communication: (1) the Ambassador and his staff, reporting directly to the Ministry of Foreign Affairs; (2) the Commercial Counsellor, reporting to the Ministry of Foreign Trade; (3) the Secret Police representative, disguised as a minor diplomat, reporting directly to the foreign section of the Security Ministry (now Committee); (4) the Attachés, reporting directly to the Director of Military Intelligence in Moscow; (5) the Party representative, also disguised as a minor diplomatic functionary, communicating directly with the foreign section of the Central Committee of the Party.

All of these representatives, with the exception of the Ambassador and the embassy staff proper, may be actively engaged in the overt or clandestine collection of intelligence information. In order to comply with the letter of their agreements with foreign countries, the Ambassador is scrupulously insulated from all knowledge of illegal espionage activities organized by the other sections, and although the Foreign Ministry Statute gives him the power to determine whether their activities are in accordance with government policy, in practice the Ambassador rarely sees the reports dispatched by the other sections through their respective channels.

In addition to espionage and intelligence activities, the Secret Police and Party sections maintain general surveillance over the other members of the mission and over each other. If the accounts of high-ranking defectors from the diplomatic and police service are accurate, Soviet missions abroad are often centers of intrigue, personal vendettas, and institutional rivalries and jealousies.

Information coming through various channels is screened, coordinated, and evaluated by a special agency of the Central Committee, which then submits its reports to the Presidium to be used as a factor in the formulation of foreign policy and in the making of decisions.

As instruments, rather than makers of policy, professional Soviet diplomats play a minor role in the formulation of foreign policy decisions. Their work is essentially technical and legalistic; the content of their reports is concerned primarily, if not exclusively, with observations and suggestions for more effective implementation of existing policy. Their area of initiative is carefully circumscribed and discouraged, and often they are themselves ignorant about the exact intentions of their superiors in the Kremlin. Their reports constitute but a minute fraction of the information upon which the Presidium takes action, and final disposition of all information from routine diplomatic channels and intelligence sources is made by the Presidium as it sees fit. As Merle Fainsod points out, accurate evaluation of information in the Soviet Union is often frustrated by special hazards:

> But the mountains of material have to be reduced to manageable proportions before they are brought to the attention of the leadership. What the rulers read reflects the selection and emphasis of an editorial staff which may be guided by its own preconditioning as well as its sensitivity to the anticipated reactions of its readers. The tendency to embrace data that confirm established predilections while rejecting the unpalatable facts that offend one's preconceptions is a weakness . . . [to] which . . . totalitarian societies appear to be particularly susceptible. . . . Every dictatorship has a tendency to breed sycophancy and discourage independence in its bureaucratic hierarchy. When the pronouncements of the dictator are sacred and unchallengeable, the words which subordinates must throw back at him tend to flatter his whims rather than challenge his analyses. . . . The ideological screen through which facts are received, filtered, and appraised constitutes an additional possibility of misrepresentation. . . . Not even the most pragmatically oriented member of the ruling group can wholly liberate himself from the frame of responses that represent the residue of a lifetime in Communist thought patterns.[57]

Khrushchev's explanation of why Stalin ignored repeated warnings from Churchill and from his own efficient espionage networks that the Nazis were planning to attack the Soviet Union appears to confirm Fainsod's perceptive appraisal when he revealed that "information of this sort concerning the threat of German armed invasion of Soviet territory was coming in also from our own military and diplomatic sources . . . [but] because the leadership was conditioned

---

[57] Fainsod, *op. cit.*, p. 283.

against such information, such data were dispatched with fear and assessed with reservation."

V. The Participation of Foreign Communist Parties in Soviet Foreign Policy Decisions

As rulers of the first country in which a Marxist revolutionary party had been elevated to power, the Bolsheviks early had to define their relationship with kindred Marxist parties engaged in revolutionary activity in other countries.

Although the international Communist movement has been institutionalized only in two organizations, the Comintern and the Cominform, Moscow's relations with foreign Communist parties falls into three distinct, but closely interrelated, periods: (1) The Leninist period (1919-1928); (2) the Stalinist period (1928-1953), and (3) the post-Stalinist period (1953-   ). These distinctions are purely arbitrary, based neither on the programmatic nor the institutional metamorphosis of the world Communist movement, but exclusively on the degree to which foreign Communist parties participated in the formulation of decisions concerning revolutionary strategy or Soviet foreign policy.

A. The Leninist period: partners in world revolution

The Comintern, founded by Lenin in 1919, was invested with two basic and interdependent functions: (1) to coordinate the strategy and direction of the world revolutionary movement, and (2) to defend the Soviet state against counterrevolution and foreign capitalist intervention. These two purposes, in turn, rested upon two fundamental assumptions concerning the world revolutionary movement: (1) the Russian Revolution was merely the first phase of a general revolution, and had neither a justification nor a purpose independent of it; (2) the revolution in Western Europe, particularly in Germany, was imminent.

The entire history of the relationship between Moscow and foreign Communist parties has been determined by the two essentially contradictory purposes of world revolution and the defense of the Soviet Union. The latter purpose, in turn, has rested upon the shifting assumptions concerning the fortune and direction of the revolutionary movement outside Russia.

When Lenin convened the first Congress of the Comintern in 1919, neither the concept of a world "Communist" movement, nor of foreign "Communist" parties, existed. Under Bolshevik sponsorship, radical or left-wing factions of the Social Democratic parties splintered off to form separate Communist parties affiliated with the new Third International. At the 2nd Congress in 1920, Statutes were drawn up defining "The Communist International [as] . . . a universal Communist party of which the parties operating in each country [including Russia] form individual sections," whose aim was "the establishment of . . . the international Soviet Republic." [58]

Although the Russian was the only ruling Party (except for the Hungarian during a brief period), and although a Russian (Grigori Zinoviev) was installed as president, the Soviet Party was not invested with a privileged and dominant status in the organization, but, like all other Parties, was subordinate to the decisions of the World Congress and its Executive Committee. The more imminent the revolution in Germany appeared, the more precarious was the "leading" role of the Russian Party. The facts, however, that it was the only Soviet state in the world and that the headquarters of the Comintern could be established only in Moscow made it inevitable that, as the prospects of the revolution faded, the position of the Soviet Party would correspondingly be enhanced.

Disagreements between Bolshevik leaders and foreign Communist parties, particularly the German, were frequent. Revolutionary doctrine and strategy and the role of Soviet diplomacy were discussed in the World Congress and in the meetings of its Executive Committee. The participation of foreign Communist parties was by no means a mere formality, and the Soviet state, which was conceived primarily as an instrument of the world revolution, frequently had to adjust its foreign policy to the views of foreign Communist parties, over which it did not exercise full control. The failure of revolution to take hold in Hungary and Germany, and the success of the Bolshevik regime to survive, forced a corresponding modification of the assumptions upon which the Comintern rested. The power struggle unleashed by Lenin's death in 1924 also found its reflection in the Comintern and within foreign Communist parties abroad. A reexamination of the previous estimates of the revolution in Germany, and the victory of Stalin's policy of "Socialism in One Country" in opposition to Trotsky's idea of "Permanent Revolution," forced leaders in the Comintern and in foreign Communist parties to choose sides. As Stalin squeezed out his rivals at home, his supporters in the Comintern and in foreign Communist parties carried out corresponding purges in their organizations. By 1930, Stalin had established his mastery over the Party ap-

---

58 W. H. Chamberlin, ed., *Blueprint for World Conquest* (Chicago, 1946), p. 36.

paratus at home and this was immediately followed by a corresponding subjugation of the Comintern.

B. The Stalinist period: instruments of Soviet diplomacy

From 1928 to 1953 foreign Communist parties, even after they
assumed power in their own countries, played little part in the formulation of Soviet foreign policy and were, on the contrary, completely
subservient to it as pliable and expendable instruments.

The world Communist movement during the Stalinist period rested
upon assumptions radically divergent from those upon which the
Comintern was originally founded. These were: (1) the Soviet Union
is the center and bulwark of the world revolution; (2) revolution independent of Moscow's support is impossible; and (3) the preservation
of the Soviet as the indispensable base of the world revolution is the
most important objective of all Communists, who must owe undeviating loyalty to Russia as the "proletarian fatherland." These new
assumptions were incorporated into the 1928 *Program of the Comintern,* and the extension of world revolution became identified with the
expansion of Soviet power:

> The U.S.S.R. inevitably becomes the base of the world revolu-
> tionary movement. . . . In the U.S.S.R., the world proletariat for
> the first time acquires a country that is really its own. . . . In the
> event of the imperialist declaring war upon and attacking the
> U.S.S.R., the international proletariat must retaliate by organizing
> bold and determined mass action and struggle for the overthrow
> of the imperialist governments.[59]

The basic philosophy justifying this submission to Moscow's control
was euphemistically defined by Stalin himself as "proletarian internationalism":

> A *revolutionary* is he who without evasions, unconditionally
> openly and honestly . . . is ready to uphold and defend the
> U.S.S.R. . . . An *internationalist* is he who unconditionally, without
> hesitation and without provisos is ready to defend the U.S.S.R. be-
> cause the U.S.S.R. is the base of the world revolutionary movement,
> and to defend and advance this movement is impossible without
> defending the U.S.S.R.[60]

Communist parties abroad were subordinated as expendable instruments manipulated in the interests of the Soviet state. Orders transmitted through the Comintern were followed with unquestioning

---

[59] *Ibid.,* pp. 220-223.
[60] J. V. Stalin, *Sochineniya* (Moscow, 1949), Vol. X, p. 61.

obedience, even if they invited self-destruction (China, Germany) or conflicted with the fundamental interests of their own people (France). As Moscow changed its policies, foreign Communists followed suit, even if the new policies were diametrically opposed to the current line. The Kremlin functioned as a GHQ of the world Communist movement, sacrificing a division or corps here and there in the interest of the movement as a whole.

The dissolution of the Comintern in 1943 did not materially alter the relationship between Moscow and foreign parties, except, as noted by Andrei Zhdanov at the founding of the Cominform in 1947, that "some comrades understood the dissolution of the Comintern to imply the elimination of all ties, of all contact, between the fraternal Communist Parties [which] . . . is wrong, harmful and . . . unnatural." [61]

After World War II, when Communist parties were installed in power in the countries of Eastern Europe and the Soviet Union was deprived of its unique position as the only Communist state in the world, the theory of "proletarian internationalism" was transformed from a system justifying Moscow's control of parties into a system justifying her control of entire countries and subordinating their interests to those of Russia. Some satellite Communist leaders considered the Soviet theory of "proletarian internationalism" applicable only to parties in capitalist countries, otherwise it became a philosophical justification for Soviet colonialism.

As satellite leaders betrayed signs of uneasiness and independence in their new role as government leaders with the interests of their own countries and peoples to consider, Stalin organized the Cominform, ostensibly as an organ of mutual consultation based on the equality and independence of its members, but in reality to solidify his control over the satellites and root out all tendencies towards independence. Unlike the Comintern, the new organization was carefully restricted to only the seven Communist states of Eastern Europe (Albania was denied membership) and to the two largest parties in the West, the Italian and the French. The refusal of Tito and other satellite leaders to place the interests of Russia above those of their own Communist countries and to act as Moscow's subservient agents of plunder and exploitation of their own people led to the expulsion of Yugoslavia from the Cominform and the wholesale slaughter of satellite leaders who showed signs of independence. "Loyalty to the Soviet Union," ran the Moscow line, "is the touchstone and criterion of proletarian internationalism." [62]

---

[61] *Strategy and Tactics*, p. 229.
[62] *For a Lasting Peace, For a People's Democracy*, June 30, 1950.

This was echoed by satellite Communists and by Communist leaders in capitalist countries, who agreed with Dimitrov that "proletarian internationalism . . . means complete coordination of the activities of Communist Parties and of the leading role of the Bolshevik [i.e. Soviet] Party." [63]

In rebuttal, Yugoslav leaders complained:

> The leaders of the U.S.S.R. consider that Yugoslavia as a state should be subordinated . . . and its entire development in a general way should be made dependent upon the U.S.S.R. At the same time, they have forced other socialist states to act in a similar manner. . . . The political relations . . . are also based upon . . . the need to maintain in the various socialist countries the kind of regimes that will always be prepared to agree . . . to accept such unequal status and exploitation of their country. Thus—subservient and vassal governments and vassal states are actually being formed.[64]

C. The post-Stalinist period: emerging polycentrism

Stalin's insistence that the Communist parties in Eastern Europe and in the Far East continue their subservience to Russia's interests introduced serious strains in the Communist orbit, of which Tito's defection was merely the most obvious manifestation. Moscow continued to interfere crudely in the internal development of the satellite states, while disclaiming interference; it plundered their economies and called it disinterested aid; and it rigidly dictated their "progress" to socialism, while paying lip-service to national peculiarities. On all these matters, satellite leaders were not consulted before decisions were taken in the Kremlin, but were simply commanded to carry them out as efficiently as possible.

Whereas the small Communist states of Eastern Europe were at the mercy of Soviet power, the attempt to dictate to Peking involved considerable resistance. Satellite leaders elsewhere were slaughtered by the score, but no Stalinist purges took place in the Chinese Party. One measure of Stalin's patent contempt for Chinese interests or national sensitivities was his refusal to relinquish the Soviet stranglehold on Manchuria, dissolve "joint stock companies," or surrender the special extraterritorial interests in Port Arthur and Darien, although this refusal was clearly resented by the Chinese. According to Walter Ulbricht, Stalin's brazen attempts to treat China like an ordinary satellite

---

[63] G. Dimitrov, *Report to the 5th Congress of the Bulgarian Communist Party* (Sofia, 1948), p. 55.

[64] Milovan Djilas, *Lenin on Relations Between Socialist States* (New York, 1949), pp. 16, 31.

almost forced Mao to desert the Soviet camp. Another clue to the deteriorated state of relations between Moscow and Peking during Stalin's lifetime was the enigmatic statement in the joint Sino-Soviet communiqué of January 19, 1957, that "since the conclusion of the Treaty of Friendship, Alliance and Mutual Assistance between the U.S.S.R. and China in 1950, the relations between the two countries have greatly developed. The events of the past few years demonstrate that the great alliance of the Soviet Union and China [is] . . . un-breakable." [65]

Stalin's successors were almost immediately confronted with the vex-ing problem of trying to perpetuate his system of vassalage or of modi-fying it. This reexamination unleashed a "great debate" within the Kremlin which divided the Soviet leadership into one faction insisting that the old system be retained with but minor adjustments and an-other advocating a "liberalization" that bordered upon revolutionizing the entire relationship between Moscow and her allies. While Malenkov was Premier no radical departures from Stalin's satellite policies could be detected, but in retrospect it appears that the faction headed by Khrushchev and Bulganin was pressing for a complete rupture with the past. Its program included: (1) elimination of the dangerously de-veloping schism with Peking; (2) rapprochement with Marshal Tito; (3) halting the outrageous economic exploitation of the satellites, and (4) permitting the gradual evolution of partial political autonomy. These proposals presupposed not only a break with the past, but an actual repudiation of Stalin's policies, and consequently they were strongly resisted by Molotov and others as dangerous to the unity of the Communist movement.

The defeat of the Malenkov-Molotov policy was clearly apparent by July, 1954. Neither Premier Malenkov nor Foreign Minister Molotov accompanied the Khrushchev-Bulganin mission to Peking in the au-tumn of 1954, whose purpose was to assuage Peking's resentments and inaugurate a new era in the relations between the two countries. The Soviet grip on Manchuria was relinquished, the joint stock companies liquidated, and full Chinese sovereignty restored over Darien and Port Arthur. Furthermore, Mao was apprised in advance of the impending changes in policy and government to be announced in February.

The most spectacular gesture of the Bulganin government was the decision to apologize to Marshal Tito, retract the accusations of treason and heresy, and make proper reparations for damages. As his

---

[65] Full text in *New York Times,* January 19, 1957.

price for a reconciliation Tito demanded, and apparently was granted, a consultative voice in the making of Soviet policy, which at one time virtually bordered on a veto privilege in affairs affecting Eastern Europe. At Tito's insistence, the following measures were taken: (1) Stalin's satellite policies were openly condemned and repudiated; (2) Stalin's victims in Eastern Europe, like Rajk in Hungary and Koslov in Bulgaria, were posthumously rehabilitated, their trials pronounced a fraud, and Tito absolved of all implications of subversion and deviation; (3) "National Deviationists" or "Titoists" still alive, like Gomulka in Poland and Kadar in Hungary, were released from prison and restored to high rank in the Party; (4) satellite "Stalinists" were, in turn, dethroned and replaced with personalities more acceptable to Tito; (5) the Cominform was liquidated; (6) Molotov was ousted as Foreign Minister because he was *persona non grata* to Tito; and (7) Moscow accepted the Yugoslav theory "that the roads and conditions of socialist development are different in different countries . . . that any tendency of imposing one's views in determining the roads and forms of socialist development is alien." [66] Never before had a foreign Communist leader—and a heretic at that—exercised such a decisive role in the deliberations of the Kremlin.

The policy of de-Stalinization not only evoked resistance from the opposing faction in the Presidium but introduced new pressures upon its deliberations from other Communist parties who disapproved of the capitulation to Tito. The decision to denounce Stalin and Stalinism at the 20th Congress carried the day in the Kremlin; and aside from Mao Tse-tung and Marshal Tito, it is unlikely that other Communist leaders were consulted in advance. However, satellite leaders who had a vested interest in the Stalinist policies resisted the rupture, but the pressures exerted by Tito upon the Khrushchev faction were sufficient to force many of them out of office. Reactions to the "de-Stalinization" program in Eastern Europe were far from uniform, and it was not entirely clear how far Moscow itself was ready to go. In Poland, Gomulka was catapulted to power; and in Hungary a national revolution threatened to sweep out the entire Communist system.

While Soviet troops succeeded in the resubjugation of Hungary, the "palace revolution" in Warsaw introduced another important and autonomous pressure upon the Soviet decision-makers—a quasi-independent Communist state of Poland which successfully defied Kremlin threats, purged Stalinists from high positions, and demanded and re-

---

[66] *New York Times,* June 21, 1956.

ceived a veto on the movement of Soviet troops in Poland. The Polish revolution was hailed in Peking and Belgrade, but it was generally condemned by the other satellite leaders.

Soviet intervention in Hungary also evoked divergent reactions in various Communist parties. Warsaw, Peking, and other influential centers privately were disturbed by the ferocity and brutality of the Soviet move, while Tito openly condemned the Soviet explanation of the revolution and deplored the use of troops. In his famous "Pula" speech,[67] Tito revealed the existence of "Stalinist" and "anti-Stalinist" factions in the Soviet hierarchy and in the Communist movement as a whole, and Yugoslavia was once again removed to the periphery of respectable Communism. The situation over Hungary was so serious that Moscow asked Peking for support. A statement was issued condoning the Hungarian repression and repudiating the Yugoslav criticisms; Chou En-lai was dispatched on a fence-mending tour through Budapest, Warsaw, and Moscow. This clearly gave Peking a voice nearly equal to that of Moscow in the Communist orbit, while that of Marshal Tito appeared to dwindle.

Since Moscow's flirtation with Tito, the entire equilibrium of power in the Communist world has undergone fundamental redistribution. Moscow has been compelled to relinquish its dictatorial control over those Communist states having a power position sufficient to establish partial independence, but the pressure of events has forced her to yield more than she anticipated and less than enough to satisfy Tito. Indications are that the Kremlin, supported by Peking, has decided to arrest further decentralization, convinced that any further concessions to Tito would unleash irreversible centrifugal forces that would disintegrate the Communist orbit.

Instead of a single dominant center of world Communism, there exist now two principal centers—Moscow and Peking—with one subsidiary center, Warsaw, and a peripheral one, Belgrade. The current aim of Moscow is to win for itself universal Communist recognition as *primus inter pares* in the Communist world as distinguished from its former autocratic position. Yugoslavia refuses to accord this recognition and will acknowledge only the chronological preeminence of the Soviet revolution. On the other hand, all other Communist parties, including the Chinese and the wavering Poles, have accepted the Soviet Union as the leading center of world Communism. The significant fact is, however, that Moscow must literally beg for this recogni-

---

[67] Full text of Tito's speech reprinted in *U.S. News and World Report*, November 30, 1956.

tion and it no longer has the power to make decisions affecting other parties without consulting them in advance; thus it must share the power of decision. The split in the Kremlin was reflected throughout the entire Communist world, producing diverse pressures upon its deliberations which it can no longer conveniently ignore.

The basic statement governing Russia's new relationship with other Communist parties was the statement of October 30, 1956, issued during the Hungarian uprising. Admitting that "downright mistakes which infringed the principle of equality in relations between Socialist States" had taken place in the past, the statement pledged that "the Soviet Government is ready to discuss, together with the governments of other Socialist States, measures . . . to remove the possibilities of violating the principle of national sovereignty and . . . equality." In place of Stalin's monolithic hegemony, the new Soviet policy would subscribe a "Great Commonwealth of Socialist Nations" based on "the principles of proletarian internationalism." [68]

Although the Soviet statement serves as the basic document, a statement of the Chinese Communist Party has been accorded the dignity of an authoritative interpretation of the new policy:

> Communist parties of all countries must be united, but at the same time must maintain their independence. . . . Solidarity among Communist parties . . . is strengthened when . . . they attain unanimity of views and action by means of real, and not formal, consultation. On the other hand, if in their mutual relations they forcibly impose their views on one another . . . then their solidarity will be harmed. . . . Stalin in his relations with fraternal parties . . . demonstrated a certain tendency toward great power chauvinism. . . . He sometimes interfered incorrectly in the internal affairs of . . . fraternal parties, an interference that resulted in serious consequences. . . . It is also necessary to overcome nationalist tendencies in the smaller countries [i.e. Titoism]. . . . For the sake of interests . . . of the proletariat of different countries . . . we must continue to strengthen the solidarity of the international proletariat with the center in the Soviet Union.[69]

The discontinuation of the Cominform and the relaxation of the Stalinist system of controls have raised the question of the future organizational forms of consultation and coordinated action. Moscow has agreed that the institutional forms of consultation are not predetermined, but she has frantically called them a matter of immediate urgency:

---

[68] Full text in *New York Times,* October 31, 1956.
[69] *Pravda,* December 31, 1956.

> The establishment of businesslike contacts between Communist, Socialist, and Workers' Parties in order to eliminate the split in the international labor movement has become one of the most urgent problems of our time. . . . The forms and ties among Marxist parties are not predetermined and immutable. They arise from the requirements of the Communist movement at each stage . . . and are determined by the parties themselves in the interest of victory of the common cause and not of course to satisfy someone's whim.[70]

These new relationships have not yet crystallized into a new supranational Communist organ of consultation, since the very nature of these consultative organs and practices remains a matter of serious dispute. The Soviet Union favors the recreation of a multinational organization, similar to the Cominform in its structural outlines, but to be based on the principles of equality, full discussion, "proletarian internationalism," and unity of action. An alternative pattern of multilateral consultation reportedly suggested by Moscow was the exchange of permanent party representatives. Both suggestions were frowned upon by Peking, Warsaw, and the Italian Communist Party, while Belgrade was not consulted.

The principal resistance to a new Cominform comes from Yugoslavia, although both Poland and China also oppose a revival of the organization in any form, which they fear may once again be employed by Moscow as an instrument of centralization and domination, since the Soviet Union can still muster the allegiance of more than a majority of the Communist parties in Europe. Opposed to the Soviet multilateral approach is the Yugoslav-Polish view that consultation be primarily a bipartisan affair:

> Both parties recognized that the bilateral interparty relations in the present conditions constitute the most appropriate form of consultation between Communist and Workers' Parties. This does not exclude, however, a broader cooperation of Communist and Workers' Parties and progressive movements in connection with individual questions of common interest.[71]

Pending the formation of definitive institutions and methods of consultation, bilateralism has been the general rule. This has followed two patterns: (1) mutual exchange of Party delegations to Party conferences and congresses; (2) bilateral discussions throughout the Communist world, followed by the issuance of joint communiqués, which have betrayed interesting deviations from the crude uniformity of the

---

[70] Mikoyan's speech to the 8th Congress of the Chinese Communist Party, *Pravda*, September 18, 1956.

[71] *New York Times*, January 1, 1957.

past. There have been only two multilateral conferences; one was held in Budapest in January, 1957, and attended only by delegates from Moscow, Budapest, Sofia, Prague, and Bucharest, and the other in Moscow in November 1957, which was more inclusive.

Regardless of what institutional forms are adopted for interparty co-operation, the Kremlin has abdicated its monopoly on making decisions for the entire Communist world and to some extent must coordinate its foreign policy with that of its allies rather than the other way around. What remains clear, however, as an aftermath of the Polish and Hungarian episodes, is that although Moscow is willing to allow considerable latitude in the internal evolution of the satellites, she has clearly laid down the outer limits beyond which the satellite states cannot go without inviting interference. These are: (1) acceptance of the basic irreconcilability of the capitalist and socialist camps; (2) recognition of the Soviet Union as the "leader" of the socialist camp; (3) intolerance of an independent or "neutralist" foreign policy for Communist states; and (4) retention of the dictatorship of the prole-tariat, i.e., the communist one-party system.[72]

These limitations apparently represent what Moscow believes to be the minimum requirements for the preservation of Communist power and Soviet security interests. By implication, the violation of any of these conditions by satellite Communist leaders will invite Soviet armed intervention. Since Tito refuses to accept the first three condi-tions, he retains his heretical status in the Communist world.

VI.   Conclusion

Since the death of Stalin the latent corrosive elements inherent in the Communist system have been activated. The centralized monopoly over decision-making in the Soviet Union has experienced a partial diffusion which is still continuing. First there was the transition from one-man decisions to collective rule and the tolerance of opposing opinions within the oligarchy. The Central Committee now exercises at least a consultative voice in decision-making which may eventually evolve into a form of participation. Informal recognition has been ac-corded special interest groups by coopting their representatives into the highest councils of the Party.

The partial decentralization of the decision-making process then had its ramifications outside the Soviet Union, particularly on questions

---

[72] Mikhail Suslov's speech on the 39th anniversary of the Bolshevik Revolution, *Pravda*, November 7, 1956.

involving other Communist states. First China, then Yugoslavia, and finally Poland and other countries were accorded a greater or lesser degree of participation and consultation in foreign policy matters of general interest. The Parties of these countries, like their Soviet prototype, in turn are under diverse factional and internal pressures.

Privileged groups, not only in the Soviet Union but in other Communist states as well, are loath to embark upon adventures likely to endanger the system from which they benefit, and hence they all have an identical interest in the preservation of the Communist system. But each national elite is preeminently concerned with its own security and self-perpetuation. Just as the transcendental goal of world revolution was subordinated to the security and power interests of the Soviet state during Stalin's lifetime, it is natural to assume that each national Communist elite will tend to identify its own survival with the ideological imperative of world revolution, subordinating the latter to its own interests.

Although it was possible for a single Communist state to rationalize the subjugation of the movement to its own impulse for survival and to gain a wide acceptance for this identification, it is hardly likely that the interests of nearly a dozen Communist states can be so harmonious that each can utilize the world Communist movement in its own interests. Inevitably, the interests of the various national Communist elites will come into conflict (as in the case of Tito and Stalin)—particularly when the interests of one Communist state endanger the survival of another—and the consequence may be either another schism (Poland), or armed intervention (Hungary).

If the interests of China and the Soviet Union ever diverge in a serious way, that may well be the end of the world Communist movement. This is recognized by both Peking and Moscow, but whether their intention to preserve solidarity can overcome the objective forces that drive them apart is questionable.

The rigidity of Soviet diplomacy has been replaced with a greater flexibility, but at the expense of abdicating its ineluctable advantage of instantaneous maneuverability. Multiple restraints have been introduced, although still in rudimentary form, in the Soviet decision-making process, and the diplomacy of Soviet Russia, like that of the United States, must now be attuned to diverse internal and external sensitivities. As a result, lapses into hesitation, vacillation, and compromise (as exhibited during the Hungarian crisis) will likely be more frequent now that a consensus must first be hammered out in the Presidium and then accommodated to similar consensuses reached by the ruling Communist elites of its coalition and ideological partners.

"Collective rule" and "polycentrism" cannot but introduce serious strains into a system whose superstructure was erected upon the foundations of one-man dictatorship and imposed uniformity. Although this basis imparted to Soviet diplomacy its greatest immediate advantage, it also threatened eventually to shatter the very edifice it supported.

Selected Bibliography

Armstrong, H. F., ed., *The Foreign Affairs Reader* (New York, 1947). Articles by Bukharin, Radek, and "X" (George Kennan).

———, *Tito and Goliath* (New York, 1951).

Barghoorn, F. C., *The Soviet Image of the United States* (New York, 1950).

———, *Soviet Russian Nationalism* (New York, 1956).

Barmine, A., *One Who Survived* (New York, 1946).

Beloff, Max, *The Foreign Policy of Soviet Russia, 1929-1941* (New York, 1947).

———, *Soviet Policy in the Far East, 1944-1951* (New York, 1953).

Borkenau, F., *The Communist International* (London, 1938).

———, *European Communism* (London, 1953).

Carr, E. H., *The Bolshevik Revolution, 1917-1923* (London, 1953), Vol. III.

———, *German-Soviet Relations Between the Two World Wars* (Baltimore, 1951).

Chamberlin, W. H., ed., *Blueprint for World Conquest* (Chicago, 1946).

Dallin, D. J., *Soviet Espionage* (New Haven, 1955).

Dedijer, V., *Tito* (New York, 1953).

Degras, Jane, ed., *Soviet Documents on Foreign Policy* (London, 1951-1953), 3 vols.

Dennet, R., and J. Johnson, eds., *Negotiating With the Russians* (Boston, 1951).

Deutscher, I., *Stalin* (New York, 1949).

Fainsod, M., *How Russia Is Ruled* (Cambridge, Mass., 1953).

Falsifiers of History (Moscow, 1948). Official Soviet explanation of the diplomacy of the Nazi-Soviet Pact and its aftermath.

Fischer, L., *The Soviets in World Affairs* (Princeton, 1951) 2 vols.

Fischer, R., *Stalin and German Communism* (Cambridge, 1948).

Garthoff, R., *Soviet Military Doctrine* (Glencoe, Illinois, 1954).

Gurian, Waldemar, ed., *Soviet Imperialism: Its Origins and Tactics* (Notre Dame, 1953).

Haines, C. G., ed., *The Threat of Soviet Imperialism* (Baltimore, 1954).

Hilger, G., and A. G. Meyer, *The Incompatible Allies* (New York, 1953).

Leites, Nathan, *A Study of Bolshevism* (Glencoe, Illinois, 1953).

Lenczowski, George, *Russia and the West in Iran, 1918-1948* (Ithaca, 1949).

Marx, K., and F. Engels, *The Russian Menace to Europe* (Glencoe, Illinois, 1952).

Moore, Barrington, *Soviet Politics: The Dilemma of Power* (Cambridge, Mass., 1950).

Moseley, Philip E., ed., *The Soviet Union Since World War II* (The Annals, May 1949).

————, *Russia Since Stalin* (The Annals, January 1956).

————, *et al., The Moscow-Peking Axis* (New York, 1957).

Nazi-Soviet Relations, 1937-1941 (Washington, D.C., 1948). Selected documents from the German archives.

North, Robert C., *Moscow and Chinese Communists* (Stanford, 1953).

Reshetar, J. S., Jr., *Problems of Analyzing and Predicting Soviet Behavior* (Garden City, 1955).

Roberts, H. L., *Russia and America* (New York, 1956).

Rossi, A., *The Russo-German Alliance, 1939-1941* (Boston, 1951).

Rostow, W. W., *The Dynamics of Soviet Society* (New York, 1953).

Russian Institute (Columbia University), *The Anti-Stalin Campaign and International Communism.* A selection of documents. (New York, 1956).

Smith, W. B., *My Three Years in Moscow* (New York, 1950).

The Soviet-Yugoslav Dispute (London: Royal Institute of International Affairs, 1948).

Stalin, J. V., *Problems of Leninism* (Moscow, 1947).

————, *The Great Patriotic War of the Soviet Union* (New York, 1945).

————, *Economic Problems of Socialism* (New York, 1952).

Stettinius, E. R., *Roosevelt and the Russians* (Garden City, 1949).

Taracouzio, T. A., *The Soviet Union and International Law* (New York, 1936).

————, *War and Peace in Soviet Diplomacy* (New York, 1940).

Towster, Julian, *Political Power in the U.S.S.R.* (New York, 1948).

Ulam, A. B., *Titoism and the Cominform* (Cambridge, Mass., 1952).

Wolfe, B. D., *Khrushchev and Stalin's Ghost* (New York, 1957). Khrushchev's secret report in full text, with commentary.

Zinner, P. E., ed., *National Communism and Popular Revolt in Eastern Europe* (New York, 1947). A selection of documents.

6 . . .

FOREIGN POLICY OF
MODERN JAPAN

. . . Robert A. Scalapino

NEARLY A CENTURY separates the end of the Tokugawa era from the Japan of today, but in some respects a full circle seems to have been turned. Once again, Japan is forced to emerge into a world from which she has been recently isolated. She must chart a new and uncertain course. Accompanying the problems of this emergence, there is again an upsurge of resentment against "excessive foreign pressures" and "inequities"; the achievement of a more independent foreign policy is a goal to which all Japanese political leaders pay some homage. Yet the need for a firm alliance with a world power is also felt in many quarters. Once more, the over-all psychology operating in Japanese foreign policy is strongly defensive, as it was in the early Meiji period. Like most historical parallels, this one should not be pushed too far, for there are substantial differences of time and circumstance. Still, the similarities that exist suggest the importance of viewing contemporary issues in Japanese foreign policy from an historical perspective.

I. The Background of Japanese Foreign Policy

In geopolitical terms, there are some obvious reasons for making a rough comparison between Japan and Great Britain. Both are island societies lying within the Temperate Zone and close to a great continental mass. From earliest times, cultural interaction with the continent has been vital in shaping the character of each society; each has definitely been a part of the larger cultural orbit centering upon the continent. The sea, however, has been both a lane and a barrier. It has prevented recent invasions, enabling the development of a relatively homogeneous people who despite many foreign adaptations have retained a strong quality of uniqueness. Thus the encircling sea has been important to culture as well as to livelihood and defense. It has also been central to the historic policy dilemma over isolation versus continental involvement. This has been the basic foreign policy issue of both societies throughout their existence. And in recent eras, the interaction between internal and external pressures has been such as to present essentially the same answer to this question in both Japan and Great Britain. The growth of foreign pressures and the needs flowing from modernization—the scarcity of certain domestic resources combined with the rise of unused power—these and other factors led to regional and then global commitment. There is the temptation to add that for both societies there now exists the need to adjust to a permanent decline in world power. This analysis, of course, stresses the similarities, not the differences. The latter will become apparent as we turn now to the Japanese scene.

A. The Tokugawa era

The diplomacy of modern Japan opened in the mid-nineteenth century on a decidedly reluctant and confused note. Prior to Perry's arrival in 1853, the Japanese government had pursued a rigorous policy of isolation toward the outside world for over two hundred years. It abandoned that policy only under strong pressure and with many misgivings. To understand the roots of Japanese isolation and the problems involved in giving it up, one requires some introduction to Tokugawa Japan.

Tokugawa foreign policy was an extension of domestic policy, and actually these two terms "foreign" and "domestic" are imprecise when applied to seventeenth-century Japan. Japan was not yet a nation in the modern sense. Provincial loyalties were deeply rooted. One's fief was one's country, and patriotism was almost wholly in local terms. In this period there were close to three hundred such fiefs, each under the control of a *daimyo* or great lord, assisted by his *samurai*, military class administrators. The Tokugawa family established their headquarters in Edo (modern Tokyo), and sought to tie these local units to the central administration by a variety of techniques. Periodically, central officials were dispatched to inspect fief activities. A special effort was made to watch those "outer lords" whose allegiance to the Tokugawa family had been given at a late date and whose true loyalties were uncertain. Another method was called *sankin kotai,* a system whereby each provincial lord was required to spend approximately half his time in Edo, thereby coming under the constant scrutiny of the central government. The lord when absent was also required to leave his family as hostages. The Emperor and his court in distant Kyoto were also carefully circumscribed in their rights and functions. Fraternization between this group and the provincial lords was strongly discouraged, as were intimate ties between the various fiefs.

Thus, isolation was used to some extent in "domestic" policy, as a technique of guarding against hostile combinations. The same concern motivated the far-reaching policy of isolation against the West. However skillful the measures of internal control, the Tokugawa regime could not be entirely stable in its opening years, nor free from the threat of revolt, especially in the southwest. Tokugawa "foreign" policy took its basic form from these facts. Foreign involvement in Japanese politics gradually came to seem as great a danger as domestic collusion. The West had been represented in Japan for fifty years before the Tokugawa (1601-1867) came to power; missionaries and traders had come in a steady stream, first from Portugal and Spain, then from the Netherlands and England. In the first years of the Tokugawa era, however, abuses were regularly reported to the government. Christian converts among the provincial nobility sought Western arms or alliances to fortify their position against the central regime. Western trade also became a means of augmenting local power, especially in the Kyushu area.

Both Western religion and commerce could be made into instruments of internal subversion at a time when power relations had not yet acquired tradition or permanence in Japan. Such fears gained additional strength in official circles with rumors of Western assaults elsewhere in Asia. By 1616, therefore, the Tokugawa government decided that Christianity must go, and the next several decades produced a series of exclusion edicts, persecutions, and waves of ruthless extermination. The anti-Christian actions were eventually followed by more sweeping injunctions against intercourse with the West. After 1641, a policy of almost total exclusion of the West was in effect. As is well known, only the Dutch were allowed a very limited trade at Nagasaki. This, together with some limited relations with China and Korea, constituted Japanese foreign relations until the middle of the nineteenth century. Even the size of Japanese ships was severely restricted so that they might not be used for foreign contacts. The unfortunate fishermen who might drift by accident to foreign shores met with many obstacles in attempting to return home.

To draw up a balance sheet upon the isolation policy is not easy. It can be argued that had Western intercourse been allowed to continue, Japan might well have plunged into chaos and warfare, subsequently suffering the colonial fate of Southeast Asia. On the other hand, isolation clearly exacted its price. This is true not merely in terms of institutions and material developments, but also in the realm of emotions and attitudes. Isolation always breeds some of the symbols of the garrison state—exclusivism, ethnocentrism, and xenophobia, accompanied by mounting fears of the unknown, outside world. Most of these factors have been present in the Japanese scene, helping to shape the foreign policies and attitudes of that nation.

But in its time, Tokugawa isolation seemed to present only one major problem to Japan: how to maintain it? The expansion of the West toward Asia was building up an intense pressure upon Japan by the beginning of the nineteenth century. From the north, the Russians were moving forward on a broad front; Saghalien, the Kuriles, and even Hokkaido seemed threatened. Overtures for trade and coaling stations were made and rejected. At the same time, English intrusions began to take place in the southwest. These events were climaxed by news of the Opium War and repeated warnings from the Dutch. A debate began to shape up in Japan over fundamental policies. It was abetted by dangerous trends in the domestic scene. A rising commercialism threatened the status and solvency of the military class. Thus unrest with Tokugawa policies—both foreign and domestic—greatly increased. To a large number of the military class, the problem lay in the inability of the Tokugawa government to maintain its original policy lines. Their solution called for a restoration of the old order: severe restrictions upon commercial expansion and the merchant class; a reunion of the military with their natural allies—the peasants and the soil; and a strict enforcement of isolation against the West. At all cost, the Western barbarians must be turned back. As the Tokugawa government seemed to waver and act in indecisive fashion, many turned away from it in anger and sought a new symbol for a romanticized *ancien régime* in the personage of the long-neglected Emperor.

Japanese nationalism now came forward, borne aloft by intellectuals from the agrarian-military class, and rooted in the primitive mythology of Shintoism. It was a movement with many facets: in part, dedicated to a restitution of Imperial prerogatives and their defense against Tokugawa usurpation; in part, an attack upon the long-standing intellectual subservience to China and an insistence upon the unique character and basic priorities of Japan; and finally, a fierce assault upon Western encroachment born out of an admixture of condescension and fear. All of these factors were implied in the chief slogan of the era, *sonno-joi*, "Revere the Emperor, Oust the Barbarians."

In the precise form just described, this movement did not enjoy complete success, but within its evolution and adaptations was carried the destiny of modern Japan. That evolution followed in some measure the broad stages characteristic of the whole panorama of Asian-Western relations during this period, whether stated in policy or intellectual terms: an initial stage dominated by the total rejection of Westernism as barbarian by definition, inferior to and completely incompatible with the Asian way of life; a second stage, in which Western science and technology—distilled into the unforgettable spectacle of Western power—were accorded a begrudging but nonetheless deeply felt respect, from which followed, after much soul-searching and confusion, a conscious majority decision to attain these sources of power while holding firmly to traditional values; and thence inevitably there developed that stage in which such a rigid and unrealistic dichotomy as that between technology and values had to be abandoned in favor of a more broadly based and integral synthesis, the exact ingredients and balance of which have depended upon the background and convictions of each individual or group. It is within this general trend—its various exceptions, time-lags, and all-important local distinctions not to be ignored—that the major elements of foreign policy in modern Asia have taken shape. Japan has been no exception.

Even before the arrival of Perry, a small group of Japanese intellectuals had begun to question the policy of rigid isolation. Out of "Dutch learning" had come exciting ideas; and there grew in some minds the desirability of leading the commercial revolution rather than fighting it, and of using foreign trade to develop power. How else could the intriguing slogan, "A rich country; a powerful soldiery" be effected; how else could Japan defend herself against Western imperialism? But this group was a small minority in the early period. Even the Tokugawa government supported the opening of the country only as a temporary expedient until force could be garnered to throw out the West. In accepting Perry's demands, it decided to accede rather than risk war, but it gave as little ground as possible. With the first step taken, however, it was imposible to retreat. Our first envoy, Townsend Harris, secured major liberalization of the Perry treaty in 1858, and similar rights were soon granted to other Western powers. From this date Japan was truly opened up to Western commerce, and shortly the Tokugawa regime was even to seek assistance in developing arsenals and shipyards. "Support the government" and "Open the country" seemed to be slogans indissolubly linked.

Yet basically, Tokugawa policy remained more a produce of pressure than of purpose, and this fact worked against the effectiveness of the policy. Beset by many problems, the regime grew steadily weaker; its capacity to act vigorously in any direction diminished. It satisfied neither the West, which complained of its inability to control unruly elements, nor the provincial samurai, who regarded the central government as archappeasers. As so often happens in history, the regime in power found by tortuous means the only feasible policy for national survival—in this case, the policy of opening the country—but in the course of reaching that policy it was itself fatally weakened so that the actual execution and fulfillment of the policy had to pass to other hands.

The fifteen years between 1853 and 1868 were years of rising confusion and political uncertainty. At the outset, the system of unequal treaties in the Chinese pattern was applied to Japan so as to guarantee Western entry on suitable terms: extraterritoriality, Western-regulated tariffs, and concessions on foreign residence and travel were a standard part of the treaty of 1858 and subsequent agreements. Ironically, they were first applied by a country (the United States) and a man (Townsend Harris) least sympathetic to this system, but they were applied because there seemed to be no alternative in an era when customs and development differed so greatly between West and East, and they were accepted because Japan had no other recourse. With these concessions in effect, a steady stream of Westerners poured into the country; treaty ports bustled with activity, and even missionary work began quietly. The antiforeign elements struck back sporadically with murder, attacks on Western shipping, and assassination of "pro-Western" officials. There was a constant danger after 1860 that Japan would succumb to the cycle of incident, Western retaliation, occupation, and colonialization. Indeed, the first two stages of this cycle were prominent aspects of the Japanese scene until the Meiji Restoration of 1867.

With the Restoration, the specter of renewed isolation was permanently laid to rest. In one sense this may seem curious, because the leaders of that movement which ended Tokugawa rule were largely younger, lower-rank samurai from the southwest, many of whom had led the assaults upon the West and upon a pusillanimous foreign policy. What prevented these young firebrands from launching an antiforeign war in the style of the Boxer Rebellion, bringing upon Japan the full fury of Western imperialism? There is no single answer to this question. From events like the Western bombardment of the Shimonoseki Straits in 1864, first-hand experience with Western power had been gained, and bravado had been somewhat diluted with realism. But probably of greater significance was the fact that the young samurai administrators of this period had an active intellectual curiosity. They were dissatisfied with certain aspects of the contemporary scene and hence were receptive to the idea of change. Against such a background, Western industrialization and science could have a remarkably rapid influence. And many new channels for receiving this influence presented themselves. Western contacts were now available in a variety of forms. Moreover, there is always a vital difference between being out of power and bearing chief responsibilities. Once the Restoration had succeeded, most of the new leaders approached their problems with realism. Abandoned was the slogan "Oust the Barbarians" which had once been theirs, and instead, the main outlines set forth by the Tokugawa were followed: intercourse with the West and an emphasis upon modernization via Western techniques as the prime methods of defense and progress. Indeed, rather than merely following, the Meiji leaders greatly expanded this policy, to the chagrin of some erstwhile comrades.

B.   Meiji foreign policy

The early Meiji era was marked by continuous experimentation and often seemed to lapse into confusion, but the Meiji leaders never lost sight of certain broad objectives. On the domestic front, the most pressing need was to reverse the recent trend toward political and economic instability. The primary weapons employed were those of nationalism, land reform, and state-supported industrialization. Each of these deserves at least brief comment because of its effect upon foreign as well as domestic policies.

In many respects, the nationalist movement dominated the era, setting the tone for all policies. The *sine qua non* of rapid and successful "modernization" lay in the ability to make and execute national policies effectively throughout the country, to demand substantial sacrifices and to obtain them with a minimum of political disorder—indeed, to obtain them most frequently through "voluntarism." The Japanese nationalist movement made these things possible. The increasing centralization of political authority was a predominant feature of the entire Meiji era. Provincial barriers were steadily worn away, local autonomy was greatly reduced, and regional officials were strictly subordinated to the dictates of national policy. Thus was the modern Japanese state created, not in leisurely fashion as in the West, but in a matter of a few decades.

Doing this required the projection and elaboration of certain traditional themes via dynamic, new techniques. And the central focus was upon the Emperor. The Throne was depicted as the essence of the Japanese soul, the spiritual repository of the Japanese race; the primitive doctrines of Shintoism were now clothed in national form. Japan was the one modern nation of the twentieth century in which the theory of divine right was still fashionable. This, however, was partly because the theory had been tied to new techniques. The Meiji leaders, with Western help, discovered the mass man. Threading their way carefully through the more dangerous democratic doctrines, they came ultimately to a modernized version of the Confucian, educative state. They perceived that a people correctly tutored in national values by means of universal education can be a source of great national strength. Thus every primary school child learned the importance of filial piety both to his parents and to the Emperor; he was also taught the supernatural origins of the Japanese race and, implicitly at least, their messianic mission.

Although the aggressive potentials of Japanese nationalism were suggested in this early period, the immediate emphasis was more defensive in character. Each individual was given to understand that the Japanese people were on trial before the world. Great sacrifices were required if Japan was to withstand the perils of Western power or to avoid the taunts of Western superiority. Only as the nation collectively "proved itself" to the West could the unequal treaties be removed. Implicit in these themes was an inferiority complex toward the West not easily conquered, a fact interrelated to those aggressive components of the nationalist movement subsequently addressed to the Asian continent. But none of this should be allowed to obscure the success with which the unique themes of Japanese nationalism were fixed in the modern Japanese mind. Before the turn of the twentieth century, there were very few Japanese who would not have died gladly for the Emperor and the nation whenever called upon to do so, whereas not too many decades earlier, there had been very few who could have identified the Emperor or understood any concept of a Japanese state. Such were the dimensions of the change.

One of the first major socio-economic reforms undertaken by the new government was that of land reform. The need was imperative; the old order had already slipped into chaos. In spite of traditional Tokugawa injunctions, *de facto* private ownership existed and required legal recognition. Taxation reform was vital if the government was to obtain uniform, regular funds with which to undertake its many plans. The Japanese farmer would have to pay the bulk of the modernization costs, and methods had to be found whereby this could be done as efficiently and smoothly as possible. Moreover, it was equally important that the farmer be liberated from the soil, so that surplus agrarian elements could move freely and fill the labor demands of the growing industries. Mobility in the rural areas was an indispensable need of the industrialization process.

Thus the government inaugurated a series of changes in the old land system only a few years after the Restoration. Private land ownership was legalized, thereby giving recognition to a trend long under way. In general, Japanese land holdings were on a small scale; there were very few large owners. Nevertheless, a comparatively wealthy landed class did emerge, serving as undisputed social and political arbitrators of the rural areas, and in many cases having military-class antecedents. This group combined with elements from the small land-owning class to constitute both in numbers and in prestige one of the most formidable pressure groups in prewar Japan. In their conservatism and their particular form of nationalism the agrarian upper class helped to set the tone for Japanese policy at home and abroad. And the agrarian lower classes helped to execute this policy in a variety of ways. From the bulging ranks of petty-owner and tenant families came the recruits for both factories and the army. With primogeniture in effect, a steady stream of second and third sons swelled the urban population and army camps. In a sense, the bond between the peasant and the soldier was renewed in modern Japan, and the impact of this bond upon Japanese foreign policy was omnipresent.

With these trends under way in the agrarian sectors, there remained the central task of industrialization. Here also the problems were immense. The old merchant class could not easily make the transition to modern industry. Thus the government embarked upon a forceful program of supplementing private capitalism with state initiative and funds. It sponsored foreign technicians and model factories; it developed certain fields under state auspices, continuing the pioneering practices first established by the Tokugawa and some of the progressive Han. It sought also to remove some of the stigma formerly attached to commercial pursuits; investment in industry was proclaimed as a patriotic duty, and progress was defined in commercial-industrial terms. Many of these appeals were directed to elements of the old military class, and they produced results. A significant portion of the new Japanese captains of industry came from this group, bearing some of its traditions and patterns of thought.

After 1880, the Japanese government withdrew to some extent from direct participation in industrialization, selling many of its holdings to private parties at low cost. Throughout the entire modern period, however, the relations between industry and government were intimate, with the early dependency of the former gradually being changed to a status of interdependence between the two. For reasons of tradition, timing, and structure, however, Japanese industry never developed the same measure of self-sufficiency or economic-political liberalism as did certain selected Western counterparts. The Japanese development is a graphic illustration of the facts that a modern industrial class is not necessarily bound to one form of political expression, and that industrialism is not necessarily the product of a single set of stimuli. In these facts also there is much that bears significantly upon the foreign policies of the modern Japanese state.

The material progress of Japanese industry during the Meiji period is common knowledge. The first major strides were made in textiles; and by the 1890's Japanese textile exports to the Asian market were of growing importance. This same period witnessed the rapid expansion of communications and the beginnings of heavy industry on an enlarged scale. While Japan was still essentially an agrarian society, its new position and strength in Asia obviously reflected this industrial progress to some degree.

How did Japanese foreign policy fit into the contours of these domestic trends? As mentioned earlier, the Meiji leaders accepted the Tokugawa program of opening the country. At the same time, however, their first major objective in foreign policy became that of removing the blemish of the unequal treaties, thereby attaining "complete independence" and equity with the Western powers. This task proved more difficult than they had expected; to accomplish it took nearly three decades. The Western powers, and particularly Great Britain, saw no reason to revise the treaties until Japanese standards came close to Western norms. The Japanese discovered that treaty revision was closely connected with basic reform in such fields as law and commerce. Thus the Iwakura mission, which left for the West so hopefully in 1871 to persuade the powers to abandon the fixed tariffs and extraterritoriality, came home realizing that many internal developments had first to be undertaken.

Through the years, "modernization" progressed by means of German, French, British, and American models. Japanese economic and military power showed remarkable gains. Law and order prevailed despite occasional domestic crises. Finally, in 1894, after repeated failures, the first great objective of Japanese foreign policy was obtained: agreements with the West were concluded on basic treaty revisions, all of which went into effect by 1899. As the nineteenth century ended, Japan had become the first nation of Asia to attain nearly complete parity with the West in legal terms. She had done so in part by satisfying the West that she was prepared to abide by the general rules of Western conduct, in part by the obvious facts of her internal progress and stability, and in part by her persistence and by certain clear signs that inequity toward Japan had reached a point of diminishing returns.

In the long struggle for treaty revision, latent elements of antiforeignism occasionally came to the surface in various forms. Officials deemed obsequious to foreign powers, too pro-Western in their own personal habits, or disrespectful of Japanese tradition ran grave risks. The history of these years is filled with records of assassination plots, some successful, against more moderate leaders. This was one price to be paid for cultivating a nationalist movement so assiduously while scarcely daring to admit its excesses. But quite apart from its extremists, Japanese society as a whole tended to react in pendulumlike fashion to the West. In many respects this was most natural. Periods of intensive borrowing and adaptation at both individual and group levels would be followed by noticeable retreats, with the primary targets being those excesses and absurdities most easily discernible, but with secondary attacks ranging over as broad a front as conditions would permit. On the one hand, Japan wanted to catch up with the West, be accepted as a "progressive" and "civilized" nation, and match the West in the areas of its own talents; in addition, a very genuine fondness for things Western was entertained by many Japanese, great and small. But on the other hand, in this period of intensive nationalist indoctrination, and when the old antiforeign traditions were not yet completely dead, the periodic cry of "excessive Europeanization!" or "un-Japanese practices!" could be rendered with telling effect. Moreover, if selected aspects of Westernism appealed to almost everyone, there was no widespread desire to abandon the main stream of Japanese culture or customs. As we shall note later, these factors are not completely absent from contemporary Japan.

Not all aspects of Japanese foreign policy in this early period were were cast in egalitarian or defensive molds. Prophetically, the first internal crisis among the Meiji leaders came in 1872-73 over the Korea issue. The refusal of Korea to satisfy Japanese desires for a reopening of relations led to the heated demand for war on the part of one group. Such a campaign was defended in terms of Japanese honor, but it had the additional advantage of providing a function for unemployed samurai. To the majority, however, who had just returned from the West empty-handed, the priorities had to be given to internal reform. They did permit samurai pressure to be released in a punitive expedition against Formosa shortly thereafter. And as it had throughout history, Korea continued to bulk large in the minds and thoughts of Japanese leadership. For the moderates, true Korean independence might be acceptable; for the zealots, only Japanese hegemony; but for none, the authority of a foreign power. Korea could be viewed either as the key to Japanese security and defense, or as the first step toward a continental policy of expansion, or perhaps as a mixture of the two.

Despite the major overtones of defensiveness in Japanese policy and psychology during this period, there were grounds for the spread of expansionism. Northeast Asia was largely a vacuum of power, tended haphazardly by the sick man of Asia, China, on the one hand, and the somewhat stronger but essentially unstable and overcommitted Czarist forces on the other. The Japanese mission seemed even clearer when it could be posed against the prospects of continuous Korean turmoil and the increasing threat of Western imperialism in this entire area. The theme of "Asia for the Asians" was first applied here, and sometimes by sincere men who had a vision of liberating other Asians from backwardness and Western domination, sharing with them the fruits of the new era in Japan. Private societies like the *Genyosha* (Black Current Society) and the *Kokuryukai* (Amur River Society) emerged to exercise a great influence on Japanese foreign policy as influential pressure groups on behalf of a forceful continental policy with some such objectives in mind.

The "ideology" of expansionism was complex, and it knew no single form of expression. From one perspective, groups like the Kokuryukai represented the past, holding firm to Japanese Confucianism, exalting the primitive mythology that surrounded the Emperor-centered state, ultranationalists of a peculiarly medieval type. Yet from another point of view these same men were radicals associated with the new era. Wherever Asian nationalism took root, they were willing to give it nourishment, even when its ideological bases were greatly different from their own. To movements as widely disparate as those of Aguinaldo and Sun Yat-sen their assistance was given freely, and in this they often went beyond what the Japanese government was willing or prepared to do. Moreover, there was an element of radicalism in their approach to internal affairs as well, though its source might be largely traditional. Decrying the corruption, materialism, and excessive wealth of the new order, they demanded stringent internal reforms, some of which could be considered national socialist in character. Thus were connected the themes of internal reform and external expansion as twins that were to have recurrent echoes throughout modern Japanese history.

The goals of the expansionists received their first major advance in the extraordinary decade between 1895 and 1905. Prior to that time, Japan had already added the Ryukyu islands and the Bonins to her domain, and made more secure her northern outpost, Hokkaido, by extensive colonization, but these were not spectacular ventures. By 1894, however, Japanese leadership was ready to challenge China, the weakest of her rivals, for influence on the Korean peninsula. For Japan, the war was unexpectedly short and easy, the first of a series of wars that "paid." The Western-style training and the nationalist indoctrination of her conscript military forces stood the initial test with flying colors. For China, defeat at the hands of a foe long regarded with some contempt, and treated at best as a pupil, was a profound shock. Demands for fundamental reform were now renewed, especially by younger intellectuals, and against Manchu resistance China was pushed toward accelerated change and revolution.

In Japan the implications of victory were fourfold. The beginnings of the Japanese Empire were laid, and the first tentative steps as a modern continental power were taken; China ceded Formosa, the Pescadores, and, for a time, the Liaotung Peninsula until the intervention of Russia, France, and Germany forced its return. And China was eliminated as a serious competitor in the Korean contest. Second, the war served as a further stimulus to industrial growth and general economic development. In an atmosphere of patriotic fervor, industrial investment and expansion were undertaken, with an emphasis upon heavy industry. The war boom brought prosperity; and afterwards, Japan received both indemnities and new China markets. Third, Japan enjoyed a sharp rise in her world prestige; most of the West looked on approvingly as their most apt pupil demonstrated her progress and valor, and it was in the aftermath of this victory that Japan began to be received in Western circles with some semblance of equality. Finally, these factors naturally accrued to the credit of the nationalist movement and to the prestige of the military class. The professional soldier, his samurai traditions now supplemented by Western science and by a new sense of mission not present in the Tokugawa era, promised to play a vital role in determining the future of his society.

In the aftermath of the Sino-Japanese War a crucial decision had to be made. Japan was dedicated to increasing her ties with other Asian societies and providing leadership for them when possible. But to obtain these objectives and to have any basic security for herself, she needed a major alliance with a non-Asian power. This was still the world of the nineteenth century, when Europe collectively exercised a global influence, and when the unfolding of European power politics had a direct and immediate effect upon the non-European world. With the United States, Japan needed only to achieve some general agreement that would serve to neutralize potential conflict; indeed, she could expect no more, since American commitments toward the Pacific were still very limited even after the annexation of the Philippines. The major powers in Asia were Great Britain and Russia, and between these two, the choice had to be made.

Initially, top political circles in Japan were divided. Men like Ito and Inoue hoped for an agreement with Russia that would establish long-term peace in northeast Asia on the basis of satisfying mutual interests. Had such an agreement been reached, Japanese expansion might have been directed toward the south at a much earlier point. An alliance with Great Britain, on the other hand, was recognized as a step toward stabilization in the south and fluidity in the northeast. Not merely in this respect, however, but in every respect, Japanese foreign policy was affected for nearly two decades by the Anglo-Japanese Alliance of 1902. This pact was widely heralded as insuring the peace of Asia. Within certain limits, perhaps it did contribute to that end. England, now finished with isolation, needed global alliances to protect her global interests. In the Western hemisphere she cultivated the United States; in Asia she directed her attentions to Japan. Once established, the alliance not only supported the *status quo* in south and southeast Asia; it also provided within the limitations of British policy some protection for China. In exchange, Japanese "special interests" in northeast Asia were given recognition by the leading power of the world. Under such conditions Japan could scarcely afford not to advance those interests.

Thus the first fruit of the Anglo-Japanese Alliance was not peace but war. The question of Japanese or Russian hegemony over northeast Asia, having its antecedents back as far as the seventeenth century, was now given over to military decision. As is well known, Japanese victory against a weary and distracted foe was swift. From the Portsmouth Treaty Japan emerged in control of much of northeast Asia as the first Asian world power. The fruits of defeat and victory were similar to those of the Sino-Japanese War: to the defeated—soul-searching, unrest, and revolution; to the victor—a new gain of territory and fame. Clear title was obtained to the Kuriles, and southern Saghalien was added to the Empire; control over Korea could no longer be challenged, although outright annexation did not come until 1910; the Manchurian-Mongolian area also fell within the shadow of expanding Japanese power, a situation placing new pressure upon China. Again, Japanese industry had enjoyed great expansion as a part of the war effort, with some support from British and American loans. And once more Japanese nationalism had risen to the test. Only a handful of intellectual pacifists and radicals denounced the war; the great majority of the people had been deeply loyal to the cause of a greater Japan.

Some costs for the victory could be tabulated. One lay on the surface. Nationalist propaganda had been carried so far during the war that many patriots assumed that the peace would be dictated in Moscow, not realizing that a long war of attrition might be dangerous for a smaller country. Consequently, ugly riots broke out over the Portsmouth settlement and the government had serious difficulty in restoring order. There were also deeper costs to be tallied. At home, militarism had grown stronger; the non-conformist had little protection, either in law or by the customs of his society. Abroad, Japan was moving into a new orbit of power and influence, but as a result, she was now the object of new suspicions and fears, some of them coming from such traditional supporters as the United States and Great Britain. Already it seemed likely that the critical test might be China.

In partial recompense, immediately ahead lay an era of unprecedented influence for Japan throughout Asia. It was an influence, moreover, derived from much more than mere military prowess. There is no doubt that most of the Asian world experienced a thrill at the Japanese victory over Russia, because it gave hope that the West could be beaten at its own game. But in the broader sense, Japan had become the symbol of the new Asia, a society that had successfully made the transition toward modernization by a process of synthesizing new ideas with its indigenous culture. In the Japanese context Western science and progress had come alive, and from this experience the rest of Asia had much to learn. The success of Japanese nationalism was also a tremendous stimulus, even though its precise ideological forms might not be acceptable elsewhere. Thus as this era unfolded Japan embarked upon an extensive career as model, tutor, and leader to eager Asians everywhere. Thousands of students flocked to Tokyo and other Japanese centers of learning and industry. The majority came from China, but every section of Asia was represented in some degree. Likewise, Asian nationalist movements found in Japan a haven and source of support. Their leaders in exile wrote polemics, collected funds, and sometimes obtained official encouragement. Tokyo became a revolutionary center for the Far East. Japan was riding the crest-tide of the developing "Asia for the Asians" movement.

Already, however, the central problem of Japanese foreign policy was becoming that of distinguishing the thin line between acceptable leadership in Asia and unwelcome domination. This problem could be put in various forms. Would Japanese national interests in the long run be made compatible with the Asian march toward independence? Would Japanese technological, economic, and political assistance to Asia rest upon mutual benefit and truly cooperative bases, or were the methods and intentions such as to be readily labelled the under-pinnings of Japanese imperialism? Did the Japanese have, or would they acquire a fitting psychology for world leadership, or would their actions and attitudes be marked by ethnocentrism, insecurity, and bru-tality, thereby producing the hatred of those whom they wished to persuade? From these, the universal questions of twentieth-century relations between advanced and lagging societies, Japanese foreign policy was by no means immune. The events of the first World War accentuated the dilemma.

C. The rise of Japan as a world power

The first World War was the third conflict within a generation to pay handsome and immediate dividends to the cause of Japanese prestige. It is not difficult to understand why later glorification of war by Japanese militarists produced such weak rebuttals from the society as a whole. Against the true desires of her ally, Japan entered the war "to fulfill her obligations under the Anglo-Japanese Alliance." She proceeded to capture without difficulty the German holdings on the Chinese Shantung Peninsula and in certain other parts of the Pacific. With this mission accomplished, she directed her energies to supply-ing the Asian markets cut off from their normal European contacts, and to providing her Western allies with the materials of war. These tasks required enormous industrial expansion. Indeed, it was at the close of this period that industrial productivity overtook agrarian pro-ductivity in yen value, and Japan could thereby claim to have moved into the ranks of industrial societies.

These trends and complemental factors elsewhere stimulated the drive for a more intensive China policy. The Manchu dynasty had fallen in the Revolution of 1911, but in its major objectives that revo-lution had failed. The Chinese scene was now marked by deep polit-ical cleavages, with rival factions striving desperately for both internal and external support. A vast section of Asia was shaking convulsively, and Japan was not likely to be unconcerned. A solution could no longer be imposed by Europe, which was engaged in a bloody "civil war." The United States would surely go no further than moral suasion in its own casual, sporadic approach to Asian problems. The Japanese case could be stated broadly as follows: A stable, friendly China is essential to Japanese interests at home and in northeast Asia; in the long run, the degree of Sino-Japanese cooperation and solidarity will determine the peace of Asia and the extent of its independence from Western control. For the moment, Japan should render financial and and technical assistance on the one hand, and provide military and political support on the other in such a manner as would enable stability to be attained under leaders friendly to these general premises.

This general policy was naturally subject to varying interpretations within the spectrum of Japanese political leadership. Was it to be read with an accent upon the more cooperative, altruistic aspects? If so, it would receive very considerable support from within China, and from almost every faction, although admittedly the element of opportunism would be strong. Even the "left-wing" nationalist movement of Sun Yat-sen had long sought intimate ties with Japan, and Sun himself during this period frequently made concrete overtures of amazing liberality to the Japanese. It is fascinating to conjecture what might have happened had Japan supported Sun instead of seeking to sustain various warlords and generally outmoded forces.

In any case, however, it was quite possible to read the general policy outlined above with less liberal overtones, and this is, of course, an understatement. Even Japanese "liberals" like Shigenobu Okuma and Takaakira Kato seemed to find it extremely difficult to relate their liberalism to the realm of Japanese foreign relations. Could the Japanese militarists be expected to do better? It was not merely that Japanese society was now deeply imbued with irrational nationalist themes and intoxicated with recent military successes. It was also that the accepted pattern of Japanese domestic relations continued to be based upon a high degree of hierarchy, paternalism, and stern discipline. The pattern of Japanese foreign relations was not likely to diverge greatly, for in the final analysis, such relations are carried out by men—men who cannot completely divorce themselves from the values and the way of life bred into them by their own society.

Some of these problems and strands of thought are illustrated by the celebrated "Twenty-one Demands" submitted by Japan to Yuan

Shih-kai in 1915.[1] What seemed to most Japanese leaders an entirely reasonable basis for future Sino-Japanese relations was regarded by almost everyone else (including most Chinese) as a flagrant example of imperialism. Some of these demands were so sweeping that if accepted, they would have placed almost every important Chinese political and military official under the guidance of a Japanese adviser. It was the additional misfortune of Japanese policy that these demands could be made to interact with the increasing unpopularity of the Yuan regime in such a manner as to render the Japanese position highly vulnerable. Having pledged herself to a more active China policy, Japan could not avoid extensive involvement in internal Chinese politics. To lend strength to one faction made her foe of another; target or rallying point, she had to make resolute efforts to understand the Chinese political whirlpool. With her prestige committed, there was a heavy premium upon selecting a winning leader and movement, or having chosen, to make them such.

Japan was prepared to experiment with a variety of techniques— technical assistance, financial aid such as the Nishihara loans, private and public gifts and advice. Yet she could not avoid appearing in the undesirable role of chief antagonist of the Chinese nationalist movement, the one movement with dynamic potentialities in the Chinese scene. Thus this era was climaxed by the historic May Fourth Movement, now widely heralded by the Chinese Communists as their point of origin, a fervent demonstration against Versailles and Japanese retention of Shantung started by thousands of Peking students, with repercussions throughout China. Instead of building friendship and influence, Japanese policy threatened to produce a hatred that would spill over in the form of attacks upon sympathetic Chinese elements, anti-Japanese riots, boycotts, and "incidents" real as well as contrived.

At the close of the first World War, however, most of these problems existed only in embryonic form, and certain trends both within Japan and abroad seemed favorable to their resolution, although the situation was complex. There could be no question that Japan was now an acknowledged world power. She was the one major nation besides the United States to emerge from the war in a stronger position. Her preeminence in East Asia could not be doubted despite the uncertain new force of Bolshevism. What were the ingredients of this power as the third decade of the twentieth century began?

One source clearly derived from the evolving economic capacities

---

[1] The "Twenty-One Demands" were a series of concessions extending over new economic, military, and political matters that the Japanese government attempted to force upon China in 1915.

of Japanese society. Perhaps the full secret of the Japanese industrial revolution still escapes us. However, in its essence, it seems to have involved the capacity of Japanese society to utilize effectively selected elements of Western technique and experience, adapting these to its own cultural and timing proclivities without duplicating either the historical context of Western development or the precise set of Western drives, impulses, and incentives. Toward this process were contributed both the conscious purposes of state and the remarkable talents of a people who could display creativeness through integration and discipline. By 1920, Japan was already becoming the workshop of Asia. Her large factories, equipped in many cases with the most modern machinery, contributed such basic products as textiles in great volume; at the same time, an infinite variety of cheap manufactured items flowed out of the thousands of small and medium plants that formed the base of the pyramidal Japanese industrial structure. Sharing with management the credit for such productivity was the new Japanese labor force, abundant in numbers, cheap in cost, malleable within limits to its new task, moving out of the paddy fields into the factories and acquiring sufficient know-how to give Japan an industrial character of which their fathers could not have dreamed.

But if manpower was a strength, it was also a problem—and one that now began to have an overt influence upon policy. Shortly after the first World War the Japanese population reached sixty million, more than double the figure at the beginning of the Meiji era. In many respects the facilities existing within Japan to accommodate this great mass already seemed greatly strained, yet no levelling-off was in sight. Increasing talk of *lebensraum* was inevitable. And if the population explosion had produced an abundance of cheap labor, by the same token, it had placed certain limits upon the consumption capacities of the domestic market, throwing increased emphasis upon foreign trade.

Other factors underlined Japanese dependence upon foreign lands. The four main islands of Japan were not richly blessed with those natural resources vital to the industrial development of this period. Coal was present in sufficient quantities except for high-grade coking coal, but iron ore was very limited, petroleum negligible, and most essential metals were either absent or available only in modest quantity. Moreover, because of her limited land space and her location, Japan had to import many of the agricultural resources to supply her industries; raw cotton and rubber were two prominent examples. The Japanese empire of this period was helpful; from Formosa, Saghalien, and particularly from Korea came important raw materials and foodstuffs. However, the larger needs lay outside these areas, and the

Manchuria-Mongolian region could be depicted in impressive economic terms.

If we revert to our discussion of the ingredients of Japanese power,
those in the military and political realm certainly cannot be over-
looked. The Japanese navy had become the third largest in the world,
and her army in size, equipment, and training dwarfed other forces
readily available in this part of the world. There was no foreign force
that seemed prepared to challenge successfully a Japanese force that
was fully committed in its own territories or in any part of East Asia.
The size and equipment of the Japanese military was a testament to
the lavish yearly budgetary contributions of the people; the morale
of that force was a tribute to intensive indoctrination, sustained by
the realities of great political power and prestige within the society.

Politics in its broader reaches also fitted into the power quotient.
For a society without totalitarian restraints (albeit one strongly pa-
ternal-authoritarian in character), Japan presented a picture of remarkable stability up to this point. Beside a handful of intellectual
radicals there were few who would dare (or think) to question
kokutai, "the national polity," or more vaguely, the Japanese Way of
Life. Thus state decisions, especially in the realm of foreign policy,
could be taken on the assumption that they would be accepted with
a maximum of conformity. The oracles of national interest could speak
without fear of discordant responses, at least so long as they spoke
within a consistently nationalist framework. What leadership group
has not found some advantage in this?

Yet as the postwar era began, there were indications that Japanese
politics might be drastically affected by the democratic tides. The
influence of Western liberalism, crowned by the global idealism of
Woodrow Wilson, was strongly felt throughout Japanese society, especially among urban and intellectual elements. Party government had
assumed new importance, the office of Premier was held for the first
time by a commoner, and the movement for universal suffrage was
receiving widespread support. Japan's "liberal era" was opening, bringing with it some serious efforts to establish parliamentary and civilian
supremacy in Japanese politics. Temporarily at least, the long-en-
trenched bureaucrats and even the military had to move to the
defensive. For the latter, the Siberian Expedition was the first clearly
unrewarding venture abroad. And however strong the attempt to
shift blame to political timidity and lack of resolution at home, the
army could not prevent some questions from arising in the public
mind.

Hence, moderation in foreign policy during this period was possible.

At the Washington Conference, Japan accepted the famous 5–5–3 naval ratio with the United States and Great Britain, despite the bitter protests of her naval authorities. She agreed to the return of the Shantung concessions. Withdrawal from Siberia was slowly and cautiously undertaken. One cabinet even had the audacity to retrench sharply the military budget, and there were some discussions (although no action) on a permanent reduction in the institutional power of the military in Japanese government. During this era no figure symbolized moderation in foreign policy more than Kijuro Shidehara, Foreign Minister under the Minseito Cabinets. Shidehara was a conservative, a nationalist, and a loyal servant of the Emperor. He believed that Japan had "special interests" in northeast Asia and a special responsibility toward China. But he wanted to avoid a "get-tough" policy which would only provoke boycotts, anti-Japanese hostility, and possibly war. Rather he hoped Japanese influence could be exerted through trade, financial agreements, and political negotiation.

D. Militarism and defeat

The "liberal era" was short-lived. With its collapse went much of the hope for moderation either at home or abroad. This is not the place to spell out the story of democratic failure in prewar Japan, but its more immediate causes are familiar: economic crisis and depression; political confusion and corruption; and the consequent rise of opponents from left and right. Repercussions were felt almost immediately in terms of Japanese foreign policy. In 1928, under the Tanaka Cabinet, there was a sharp turn toward a more militant nationalism in both the economic and political fields. State support to home industry was combined with a more "positive" program of support for Japanese interests abroad, especially in China. Overtures from Chiang Kai-shek—who had just broken with the Communists—were rejected, partly because of fear that a successful northern expedition would jeopardize the future Japanese position in Manchuria and north China. Ironically, while the Tanaka China policy was provoking sharp Chinese reaction because of its "strengths," it was under simultaneous attack by Japanese military extremists because of its "weaknesses." When some of these elements working through the Kwantung Army in Manchuria engineered the murder of Chang Tso-lin in June, 1928, young radicals hoped to force a decisive Japanese move in this area. The Japanese government was posed with the first of a series of direct military challenges to civilian control, challenges which went unmet.

Japanese foreign policy in the fifteen years between 1930 and 1945 represented the natural culmination of these new trends. To be sure, not all the old themes were reversed, particularly those that could be read with different inflections. Stress continued to be placed upon Sino-Japanese cooperation, and on the need for a stable, friendly China, purged of Communist and anti-Japanese elements. But actions continually interfered with words. As the Japanese militarists gained control of the strategic heights of policy, especially in the field, any cooperation had to be strained through the tightening net of aggression, fanatical "patriotism," and individual—sometimes mass—acts of brutality. Through these field actions, and as a result of a contrived "incident," war came to Manchuria in September, 1931. Weaker Chinese forces were quickly defeated, but Manchukuo remained to the great body of the Chinese an unacceptable symbol of Japanese aggression.

With the Manchurian region at last under complete Japanese control, the militarists could not avoid spreading outward toward Mongolia and north China. Thus the "Second China Incident" erupted in 1937 and led eventually to total war and defeat. Throughout this entire era, Japan could always find some Chinese allies, whether as a result of the acrid internal rivalries for power in China, sheer opportunism, or some genuine hopes that this route might lead to a new and better Asia, freed from Western control. Indeed, the allies garnered from all of these sources were not inconsiderable either in numbers or in influence. In a man like Wang Ch'ing-wei Japan finally found an able if embittered leader. But as against these facts, Japanese policy achieved what had always been feared most: a union of the dominant wing of the Kuomintang with the Communists and many independents into a nationalist popular front that was bitterly anti-Japanese. And having as one of its supreme goals the salvation of Asia from Communism, ironically, Japanese policy in the end contributed more than any other single factor to Communist success.

To concentrate solely upon China policy, however, would be to examine only the weakest link of a general Asian policy which for all its militant aggressive qualities had elements of real power and appeal. Building from the old "Asia for the Asians" theme, Japanese policy in the 1930's moved toward the concept of a Greater East Asia Co-Prosperity Sphere. The economic background for this policy lay in the rapid strides made by Japanese trade throughout Asia. By means of general deflation, changes in currency valuation, industrial rationalization, and extensive state support, Japanese trade came to enjoy highly favorable competitive conditions in East Asia by the mid-'thirties. Western Europe complained vigorously about the practice of "social dumping" onto the colonial markets. Japan retorted with charges of economic discrimination and attempted monopoly. The fact remained, however, that Japanese penetration of the Asian market during this period was substantial. The basis was thus provided for later proposals of greater economic integration under an Asian regionalism led by Japan and divorced from Western control.

The center of the Japanese appeal to greater Asia, however, remained in the sphere of political nationalism. As Japan drifted toward the Fascist bloc, Western imperialism in Asia could be attacked with less inhibitions than in the past. These attacks were particularly effective in areas where nationalism was still treated as subversive by Western governors, and where Japanese policies could not yet be tested. Once again, an attempt was made to develop an expanded program of cultural relations and technical assistance. Students flocked to Japan from all parts of Asia; cultural missions were exchanged on an increasing scale; Japanese technicians went forth; and as the Pacific War approached, the Japanese government provided underground assistance to various Asian nationalist movements in the form of funds, political advice, and even the training and equipping of military forces.

Most of the present independent governments of south and southeast Asia owe an enormous debt to Japanese propaganda, military successes, and political concessions—even when the latter were self-serving, empty, or last-minute gestures. There can be no doubt that Japan both in victory and in defeat contributed mightily to the end of the old era and the emergence of a more independent, dynamic Asia. Yet her record was tarnished, and today she must combat a legacy of suspicion and even hatred in many of these countries. In part this can be attributed to such factors as the misconduct of her troops, but writ large, it is the product of the great cultural barriers that separated her from the regions she occupied and of her inability—through lack of experience, insecurity, and because of her own traditions—to develop the type of flexibility and broad tolerance necessary in leadership. In considerable degree, Japanese hopes for cooperation and friendship were strangled by the very force of nationalism that pushed them forward.

As a corollary to her new Asian policy Japan naturally developed a new policy with respect to the West. Nearly a decade earlier, at the time of the Washington Conference of 1921, Japan had reluctantly given up the Anglo-Japanese Alliance, her shield and support for twenty years. In its place were substituted the more general agreements among the major powers. This concept of collective agreement (not, it should be emphasized, collective security) was especially attuned to the American position. The United States wanted an end to exclusive alliances, but it was prepared to undertake only the most limited of commitments, and it still wished to rely essentially upon moral suasion for policy enforcement. The great symbol of this hope and this era was the famous Kellogg-Briand Peace Pact, outlawing war.

Thus the decline of Japanese liberalism at home was complemented by the absence of effective external checks or controls. The old system of alliances and the type of checks they imposed upon unilateral action had been declared obsolete in the Pacific, but no effective international order had replaced them. Consequently, in the name of her national interests, Japan could successfully defy the Nine Power Agreement and the League of Nations, with no single nation or group making an effective stand against her. Inevitably as she challenged "the *status-quo powers*," Japan gravitated toward Germany and Italy, the dissidents of Europe. The Anti-Comintern Pact sealed an alliance of mutual interest, though not one of great intimacy.

But the real decision that confronted Japan as the Pacific War approached had a familiar ring: was she to seek a stabilization of her northern or her southern flanks; who was to be engaged, the Soviet Union or the Western allies? The decision was not an easy one. In the late 1930's, Japan had participated in large-scale clashes with Russian forces in the Mongolian region; her historic rivalry was augmented by her hatred of Communism. In the final analysis, however, she decided to count upon a German victory on the steppes of Russia, and she turned to the south whose resources had to be unlocked and whose Western masters had to be overthrown if the Japanese vision of the future were to be attained. Possibilities for agreement with the West to avoid this fateful step were explored, as all the moderates desired, but hopes were broken on the rock of China. Too much had been invested in blood and treasure to concede to Chiang Kai-shek, and so, infinitely more was to be invested—and all in vain.

II.   The Formulation of Foreign Policy
in Prewar Japan

In the Tokyo trials of "major war criminals" that followed the Japanese surrender, the Allied prosecutors repeatedly sought the answer to one central question: "Who bears the responsibility for leading Japan toward aggression and war?" If they did not obtain a completely satisfactory answer, no blame should be assigned. Few questions involve greater difficulties. The problem has taken on universal dimensions as the modern state has grown in conscious complexity and as foreign policy has developed into the composite, uncertain product of a myriad of "technicians," often compartmentalized, skilled and jealous of these skills, but almost always frustrated by the limits of their power; an indeterminate number of free-roaming "generalists," yet not so free, being bound by the limits of the single mind, the niceties of group decision, and the pressures—subtle or direct—of subalterns; finally, the larger, vaguer "public," varying in size but never comprising the whole of its society nor the sum of its parts—alternately indifferent and excited, overwhelmed by the complexities and focusing directly upon some vital issue, ignored and watched with anxiety, molded and breaking out of molds.

Japan partook of this central problem in high degree, and with some differences of kind. Here only its broader dimensions can be sketched. In the narrow sense, Japan appeared as a society of great personal absolutism. At both the familial and the national levels the head of the house (state) was invested with absolute powers. The injunction upon inferiors was complete and unswerving obedience. There seemed no measure of egalitarianism or individualism to alleviate the rigidities of an hierarchical system which through primogeniture and an Emperor-centered mythology found its apex in a single source. But in fact, the essence of power in Japanese society has not been that of personal absolutism. The vital center of decision-making has uniformly lain in its collective or group character, and in its extensive reliance upon consensus as the primary technique. It is critical to understand that despite all superficial signs to the contrary, the basic nature of Japanese society can only be approached by a thorough appreciation of the intricate refinements of group interaction, the high importance in induced voluntarism, and the generally eclectic quality of final agreements.

In all likelihood, only if these things were true could the outward signs of rigid hierarchy and absolutism have been so well maintained into the modern era. Elaborate methods had already been developed to integrate theory and appearance with the needs of a dynamic society. Just as the system of adopted sons had long preserved the necessary flexibility in the Japanese family, so the institutions of senior councilor, adviser, and go-between had each, in its own way, facilitated the making of group decisions. That process, giving extraordinary attention to form and status, was often wearisome and prolonged, but every care had to be taken to make concessions and consensus possible with minimal violence to the position and prestige of those involved. Necessarily, "equals" were wary of confronting each other in person until the formula for consensus seemed assured; and "inferiors" developed to a fine art all forms of subtle pressures and persuasive devices, with successful "superiors" paying silent homage to these in the course of final action.

Not all of these conditions sound totally strange to Western ears, although the aggregate process might seem foreign or extreme. In any case, how were such basic factors in Japanese social relations translated into politics and the making of foreign policy? In theory, the Meiji Constitution of 1889 paid its highest tributes to Imperial absolutism, but for successful practice it demanded a unity or consensus of its disparate working parts. The weakest of these, the two-house Diet, with its lower house elective, had at least the power to withhold its consent from basic policies. The administrative bureaucracy, culminating in such executive offices as the Prime Ministership, Cabinet, and Privy Council, had a vast range of powers and had legal responsibility only to the Emperor, but could not be effective alone. The military also drew their power from the Emperor, and had direct access to him; in practice, moreover, this branch acquired a potent weapon in that Ministers of War and Navy had to come from its ranks, which served to limit sharply the independent power of the Japanese Cabinet. The military, however, could operate effectively only in conjunction with the other major branches.

There was never any serious thought of having these forces coordinated by the Emperor personally, despite the awesome nature of his stipulated powers. Instead, that task was handled for some thirty years by a small oligarchy of Restoration leaders who acted in the name of the Emperor as his "chief advisers." Ultimately, this group came to be known as the *Genro* or Senior Councillors, an institution without a vestige of legal recognition or responsibility, but central to the process of Japanese politics. Every basic policy decision was placed before the Genro, and their approval was a prerequisite to action. Even the daily affairs of state frequently engaged their attention. With protégés in every branch of government and with their own vast accumulation of experience, these men were at once the source of integration, the court of final appeal, and the summit of power. To be sure, agreement among them was not always easy; there were deep personal and policy cleavages in this as in other Japanese groups. Timed withdrawals and temporary concessions, however, enabled the consensus process to operate with a minimum of crises. Until the close of the first World War, with rare exceptions, the fountainhead of Japanese foreign policy existed within this group.

With the postwar era, however, basic changes in government began to emerge, paralleling those in society. The Genro became old men, and their ranks were not refurbished. No group came forth to undertake the integrative role. Instead, Japanese politics was marked by an increasing struggle for supremacy and control among the parties, the bureaucracy, and the military. It is interesting to note that at the outset of this era an attempt was made to establish a liaison council under the aegis of the Prime Minister for the development of a "unified" foreign policy. It was intended to include major party, official, and military representation, but it was never accepted by the major opposition party and ultimately faded away.

Without a supreme coordinator such as the Genro, Japanese constitutionalism, in both its written and unwritten aspects, revealed serious flaws. In the hectic party era, foreign policy decisions taken in Cabinet or government party circles were not only subject to legitimate attacks in the Diet, but also to extensive sabotage by the ranks of the subordinate bureaucracy and to angry challenges by the military groups. The parties never attained more than a quasi-supremacy, and as they faded, the military moved from verbal challenge to open defiance. Japanese society in the period after 1928 represented a classic example of a government divided against itself. Important segments of the military operated both in the field and at home in such a manner as to scorn the government. They received substantial support from within the bureaucracy, and from certain party figures as well. Every branch of government was riddled with dissension. Within the Ministry of Foreign Affairs various cliques maneuvered for position— the militarist clique, the Anglo-American clique, and numerous others. For a time, consensus was impossible, and conditions close to anarchy prevailed.

Gradually, however, greater stability was achieved. Making full use of traditional procedures, top court officials surrounding the Emperor involved themselves in unending conferences with representatives of all major groups; innumerable go-betweens explored the possible bases of compromise; certain voluntary withdrawals, strategic retreats, and silent acquiescences were effected. Slowly a new basis for interaction developed, one which gave due recognition to military superiority but still was broad enough to include essential elements of the civil bureaucracy, court officials, and important pressure groups. Once again the basic decisions were reached through the consensus process, but with somewhat greater cognizance than usual for the realities of power. In this period a new group of senior councilors, the *Jushin*, was organized. Although lacking the influence of the Genro, it was fashioned after its model, indicating the continuing search for an integrative center. That search was destined never to be completely successful. Another experiment was conducted in a liaison council, the purpose being to pool military and civilian policy with particular reference to the foreign scene. *Ultimately, the Imperial Conference, with the Emperor himself presiding over a small group of top military and administrative officials, became the final decision-making body.* Indeed, it was this group that determined the Japanese surrender, with the Emperor personally settling this great issue. Perhaps this was the only basis left for the organic unity envisaged by the Meiji Constitution.

The foregoing trends are not completely meaningful without some brief reference to other important socio-economic groups. First, however, it should be noted that the type of consensus being developed during the militarist era was abetted by an increasing control over all communications media. As one of the most literate societies in the world, Japan had national newspapers and magazines with massive circulation. After the early thirties, prominent dissent from ultranationalism became increasingly dangerous, and after the "Second China Incident" all public organs were echoing the official line.

Meanwhile, a process of accommodation had been taking place between conservative militarists and the industrial-commercial world of Japan. In the initial stages of the military revolt against liberalism and a "weak-kneed" foreign policy, the strong notes of a radical, anti-capitalist theme were heard; the historic cry of "internal reform, external expansion" once again sounded forth. However, after the February 26th Incident of 1936, when army units in Tokyo under radical command rebelled, this type of revolutionary activity was suppressed. Although some "liberal" business elements were regarded with suspicion and certain onerous controls were sharply protested by entrepreneurs, still the necessary compromises were made, and Japanese industry at all levels rose to the war effort.

Japanese labor reacted in the same way. Its radical and liberal elements had long since been silenced, and the great masses worked with patriotic fervor. It was from the rural areas, however, that the bedrock of Japanese conservatism derived, as we noted earlier. The peasant-soldier alliance now held more meaning than at any time since the Restoration. As is so frequently the case, rural provincialism bred its own type of ultranationalism. The Japanese common man played a role in the formulation of foreign policy in his own way: he posed no obstacles to expansionism, his complete loyalty was assured, and no sacrifice would be too great if it contributed to the nationalist cause.

III.   Japan Under Foreign Occupation

When Japan surrendered in August, 1945, both her leaders and her people were forced to reconcile themselves to the status of a vanquished nation. By the terms of the Yalta and Potsdam agreements, the Japanese Empire was to be destroyed and Japan reduced in size to the approximate boundaries of the Restoration era. The homeland was to be occupied for an indefinite period by foreign forces. For the first time in recorded history, Japanese sovereignty was to be superseded by foreign rule. Some of the broad objectives of this rule had already been stipulated: action was to be taken to insure that Japan never again would become a world menace (or world power). Total disarmament was to be carried out, and those responsible for past aggression were to be punished; even the fate of the Emperor was unclear, although Japanese leaders sought desperately to gain assurances on this point during the surrender negotiations. Along with these essentially negative tasks, the occupation was also to encourage Japanese democratic forces and movements, so that Japan could eventually take her place in a peaceful world. Thus was inaugurated in September, 1945, a radically new era for Japan, one that might well be labelled "the era of the American Revolution."

If the contemporary issues, problems, and mechanism of Japanese foreign policy are to be discussed meaningfully, certain pertinent aspects of this period must be set forth. In the first place, the American occupation and its aftermath can easily be divided into three broad phases: (1) the early revolutionary era, when the emphasis was upon punishment and reform; (2) the era of reconstruction, when the stress was shifted to stabilization and economic recovery; and (3) the era of proffered alliance, which is continuing at present. Each of these eras, in its own way, contributed to the current nature and problems of Japanese society.

A.   The revolutionary era

The American Revolution in Japan was that of 1932, not that of 1776, although some of the spirit of the latter as it applied to basic democratic values was certainly present. The New Deal had new opportunities along the bombed-out Ginza and in the rice fields. But first, the old order had to be eradicated. Japanese military forces were totally disbanded in a remarkably short time; before the end of 1947, some six million Japanese troops and civilians had been returned from overseas, demobilized, and poured into the homeland. The military forces within Japan proper had also been completely dissolved. The Ministries of War and Navy were abolished. And in an effort to seal these actions with the stamp of permanency, the now-famous Article Nine was written into the new Japanese Constitution:

> Aspiring sincerely to an international peace based on justice and order, the Japanese people forever renounce war as a sovereign right of the nation and the threat or use of force as means of settling international disputes.
> In order to accomplish the aim of the preceding paragraph, land, sea, and air forces, as well as other war potential, will never be maintained. The right of belligerency of the state will not be recognized.

The American vision for Japan during this period became widely associated with the phrase, "The Switzerland of the Far East," although in this case pacifism was added to neutralization. It was a vision that had a powerful appeal to many Japanese who lived amidst rubble, without adequate food or warmth, and with vivid memories of lost ones, fire raids, and the final atomic holocaust. There could be no question as to whether this war had paid, and the extraordinary vulnerability of the great Japanese cities had been fully demonstrated during the war's last terrible months. For most thoughtful Japanese, the early postwar era was a period of deep reflection. Its dominant theme was one of trenchant criticism of past leaders and institutions. Once more there was a Japanese surge toward new ideas and ways; MacArthur no less than Perry symbolized the end of an old order, and a war-weary people turned hopefully to "demokurashi," without being precisely sure of its contents. These sentiments, widespread as they were, aided the revolution that was getting under way.

Among the various SCAP [2] actions, none had more long-range implications than those which affected the nature and position of Japanese pressure groups. As we have noted, for more than a decade the most powerful group in Japanese society had been the military. Suddenly it was entirely liquidated, and in the late 1950's more than a decade later it had not yet reappeared as a significant force. The process of liquidation was not merely in demobilization, but also in the purge that barred all professional military officers from future political activity, and in the war crimes trials, which saw the top military men of the nation executed or sentenced to prison. Although some of these actions were subsequently modified or rescinded, still

---

[2] SCAP is the commonly used abbreviation for the term, Supreme Commander of the Allied Powers. It is used to designate not only General MacArthur personally, but the Occupation Force collectively.

their total effect, combined with other circumstances, has thus far been sufficient to render postwar militarism in Japan impotent.

Through the purge and other measures, SCAP ate still further into prewar conservative ranks. For the old guard it seemed like the reign of terror, though without violence or brutality. Most professional politicians of the old conservative parties had to step aside because they had belonged to some ultranationalist group or had been endorsed by the Tojo government in the elections of 1942. Conservative leadership was hastily thrust into the hands of the one group that could be cleared: the so-called Anglo-American group from within the Foreign Ministry. Kijuro Shidehara, Shigeru Yoshida, and Hisashi Ashida, all from this group, became the top conservative leaders of Japan for nearly a decade. Even the commercial-industrial world felt the shock of reform. In the midst of purges, a deconcentration program to break down the *zaibatsu* or big combines, and the general toll of wartime ravage and postwar inflation, most business elements sought merely to survive, in the manner of seeking shelter during a gale.

Meanwhile, under American encouragement, the labor union movement attained a massive size; within a brief period it numbered some six million workers, whereas in the prewar period bonafide union membership had never exceeded one-half million. These postwar figures masked many divisions and weaknesses, but nonetheless there could be no doubt that Japanese organized labor was a new force with which to reckon on the economic and political scene. And in the rural areas the American Revolution was operating in the most forceful fashion. Under a far-reaching program of land reform, absentee landlordism was almost completely abolished, tenancy was reduced to less than 10 per cent of total agrarian families, and land holdings were equalized beyond the wildest imagination of prewar land-reform advocates. Basically, this program was dedicated to the creation of a huge independent yeomanry. Socio-economic repercussions in the rural areas over this upheaval, especially among younger age groups, are only now measurable in some degree.

Certain reforms cut across economic class lines and into the broadest categories of society. Legal attempts were made to abandon primogeniture and also to emancipate women. The latter were given full equality before the law, including equal rights of inheritance, divorce, and suffrage. Sweeping reforms in education were inaugurated, dedicated to the development of freer, more independent students, unshackled from the old chauvinism and submissiveness. Even that very special category of men, the subordinate government officials, were given lectures on democracy, in the hope that some of the old attitude of *kanson mimpi*, "officials honored, people despised," could be removed.

To recite these various efforts in such bald fashion may lead to the supposition that a total social revolution took place in Japan during the first years after 1945. Any such impression would be false. Conservatism both in the form of certain dominant classes and in the form of certain traditions that operated in every class was a sturdy force. Moreover, as might be surmised, not all SCAP experiments were successful, and by the end of 1947, in any case, the era emphasizing reform was drawing to a close. In its ripest forms, it had lasted only about two years, and the conservatives definitely survived.

It would be equally misleading, however, to underestimate the changes that have been wrought, whether by SCAP reforms or by the total complex of postwar circumstances. Some of these changes are only now capable of being seen as continuing processes. With respect to pressure groups, important differences in comparison with the pre-1945 period can be discerned, and these quite naturally have their influence upon the formulation of foreign and domestic policy. On the right, there is the demise of the military for more than a decade, the levelling process that was used against the landowner classes, and the disappearance of most prewar political leaders. These changes have affected the nature and potentialities of postwar Japanese conservatism, and they may affect it even more as time passes. Correspondingly, the rise of organized labor among Japanese young people of almost every class, including those from the rural areas, has given heightened significance to the political left in Japan. It is yet too early, perhaps, to say whether these various pressure groups will in the long run exercise themselves on behalf of democracy or some other system, but one thing seems apparent: the trend is toward the closer balance of competing pressure groups within Japanese society as compared to the prewar era, and partly as a result of this, the Japanese common man of whatever socio-economic category is increasingly the object of political solicitation and concern in policy-making. In discussing current foreign policy issues, this fact must be kept very much in mind.

Some of these factors acquire added significance when the changes made in Japanese political institutions during this period are noted. The Meiji Constitution was replaced by the required procedures, and in May, 1947, the new Japanese Constitution came into effect. Patterned almost wholly after Anglo-American institutions, it drastically altered the old system. Under its provisions, the Emperor was relegated to ceremonial and symbolic functions; sovereignty was bequeathed solely upon the people. A parliamentary system modelled after that of Great Britain was established, with certain modifications of a distinctly American flavor.

The new Diet, instead of being peripheral to the political process, is now its center. Both houses of the Diet are elective. The upper house, the House of Councilors, is constructed in a complicated fashion, with both nation-wide and prefectural constituencies; the lower house, the House of Representatives, has been based upon medium-sized election districts (although there is a current attempt by the conservatives to change this to a single member district system). Executive responsibility to the Diet is clearly stipulated. The Prime Minister must be approved by the Diet, and if the houses disagree, by the lower house. If there is a vote of no-confidence, the government must either dissolve the lower house and call for new elections, or resign.

A new Diet Law was enacted to accompany the Constitution of 1947. Among other things, it provided for a system of permanent committees, similar to the system operative in the United States, and differing from past Japanese practice. Thus, a Foreign Affairs Committee for each house now has a permanent staff and membership based upon the seniority and party quota systems. It holds hearings upon government legislation or on any policy matters within its general jurisdiction. In practice, however, initiative on foreign policy matters still rests strongly with the executive branch.

The new Constitution guarantees the Japanese political parties a much more important position. In their collective hands the real locus of supreme power lies. As might be expected, the history of the postwar parties has been complicated and at times hectic. Four general trends, however, are significant for purposes of a consideration of Japanese foreign policy.

First, the conservatives have continued up to this point to hold a commanding lead in political strength. They have consistently polled close to two-thirds of the votes, and they have held a majority of the seats in both houses of the Diet by a considerable margin at all times. As noted earlier, the Japanese socio-economic revolution has had its limits. Perhaps the major causes for continued conservative victories have been their prewar ties and strength at local levels, especially in the rural areas; their prominent, "name" candidates; the funds at their disposal; the relative prosperity in Japan since 1950; and the divisions within the opposition. At the same time, the importance of the postwar socialists cannot be ignored. They have made consistent if modest gains since 1949, a low ebb for them, and now hold approximately one-third of the Diet seats. If the trends among younger Japanese voters hold, they may come to power within the next decade.

Second, after much travail, a two-party system has finally been achieved in Japan. It is not clear, however, whether it can endure. The conservatives are now united as the Liberal-Democratic Party and the various major socialist factions have also come together in the Socialist Party. There remain some minor parties, such as the Communists, but they do not poll a sufficient number of votes to count. Both personal factionalism and policy differences plague the major parties internally, the former being more important to the conservatives and the latter to the socialists.

Third, the party system as a whole is still on trial with the Japanese people. It is not yet thoroughly engrained either in institutional practice or in public behavior. Popular commitments are not yet strong to individual parties or to the party concept. And at every level of government, the bureaucracy still plays a tremendously important role, with its own dominant values unsettled. Political fluidity remains the keynote to Japanese politics.

Finally, bipartisanship on policy issues, either domestic or foreign, does not exist in Japanese politics. Thus when we talk about Japanese policy or government attitudes, it must be constantly borne in mind that there is a vigorous and adamant opposition with its own channels to public opinion. The Japanese press and other media of public communication have never had such freedom, and they use it to express the whole range of political views. The Japanese left wing is not inadequately represented; and in some media, indeed, it has signal advantages over the conservatives. Meanwhile, the split over issues between the two major parties is the greater because the Socialists are currently under the control of their left wing. However, it is still possible to refer to certain broad trends or tendencies in foreign policy thinking or action that cut across partisan lines, as we shall shortly note.

From these facts it can be seen that Japanese foreign policy is conceived and executed today in an atmosphere considerably different from that of the prewar period. Perhaps most of the changes are indicative of the greater degree of democracy prevailing. Interrelated institutional and pressure-group changes have produced heightened political competition. As one result, public opinion must now be more carefully considered by political leaders in policy formation. And at the same time, less control can be exercised over the public mind by those in power, owing to the new freedom in education, the press, and public speech. This is a matter of great concern to some conservatives who fear that the loss of unity and "patriotism" will result in the weakening of Japanese foreign policy and ultimately in the destruction of the Japanese state. Underwriting the new importance of the public is the legal supremacy of their representatives, the political parties, in the current institutional structure. Japanese foreign policy is now heavily dependent upon the policy decisions and performance of the major parties, and upon which party is in power. In every election since 1949 foreign policy issues have been in the forefront, and this is likely to continue. Under these conditions there has been a tendency recently for conservative leaders to engage in personalized diplomacy both as a means of dramatizing policy before the public and as a method of scoring personal political triumph. Does this betoken the rise of greater individualism in Japanese politics? Party leaders, however, are still heavily dependent upon the "technicians" for basic details, briefing, and guidance. During the occupation, the Foreign Affairs Ministry necessarily went into an eclipse, and it has been a very difficult struggle for it to regain its previous prerogatives. Foreign policy in its composite form involves almost every major ministry, and jurisdictional issues in Japan as elsewhere are rife. In the final analysis, however, the Prime Minister and his party now have an unprecedented power in terms of past Japanese experience to set the dominant tone of foreign policy, as long as they can command success at the polls.

B.   The stabilization era

Before we turn to the current substantive issues of Japanese foreign policy, some brief consideration should be given to the second and third phases of the Occupation, which set many of these in motion. The shift to an emphasis upon stabilization and economic recovery began as early as 1947. The change was motivated by many problems. Certain earlier American premises about the postwar world now seemed unjustified: the prospects were dim for a China that would be friendly and democratic by any American definition; the honeymoon with the Soviet Union was clearly over and the cold war was beginning; the threat of Communism throughout Europe and Asia as a result of postwar chaos and economic misery was a matter of profound concern. With respect to Japan itself, the close relation between economic recovery and the prospects for democratic success could no longer be slighted or ignored. In addition, as long as the Japanese economy was in the doldrums, occupational expenses and relief under-takings constituted a heavy burden for the American taxpayer; at its peak, the cost was running close to one-half billion dollars per year.

The new emphasis brought many changes in policies and techniques. Increasingly, the supreme test to which any policy could be put was, "Does it advance productivity and economic stabilization?" Some assessment was made of the primary obstacles—war damage, inflation, the lack of raw materials, and low morale owing to miserable condi-tions for workers and uncertainties for capitalists. First, SCAP began to interest itself in problems of productive efficiency, and moved from merely keeping Japan alive to furnishing her with some industrial raw materials in lieu of the vanished products of continental Asia and the old Japanese Empire. Belatedly, the complex problem of infla-tion was squarely faced, and finally a comprehensive American answer was put forth in the form of the Dodge Nine-Point Stabilization Program. This plan called for many stringent reforms and was very unpopular in some quarters, but the inflationary tide was at last turned.

Meanwhile, other "disruptions" to production were treated. The deconcentration program was relaxed and gradually abandoned after initial attempts to reduce certain large *zaibatsu* families and cartels had been effected; reliance henceforth was to be placed upon anti-trust and monopoly laws. The United States also progressively re-ceded from its early attitude of severity on the issue of reparations. By the end of this era, the American government had indicated its acceptance of the thesis that the Japanese ability to repay war dam-ages was strictly limited, that heavy reparations would indirectly become a responsibility of the United States, and that in any case, the basic heavy industrial complex upon which Japan was so de-pendent for her future could not be used for these purposes. Finally, SCAP took a sterner attitude toward radicalism in the labor movement, amending its earlier, generous legislation on unionism so as to give the employer and especially the government a stronger position.

The net effect of these actions, when accompanied by certain broader trends at home and abroad, was to stimulate rapid economic recovery. Japanese society could build upon the heritage of an industrial revo-lution and a legacy of technical know-how. Deflation and internal readjustments were followed by the opportunities for industrial ex-pansion provided by the Korean war and the great prosperity of the free world. Controls were unduly relaxed during the war, and another retrenchment followed, but still the statistics on industrial production showed amazing gains. In many fields, especially heavy industry and chemicals, productivity exceeded pre-1945 heights. The most serious problem was that of foreign trade, which lagged in recovery. The import-export balance remained adverse to Japan, and extensive dependence upon the United States both for raw materials and general aid remained. In large measure, Japanese economic recovery was both due to and continuously dependent upon such aid, particularly American procurement demand for the Occupation, Korean war needs, and other parts of Asia.

These developments were not without internal political reverberations. In the revolutionary era, American actions had been an anathema to the conservatives; now, they were the new allies. And the liberal left, which had cheered in the early days, was filled with dismay and resentment at many actions of which it did not approve but from which it had no recourse. Japanese democracy was still under the tutelage of American military rule. The methods of permissible criticism and opposition were restrained by that fact. Nevertheless, the issue of American involvement in internal politics gradually built up as the Occupation continued, paving the way for the sharp divergencies that came out into the open in the post-independence period. For every political group, however, this second era was one of reflection and reconsideration of Western values. There was an unmistakable tendency at all levels to emphasize synthesis and adjustment rather than uncritical acceptance of foreign concepts. The pendulum had begun to swing back.

As can be noted, the beginnings of postwar Japanese foreign policy were established in this era, albeit under American direction. These beginnings followed a course that Japanese leadership itself might well have taken and labelled "in the national interest" had it been an independent agent. Indeed, on issues like reparations, the United States was widely accused of being excessively "pro-Japanese," and some apprehensions were felt upon other issues as well. The most prominent pattern being established was that of rehabilitating Japanese heavy industry and encouraging its orientation again toward the needs and markets of the "late developing" societies, particularly those of non-Communist Asia. Again the concept of Japan as the workshop of Asia was being heard, but with certain new connotations. As a concomitant to this policy, the United States also took steps to adjust Japanese political and economic relations with erstwhile enemies whenever possible; like the kindly warden who is convinced of the successful rehabilitation of his charge, the United States now pressed for Japanese reentry into the world community on terms of equality.

C.   The era of alliance

Within this trend lay the seeds of the third era, that of proffered alliance by the United States to Japan. By 1949, American authorities realized on the one hand that the Occupation was reaching a point of diminishing returns, and on the other, that continuing political and economic ties between the United States and Japan were a mutual necessity. Explorations were begun which led to the San Francisco Peace Treaty of 1951. In the process, a series of decisions were reached between Japanese and American authorities that added further important dimensions to the new Japanese foreign policy and provoked violent political debate. One critical issue pertained to the question of Japanese defense. Two broad alternatives seemed to exist. One would be to continue a reliance upon pacifism, seeking universal agreements upon the sanctity of Japanese territory and backing these with pledges of protection through the auspices of the United Nations, and possibly of the United States separately. The other would be to move away from pacifism and neutralization, acknowledging the Japanese need for, and right to military defense forces, and underwriting Japanese rearmament efforts with American power until these could reach some degree of self-sufficiency. Obviously, a choice between these two broad courses involved many factors and might be decisive in shaping most other aspects of Japanese foreign policy.

To the socialists, the dangers of rearmament, total commitment to the Western camp, and dependence upon American power outweighed the threats of external aggression, Japanese isolation, and impotence. They favored retention of the constitutional antiwar clause, a permanent commitment to pacifism and neutrality, and the solicitation of international support through the United Nations; they opposed rearmament in any form, post-independence American bases in Japan, or any bilateral security pact with the United States. The dominant conservative forces in Japan, however, together with the American government, viewed the second alternative outlined above as the only one compatible with world conditions and Japanese needs. At least as early as 1949, the creation of a Japanese defense force was being urged in some American and Japanese circles. Shortly after the outbreak of the Korean war, SCAP authorized the establishment of a "National Police Reserve" as the first step in this direction.

Meanwhile, negotiations for Japanese independence were proceeding when the cold war became hot in Korea. No attempt was made to obtain Russian approval for the treaty draft as the Japanese socialists wished. When the treaty was put in final form for acceptance at San

Francisco in September, 1951, it contained no barriers to Japanese rearmament or to other changes in SCAP reforms. Reparations and certain territorial issues were left open, providing Japan with some bargaining power. Accompanying the main treaty was a bilateral Mutual Security Treaty with the United States providing for continuance of American bases in Japan proper until adequate defenses were prepared. Official independence for Japan finally came on April 28, 1952, the day on which the Treaty of San Francisco came into effect. In the course of reaching that independence, Japanese leadership had had to make some basic decisions respecting the future foreign policy of their nation. The conservatives in power had not hesitated in committing Japan to the general position of the West, and especially to close ties with the United States. Prime Minister Yoshida had denounced "neutralism" as unwise and impossible. With some reservations, which remain to be explored, the Japanese conservatives had accepted the proffered alliance.

Events of this period produced a definite split in the socialist ranks. The right-wing socialists, who leaned plainly toward the West in an ideological sense, were willing to accept the peace treaty even though it did not constitute an over-all agreement. The left-wing socialists, who sought to adhere closely to the "neutralist" position and contained within their ranks some extremely orthodox Marxists, remained sharply opposed to the treaty. Both groups rejected the Mutual Security Treaty and its implications. However, the arguments over the peace treaty both exacerbated and reflected a wide range of differences within socialist ranks. The party split into two wings and was not reunited until 1954.

Even for the conservatives, many issues pertaining to the future Japanese course remained unsettled, although the broad contours had been drawn. The Communist bloc naturally refused to ratify the treaty, and Japan faced the prospect of negotiating with the U.S.S.R. on such vital problems as fishing rights and northern boundaries. The problem of China (or the two Chinas?) with all its complexities remained to be approached. Relations with South Korea were regrettably bad. And Japan had a long distance to go in terms of her relations with south and southeast Asia. Some of the Asian neutrals, notably India and Burma, had refused to participate in the San Francisco conference because they disapproved the drafting procedure, and thus separate negotiations with them were necessary. Others such as Indonesia and the Phillipines remained firm on the subject of reparations. With the United States itself, there were such unresolved questions as the future of the Ryukyu Islands.

IV.   Contemporary Issues in Japanese Foreign Policy

Against this background unfold the current issues and problems of Japanese foreign policy. Today there appear to be three overriding considerations that shape the general character of that policy and produce its particular flavor. The first of these is the high priority accorded the economic component of foreign policy—the extreme importance attached to such matters as trade and the opportunity for technical assistance. The second relates to the sharp rise of Japanese nationalism and its reverberations in nearly every aspect of external policy. Finally, there exists within Japanese foreign policy an ardent search for some basic purpose or function, especially one that will relate Japan in a suitable manner to the Asian world, catering to her "special interests" there, while at the same time allowing her a place on the world stage in concert with other major societies. We must study these general considerations further in the context of specific policy issues, for they are likely to be the enduring as well as the underlying forces motivating Japanese society. Indeed, if the background that we have projected is examined closely, these forces will be seen in different forms throughout the history of modern Japan.

A.   The economic basis of
Japanese foreign policy

Economic priorities for Japan stem from many somber facts. In June, 1956, the Japanese population surpassed the 90 million mark. This vast number of people now live in a country the size of California with approximately 16 per cent of the land arable. If present calculations are correct, population stability will probably be attained within the next twenty to thirty years, but the stabilized figure is not likely to be less than 110 to 120 million people. Meanwhile, for the decade after 1955, the average yearly increase of workers on the labor market will be some 900,000. Already the Japanese rural areas are greatly overpopulated; it has even been suggested that the marginal productivity of the present agrarian worker may be zero. After a period of near-stability since the early Meiji era, the rural population of Japan suddenly increased about 20 per cent after 1945. Under present productive methods, the land is overburdened with people, and relief appears possible only through further industrialization.

Japanese industry cannot avoid a heavy dependence upon foreign trade. As noted earlier, there are critical shortages of natural resources. Japan can presently provide only 20 per cent of her needed

iron ore, and lesser amounts of many other vital metals; 95 per cent
of her petroleum must be imported; raw cotton and wool come wholly
from abroad; although furnishing about 90 per cent of her rice needs
now, she must import a sizeable amount of wheat, other cereals, and
general foodstuffs. Industrial expansion increases the need for raw
materials, putting additional strains upon Japanese currency reserves.
It is possible that the continuous scientific revolution will enable a
bold breakthrough on economic problems involving present resources,
techniques, and population; no one can be certain how much to expect
from the atomic-hydrogen age in this respect. Already in the postwar
period scientific developments have made possible some modest de-
creases in raw material imports for a few products. Probably also the
Japanese domestic market can be expanded. In the period since 1950
there has been some improvement in the Japanese standard of living;
the prewar peak figure has now been surpassed. In this connection,
a certain process of equalization seems to have taken place, with
improvements occurring largely in the rural areas and among the low-
income groups. Thus the internal consumer market has enjoyed an
expansion, and current Japanese economic planning is based upon the
assumption that this trend can and should be accelerated so as to
reduce somewhat the dependency upon foreign trade.

It must be quickly added, however, that internal Japanese prosperity is a relative matter. The average Japanese family has a long
distance to go before approximating Western European standards
even at their more modest levels. Per capita incomes translated into
dollars are of limited meaning, but it might be interesting to note
that in 1954 the Japanese per capita national income was close to
U.S. $200, whereas the figure for the United States was some $1,850;
Great Britain—$850; France—$700; and Italy—$300.

When all factors have been assessed, the importance of foreign trade
becomes apparent. Yet in 1955 only 13 per cent of the Japanese national product went to export, a figure much lower than that for
Western societies with comparable economic needs. And although
heavy increases brought trade figures for that year ahead of prewar
figures in adjusted value, Japanese economists were quick to point
out that Japanese trade increases still lagged behind the rate of increase for total world trade and also behind the general rate of
Japanese economic progress. The problem of import surpluses, moreover, has remained, and recently it has grown more serious. In the
postwar period, as was noted, only the tremendous flow of American
funds has preserved the Japanese economy from bankruptcy, and
the need for aid in some forms continues.

The character of postwar Japanese trade can be rather easily summarized. First, the American quotient in total trade has substantially increased, especially in terms of Japanese imports. Thus far, Japan has been forced to buy a much larger percentage of her raw materials from the United States. Consequently, she continues to have a large trade deficit with this country despite recent relatively successful attempts to increase her exports. Second, the remainder of Japanese trade is marked by great diversity, both of product and of area. Outside of the United States, no single country at present accounts for more than 4 per cent of Japanese exports. In part, this pattern reflects the serious decline in Japanese trade with the northeast Asian area, including China-Manchuria and the former Japanese Empire. Finally, Japanese exports, while diversified, show a decided shift toward heavy industry and chemicals, and market trends suggest a growing interrelation between Japan and various "late developing" societies.

Each of these facts has a direct bearing upon Japanese foreign policy today and for the foreseeable future. Political ties with the United States are and must be underwritten with economic ones. Understandably, however, Japan hopes to reduce her recent heavy dependency upon American aid while still retaining a high level of economic interchange with this country. Thus she insists upon maximum export opportunities; "Trade not Aid" is also a slogan that Japan currently likes to use. But there are political problems in this connection. If total Japanese trade with the United States shows a deficit, certain Japanese exports have shot up in volume and frightened some American producers who assert that they cannot compete with Japanese wages and working conditions. The problem has been most acute recently with respect to textiles and chinaware. There has been some discriminatory state legislation and heightened pressure for more tariff protection. Thus far the issue has been kept within bounds by the strong desire of both governments to work out a compromise, and by Japan's acceptance of a quota system to limit further increases in textiles. It cannot be considered "solved," however, or susceptible to easy solution. The diversification of Japanese exports to the United States continues, with advantage being taken both of new American tastes for oriental objects and of the absence of Chinese products. Another aspect of Japanese policy, however, must be the increasingly active search for lower-priced alternatives to the American market for basic raw materials.

Economic relations with the United States are likely to remain the single most important factor in determining the fate of the Japanese economy. This is widely recognized by present Japanese officials, and among the conservatives at least, there is every desire to keep these ties strong. At the same time, however, there is a natural tendency in Japan to think of economic problems, and particularly trade, as susceptible only to a multipronged attack. Every possibility must be explored and even modest increases must be treated with respect. This attitude, together with certain political pressures that provide additional strength, explains the position of the Japanese conservatives on the question of trade with Communist China.

In the prewar period when Japan controlled Manchuria and used China as an area both for investment and markets, that trade was of great importance. Japan recognizes that the old trade pattern, which rested upon vastly different conditions, cannot be reestablished. There is considerable doubt in some circles whether trade with Communist China under any conditions can be very significant. So far as can be seen, Sino-Soviet relations are likely to remain close, both politically and economically. If history is a reliable guide in this respect, economic relations between Japan and China under these conditions could not be extensive. Many Japanese business interests, however, in company with other groups in the society are anxious to explore this question in concrete terms. Communist China has made recent offers to buy Japanese heavy industrial products and even to use Japanese technicians if the U.N.-sponsored embargo on strategic items to China were removed. There is a strong Japanese desire to test these promises.

The immediate answer to this question may be fashioned as much by political as by economic factors. Will Communist China seek Japanese friendship or neutralization through economic ties? If, for whatever reasons, Communist China were to desire a supplement to Soviet-bloc trade and assistance, Japan might be a more logical source of heavy machinery, chemicals, and technicians than the West. In measuring all of these possibilities, the Japanese conservatives are not seriously afraid of the political dangers of Communist trade, giving Japanese economic needs a much higher priority. Naturally, internal politics enters the picture. The socialist opposition maximizes trade possibilities and accuses the government of bowing to American pressure. The government encourages various unofficial trade missions while voicing caution about long-range prospects. Amidst all of the present uncertainty, one basic fact stands out: Japan will continue to explore methods of improving her economic relations with Communist China and exert growing pressure to remove such obstacles as the embargo. Even if the China trade does not reach prewar percentages, any improvement over the present 2 or 3 per cent will be welcomed.

This refusal to overlook any economic possibility applies to other areas as well. In the postwar period, and particularly since 1949, Japanese businessmen have canvassed possibilities in earnest on every continent. New markets have been developed in Africa, Latin America, the Middle East, and southern Asia. Indeed, it is in these areas that Japan places her greatest hope, particularly in South and Southeast Asia. She expects to find her major export in goods and services to societies enroute to modernization. Consequently, she is continuing to shift her emphasis toward heavy industrial and chemical products, recognizing that in the light industrial field, new competition and self-sufficiency are growing. The premium, however, will be upon diversity and flexibility, with the hope that her know-how will assist in developing and holding new markets.

B.   Nationalism and foreign policy

When one turns to the political realm, nothing stands out more sharply than the resurgence of Japanese nationalism. Given the years of defeat, occupation, and Americanization, this is completely understandable. Nor is it an isolated phenomenon. As the fear of global war in the world has receded, centrifugal forces have operated within both major power groupings with greater intensity. In this age of interdependence, the force of nationalism is still potent, and neither the Russians nor the major Western democracies dare forget it unless they want more trouble. Perhaps the greatest political competition within Japan today in the broad field of foreign policy is that between "neutralism" and alliance with the United States. Neutralism has a nationalist appeal in addition to its Afro-Asian orientation and its pacifist idealism. But conservative foreign policy is not bereft of a nationalist note. The new conservative program calls for "an independent foreign policy within the framework of cooperation with the West, and particularly the United States."

Today, in contrast to the prewar situation, Japanese nationalism is based upon no single ideology or line of attack. Rather, in some degree, it is a weapon both for and against all parties in the political arena. Perhaps for this very reason it can become more compatible with democracy. When the Liberal-Democrats attack the new Constitution, they do so in nationalist terms, referring to it as "the translation" and unsuitable for Japan in some of its provisions. It is the socialists who defend this document as representing the true will of the Japanese people. There are many other respects in which the Japanese nationalist mantle seems to be worn by the conservatives. Yet on foreign policy issues, the socialist attack is generally spearheaded by nationalist slogans. American bases in Japan, the Okinawan problem, and all issues revolving around the so-called "dependency upon America" are brought under this assault. The conservative reply has been to insist upon the need for an alliance with the United States, but to assert that the goal must be cooperation, not subordination. To uphold their case, as well as to give voice to their true sentiments, the conservatives have moved toward a stronger assertion of Japanese interests and needs as they view them, even when these do not coincide with American policy.

In some respects, nationalism in this period is reminiscent of the Meiji era. Once again, its dominant notes are defensive in character. Japan is an island of weakness surrounded by a sea of power. But this time the power is Asian as well as Western. The continent is no longer a vacuum; Communist China in itself is a major power, and behind it stands the Soviet Union. Under these conditions, it seems highly unlikely that Japanese nationalism will revert quickly or easily to its former notes of expansionism and a militant messianic mission. The burning issues are more likely to concern the best way in which to preserve the territorial integrity of Japan and her true independence. And these are the issues of the day. On the one hand, questions of extraterritoriality, foreign residency and bases, and equality of treatment once again have come to the forefront. On the other hand, another question has been posed: how can Japan attain real security under present conditions without an American alliance?

Within this context the problems of Japanese defense and related issues are being debated. There is no doubt that the presence of American troops and bases in Japan complicates relations between the two countries. Until these are removed or at least greatly reduced, they will constitute a political hazard to American-Japanese relations. This is not to assert that anti-Americanism is rampant. In general, personal relations between Americans and Japanese have been very good, and history will probably record the Occupation as one of the most successful of its type. But a decade is a long time, and the nationalist pendulum is swinging back. As just one indication, it is now common for the Japanese press and other public media to feature the inevitable personal incidents involving American soldiers, the farmers' protests against land use for base expansion, and a wide range of other problems some of which involve jurisdictional or sovereign rights. Over a period of time—perhaps from one dramatic episode—the public mind can be deeply affected.

What alternatives are being considered by Japanese spokesmen? As noted earlier, the question of Japanese defense seemed susceptible at one point to two broad alternatives—pacifism under international guarantee, or limited rearmament probably in concert with the United States. Despite the position of the socialists, who continue to adhere to pacifism, it seems unlikely that the clock can now be turned back. Japanese rearmament was first started in the summer of 1950. The National Police Reserve was activated in August of that year with an authorized component of 75,000 men. With the coming of Japanese independence in May, 1952, this number was increased to 110,000, and a small Maritime Safety Force was established. In August, these were brought together under the National Safety Agency. Two years later, on July 1, 1954, the name was changed to the Defense Agency, brought directly under the office of the Prime Minister, and authorized to have a small Air Self-Defense Force in addition to its other units. By the end of 1955 there were about 200,000 men in the Defense Force, and the number has been slightly augmented since that time. It does not seem likely that Japan will revert to complete pacifism unless the socialists come to power very quickly, and even then, certain doubts can be held.

On the other hand, however, long-range questions of Japanese defense remain unsettled. Up to this point, rearmament has been rather slow and reluctant. From all indications this is in tune with Japanese public opinion. Even the conservatives have hesitated in speeding up the tempo, although they are strongly championing a constitutional revision to remove any doubts about the legality of a defense force. Conservative arguments on behalf of defensive rearmament, incidentally, also make use of nationalist themes—that only in this fashion can Japan regain true sovereignty and play her proper role in world affairs. But if it is assumed that a defense program will continue, ultimately certain basic decisions regarding that program must be made. Shall it continue in the conventional mold, and if so, at what speed, with what maximal goals, and with what type of American assistance? There is one alternative that has already been mentioned, namely a Japanese defense based upon the more radical principle of selected atomic-hydrogen weapons that would serve as devastating deterrents to aggressors. The disadvantage of conventional armament is the improbability that it would represent an effective defense against any emergency other than civil uprising. This seems particularly evident if one recalls the proximity and nature of the Communist forces. But the problem of atomic weapons for Japan lies not only in the high sensitivity of the Japanese people to these as a result of past experiences, but equally in the fact that an atomic war for Japan, whatever its causes, would be an almost unthinkable disaster for a society so densely concentrated into major industrial centers.

For the moment, Japanese military policy is predicated upon limited, conventional rearmament, for defense purposes only, with the defense force gradually increasing in size to the point where American troops and bases can be removed from Japan proper. The speed of that removal has recently been accelerated; before the beginning of 1958, all American ground troops were to have been taken out of Japan. It is assumed that the United States will continue to give assistance in rearmament and will be willing to negotiate certain inequities out of the Mutual Security Treaty. The government has stated that it would oppose the storage of American atomic weapons in Japan. From these facts it is clear that Japanese defense in the broader sense hinges very slightly upon the "National Defense Force," and very greatly upon such factors as internal stability, general world trends, Communist intentions, and American power.

Nationalism is not only inextricably involved in Japanese defense issues but it is also clearly depicted in attitudes over certain territories. Japan has buried or hidden any bitterness over the loss of the greater Empire, at least for the time being, but she has no intention of giving up her claims to areas that she considers to have been taken from her wrongfully. In the north, this involves South Saghalien and especially the Kuriles. In the south, the issues are the Bonins and Okinawa. Upon this general issue there is a broad measure of agreement among various Japanese political groups. When peace with the Soviet Union was finally achieved in 1956, there was strong disappointment in Japan because of the meager nature of Soviet concessions. However ineffectively, her rights to northern fishing waters and islands will continue to be pressed. These issues will remain among the many that inhibit cordial Russo-Japanese relations. Once again, Russia stands on the threshold of Japan, with all efforts to remove her seemingly in vain.

The issue in the south, however, is at least as close to the Japanese heart. In contrast to the rather barren northern regions, Okinawa has a population of considerably more than one-half million people who are culturally Japanese. Unlike the Soviet Union, the United States has recognized the "residual sovereignty" of Japan to this island. But now there is mounting demand that the residual become actual. Again, domestic politics enters the picture. The serious friction between the American military and the Okinawan people which has developed recently over problems of land usage and compensation has been freely and effectively used by the political left, both in Japan and in Okinawa. This campaign has had wide support from independent elements in the press and elsewhere. The results of recent Okinawan elections have shocked many Americans who were previously complacent. The Japanese conservatives have taken a stand on behalf of immediate restoration of Japanese control, in exchange for the granting of long-term leases of military bases and installations. Until the issue is approached in some such fashion as this, Okinawa will be a major source of friction in American-Japanese relations. Indeed, as long as Americans remain on the island in large numbers, under whatever auspices, there is likely to be trouble.

In a broader sense, Japanese nationalism can also be seen in many other aspects of Japanese diplomacy since 1954. It was during this period that the phrase "an independent foreign policy" first began to be used openly by the Japanese conservatives. One of its manifestations has been the policy of seeking "normalization" of relations with the Communist bloc. Negotiations with the Soviet Union culminating in the Treaty of 1956 constituted the opening and rather frustrating move. As noted earlier, Russia made very few concessions. In general, the future of Russo-Japanese relations is likely to resemble the past. Within Japan, antipathy to the U.S.S.R. is relatively strong, a product of historic rivalries, the last-minute attack in 1945, Russian treatment of Japanese prisoners, and its "get-tough" policy toward Japan on most matters. Japan cannot ignore such issues as fishery rights and boundaries; they are of economic significance to every citizen. There is every indication, however, that Russo-Japanese relations will not go far beyond the levels of correct formality and minimal concessions. Japanese policy will be marked by vigilance, determined bargaining, and the hope for Soviet containment.

Relations with Communist China are regarded as much more important and potentially different. Once again, Japan is faced with the prospect of seeking a workable China policy, and this time it must be based more upon the strength than the weakness of that nation. A Sino-Soviet Communist alliance poses a considerable long-range threat to the non-Communist world, and to Japan in particular. Can "normalization" only mean an effort at co-existence, or are there some possibilities of mutually beneficial interaction, despite ideological differences? In approaching this and related questions, Japan has inclined thus far toward ruling out only one possibility—that of ignoring the new regime and treating the nationalist government on Formosa as if it were China. While Japan still has formal diplomatic relations only with the nationalist government, its *de facto* cultural and economic relations with the Communist government have been expanding with official approval. In reality, Japanese foreign policy toward China today is based upon the "Two Chinas" theory.

Many socialists and some independents envisage the possibility of Sino-Japanese cooperation and friendship, despite the differences now existing. As we have seen, this has been a recurrent theme throughout the modern period, but one never realized. Chinese Communist foreign policy is likely to give encouragement to this theme, at least for the near future. The Communists would like to strike a fatal blow at the American-Japanese Alliance. They may be prepared to go a considerable distance, policy-wise, in attempting this. Given the political realities of the present, however, it seems doubtful that Sino-Japanese relations will be marked by great intimacy. The chances are strong that China will remain Communist and Japan anti-Communist; that economic as well as political rivalries will build up in the Asian area; that both states will reflect their differences within Asia through alliances out of Asia. But even if this proves to be the case, Japan will seek to follow a flexible, realistic policy under conservative leadership, exploring all economic opportunities and moving toward recognition.

C. Basic Japanese goals

Any discussion of the China problem inevitably leads to the larger issue of basic Japanese goals or functions in the current world. With the present psychology of defensiveness, there is a certain tendency in Japan to go from moods of black despair to quests for lofty, idealistic solutions. Most concepts like world brotherhood strike a strong emotional note in Japan. The desires to be recognized, to be equal, to be loved are all present in high degree. There was great enthusiasm over the admission of Japan into the United Nations. Japan hopes to play a considerable role in this and other international bodies, in part as middle man and interpreter betwen Asia and the West. She knows that she has various competitors for this role, and that she has some lost ground to regain. However, she has certain unique capacities, among them the fact that she is still the only industrial society in the Asian area.

Partly for this reason, Japan does not think of herself as a totally Asian society, but rather as a mixture, as a kind of universal state. This does not mean that she wishes to be divorced from Asia. On the contrary, she believes that her special interests continue to reside in this area, and that she can find her greatest function in technical-economic interaction with those societies now embarking upon a modernization program. To do this she requires international assistance herself, and most especially the broad protection of an American alliance. For twenty years the Anglo-Japanese Alliance underwrote Japanese policy in Asia. Then through the disintegration of that alliance and the abuses of Japanese policy, Japanese plans and hopes came to nought. Now an American alliance may give her a second opportunity for an Asian policy which, if it is to be successful, must be marked by moderation and a cooperative spirit.

An American-Japanese alliance is rendered logical not only by the goals of Japanese policy and the needs of Japanese security, but also by certain cultural trends of the past decade. These two societies, thrown closely together by war and occupation, have emerged with a much greater appreciation of each other, and there has been extensive cultural borrowing on both sides. There remain, of course, substantial differences of language, custom, and race. And even the most logical alliances can be destroyed by carelessness or by lack of homage to important emotional and value positions. If these dangers can be surmounted, however, the American-Japanese alliance should have a longer life than the earlier alliance with Great Britain and—one would hope—serve as a greater instrument of peace.

Selected Bibliography

There is a great wealth of primary and secondary source materials on Japanese foreign policy for the reader who can use the Japanese language. Memoirs of prominent statesmen are abundant; a number of documentary collections and good secondary works exist; and many of the Japanese Foreign Office Archives, having been microfilmed during the Occupation, are obtainable through the Library of Congress. To list even the most essential Japanese materials would be a lengthy task, and one not appropriate here. Fortunately, the reader of Japanese can refer to a number of sources for bibliographic assistance. We shall merely suggest some English-language materials, with emphasis upon more recent books.

Although English materials are still far too limited, the last ten years have seen an increasing number of worthy articles, monographs, and general studies, many of which deal in some fashion with Japanese foreign policy. To start with the historical background of Japanese international relations, one might mention the older work of R. H. Akagi, *Japan's Foreign Relations: 1542-1936* (New York, 1936), but two more recent works by Sir George Sansom provide an excellent introduction to this as to other facets of historic Japan: *Japan—A Short*

Cultural History (New York, 1943), and *The Western World and Japan* (New York, 1950). To these should be added C. R. Boxer's *Christian Century in Japan* (Berkeley, 1951) for a careful exposition of initial Western contacts.

Turning to the modern period, there are a few general works that include materials on foreign policy. One might select Hugh Borton's *Japan's Modern Century* (New York, 1955) and Chitoshi Yanaga's *Japan Since Perry* (New York, 1949) as recent works of this type. For those particularly interested in the early Meiji period, we are fortunate in having the work of W. G. Beasley: his *Great Britain and the Opening of Japan, 1834-1858* (London, 1951) has been followed by *Select Documents on Japanese Foreign Policy, 1853-1868;* these serve as an admirable introduction to the problems of the early Meiji era, which began in 1867. The memoirs and accounts of Western diplomats and other residents are also of interest: E. M. Satow, *A Diplomat in Japan* (London, 1921); Sir Rutherford Alcock, *The Capital of the Tycoon,* 2 vols. (London, 1863); J. H. Gubbins, *The Progress of Japan, 1853-1871.* There are also a few monographs of special interest, mainly pertaining to the later Meiji period. One of these is Marius B. Jansen, *The Japanese and the Chinese Revolutionary Movement, 1895-1915.* The Taisho period (1912-1926) is rather sparsely covered as yet. Masamichi Royama has written one work in English entitled *The Foreign Policy of Japan, 1914-1939* (Tokyo, 1941); the older work by T. Takeuchi, *War and Diplomacy in the Japanese Empire* (New York, 1935), may still have some utility. The books by A. M. Young, especially his *Japan under Taisho Tenno* (London, 1928), are of interest as contemporary accounts, and the Young newspaper, the *Kobe* (later *Japan*) *Chronicle,* is a most important source for many events of the entire period between the mid-Meiji and prewar Showa eras.

For most readers the Showa period is likely to be of greatest interest. For the militarist era of the 1930's the most important materials are contained in two memoirs: the so-called *Harada-Saionji Memoirs* and the *Kido Diary;* neither of these has been published in English, but both are available at certain leading libraries in the United States in mimeographed form, in whole or in part. Perhaps no single English source is as valuable as the voluminous War Crimes Trial Documents, running into thousands of pages, which were translated for purposes of the famous Tokyo trials. These also can be obtained; a complete set exists, for instance, at the Berkeley library. Among existing Western memoirs special mention should be made of J. C. Grew, *Ten Years in Japan* (New York, 1944), and Sir R. Craigie, *Behind the Japanese*

Mask (London, 1946). We have a new general account of this war-time period in F. C. Jones *Japan's New Order in East Asia; Its Rise and Fall, 1937-1945* (New York, 1954). Two worthy monographs are Willard H. Elsbree, *Japan's Role in Southeast Asian Nationalist Movements, 1940-1945* (Cambridge, 1953), and Robert Butow, *Japan's Decision to Surrender* (New York, 1955). Japanese accounts of the war can be obtained from T. Kase, *Journey to the Missouri* (New Haven, 1950), and M. Kato, *The Lost War* (New York, 1946).

Naturally, the American reader will tend to have a special interest in American-Japanese relations. A substantial number of books have been written on this subject. Among the older works, those of Payson J. Treat are well known: *Japan and the United States* (rev. ed.; Stanford, 1928), and *Diplomatic Relations between the United States and Japan*, 3 vols. (Stanford, 1932, 1938); there is also Foster Rhea Dulles, *Forty Years of American-Japanese Relations* (New York, 1937); and a broad cultural account is to be found in T. Dennett, *Americans in Eastern Asia* (New York, 1922). More recently, such an approach has been effectively used by Robert Schwantes in his *Japanese and Americans; A Century of Cultural Relations* (New York, 1955). In terms of cultural and political relations, the reader can refer to E. O. Reischauer, *The United States and Japan* (Cambridge, 1950), and a section entitled *The United States and Japan* by the present author in the American Assembly publication, *The United States and the Far East* (New York, 1957). Official publications from the State Department, such as the series on *Foreign Relations of the United States and Japan*, are naturally useful for major documents.

In addition there are a number of more specialized accounts, limited in scope or time. Only two will be mentioned here: H. L. Stimson, *The Far Eastern Crisis* (New York, 1936), and Herbert Feis, *The Road to Pearl Harbor* (Princeton, 1950).

No serious study of Japanese foreign policy should be undertaken, of course, without reference to the periodical literature. Among the English-language journals, those carrying articles of significance at rather regular intervals include *Contemporary Japan, The Japan Quarterly, The Asian Quarterly* (formerly *The Far Eastern Quarterly*), *Foreign Affairs, Pacific Affairs,* and the *Far Eastern Survey.* Some reference should also be made to the increasing number of English-language materials being published by the Japanese government, including valuable items pertaining to foreign policy problems and policies from the Ministries of Finance, Trade and Commerce, and the Foreign Office. In reference to contemporary issues it will be helpful to consult the translations of the Vernacular Press and translations of selected articles from Japanese vernacular magazines, put out by the American Embassy, if one can obtain access to these. Such newspapers as the *Japan Times* (formerly *Nippon Times*), the *Osaka Mainichi* English edition, and the *Asahi Evening News* should also be examined. Naturally, many of the above materials will contain further leads and much fuller bibliographies.

7 . . .

FOREIGN POLICY OF COMMUNIST CHINA

. . . *Allen S. Whiting*

I. Scope of Study: 1949 to Present

CHINA, LIKE JAPAN, is a relative newcomer to orthodox conduct of foreign relations. For centuries relations between the imperial court at Peking and the outside world remained tributary in nature. No concept of sovereignty or equality interfered with domination by the Middle Kingdom over dependencies such as Tibet and Mongolia, or vassal states such as Korea and Annam. Beyond these peripheral areas the presence of "foreign barbarians" only occasionally interrupted the splendid isolation of the emperor.

Not until the nineteenth century did Western pressure forcefully break down this isolation. During the first decades demands for trade, backed with arms, won limited concessions from Peking, but negotiations were restricted to provincial officials immediately concerned with coastal areas. Even when British and French troops shot their way to Peking, forcing establishment of the Tsungli Yamen as an office to deal with foreign governments, Chinese officialdom remained hostile to conventional Western practices of international law and comity.

Collapse of the Manchu Empire and birth of the Republic of China in 1912 offer a convenient point of demarcation in the foreign relations of modern China. Still, the resemblance with Western states is more apparent than real. To be sure the Waichiao Pu with its consular establishments abroad and its acceptance of international protocol at home functioned as did most ministries of foreign affairs. The difference lay in China's political fragmentation, which left nominal authority with a central government but permitted local warlords to conduct *de facto* if not *de jure* foreign relations.

Civil war rent China apart during the decade 1918-1928 as a northern government at Peking, dominated by shifting military factions, vied for power with a southern government at Canton, headed by Sun Yat-sen and his Kuomintang cohorts. Officially Peking enjoyed recognition as the legal voice of China until its final defeat by the Nationalist Army in 1928. Its actual power, however, extended through only a small section of the country. During the turbulent 'twenties most of South China, Tibet, Sinkiang, Mongolia, and Manchuria lay beyond control from the capital.

Thus, examination of foreign policy during this period would have to consider not only Waichiao Pu activities but also relations between Soviet advisors and the Canton government. These important clandestine relations continued even after recognition was established between Moscow and Peking in 1924. Similarly, Russian troops assisted a revolutionary regime in Outer Mongolia to oust Chinese control in 1921. Despite recognition in 1924 of Peking's sovereignty over the area, the Soviet Commissar for Foreign Affairs continued to describe its "autonomy" as permitting "independence in its foreign policy." [1] In like fashion Moscow ignored Chinese protests and concluded an agreement with Marshal Chang Tso-lin for operation of the Chinese Eastern Railway which ran through his bailiwick of Manchuria, although a similar agreement had been concluded with Peking only four months before.

In fact, the history of modern China down to 1949 finds few years wherein a central government exercised sufficient authority throughout the legal limits of its declared competence to preclude local conduct of foreign affairs. Japan overran Manchuria in 1931, setting up the independent state of Manchukuo. Soviet authorities concluded extensive agreements with local governors in the border province of Sinkiang, covering loans, trading privileges, and mineral exploitation rights all without reference to the central government. Even the miniscule Chinese Communist Party took upon itself the power to declare war against Japan in 1932, acting as a Chinese Soviet Republic.

We see that analysis of Chinese foreign policy requires a continual adjustment of scope depending upon the time-span considered, for it would be a fiction to ignore these side-currents, some of which proved

---

[1] Commissar for Foreign Affairs Chicherin to the Congress of Soviets, *Pravda*, No. 54 (2985), March 6, 1925, p. 5.

rather critical in determining the fate of large sectors of China. Communist victory over the forces of Chiang Kai-shek in 1949, however, provides a partial solution to the problem, albeit not a wholly successful one. Communist control over the mainland of China and its general acceptance by Asia, if not by the world, as the *de jure* as well as the *de facto* government, compels our studying the regime of Mao Tsetung. Yet another claimant to China conducts foreign policy in its name—the regime of Chiang Kai-shek, who withdrew to Taiwan in 1949 and continued to function there as the Republic of China. In view of the relatively small domain under Nationalist control and the impossibility of this group reconquering the mainland, we shall focus solely on the Communist People's Republic of China (PRC).

II.   Problems of Analysis

[Obstacles to analysis of Chinese Communist foreign policy are several and severe. Our perspective of Chinese foreign policy in general is limited by the formidable language barrier, which reduces the number of Western scholars able to read original documents.] Extensive translation of nineteenth-century materials on foreign policy occurred only during the past decade. Furthermore, the turbulence of recent [Chinese politics and the authoritarian tendencies of most regimes concerned combined to place serious limitations on the availability of materials.] Again it has been only in the past decade that volumes of documents on the important T'ai P'ing rebellion of a century ago were published by the Peking regime.

The present government of China is as secretive about its foreign policy process as is its mentor, the Soviet Union. A determined appearance of "monolithic unity" within the authoritarian elite masks whatever differences may exist. [Complete control over all media of communication censors information made available to the West.] Public discussion comes only after policy has been decided within the highest levels of the Chinese Party. Government spokesmen rationalize but need not defend policy in the absence of an organized opposition.

[Compounding these physical obstacles to analysis is the interpretive debate among non-Communists as to the nature of policy-making in Peking.] Is it principally Chinese and therefore comprehensible only within a continuous flow of policies preceding it from Nationalist or even Manchu days? Or is it principally Communist, necessitating close study of Marxist-Leninist-Stalinist precedents for clues and insights?

Our analysis admits elements of both arguments without supporting either side exclusively. The present rulers of China are Chinese. They have lived there, with few exceptions, during most of their past. The environment within which they operate is essentially the same as that which prevailed in China for the previous century. At the same time, they view that environment through Communist lenses. The elite possesses a highly articulated ideology which it consciously proclaims as the basis of behavior: the Marxist-Leninist creed of Communism.

Therefore we must examine the Chinese component of policy in terms of the external environment within which it operates. Part of this may be termed objective—the physical factors such as territory, accessibility, and material development, which confront all elites with certain tangibles. Part of this environment is subjective in the way in which historical trends are experienced and perceived by decision-makers. Insofar as the subjective factor remains relatively constant in groups preceding the Communists, we may term it a Chinese component of policy.

Then we shall analyze the Communist component of policy. Its ideological content is defined by the canons of Marx, Lenin, Stalin, and Mao. Its institutional structure springs from ideological convictions about the role of the Party, the nature of government, and the function of authoritarian rule—or "democratic centralism" as it is termed by the ideology. By combining these varied factors we can discern more clearly not only the goals of Chinese Communist foreign policy, but the means available to and likely to be adapted by the elite in support of that policy.

III.   External Environment: The Chinese Component

A.   Physical factors

Although the days of the Chinese Empire are long past, contemporary elites continue to pay obeisance to the memory of vanished glory in their delineation of China's territorial sovereignty. Chiang Kai-shek, borrowing Adolf Hitler's concept of *lebensraum,* or "living-space," laid claim to past holdings on the basis of population pressure as well as of historical possession:

> In regard to the living space essential for the nation's existence, the territory of the Chinese state is determined by the requirements for national survival and by the limits of Chinese cultural bonds. Thus, in the territory of China a hundred years ago [*circa* 1840], comprising more than ten million square kilometers, there was not a single district that was not essential to the survival of the Chinese nation, and none that was not permeated by our culture. The breaking up of this territory meant the undermining of the nation's security as well as the decline of the nation's culture. Thus, the people

as a whole must regard this as a national humiliation, and not until all lost territories have been recovered can we relax our efforts to wipe out this humiliation and save ourselves from destruction.[2]

Although Chiang does not specify his "lost territories," a Chinese textbook published shortly after his statement contains a table listing them (see Table 1).

Table 1.   CHINA'S "LOST TERRITORIES" [3]

Date	Area, in square kilometers	Location	New ownership
1689........	240,000	North side Khingan Mountains	Russia
1727........	100,000	Lower Selenga Valley	Russia
1842........	83	Hong Kong	United Kingdom
1858........	480,000	North of Heilungkiang	Russia
1858........	8	Kowloon	United Kingdom
1860........	344,000	East of Ussuri River	Russia
1864........	900,000	North of Lake Balkhash	Russia
1879........	2,386	Liuchiu Islands	Japan
1882–1883....	21,000	Lower Ili Valley	Russia
1883........	20,000	Irtysh Valley east of Lake Zaysan	Russia
1884........	9,000	Upper Koksol Valley	Russia
1885–1889....	738,000	Annam and all Indochina	France
1886........	574,000	Burma	United Kingdom
1890........	7,550	Sikkim	United Kingdom
1894........	122,400	West of the Upper Salween	United Kingdom
1894........	91,300	West of the Upper Yangtze	United Kingdom
1894........	100,000	Upper Burma, Savage Mountains	United Kingdom
1895........	220,334	Korea	Japan
1895........	35,845	Taiwan	Japan
1895........	127	Pescadores	Japan
1897........	760	The edge of Burma	United Kingdom
1897........	2,300	The edge of Burma	United Kingdom
Total......	4,009,093		

Nor do Communist leaders remain indifferent to China's past holdings, although they temper their immediate claims according to time and place. Thus Mao Tse-tung staked out his future realm in an interview more than twenty years ago:

It is the immediate task of China to regain all our lost territories. . . . We do not, however, include Korea, formerly a Chinese colony, but when we have reestablished the independence of the lost

---

[2] Chiang Kai-shek, *China's Destiny* (New York: Roy Publishers, 1947), p. 34.
[3] Hou Ming-chiu, Chen Erh-shiu, and Lu Chen, *General Geography of China* (in Chinese), 1946, as cited in G. B. Cressey, *Land of the 500 Million* (New York: McGraw-Hill, 1955), p. 39.

territories of China, and if the Koreans wish to break away from the chains of Japanese imperialism, we will extend them our enthusiastic help in their struggle for independence. The same thing applies for Formosa. . . . The Outer Mongolian republic will automatically become a part of the Chinese federation, at their own will. The Mohammedan and Tibetan peoples, likewise, will form autonomous republics attached to the Chinese federation.[4]

True to his word, at least in part, Mao drove his Red Armies to the Tibetan heights despite Indian protests one year after establishment of the People's Republic of China in 1949. His implicit definition of Korea as within China's sphere of interest received implementation when Chinese armies hurled back United Nations troops from the Yalu River to the thirty-eighth parallel during 1950-51. Sinkiang, presumably referred to above as "the Mohammedan people" because of its predominantly Moslem population, became an autonomous region in 1955 after considerable "pacification" by the Red Army. Only Formosa, held by Chiang Kai-shek, and Outer Mongolia, recognized as independent by the Treaty of Friendship and Alliance concluded between the Nationalist Government and Moscow in 1945 and adhered to in this particular by Peking, remained beyond Mao's control in 1958.

Similarly, both Nationalist and Communist maps place China's borders far down in the South China Sea, off the shores of Borneo. Mao would subscribe to the statements of the official Nationalist handbook, "Both the southernmost and westernmost borders remain to be defined. The Pamirs in the west constitute a contested area among China, the U.S.S.R., and Afghanistan. The sovereignty of the Tuansha Islands (the Coral Islands) in the south is sought by China, the Republic of the Philippines, and Indo-China. The boundary between China and Burma also remains to be demarcated."[5] Movement of Chinese Communist forces into this disputed area bordering Burma during 1955-56 aroused protests in Rangoon. Lengthy negotiations demonstrated Peking's unwillingness to renounce any territorial demands, even when they possess little economic or strategic value and when they bring unfavorable political repercussions.

This persistent pattern of behavior stems from the traditional Chinese definition of a government possessing the Mandate of Heaven as one capable of defending the frontiers against barbarian incursions while maintaining the peace against domestic insurrection. So remote

---

[4] E. Snow, *Red Star Over China* (Modern Library Edition, 1944), p. 96; interviews with Mao Tse-tung in 1936.

[5] *China Handbook, 1955-56* (Taipei, Taiwan, 1955), p. 15.

an area as Outer Mongolia became the subject of political controversy in 1912 when young nationalists agitated against Peking's concessions to Mongolian demands for autonomy under Russian protection. These nationwide protests proved a useful political weapon against the regime of Yuan Shih-k'ai. Similarly in 1950 Nationalist propaganda sought to embarrass Communist Peking by charges of "selling out" Chinese soil to the Soviet Union through acceptance of Outer Mongolian independence.

The leaders may not believe in this expansive definition of China's territory, but its acceptance may be dictated by political expediency. Whatever the cause, the effect is to saddle the government with serious international problems. Vague territorial claims based on concepts of suzerainty and tributary relations or on disputed treaties give no objective basis for determining international boundaries. Thus it is a moot question whether "aggression" in the conventional usage could be legally charged against Chinese Communist invasion of Tibet in 1950.

Where such boundaries are fixed with rough approximation, precise definition is impeded by the absence of natural lines of demarcation. Except for the coast and the relatively short Yalu and Amur rivers in the northeast, none of China's frontiers can be readily identified by natural phenomena. They twist tortuously through jungle, mountain, and desert according to the temporary dictates of local needs and the relative power available to interested parties. The absence of natural demarcation is paralleled by an absence of natural barriers against migration or invasion, complicating the responsibilities facing the central government responsible for its citizens' welfare and defense.

Few lines of communication traverse the great distances from China's traditional capitals to its remote border provinces. At the same time, these remote provinces are relatively close to rival centers of power. Not until Chinese Communist rule was a railroad constructed linking Outer Mongolia with North China. At this same time the first rough road joined Tibet with South China. Currently, Russian assistance enables Peking to lay a railroad through the desert wastes into Sinkiang where it will meet a trunk line from the Turk-Sib railroad in the Soviet Union. Even Manchuria's transport ties with China proper, although infinitely better than those to other areas, were weak considering the strategic importance of this region.

Beside these obstacles those responsible for China's security have been confronted with British pressure upon Tibet from India; Russian pressure upon Sinkiang from adjacent Kazakhstan, upon Mongolia from Siberia, and upon Manchuria from the Far Eastern territories; and Japanese pressure first upon Korea and from there upon Manchuria, as well as upon the Ryukyu Islands and Formosa. China's attraction for invaders traditionally was one of food and wealth, luring from the interior certain nomadic groups against whom the Great Wall was originally designed. Modern invaders came after markets (Great Britain), raw materials (Japan), or imperialist prestige (Germany).

Throughout the past 300 years these conditions have been magnified in their seriousness by the inferiority of China's economic development compared with that of predatory powers arraigned against her. Russia's piecemeal nibbling at Chinese territory was facilitated by the remoteness of Sinkiang and Outer Mongolia from the base of China's strength. Bringing the contest nearer this base, however, revealed that the strength was more apparent than real. Despite the striking disparity of populations, Japanese offensives took Korea, Manchuria, and finally much of China proper from the "land of the four hundred million." Only industrialization could remedy this material weakness which left China vulnerable to all comers.

Thus Chinese foreign policy during the nineteenth and twentieth centuries grappled with problems of defense against outer pressures to a degree unique among the countries under survey. These pressures were varied, but alike in their threat to Chinese civilization. Military attack literally tore off chunks of territory. Economic concessions carved out sheltered spheres of influence, disrupting domestic economic development through artificial emphasis upon coastal points of foreign control. Finally, ideological pressures were exerted by foreign missionaries, who, protected with force when necessary, challenged the Confucian order with destructive vigor.

Virtually no point along the 12,600 miles of China's perimeter has been safe from one or another of these pressures during the last 300 years. So vulnerable were they at the turn of the century that many wondered whether China was not to be the "sick man" of Asia, to be carved up by other countries as was the Ottoman Empire. These physical factors pose an objective challenge for Chinese foreign policy, be it Manchu, Nationalist, or Communist. Taken in conjunction with the subjective factor of historical experience, they provide an important clue to the behavior of Mao Tse-tung and his followers.

B.   Historical factors

More than objective concerns explain defensive attitudes in China, which intermittently explode into xenophobia. Subjective evaluation of events during the past century convinces Nationalist and Communist alike that many, if not all of China's ills stem from contact with the "foreign devil," now castigated as "Western imperialism." Two hun-

dred years ago Li Shih-yao, viceroy of Kwangtung and Kwangsi, memorialized the throne on regulations for the control of foreigners, warning, "It is my most humble opinion that when uncultured barbarians, who live far beyond the borders of China, come to our country to trade, they should establish no contact with the population, except for business purposes."

Events since Li Shih-yao's day show little break in continuity so far as interpretation of foreign relations is concerned. Chiang Kai-shek blamed the chaotic years of interregnum following collapse of the Manchu Dynasty upon "secret activities of the Imperialists . . . the chief cause of civil wars among the warlords." Indeed, he attributed the Empire's disintegration to the so-called "unequal treaties" which "completely destroyed our nationhood, and our sense of honor and shame was lost. . . . The traditional structure of the family, the village, and the community was disrupted. The virtue of mutual help was replaced by competition and jealousy. Public planning was neglected and no one took an interest in public affairs." *sounds familiar*
doesn't fit

This simplistic explanation errs in attributing cause and effect where coincidence is the phenomenon. Western pressures hastened collapse of the Empire with its Confucian traditions, but they came after the process of disintegration had begun. By contrast, the ability of Japanese society to adapt new forms with old content under the combined impact of feudal decline and Western influence demonstrates the distortion of history in Chiang's analysis.

However, it is not the facts of history that condition political behavior but the way in which men view those facts. Hence the similarity of the following Communist analysis with those mentioned above, preceding it in time, is highly suggestive of xenophobia as a Chinese component of policy:

> They [the imperialists] will not only send their running-dogs to bore inside China to carry out disruptive work and to cause trouble. They will not only use the Chiang Kai-shek bandit remnants to blockade our coastal ports, but they will send their totally hopeless adventurist elements and troops to raid and to cause trouble along our borders. They seek by every means and at all times to restore their position in China. They use every means to plot the destruction of China's independence, freedom, and territorial integrity and to restore their private interests in China. We must exercise the highest

---

6 Hu Sheng, *Imperialism and Chinese Politics* (Peking, 1955), p. 9.
7 Chiang Kai-shek, *op. cit.*, p. 78.
8 *Ibid.*, pp. 79 and 88.

vigilance. . . . They cannot possibly be true friends of the Chinese people. They are the deadly enemies of the Chinese people's liberation movement.[9]

[Thus the Chinese Communist devil-theory of imperialism coincides with popular mythology of evil inherent in foreign contacts to produce attitudes of suspicion and hostility at various levels of action.]This popular mythology derives from perceived experience, which generalized foreign behavior on the basis of rape and pillage by Western troops during the nineteenth century. Western insistence on extraterritorial privileges to try persons by foreign law for crimes committed on Chinese territory rubbed salt in the wound. Insult was added to injury.[While Chinese viewed white behavior as "barbaric," whites viewed Chinese punishment as "brutal." The inevitable cultural gap, widened by racial prejudice, reinforced hostility on both sides.]

[Injustice was also encountered at higher levels of diplomatic relations. Chinese experience in the international arena gave good reason for bitter resentment at being cast in the role of "a melon to be carved up by the powers."] Throughout the nineteenth century, gunboat diplomacy forced abdication of customary rights of sovereignty without reciprocal privileges for China. Extraterritorial law, economic concessions, and the stationing of foreign troops in Chinese cities were sanctified by treaty but won by force. Punitive expeditions in 1860 and 1900 delivered the supreme insult of foreign military occupation in the venerated capital of Peking.

The twentieth century brought little relief. Japan fought Russia on Chinese soil for control of the rich provinces of Manchuria. China's own allies in World War I swept aside her protests at Versailles to award Japan concessions in China held by defeated Germany. World War II saw the Yalta Conference of 1945 reward Soviet Russia with important military, economic, and political privileges in China, all without consultation with Chiang Kai-shek. Although President Roosevelt reminded Premier Stalin that those inducements for Russian entry into the war against Japan would have to be affirmed by Chiang, it was a foregone conclusion that allied pressure left China no alternative but capitulation.

[In sum, China was the object of international relations but seldom the subject.] Acted upon by others, she was unable to act in her own

---

[9] K'o Pai-nien, "Hsin min chu chu yi te wai chiao tse" (The Foreign Policy of the New People's Democracy), *Hsüeh Hsi* (Study), Vol. I, No. 2, October 1949, pp. 13-15.

right. Long the primary power in Asia, she has been cut deeply during the past century by this induced feeling of inferiority. Fear of Japan followed a defeat caused by material inferiority. Resentment against the West followed capitulation caused by military inferiority and humiliation caused by sensed cultural and ideological inferiority. Small wonder that today Peking's militant insistence upon being heard in regional and world councils strikes a responsive chord among wide sectors of the populace. At long last a determined elite is working to restore China's place in the sun.

To be sure, irredentist claims to "lost territories," denunciation of "unequal treaties," and the playing off of power against power—"use barbarians against barbarians"—are all traditional techniques of foreign policy. The difference in their use by Chinese elites lies in the psychological convictions behind these techniques. Among Western states, exploitation of grievance occurs as an accepted stratagem among assumed equals, struggling for limited gains and for the coveted position of *primus inter pares*. Between China and the rest of the world, however, the bitter remembrance of things past heightens the defensive-offensive aspects of foreign policy.

Communist emphasis upon imperialist aggression fits well into the objective and subjective factors conditioning Chinese views of world politics. Resulting xenophobia, manifested in exaggerated attitudes of belligerence, may ultimately work to Russia's disadvantage. Thus far it has been exploited by Soviet leaders against the West. Study of the Chinese Communist press over the past decade, however, reveals evidence of mutterings against Soviet behavior in Manchuria, concern over continued dependence on Russian economic assistance, and open protests against Red Army suppression of the Hungarian uprising in 1956. Official affirmation of the "monolithic unity of Sino-Soviet Friendship" seeks to repress the hostility with which many Chinese apparently view the Sino-Soviet Alliance. Chinese historians describing nineteenth-century imperialism do not exempt Tsarist Russia from criticism, to the dismay of Soviet writers. A question for continual study, therefore, is the degree to which Russia, like other nations, will suffer the consequences of the dragon's teeth sown in the past in China.

IV.   The Process of Policy: The Communist Component

A.   Ideological content:
Marxism-Leninism

Beside those aspects of continuity in policy which we ascribe to the Chinese component, differences in degree or substance stem from the dedication of this elite to Communism. As Mao Tse-tung declared in 1945, "From the very beginning, our Party has based itself on the theories of Marxism, because Marxism is the crystallization of the world proletariat's most impeccable revolutionary scientific thought." [10]

General protestations of fidelity to Christianity, international law, and justice appear throughout statements of Western political figures. Rarely do these protestations enable us to determine the ends and means of these elites, especially in foreign policy. Marxism-Leninism, however, carries with it a construct of goals and ways of seeking those goals that structures ideology and institution for Communist elites to a degree unknown in the non-Communist world.

Foremost in this ideology is its determination to advance Communism throughout the world. Almost three decades ago the fugitive Chinese Communist Party, beleaguered by Nationalist armies in Kiangsi, proclaimed, "The Provisional Government of the Soviet Republic of China declares that it will, under no condition, remain content with the overthrow of imperialism in China, but, on the contrary, will aim as its ultimate objective in waging a war against world imperialism until the latter is all blown up." [11]

In terms of "progress" and "revolutionary scientific thought" this goal is justified as a desirable one, the "good society" found in utopian drives common to world philosophies. An additional element, however, distinguishes this compulsion toward ideological expansion from counterparts in Islam, Christianity, Wilsonian democracy, and Nazism. For the Marxist, destruction of the imperialist is not only desirable but necessary. The maximum goal of world conquest is the only guarantee for achieving the minimum goal of Communist survival.

Basic to this argument is the assumption of conflict as omnipresent in human relations. The "contradictions of the dialectical process" exist in various forms; conflict need not be military in manifestation. Yet Marx posited all historical development as a process of struggle, whether between classes within a nation or between nations themselves. The highest and final conflict is to come between classes on the international plane, in the world revolution springing from the basic contradiction between international Communism and international capitalism.

[10] Mao-Tze-Tung [Mao Tse-tung], *The Fight for a New China* (report of April 24, 1945, to the Seventh National Congress of the Chinese Communist Party) (New York, 1945), p. 76, as quoted in O. Edmund Clubb, "Chinese Communist Strategy in Foreign Relations," in "Report on China," *The Annals*, Vol. 277, September 1951, p. 156.

[11] *Central China Post* (Hankow), November 25, 1931, as quoted in O. E. Clubb, *op. cit.*, p. 157.

This struggle is not one that is "created" by the Communists. According to their credo, it is the imperialists who are to blame, engaging in a death-struggle to stave off the "inevitable victory" of the Communist ideal. As expressed by Peking's official voice, the *Jen Min Jih Pao* (Peking People's Daily), "Although we have consistently held and still hold that the socialist and capitalist countries should co-exist in peace and carry out peaceful competition, the imperialists are bent on destroying us. We must therefore never forget the stern struggle with the enemy, *i.e.*, the class struggle on a world scale." [12]

Thus defensive dictates for the minimum goal of survival require policies employing offensive means, which simultaneously serve the maximum goal of world Communist domination. One such means is that of applying the classic Chinese dictum of "using barbarian against barbarian" so as to take advantage of the conflict that assumedly exists among capitalists. Mao Tse-tung wrote in 1940, "Our tactical principle remains one of exploiting the contradictions among them [the imperialists] in order to win over the majority, oppose the minority, and crush the enemies separately." [13]

[However, "the enemy" will not rest content and permit the socialist camp to develop peacefully. His efforts to split that camp apart compel a corollary defensive response of unity among Communist elites in general and support for the Soviet Union in particular.] An important statement of this principle came after the Hungarian uprising of 1956 when Peking justified Moscow's armed suppression of the insurgents:

> There are before us two types of contradictions which are different in nature. The first type consists of contradictions between our enemy and ourselves (contradictions between the camp of imperialism and that of socialism, contradictions between imperialism and the people and oppressed nations of the world, contradictions between the bourgeoisie and the proletariat in the imperialist countries, etc.). *This is the fundamental type of contradiction, based on the clash of interests between antagonistic classes.* The second type consists of contradictions within the ranks of the people (contradictions between different sections of the people, between comrades within the Communist Party, or in socialist countries, contradictions between the government and the people, contradictions between socialist countries, contradictions between Communist Parties, etc.)

---

[12] "More on Historical Experience of Proletarian Dictatorship" (article prepared by the Editorial Department of the *Jen Min Jih Pao* on the basis of a discussion at an enlarged meeting of the Political Bureau of the Central Committee of the Communist Party of China), Peking *Jen Min Jih Pao*, December 29, 1956.

[13] Mao Tse-tung, "On Policy," December 25, 1940, as translated in *Selected Works of Mao Tse-tung* (Bombay, India, 1954), Vol. III, p. 218.

This type of contradiction is not basic; it is not the result of a fundamental clash of interests between classes, but of conflicts between right and wrong opinions or of a partial contradiction of interests. It is a type of contradiction whose solution must, first and foremost, be subordinated to the over-all interests of the struggle against the enemy. . . .[14]

These assumptions of conflict receive reinforcement from attitudes and actions of the non-Communist world. In part this results from Chinese Communist behavior, the phenomenon of the "self-fulfilling prophecy." When Mao Tse-tung proclaimed establishment of the People's Republic of China in October 1949, Great Britain extended recognition. Twisting the lion's tail, Peking rejected recognition with spurious protests against phraseology contained in the British note as well as against British consular relations with the Nationalist authorities on Taiwan. Maltreatment of British business concerns in China undermined economic arguments advanced in England for wooing Peking in contrast with American hostility to the Communists. Subsequent British refusal to vote for Peking's admission to United Nations chambers and British support for United States action in the Korean war aroused violent reaction in China against the "Anglo-American imperialist bloc." In one sense that bloc came about in spite of the "contradictions" within it, largely because of Chinese Communist predispositions to hostility.

To a lesser extent United States relations with the new regime were a product of its own actions. As early as 1948 American consular officials were put under house arrest in Communist-held Mukden, jailed, tried, and eventually expelled from China. The seizure of Economic Cooperation Administration stocks in 1949, the inflaming of public opinion against United States personnel, both official and unofficial, and the confiscation of American consular property, held through treaty agreement, in January 1950 all served to obstruct a *rapprochement* between Washington and Peking. Chinese intervention in the Korean war with its attendant defeat of American troops at the Yalu in November 1950 wiped out whatever possibility remained of normal relations between the two countries, at least for many years to come. Yet prior to this war the record shows a number of instances where normal adherence by Peking to international custom might have strengthened the hands of groups within the United States seeking to establish ties with the new regime.

It would be misleading to attribute all Chinese Communist fears and resentments against the United States to this "self-fulfilling proph-

---

[14] *Jen Min Jih Pao*, December 29, 1956, *op. cit.*, italics added.

ecy." America's support of Chiang Kai-shek in the civil war, its obstruction of Chinese Communist representation in the United Nations, and its promulgation of an economic embargo against Peking exacerbated relations between the two countries during the 1950's. The combination of expectation and realization reinforced the ideological content of Chinese Communist policy which posits conflict, overt or covert, inherent in relations with the non-Communist world.

The most famous formulation of this principle came in Mao Tse-tung's "lean to one side" declaration on July 1, 1949:

> "You lean to one side." Precisely so . . . Chinese people either lean to the side of imperialism or to the side of socialism. To sit on the fence is impossible; a third road does not exist. . . . Internationally we belong to the anti-imperialist front headed by the U.S.S.R. and we can look for genuine friendly aid only from that front, and not from the imperialist front.[15]

Implementation of the principle came quickly with the signing of the Treaty of Friendship, Alliance, and Mutual Aid of February 14, 1950, between the Chinese People's Republic and the Union of Soviet Socialist Republics. Mao and Stalin agreed that "in the event of one of the Contracting Parties being attacked by Japan or any state allied with her and thus being involved in a state of war, the other Contracting Party shall immediately render military and other assistance by all means at its disposal." A proliferation of subsequent agreements regulate Soviet economic assistance to China in the form of loans, technical assistance, military aid, and cultural exchange, as well as routine agreements on telecommunications and postal regulations.

This "lean to one side" policy, excluding assistance from, much less alliance with, non-Communist countries, is antithetical to traditional Chinese politics of playing off one country against another. It can only be explained in terms of the Communist component of policy.

B. Ideology: Maoism

So far we have been discussing aspects of Chinese Communist policy that stem from the Communist component as developed in Marxism-Leninism. Assumptions of conflict, antagonism against capitalism, and unity within the socialist camp are all compatible with ideological concepts dominant in Soviet policy, at least to the death of Stalin in 1953. Indeed, on these three points there is no evidence of major revision in post-Stalin developments despite attempts by Khrushchev to temper

---

[15] Mao Tse-tung, "On People's Democratic Dictatorship," July 1, 1949, as translated in C. Brandt, B. Schwartz, and J. K. Fairbank, *A Documentary History of Chinese Communism* (Harvard University Press, 1952), pp. 449 ff.

expectations of Communist-capitalist conflict at the 20th Party Congress in 1956 with his disquisition on the "absence of fatal inevitability" of conflict between the two camps.

Within the Marxist-Leninist framework, however, divergent strategies appear to have developed as evidenced by the practices of the Soviet elite compared with those of the Chinese elite. Admittedly, proof of divergence is complicated by a number of factors. The proliferation and vagueness of Marxist-Leninist scriptures permit almost any action to be interpreted as being sanctioned, explicitly or implicitly. Furthermore, insistence upon ideological conformity at the surface masks subsurface differences within the Communist bloc.

Yet the course of Chinese Communism over the past decades suggests a number of points in domestic and foreign policy that conflict with the Soviet view. Although divergencies on conduct of the Chinese revolution appear as far back as the 1930's, foreign policy disagreements remained hidden until the mid-'50's. Isolated from the outside world during most of the civil war, the elite faced no need and experienced no contradicting evidence to challenge Soviet interpretations of foreign affairs. With victory came pressing reliance upon Soviet economic and military aid, precluding disagreement with Stalin's policies. Seconding Kremlin expulsion of Tito from the Cominform proved politically expedient for Peking even were it informed of the actual roots of the dispute, which is doubtful.

[Involvement in the Korean war, combined with the United Nations embargo, furthered Peking's dependence upon Moscow.] As the official *Handbook of World Knowledge, 1954* stated, "It is erroneous to think that we have no need for international assistance and can still succeed. . . . Who can help us? Only the camp of peace, democracy, and socialism under the leadership of the Soviet Union can give us genuine friendly assistance." [16]

Beneath the surface, however, relations were strained[One bone of contention within China was the establishment of joint Sino-Soviet stock companies in 1950 to exploit oil and nonferrous metals in Sinkiang, as well as to operate a civil airline.][17] It is significant that these companies, established in 1950 for a period of thirty years, were dissolved by joint agreement in 1954 when Khrushchev and Bulganin visited Peking after the death of Stalin.

---

[16] *Shih chieh chih shih shou p'eng, 1954* (Handbook of World Knowledge) (Peking, 1954), p. 7.

[17] For a sampling of adverse comment reported by the Chinese Communist press, see A. S. Whiting, "Communist China and 'Big Brother,'" *Far Eastern Survey,* No. 10, October 1955.

In addition, Chinese participation in the Korean war, albeit aided by Soviet military deliveries, saddled Peking with debts compounded by large Russian deliveries in 1954-55. By 1957 China owed the Soviet Union more than U.S. $2.4 billion, and open criticism within China received no factual contradiction from the elite.[18] The belated revelation of past grievance merits quotation at length:

> It was unreasonable for China to bear all the expenses of the Korean war. . . . During the First and Second World War, the United States lent funds to its allies. . . . Afterward some of the countries repudiated their debts while in some cases the United States waived its claim for repayment. The Soviet loan . . . is repayable in full in ten years. The time is too short and moreover interest has to be paid. I propose that repayment be extended to 20 or 30 years so as to ease the tense economic situation in our country. . . . When the Soviet Union liberated our Northeast [Manchuria], it dismantled some machinery equipment in our factories. Was there compensation for it? Will there be repayment? [19]

The dramatic events of 1956, commencing with Khrushchev's denunciation of Stalin at the 20th Congress in February and climaxed in the Hungarian revolt of November brought Sino-Soviet differences to the fore. Commenting on Stalin's "cult of personality" *Jen Min Jih Pao* saw his errors not merely as the result of personality but as a product of "contradictions" in the socialist system.[20] Reviving Mao Tse-tung's 1937 theory on the "universality of contradiction," the editorial stated, "It is naive to assume that contradictions can no longer exist in a socialist society. To deny the existence of contradictions is to deny dialectics."

---

[18] For China's indebtedness to the Soviet Union see Li Hsien-nien, "Final Accounts for 1956 and the 1957 State Budget," delivered to the fourth session of the First National People's Congress on June 29, 1957; NCNA, Peking, June 29, 1957. Calculation of loan receipts as revealed by Li's report of timing, compared with previously announced loans and related references to military assistance from Russia, compels the conclusion that almost U.S. $2 billion covered military, as distinguished from purely economic, aid.

[19] Lung Yün, "My Ideological Review," *Jen Min Jih Pao*, July 14, 1957 as translated in *Current Background*, No. 470, July 26, 1957. Lung here recapitulated his criticisms voiced before the Standing Committee of the National People's Congress of which he is a member. As vice-chairman of the National Defense Council and travelling companion of Politburo member Peng Chen on a tour of Soviet Russia and East Europe in late 1956, Lung's words merit attention. He recanted in this article but only "subjectively," leaving intact his factual assertions as quoted. No official refutation of these facts occurred although he was criticized for his motives.

[20] *Jen Min Jih Pao*, "On Historical Experience Concerning the Dictatorship of the Proletariat," April 5, 1956, in *Current Background*, No. 403. Mao's original statement of this theory is in his essay *On Contradictions*, August 1937 (English edition—Peking, 1952).

Yet *Pravda* implicitly denied this assertion by deleting all portions relating to it from its translation of the editorial. Although a fuller version was subsequently published in Russia, Khrushchev explicitly denied applicability of the formula to the Soviet Union in a television interview one year later.[21]

Soviet sensitivity to this analysis from Peking is understandable in view of its implications for relations within the bloc, since it postulated "contradictions" among socialist countries rather than Stalinism as basic to the cause of tension. Explicit attention to Yugoslavia's difficulties in this editorial signalled growing Chinese concern with East European developments, vital to China's own economic development as well as to its strategic interests.

Despite Khrushchev's open hostility to Gomulka, reliable reports indicated encouragement for independence on the part of the Polish leader from Mao Tse-tung personally.[22] When Hungary erupted in revolt, Peking press coverage offered a fuller version of events and one different from that of Moscow. Recalling its ambassador to the Soviet Union for consultation, the Chinese elite formulated an analysis in the *Jen Min Jih Pao* editorial of December 29, 1956, which marked the fullest statement to date of disagreement with Soviet policy, albeit tempered by a desire to compromise for the sake of unity within the bloc:

> . . . Contradictions between socialist countries, between Communist Parties . . . are not basic, not the result of a fundamental clash of interests but . . . of a *partial* contradiction of interests. . . . Recent controversies in the international Communist movement, for the most part, have had to do with one's appraisal of the Soviet Union. . . . The Communist Party of the Soviet Union has been taking measures to correct Stalin's mistakes and eliminate their consequences. *These measures are beginning to bear fruit.* . . . Since Stalin's mistakes were not of short duration, their thorough correction cannot be achieved overnight but demands fairly protracted efforts and thoroughgoing ideological education. . . . Only by adopting an objective and analytical attitude can we correctly appraise Stalin and *all those comrades who made similar mistakes under his influence.* . . . We need therefore to adopt a comradely

---

[21] R. Schlesinger, "Soviet Historians Before and After the XX Congress," in *Soviet Studies*, Vol. VII, No. 2, October 1956, pp. 165-66 and ftn. 31. *Pravda* published the full text as a pamphlet that went to press on June 10, 1956. Khrushchev's denial was deleted in all Soviet and Chinese versions of the interview.

[22] The *New York Times* issues of October 16, 1956, and January 11, 1957, tell of two instances of intervention by Mao on behalf of Gomulka, both apparently related by authoritative sources.

attitude towards these people and *should not treat them as enemies* . . . should not blankly denounce everything they did. . . . Their mistakes have a social and historical background.[23] [*Italics added*]

The faint touch of condescension and paternalism is apparent. For Peking the case was far from closed on Stalin or on Soviet policy. As another comment on Soviet-Polish relations noted, "In future relations between socialist countries, if only the bigger nations pay more attention to avoiding the mistake of big-nation chauvinism (this is the main thing) and the smaller nations avoid the mistake of nationalism (this is also important), friendship and solidarity based upon equality will undoubtedly become consolidated." [24] The source of such "big-nation chauvinism" was explained by *Jen Min Jih Pao*, "The time-worn habits of big countries in their relations with small countries continue to make their influence felt in certain ways, while a series of victories achieved by a Party of a country in its revolutionary cause is apt to give rise to a certain sense of superiority." [25]

In keeping with its insistence upon "equality" and "independence" in relations among socialist countries, *Jen Min Jih Pao* in the December 29 editorial dealt relatively lightly with Tito's criticism of the Soviet Union. Expressing "amazement," the editorial termed his views "wrong" insofar as they could "only lead to a split in the Communist movement. . . . Clearly the Yugoslav comrades are going too far. Even if some part of their criticism of brother parties is reasonable, the basic stand and method they adopt infringe the principles of comradely discussion." Thus Peking did not castigate Belgrade in the same severe terms of censure used by Moscow, but reproached "Comrade Tito" with "our brotherly advice" for washing dirty linen in public. As Chou En-lai observed after his sudden trip to Russia and Eastern Europe in January 1957, "Even if no unanimity can be reached for the time being, it would also be normal to reserve the differences while upholding our solidarity." [26]

So long as the Communist component compels Peking to view the outside world as a hostile camp headed by a United States possessing weapons of devastating destruction, "solidarity" within the socialist

---

[23] *Jen Min Jih Pao*, December 29, 1956, *op. cit.* Although Ambassador Liu Hsiao's return to Peking went unreported in the press, his presence at a Moscow reception in November and his subsequent departure from Peking with Chou En-lai, for Moscow, January 7, 1957, give support for this analysis.

[24] NCNA, Peking, November 21, 1956, "International Significance of the Soviet-Polish Talks."

[25] *JMJP*, December 29, 1956.

[26] Chou En-lai to the third annual plenary session of the Second National Committee of the CPPC on March 5, 1957, in *Current Background*, No. 439.

camp is mandatory for China] Lacking any prospect of overtaking America in missile and thermonuclear development, reliance upon Russian protection is the only guarantee of survival, given this view of the world.[Yet short of dissolution of the alliance, the dynamics of inner tension and Chinese response to it argue for identifying Peking separately from the so-called satellites of East Europe. Nor is the independence of Peking from Moscow more apparent than real.] A concatenation of military, economic, and political trends during the first decade of the Sino-Soviet alliance provides a continual and consistent altering of the relationship between Moscow and Peking. The net effect is to increase the ability of the Chinese Communist elite to differ with its Soviet counterpart, never going so far as to cause a "Titoist" break but opening areas of disagreement pertinent for interested third parties, whether Polish or American.[27]

Rather than being scrapped, then, the alliance is being reconstructed with time. Chinese observance of its formation was almost perfunctory in 1957, in contrast with 1955 and 1956. No Politburo members attended the anniversary receptions in Peking nor did any high-level officials write articles summarizing its achievements. Instead, a major speech by Mao Tse-tung the same month included revision of a traditional formulation, a revision suggesting reduction in the status of the Sino-Soviet alliance. After speaking of "socialist countries" and "Asian-African countries," Mao declared, "United with these *two* forces, we will not stand alone." [28] [*Italics added.*] In the same address he cautioned against "criticism . . . harmful to international Socialist solidarity" but did not include this criterion as among "the most important" for determining "right from wrong.[His routine references to the Soviet Union paralleled a shift in emphasis throughout China from the motto, "Study advanced Soviet experience," to injunctions against "mechanical and dogmatic copying of foreign countries."

What has been termed "Maoism" in distinguishing domestic Chinese Communist policy from strictly applied Marxist-Leninist precepts may well prove applicable to the foreign policy area] Absence of schism between Peking and Moscow before 1955 is readily understandable in terms of Chinese reliance upon Russian aid and preoccupation with domestic problems. Growing industrialization, removal of foreign em-

---

[27] For detailed examination of these military, economic, and ideological trends in the Sino-Soviet alliance as they appeared during 1955-57, see A. S. Whiting, "Contradictions in the Moscow-Peking Axis," *Journal of Politics*, February 1958.

[28] Mao Tse-tung, "On the Correct Handling of Contradictions among the People," delivered at a closed session of the Supreme State Conference, February 27, 1957, and released "with revisions" by NCNA, June 18, 1957. Apparently most foreign affairs references were deleted in the final version.

bargo, and increased experience in managing China all provide opportunity for differing with Russia at relatively less cost. At the same time, increasing attention to foreign affairs, whether in East Europe, the Middle East, or Asia, heightens the probability of divergent views within the alliance. Soviet control of such divergency becomes reduced with the decline of Chinese dependence upon Russia. Conversely, China becomes more of an asset as its military and political stature grows, not only within the bloc but in the world at large.

In sum, the ideological ingredients that posit similar ends of policy for the two elites do not necessarily posit identical means or identical timing. The "partial contradiction of interests" seen by Peking as characterizing "relations among socialist countries" compels us to consider China's alliance with Soviet Russia one of voluntary partnership, subject to cohesive and divisive forces which keep that partnership in constant flux. The content of Chinese Communist foreign policy will remain related to, but not dictated by, that of the Soviet Union.

C. Institutional structure

Decision-making in the People's Republic of China is the exclusive prerogative of the CCP, within that Party being confined principally to the Political Bureau (Politburo) or more probably its Standing Committee. Teng Hsiao-p'ing analyzed the relationship between party and state in his report to the 8th National Congress of the CCP in September 1956 as follows:

> The Party is the highest form of class organization. It is particularly important to point this out today when our Party has assumed the leading role in state affairs. . . . [This] means first, that Party members in state organs and particularly the leading Party members' groups formed by those in responsible positions in such departments should follow the unified leadership of the Party. Secondly, the Party must regularly discuss and decide on questions with regard to the guiding principles, policies, and important organizational matters in state affairs, and the leading Party members' groups in the state organs must see to it that these decisions are put into effect with the harmonious cooperation of non-Party personalities. Thirdly, the Party must . . . exercise constant supervision over the work of state organs.[29]

This frank analysis lends substance to analysis of Party control of state organs based upon interlocking direction by high-ranking Party members. The State Council, corresponding to the Council of Min-

---

[29] Teng Hsiao-p'ing, "Report on Revision of Party Constitution," delivered to the CCP Eighth National Congress on September 16, 1956, as quoted by NCNA, Peking, September 18, 1956.

isters in the Soviet Union or the Western cabinet, allocates controlling positions to Party members in the case of the premiership, all ten vice-premiers, and such key ministries as foreign affairs, defense, public security, finance, state planning agencies, machine industries, electric power, railways, and foreign trade. Non-Communists hold ministries concerned primarily with consumption, such as food, textiles, and building materials, or posts concerned with cultural affairs, health, and overseas Chinese.

Similarly, the Standing Committee of the National People's Congress is studded both with Politburo personalities (in its chairman and secretary-general) and with Party members (in five of its twelve vice-chairmen). Although this group is vested by the constitution of 1954 with powers akin to those of legislative bodies in the West, its membership seems relatively impotent in view of the extreme range of decree power held by the State Council. Inclusion of such dignitaries as Madame Sun Yat-sen (Soong Ch'ing-ling); China's outstanding literary polemicist, Kuo Mo-jo; and Tibet's Dalai Lama Dantzenjiatso among its vice-chairmen suggests the nature of this body as an honorific gathering to provide public sanction for decisions arrived at elsewhere.

The Party's constitution makes clear the absolute duty of all members to carry out policies and practices decreed by the Central Committee or, in its absence, by the Politburo:

> Article 19. (6) The decisions of the Party must be carried out unconditionally. Individual Party members must yield to Party organizations, the minority to the majority, the lower organizations to the higher organizations, and all the organizations throughout the country must yield centrally to the National Congress and the Central Committee.[30]

That such decisions are seldom those of the Central Committee is evidenced by the infrequency of its sessions, the size of its membership, and the relatively short intervals during which lengthy reports are read and accepted with little discussion. The Seventh Central Committee, elected in 1945 with more than 75 members and alternates, met in plenary session only seven times in the decade 1945-1956, although the Party constitution called for sessions every six months. The average length of these meetings was one week.

With election of 166 regular and alternate members to the Eighth

---

[30] "The Constitution of the Communist Party of China," adopted by the Eighth National Congress of the CCP on September 26, 1956, as translated by the United States Consulate General, Hong Kong, in *Current Background*, No. 417, October 10, 1956.

Central Committee in 1956, it seemed unlikely the pattern of decision-making by an inner elite would change. This elite is composed of 17 regular and six alternate members of the Politburo. Of its workings we know virtually nothing except that only once in the past two decades has its composition been shaken by purge, and then only two fell from power. Essentially the core, represented by the Politburo Standing Committee of Mao Tse-tung, Liu Shao-ch'i, Chou En-lai, Chu Teh, and Ch'en Yun, is a united group whose internal differences have remained concealed through more than twenty years of civil war and ruling responsibilities.

Political institutions of the PRC resemble those of non-Communist countries in name only. To be sure, other "democratic parties" exist, as in the Soviet Union they do not, but they play no part in policy formation. These groupings, such as the China Democratic League and the Revolutionary Committee of Kuomintang, are small in membership and limited in function. Approximately one-third of the government ministries and chairmen of commissions under the State Council are headed by representatives of these party and so-called "nonparty" persons.[31] Of the 1,226 deputies in the National People's Congress, only 269 came from the "democratic parties" in 1956.

Basically these organizations communicate from the center to the periphery according to the nature of their membership, which may concentrate on intellectuals, businessmen, or overseas Chinese. Control of these "parties" is facilitated by double enrollment of some members in the CCP. In addition the CCP never neglects its role as political leader, even while stressing "long-term co-existence and mutual supervision" between the CCP and the "democratic parties." As a spokesman for one of these groups warned, "We must not one-sidedly emphasize the political freedom and organizational independence of the democratic parties." [32] Their passive role in implementing but not formulating policy is clear from an official explanation of their responsibility "following the victory of socialism . . . Important results might be obtained then in our task of ideological remoulding if education and transformation is conducted through the democratic parties." [33]

These groupings perform on a limited scale functions parallel to those carried out by mass organizations throughout large sectors of

31 NCNA, Peking, March 4, 1957.

32 Huang Ch'i-hsiang, "Two Problems in Work of Democratic Parties," Peking Kuang Ming Jih Pao, January 3, 1957.

33 Shih Ch'i and Sun Nan, "How to Understand the Policy of Long-Term Co-existence Between the Communist Party and the Democratic Parties," Cheng Chih Hsueh Hsi (Political Study), No. 9, September 13, 1956.

the Chinese populace. The Communist Youth League, the Sino-Soviet Friendship Association, the All-China Federation of Trade Unions, and the All-China Democratic Women's Federation enmesh millions in a closely coordinated network of communications media directed from the Department of Propaganda of the CCP. Annual gatherings, such as the National Committee of the Chinese People's Political Consultative Conference, bring together representatives of "democratic parties and mass organizations" to receive reports from government leaders and to endorse the contemporary program of the CCP. Additional *ad hoc* meetings convene these groups for ritualized avowals of support for particular campaigns of domestic or international import.

Thus both parties and interest-group organizations exist in the PRC, but their function is basically one-way communication from the top downwards, as distinguished from their dual role of influencing policy and explaining policy in the West. In this sense public opinion exists to be mobilized by the Party but not to direct the Party. It may fail to respond to Party propaganda, thereby compelling some revision of policy. It may articulate grievances by indirection, thereby stimulating examination of policy at the top. As an external pressure upon the government, however, public opinion cannot be identified in China as an articulate force.

The relevance of parties, interest groups, and public opinion to foreign policy is realized by the elite primarily as a means of affecting the cohesion of the populace. Mass campaigns carried out for months at a time over all communications media and with thousands of "study groups" characterize this effort to reduce dissent and maximize support for policy. These means are useful in three different situations.

Mass campaigns may serve a contingency purpose, preparing the populace for possible action without committing the government to such action. In 1954-55 all China signed petitions in blood, applauded speeches, and endorsed resolutions calling for "immediate liberation of Taiwan." No invasion of Taiwan followed nor were any decisive preparations for invasion evident. Similarly in 1956 a shorter, less intensive campaign pledged "volunteers for "Egypt" during the Anglo-French attack upon that country. Again no action followed words. Such instances serve to confuse the outside world as to the intent of Chinese policy, in addition to whatever domestic stimuli they may provide for higher production, renewing bonds of allegiance, or promulgating symbols of unity for the regime.

Such campaigns may also serve a preparatory function of whipping up public support for a decided action. In 1950, attack upon Tibet was preceded by public rallies, exhortatory articles, and ringing declarations by prominent leaders. Undoubtedly the most extensive use of this technique came in the celebrated "Resist-America-Aid-Korea" movement which accompanied Chinese intervention in the Korean war. During the three years of that action a steady drum-fire of propaganda carried the movement to every corner of China.

Finally, these campaigns serve a purpose of "feedback" similar to the presumed role of public opinion in the non-Communist world. Study groups are not passive lecture-audience sessions but active discussion meetings. They seek to bring out all question of doubt and opposition for the purpose of achieving final unity under the skilled leadership of prepared Party personnel, activists, and cadres. Following Soviet intervention in the abortive Hungarian revolt of 1956 meetings at Chinese universities, factories, and farms discussed Peking's support for Soviet action and attempted to quell what was reported by the Communist press as "shock and confusion."

The limits upon public participation in policy are extreme and explicit, however. An authoritative Chinese analysis warned against "practicing democracy merely for the sake of democracy." Specifically, it advised the youth:

> Before the liberation the forms used by the people in demanding democracy from the Kuomintang consisted mainly of strikes (of workers and students), demonstrations, and parades, bringing loss to the Kuomintang and applying pressure on the enemy so that they had to accept our demands. Today, in dealing with the Anglo-French imperialists who carry out aggression against Egypt, we still adopt the form of demonstration and parade. However, in dealing with divergences of views within the internal ranks of the people, the defects and mistakes of the people, we must resort principally to argument . . . and not the form of applying pressure. . . . The country today belongs to us, and we ourselves will bear the losses, political and economic, arising out of such forms as strikes of workers, strikes of students, and demonstrations and parades for the solution of questions.[34]

Another caveat cautioned against "exaggerating" defects, particularly in Chinese or Soviet policy:

> Some people find certain inappropriate measures carried out by individual socialist countries, and begin to doubt the superiority of the socialist system, and lose confidence. . . . Those who begin to waver as soon as they see mistakes in socialist countries are even more susceptible to pessimism and despair, and lose their political direction. And if counter revolutionaries should be watching at the

---

[34] Chiang Ming, "Democracy Is the Means, Not the End," *Chung Kuo Ching Nien* (China Youth), No. 23, December, 1 1956.

time, who can say but such young people will be utilized by the counter revolutionaries? The experiences of some Hungarian youth these past few weeks should give us cause for vigilance.[35]

The interaction of institution and ideology produce a foreign policy, formulated by a small, authoritarian, continuously functioning elite, whose ends and means are basically those followed by the Soviet elite with such modifications as are affected by the Chinese component of policy. The process of policy as such remains veiled from observation, but the content of policy may be determined with a high degree of probability because of the explicit and detailed nature of the Communist ideology and the conscious dedication of this relatively stable elite to that ideology. Allowing for the modifications of time, then, we may now proceed to examine the most likely alternatives of policy to be anticipated from the People's Republic of China in the near future.

V. The Substance of Policy

A. Ends

[The foreign policy of the People's Republic of China embraces a range of goals extending along a minimum-maximum continuum. Maintenance of internal security as a minimum goal is not peculiar to the elite in Peking.] Intermediate-range goals, however, projecting what might be called "friendly domination" of Asian political and economic developments, stem from Chinese as well as Communist components of policy. They are not, for instance, evident to any comparable degree in the range of goals held by Burmese or Thai elites. Finally, the maximum goal of Peking, direct control of Asia through Communist regimes that are political and economic satellites of China, is a more ambitious aim than is evident in any other ruling group in the area.

These different goals may employ similar means. Wooing the uncommitted or neutral groups of Southeast Asia following the Korean armistice in 1953 not only served the minimum goal of security by offsetting United States negotiations for the Southeast Asian Treaty Organization. It also smoothed the way for the increase of Peking's prestige and influence as an intermediate-range goal in the move to dominate governments in the area.

Yet it is important to recognize that this priority of goals is dictated by the necessity of circumstance. The first decade of PRC foreign policy grappled with problems of uniting traditionally Chinese terri-

---

[35] Fang Chun, "Do Not Deny Everything," *ibid.*, No. 23, December 1, 1956.

tory on the Asian mainland while reducing the external threat as perceived by the ruling elite. Chou En-lai's skillful diplomacy at Geneva and Bandung provided a peaceful counterpart to military intervention in Korea, but both aimed basically at the minimum goal of internal security.

The intermediate goal is capable of realization only with economic development hoped for in the Second and Third Five Year Plans, and with the achievement of a more flexible political atmosphere within China following elimination of counterrevolution and completion of collectivization. These domestic developments, accompanied by armistices in Korea and Indochina, are a prerequisite for extending Peking's leadership in Asian affairs. Not until this process is completed, perhaps several decades distant, can the maximum goal of a Chinese "bloc" of Communist regimes in Asia be realistically contemplated by Peking.

Thus although both China and the Soviet Union may hold identical maximum goals of extending Communism throughout the world, they are not in the same stage of development toward attaining this goal. Moscow has long since disposed of its minimum concern for internal security and has advanced well along the path of attaining intermediate goals of influencing governments along its periphery in Europe and the Middle East. Its economic and military means of policy are far ahead of those available to China. This differentiation of ends attainable within a given time-period provides further justification for distinguishing between Moscow and Peking, not only in our present analysis but in formulating future policy.

This difference in development, carrying with it difference in goals, may provide conflict in specific policy between the two Communist capitals. Prolongation of the Korean war in 1952-53 may have served Soviet ends of increasing strains in the North Atlantic Treaty Organization and of weakening its available force in Europe. This would facilitate Soviet influence over its East European satellites and extend its influence, at least negatively, into West Europe. For China, however, internal security called for throwing back United Nations troops from the Yalu but not necessarily beyond the thirty-eighth parallel. Continuation of the war drained the Chinese economy, shaky at the start, and increased the danger of retaliation upon China proper by United States airpower. Not until the death of Stalin in March 1953 did Peking's negotiators at Panmunjom agree to armistice terms essentially similar to those they had rejected months previously. Although not conclusive, the timing of this move lends credibility to our analysis.

This example suggests a spatial difference in goals in addition to one derived from time differences of development. For the Soviet Union, Europe remains its primary sphere of interest and concern, offensively and defensively. For China, the Asian periphery extending from Tokyo to Kabul demands prior attention. Both countries share interests as well as concern with Japan, but basically they are oriented in opposite directions. This increases the possibility of conflict of goals between Peking and Moscow, at least with respect to specific points of policy. It also suggests differences in the degree of conflict anticipated with United States interests aligned against those of Peking as compared with those of Moscow.

B. Means

Any construct of probable means to be adopted must take into consideration the availability of means as well as the likelihood of their being adopted. The latter consideration assumes rationality of decision-making insofar as a decision is logically consistent with the ideology of the elite. For reasons stated earlier, we cannot assume such rationality to be uniformly present in Chinese foreign policy. Compulsive belligerency, for instance, during the early years of the People's Republic of China was irrational even from the point of view of Peking's perceived interests, much more so in terms of objective appraisal of its assets and liabilities. However, such behavior seems less evident with the elite's maturing responsibility and its growing experience with international affairs. Therefore the likelihood of rash or essentially irrational action lessens with time, although it by no means disappears entirely.

The means least likely to be employed by Peking in pursuit of goals in Asia are those of open military force. In the northeast, only South Korea and Japan might be targets of aggression from China. The former is definitely under United States protection; the latter is less vulnerable given the relative air and sea weakness of Chinese military forces. In South Asia, transportation media are few and primitive. The only rail lines venture from China into North Viet Nam. Air bases are scattered and isolated from supply sources. Terrain along the frontier is predominantly thick jungle or rugged mountains. Although this favors border incursions, it argues against mass invasion directed at the distant capitals of Delhi, Rangoon, Bangkok, or Phnom Penh.

In addition, the base strength of China, presently located along the coast and northeastern sectors, is moving gradually toward the north and northwest. This is more secure from United States bases of attack and closer to the Soviet hinterland, safeguarded by alliance. It leaves China's south and southwestern areas extremely deficient in the manpower and economic strength necessary for supporting large-scale military action.

Finally, open use of force would risk the loss of influence and prestige that might otherwise be won through less costly alternative political and economic means. It might drive presently uncommitted countries to the side of the United States. If Soviet precedent serves as example, such use of military force enters only as an exceptional means of strategy when all other alternatives are exhausted. The Russian attack upon Finland in 1939 provides this precedent, but the singularity of such an occurrence argues against assuming high probability of military means being used in support of policy.

More likely is the use of Chinese military assistance to local insurrections or civil wars that advance Peking's interests. Strengthening North Viet Nam, bolstering insurgent Pathet Laos forces, and aiding guerilla groups in Malaya served China well during 1950-1956. Increased emphasis on the so-called "Bandung Spirit," however, brought a diminution in this strategy, at least for several years. Resumption of conflict endangers the positive influence won by Peking in circles sensitive to armed insurrection, such as Nehru of India and U Nu of Burma.

The least expensive and the least dangerous means of advancing intermediate-range goals would appear to be those employing economic and political techniques. Dramatic announcements of economic assistance, as in the case of India's famine of 1954, or token teams of technical experts accompanied by loans or grants, as with Cambodia in 1957, reap rewards far out of proportion to their expense. Chinese experience is closer than that of Western countries to the experience of underdeveloped countries of Asia. The cultural gap is easier to bridge, given the absence of racial or religious barriers between China and her neighbors. Finally, accomplishments by Chinese Communists appear more striking in contrast with recent conditions in their country than does continued industrial expansion by the United States.

Political channels available for exporting influence are several. Much of Asia is opposed to private capital and foreign investment. Communist credo supports this prejudice. Key groups in India, Burma, Indonesia, and Japan support varying degrees of Marxist or socialist ideology and are responsive to Peking's planned economy. Chinese tolerance of Buddhism and Islam lessens the antipathy of Burmese and Indonesians, while Communist strictures against corruption, nepotism, and sloth provide a positive appeal throughout Asia.

Local agents for communicating Chinese messages may be found in various cultural groups organized ostensibly to promote Sino-Indian or Sino-Burmese friendship. They may be assisted by local Communist parties of some strength, as in Indonesia, or by overseas Chinese who are assimilated into the domestic society, as in Thailand. In any event, interpersonal contact at the popular level provides Peking with an advantage in political warfare generally denied Western capitals.

Furthermore, personal contact at the elite level has appeared to be an increasingly favored means of Chinese Communist diplomacy, as it has come to appreciate the advantages of exploiting shared attitudes of anticolonialism and pan-Asianism. It is no accident that of thirty states recognizing the People's Republic of China as of March 1, 1957, eleven belonged to the Soviet bloc, and another eleven belonged to the so-called Arab-Asian bloc. Only United States pressure continued to keep Japan from recognition, while Laos and Cambodia were expected to swell the list shortly. Although lacking enough votes for seating in United Nations organs, Peking could still claim admission to Asian councils on an equal basis.

Exploiting these contacts to the fullest, Chou En-lai secured a number of joint statements from Asian leaders, exchanging support for grievances against the West as with Goa in India or West Irian in Indonesia, for their support of Chinese claims to Taiwan and representation in the United Nations. In addition, interpersonal relations helped to reduce the negative picture of Chinese Communists acquired through action in the Korean war accompanied by mass executions at home. Suave and sophisticated in his manner, Chou En-lai has repeatedly visited Nehru in Delhi, lingered for days in little Cambodia, and sipped long cups of tea in Rangoon, seeking to assure his audience of China's exclusive concern with domestic problems and her common interest in friendly assistance to fellow Asians. This strategy pays dividends in countries where personal figures play an important role in policy, unimpeded by opposition parties of stature or by rival leaders in the bureaucracy. Furthermore, the political instability of a leader such as Sukarno may necessitate his seeking Chinese support in a marriage of convenience.

These various tactics serve the familiar united-front strategy employed by Communists throughout the world intermittently since the days of Lenin. They may act from above, joining forces at the elite level. Or they may act from below, infiltrating mass organizations to undermine present leadership. Either strategy is a temporary one designed to facilitate ultimate overthrow of the government.

In view of China's power compared with that confronting it, both from local sources and from the United States, this strategy maximizes Peking's assets while minimizing its liabilities. So long as societies in South and Southeast Asia continue to suffer from political and economic instability, and so long as the United States places primary emphasis upon military development within the area, we may expect increased economic and political action from the People's Republic of China.

Selected Bibliography

Boormann, H., A. Eckstein, P. E. Mosely, B. Schwartz, *Moscow-Peking Axis,* published for the Council on Foreign Relations by Harper & Bros., New York, 1957.

Levi, Werner, *Modern China's Foreign Policy* (Minneapolis: University of Minnesota Press, 1953).

North, Robert C., *Moscow and Chinese Communists* (Stanford: Stanford University Press, 1953).

Wei, Henry, *China and Soviet Russia* (Princeton, New Jersey: D. Van Nostrand Company, Inc., 1956).

In addition, the reader should consult the bibliographies published each August in *The Far Eastern Quarterly,* renamed *The Journal of Asian Studies* in 1957.

8 . . .

FOREIGN POLICY OF THE TURKISH REPUBLIC

. . . Dankwart A. Rustow[1]

I.   From Empire to Republic

"WE HAVE ON OUR hands a sick man, a very sick man," Czar Nicholas I is reported to have said in 1853 when discussing the fate of the Ottoman Empire with a Western ambassador. Today, by contrast, the Turkish Republic is widely hailed as a pivot of stability in a proverbially unstable Near East. At a time when two-thirds of mankind in Asia and Africa are agonizingly reappraising their relations with Europe and North America, Turkey stands out as the only non-European and non-Christian country to have been fully accepted into the diplomatic family of European nations. Turkey's present role in international affairs provides an impressive illustration of how a small country, poor in natural resources but strong in its unity of purpose, can, through circumspection and good fortune, survive amidst the intersecting pressures of great-power politics.

The collapse of the Ottoman Empire had been anticipated by its antagonists long before the first World War. A cumulative series of military defeats in the seventeenth and eighteenth centuries disrupted the once-dynamic administrative structure. Napoleon's invasion of Egypt in 1798, unlike the earlier defeats, could no longer be passed over as a temporary setback at the outer frontier. It furnished an un-

---

[1] The writer would like to express his gratitude to the Center of International Studies, Princeton University, for its support of research preliminary to the preparation of this chapter.

deniable demonstration of European military superiority (based on the discoveries of the Industrial Revolution) and of European social organization (based on the growing strength of nationalism). The attempt of the nineteenth-century sultans to introduce European reforms into their army and administration at first only added to the weakness and confusion. The reforms also constituted a growing drain on the Empire's finances, and by 1881 the sultan was forced to turn over the collection of most of his revenues to a European debt administration. Unable to ward off its powerful enemies, the Empire survived precariously by dint of the rivalries among them.

The one force that might have shaken the Empire out of its torpor was the rising class of Westernized officers of its reorganized army. Yet the program of the Young Turk officers who came to power after 1908—"Turkification, Islamization, Modernization"—amounted to a bland juxtaposition of opposite aims, each one in potential conflict with the traditional basis of the Ottoman Empire and with the multifarious aspirations of its polyglot subjects. In the end the Young Turks' ill-calculated gamble in entering the first World War on the German side cut short the agony of the dying Empire. The armistice of Mudros in 1918 detached most of the Empire's non-Turkish territories and placed Allied troops at strategic points throughout the remainder. The anti-Young Turk party, which took over in Istanbul, tried to win Allied favor by abject collaboration. Yet the peace terms, announced in May 1920, amounted to the complete dismemberment even of the Turkish-inhabited Anatolian parts of the Empire.

The delay of a year and a half between armistice and announcement of the peace terms provided the crucial breathing spell for the formation of a national resistance movement in Anatolia. It derived from numerous small-town patriotic societies rallying to the slogans of "Rejection of Annexation" and "Defense of Rights"; it received the support of the majority of the officers' corps and the remainders of the demobilized army; and Mustafa Kemal Atatürk, one of the few undefeated Turkish generals of the first World War, provided it with circumspect and energetic leadership. Kemal's program, known as the National Pact, called for full national sovereignty for the "Ottoman-Muslim" (*i.e.* Turkish and Kurdish) parts of the Empire, and for the abolition of all capitulations and economic servitudes; it is considered the cornerstone of Turkish foreign policy to this day.

The National Pact signified a defiant challenge to the victorious Allies; a slap at the collaborationist policy of the sultan in Istanbul; and a resolute break with the Ottoman Imperial tradition. Instead of a multinational Empire with pretentions to all-Islamic leadership,

Turkey was to be a much more nearly homogeneous nation-state. In a realistic limitation of its aspirations the nation was to find new strength. The sultan's ministers, in accepting the Allied peace terms, declared that "a weak existence is preferable to total annihilation." Kemal's language, by contrast, was clearly reminiscent of that of Patrick Henry a century and a half before:

> The basic goal was that the Turkish nation should survive in dignity and honor. This goal could only be achieved by the possession of complete independence. A nation deprived of its independence— however wealthy and prosperous it may be—is not entitled to be regarded in the eyes of civilized humanity as anything better than a slave.
>
> To accept the protection and suzerainty of a foreign state is tantamount to admitting one's lack of all human qualities, one's impotence and dejection. It is inconceivable that those who have not already sunk to this condition would willingly accept a foreign master.
>
> But in fact the Turk possesses honor, self-respect, and ability to a high degree. Rather than live in servitude it is better that such a nation should perish.
>
> Therefore: Independence or Death! This was to become the rallying cry of all those who desired true salvation for their nation.

The Kemalists, profiting from the many latent divisions among the victor powers, managed to take on their opponents one at a time. The Armenian nationalists, defeated by Turkish forces, sued for peace in December 1920. Three months later the Ankara government concluded a friendship treaty with Soviet Russia. To the south the French, fully occupied with establishing their rule over Syria, abandoned their military campaign in Anatolia and, in a separate treaty, recognized most of Kemal's territorial claims. When the Greek armies, in an ambitious attempt to resurrect a latter-day Byzantine Empire, penetrated deep into Western Turkey in 1921 and 1922, Kemal was able to mass all his forces to drive them back to the Aegean. The peace treaty of Lausanne of 1923 confirmed these victories of the battlefield. A mere five years after the end of the first World War, Turkey—by all appearances the weakest of the defeated powers—became the first and only one to obtain a negotiated peace settlement.

II.   Turkish Foreign Policy, 1923-1939

With their victory in the War of Independence thus secured and recognized, the Turkish leaders could proceed to consolidate their internal regime. One by one the Ankara Assembly and its executive committee had assumed the attributes of sovereignty; a provisional constitution had been adopted early in 1921. Following the armistice with Greece the Sultanate was abolished on 1 November 1922—significantly with retroactive effect as of the date of the Allied occupation of Istanbul. Three months after Lausanne Turkey was officially proclaimed a republic (29 October 1923), with Ankara its permanent capital, Kemal its first president, and Ismet Inönü its first prime minister. Somewhat earlier the Defense of Rights society had been transformed under Kemal's leadership into the more permanent People's Party. And as the wartime spontaneous unity of purpose gave way before the problems of reconstruction, political power in effect came to be concentrated in the hands of Kemal, the Victor (*Gazi*), the Savior of his nation.

Preservation and protection of Turkish national independence was the aim, whose active and imaginative pursuit had led Kemal and his adherents to found the Turkish Republic. Preservation and protection of the integrity of the Republic has remained the major aim of Turkish foreign policy since 1923. The goal has been pursued with a level-headedness and steadfastness, a sober acceptance of limitations and a shrewd assessment of opportunities, that are far from characteristic of all nations that have so recently asserted their sovereignty. No less remarkable, perhaps, was the single-mindedness with which Kemal and his followers worked to make over all of Turkish society in the image of that very Europe against which the fierce battle for independence had only just been fought. For nothing short of a cultural surrender was implied in the measures that followed in staccato rhythm upon the proclamation of the Republic: the Caliphate abolished; Muslim seminaries closed (1924); Dervish orders prohibited; the hat for the accustomed fez (1925); the Christian instead of the Muhammadan era; European legal codes replacing the Muslim holy law (1926); Roman letters instead of the Arabic script in which Turkish had been written for a millennium (1928). But to Kemal both the external struggle that led to the formation of the new state and the internal reforms that followed proceeded from a single assumption: "Our overriding aim," he declared in his monumental Six-Day Speech of 1927, is "to bestow upon the Turkish nation its rightful place in the civilized world."

The diplomacy of nationalist Turkey from the defeat in the first World War to the victory in the War of Independence forms a clear-cut, cogent pattern. The threat of national extinction was acute, the nationalist response unequivocal, and the denouement highly dramatic. No threat of equal magnitude has faced Turkey since then, and indeed no serious threat to her territory or of involvement in war reappeared until the time of the second World War. Turkish diplomacy in the interwar period thus cannot but seem slow-moving, tedious, and complex. Workmanlike consular agreements and treaties of commerce and navigation took the place of armistices. Instead of peace treaties we find friendship and nonaggression pacts. Yet it was during this period that Turkey, already respected for her valor and tenacity on the battlefield, established within the European and international community a solid reputation for reliability, for responsibility in her undertakings, and for devotion to peace—a reputation that was to prove a valuable asset for the future.

The post-Lausanne decade saw a gradual relaxation and normalization of relations both with Turkey's immediate neighbors and with the powers of Western Europe. Late in 1925 the Council of the League awarded the disputed Mosul area to Iraq, a ruling which Turkey reluctantly accepted the following year. The original agreement gave Turkey a 10 per cent share in the area's oil production; but she later settled this claim for a lump-sum payment of half a million pounds sterling. In 1933 Turkey worked out an agreement with the bondholders of the Ottoman debt concerning her share of the payments. A year earlier she had been admitted to the League of Nations—a visible token of her newly won respect among the "civilized world."

The details of the gigantic population-exchange scheme with Greece laid down at Lausanne gave rise to considerable temporary friction. Thus in 1925 the Greek government sharply protested the Turkish government's action in expelling the Greek Orthodox patriarch of Istanbul on the basis that he belonged to one of the exchangeable categories; and in 1929 it briefly looked as if Greece and Turkey were about to engage in a small-scale naval armaments race. Nevertheless, by the end of 1924 nearly a million nationals from either side of the border had been exchanged, and another million Greeks who had fled Anatolia with the retreating armies in 1922 were permanently resettled in Greece. Only the Greek minority in Istanbul (about 100,000 persons) and the Turks in the Greek portion of Thrace were allowed to remain. A final agreement of 1930 regulated the financial questions arising from the resettlement operation. Despite the disruptive effects of the population exchange on the economies of the areas of mixed population, there is no question that this act of plastic surgery greatly reduced the potential for future friction.

The Greek-Turkish *détente* made possible a general *rapprochement* among the Balkan powers, and Turkey took an extremely active part in the negotiations resulting in the Balkan Entente of 1934 among Greece, Rumania, Turkey, and Yugoslavia. The four nations by this treaty guaranteed one another's frontiers and undertook to consult with one another in the event of any threat to the peace in the Balkan area. Various schemes for cultural and economic cooperation were taken up to foster a greater spirit of unity and prepare a possible Balkan federation. Two of the Balkan countries remained outside of the Entente from the beginning—Albania, because she was increasingly being absorbed within the Italian orbit; and Bulgaria, because she was unwilling to accept her existing frontiers as final. Furthermore, in the words of an acute observer:

> . . . the Balkan Entente [was] a fragile combination of small states having a definite and limited objective, namely, to guarantee some of their frontiers against the possible aggression of certain small and weak states. The members . . . seem to have completely ignored the fact that they have other frontiers to guard against the aggression of great and predatory states.[2]

A second quadripartite regional agreement that Turkey joined had far more modest pretensions from the outset. In 1937, after two years of preliminary contacts, Turkey, Iraq, Iran, and Afghanistan signed a nonaggression pact at Sa'dabad. They undertook to refrain from interfering or using force in one another's internal affairs, and to "consult together in all international disputes affecting their common interests." They also cooperated in supporting the candidacy of pact members in elections for the League of Nations Council. There is no record of consultations concerning international disputes ever having been held under the Sa'dabad Pact. It never was denounced; with the advent of the second World War it was simply forgotten.

Security for Turkey, as well as for her small-power neighbors to the northwest and southeast, depended only to a negligible extent upon intraregional agreements, however sincere, well-intentioned, or ingenious. Turkey's highly strategic location put her in the extraordinary position of having for immediate neighbors the Soviet Union (in the Caucasus), France (through the Syrian mandate), Britain (in Cyprus, and also as mandatory over Iraq and after 1932 as senior partner in the British-Iraqi alliance), and Italy (on the Dodecanese). Germany, the fifth great power on the continent, was systematically extending her commercial and political influence toward southeastern Europe throughout the 'thirties. Within a few years the outbreak of the second World War all but eclipsed the smaller Balkan and Near Eastern countries and left Turkey face to face with the major belligerents.

---

[2] Theodore I. Geshkoff, *Balkan Union* (New York: Columbia University Press, 1940), p. 228.

During the War of Independence Turkey, in fighting against Greece and her Western protectors, had sought the aid and encouragement of the Soviet Union. Atatürk and other Turkish leaders had few illusions about the Soviets' ulterior motives. But by 1921 the Bolsheviks had given up their initial bid for world revolution in Europe and the Near East. For two decades Russia's forces were fully absorbed by her momentous internal problems—the New Economic Policy and the liquidation of the kulaks, the struggle for Lenin's succession and the Great Purge. Official diplomatic relations between Turkey and Russia thus remained cordial. Following the League's irritating award in the Mosul dispute in 1925 Turkey signed a friendship and neutrality treaty with the Soviets. Under a 1934 loan agreement the Russians furnished Turkey some $8 million of industrial equipment, free of interest and repayable in goods. In referring to this loan agreement in 1935 Premier Ismet Inönü stated: "The beautiful products of Soviet industry are rising in our new industrial life as tokens of eternal friendship. Our close and sincere friendship with the great Soviet Union is every day becoming more extensive and more intensive both in the political and in every other sphere." And as late as June 1937 he denied rumors of any cooling of relations, asserting that Turco-Soviet friendship "has recently come alive with new sincerity." Conversely, Maxim Litvinov, in a statement to the Soviet Central Executive Committee in December 1933, could hold up Soviet "relations with the great Turkish Republic as a model of relations with foreign states." [3] Yet this official cordiality did not prevent Turkey from asserting her independence in a variety of ways —including the arrest of sporadic Communist agitators and the decision to provide asylum for Trotsky who, following his flight from Russia in 1929, spent seven years in a resort island near Istanbul.

It was the growing threat of Fascist expansion—implicit in Mussolini's flamboyant talk about Italy's destiny in Africa and Asia, and manifest in his attack on Ethiopia (1935-36)—that brought Turkey closer to Britain and France and indirectly led to a growing coolness in Turco-Soviet relations. Turkey as early as 1933 had pressed for a revision of the Straits regime agreed upon at Lausanne. Following the Ethiopian War Britain and other maritime powers were inclined to consider this demand. A conference at Montreux, boycotted by Italy, adopted a revised Straits Convention on 20 July 1936. Turkey regained the right to fortify the Straits zone and assumed the super-

---

[3] Jane Degras, ed., *Soviet Documents of Foreign Policy* (London: Royal Institute of International Affairs, 1953), Vol. 3, p. 52.

visory functions hitherto entrusted to an international commission. The principle of free passage through the Straits was maintained; Turkey, however, was granted the right to bar passage to warships not only in time of war but also when she considered "herself to be threatened with imminent danger of war."

A potential dispute with France was resolved when Turkey obtained another significant revision of the postwar settlement. The French in 1936 had negotiated an agreement whereby they promised full independence to Syria. The Ankara government had secured as early as 1921 recognition for the special status within the Syrian mandate of the Turkish population of the border district of Alexandrette, and this arrangement had been confirmed at Lausanne. The League of Nations, to which Turkey appealed, proposed autonomy for the district. But France, which together with Britain just then was negotiating for a military alliance at Ankara, agreed in 1938 to joint Franco-Turkish administration pending general elections. The newly chosen Alexandrette assembly, with a bare pro-Turkish majority, promptly applied for incorporation into Turkey, which was consummated in July 1939.

Having just regained full sovereignty over the Black Sea Straits, Turkey now obtained in Alexandrette a third major natural harbor. The Alexandrette question has caused lasting resentment in Syria— both against France, which was held to have sacrificed Syrian interests to her own strategic advantage, and against Turkey, which has been charged with exacting an unrelated concession in return for her alliance with France. Yet from Turkey's point of view there was a perfect legal basis for her policy. She had entrusted the fate of the Alexandrette Turks to France, not to an independent Syria. Now that the French were about to relinquish their mandate the future of the district, the Turks insisted, was subject to renegotiation. In the eyes of Western observers Turkey's legal approach to the Straits and Alexandrette questions provided a marked and welcome contrast with Hitler's unilateral action in the Rhineland, in Austria, and in Czechoslovakia, and to Mussolini's aggression in Ethiopia and Albania.

III.   Turkey's Neutrality in the Second World War

Before concluding the proposed alliance with the Western powers, Turkey made a determined attempt to clarify her relations with Russia. The Russians took the occasion to propose a joint Russo-Turkish arrangement for the Straits which, in clear violation of the Montreux convention, would have closed the Black Sea to outside shipping. While Turkish Foreign Minister Şükrü Saracoğlu had been kept waiting in Moscow antechambers, Russia had announced her infamous agreement with Nazi Germany. The Turks were not mistaken in sensing in this massive totalitarian alignment an imminent threat to their security. In secret negotiations at Berlin a year later, Russia was to state as her price for supporting Hitler's New Order "the establishment of a base for land and naval forces of the U.S.S.R. within range of the Bosporus and the Dardanelles," as well as recognition of "the area south of Batum and Baku in the general direction of the Persian Gulf" as "the center of the aspirations of the Soviet Union." In October 1939 Turkey signed an alliance with Great Britain and France. The three partners undertook to come to one another's assistance if they were involved in war as a result of aggression in the Mediterranean or against Turkey, or as a result of the earlier Franco-British guarantees of the integrity of Greece and Rumania. Yet the Turks realistically insisted on the addition of a protocol exempting them from any action under the alliance that would involve them in armed conflict with the Soviets.

When the war in fact spread to the Mediterranean and the Balkans with Italy's attack on France and on Greece through Albania, neither the British-French-Turkish alliance of 1939 nor the Balkan pact of 1934 was brought into play. At the final Balkan conference in February 1940 Yugoslavia had opposed all attempts to strengthen Balkan solidarity; by autumn she concluded economic and political agreements with Germany that put her clearly in the Axis camp. On 21 June 1940 France surrendered to the Germans. Turkey, facing not only a potential threat from Germany and Italy but also the direct proximity of a hostile Russia, kept her forces fully mobilized and left little doubt of her readiness for self-defense. Yet short of direct aggression against her territory she was determined to stay out of the conflict, earlier treaty engagements notwithstanding. After Italy's entry into the war, Turkey made use of the reserve clause of the 1939 treaty to resist British-French pressure to break off relations with Rome or to close the Straits to Axis shipping. When Italy invaded Greece, Britain did not call for Turkish assistance for fear that any diversion of Turkish troops from Thrace would lay her open to Axis attack.

If Turkey in her mounting predicament clung to her neutrality in disregard of her twofold obligation toward Greece, she was equally firm in resisting German pressure to cooperate with the Axis camp. In April 1941 anti-British rebels had taken over the government of Iraq—at a time when German troops were invading Yugoslavia and Greece, when Rommel was menacing Egypt, and when Vichy French forces were still in control of Syria. Prompt German military aid to the Iraqi rebels might well have brought total control of the Near East within their reach. The Germans, who had just taken over the entire Danubian area (Hungary, Rumania, Bulgaria) by military threats and promises of territorial aggrandizement, would evidently have liked to apply the same combination to Turkey. But Turkey's difficult terrain, her defensive preparedness, and above all her marked lack of interest in any petty schemes of annexation proved utterly baffling. Italy's Foreign Minister Ciano has summarized a conversation with Hitler during this period as follows:

> The possibility of attempting the operation by force can be ruled out. Independently of Turkish resistance, which would be considerable, the distances would make any military operation uncertain and dangerous. Diplomatically, too, it seems difficult to draw Turkey into the orbit of the Axis, at least within a short space of time. Difficult . . . because it is impossible to see what political advantage could be offered to Turkey in exchange. The Fuehrer knows that Turkey would not even like the promise of Syria, and in any case that would raise an infinite series of complications in the Arab world.[4]

At the minimum the Germans were eager to secure Turkish permission for sending troops and materiel to Iraq across the Turkish railways. The Turks, however, systematically stalled negotiations until, by early June, British control had been restored in Iraq. After weeks of protracted negotiations the German Ambassador had to be content with a rather meaningless friendship treaty (signed in June 1941), whose preamble expressly reserved "the already existing engagements of each party"—including, that is, Turkey's earlier alliance with Britain and France.

In evaluating Turkey's neutralist course during this phase of the war, the wartime British Ambassador to Ankara has written:

> To plunge . . . into the melee at the moment when one of their Allies [France] was down and out and the other [Britain] in deadly danger might have earned for Turkey imperishable memories of heroic self-sacrifice, but it would have done little good. Indeed, by becoming a liability to their already strained ally [Britain] they might have done incalculable harm.[5]

Turkey probably at no time came closer to being forced into the war than in those tense spring days of 1941. Four days after the signature

---

[4] *Ciano's Diplomatic Papers* (London: Odhams Press, 1948), p. 435.
[5] Sir Hughe Knatchbull-Hugessen, *Diplomat in Peace and War* (London: J. Murray, 1949), p. 167.

of the Turco-German treaty Hitler launched his long-prepared offensive against Russia. It became clear that Nazi operations in the Balkans had been designed chiefly to secure the right flank of the Russian attack, rather than as the spearhead for any major offensive southeastward. After less than two years of an unholy alliance Turkey's most formidable potential enemies were absorbed in mutual combat; the most immediate danger was past.

The winter of 1942 brought the decisive turning point in the European war with Allied victories at el-Alamein and Stalingrad—both, incidentally, fought within less than 500 air miles of Turkey's borders. It now was the Allies' turn to prod Turkey into a more active participation in the war. Following conversations between President Inönü and Prime Minister Churchill in the southern Turkish town of Adana in January 1943 Britain agreed to supply the Turkish army with a year's reserve equipment and with fighter aircraft. But Churchill's pet strategic plan of this period—an attack through the "soft underbelly" of southeastern Europe—was running into American objections on strategic grounds and warnings from his own military mission that the Turkish army was ill-prepared to play its part in such operations. At one point the three Allied foreign ministers agreed to put pressure on Turkey to enter the war; but they were promptly reversed by their chiefs who assigned definite priority to the proposed second front in Western Europe. Churchill made a final attempt at persuasion in a second conference with Inönü. Yet the Turks, little encouraged by the recent failure of Allied landing attempts on the Dodecanese, appeared reluctant to run the full risks of belligerency for the sake of a secondary operation in which they would perform no essential strategic role. In the meantime they stepped up their requests for military equipment beyond what the Allies were prepared to furnish.

By 1944 Allied pressure for Turkish cooperation became more insistent and the earlier risks in a more active attitude had largely disappeared. Two months before the Normandy landings, Turkey discontinued all shipments of strategic materials to Germany in response to firm Allied demands. In June sharp British protests against the passage of a number of disguised Axis naval craft through the Straits resulted in the dismissal of the Turkish foreign minister. On 2 August 1944, Turkey broke off diplomatic relations with the Axis. On 23 February 1945—six days before the deadline set at Yalta for participation in the San Francisco Conference and ten weeks before V-E Day—Turkey at length declared war on Germany and Japan.

Turkish foreign policy during the second World War followed a course consistently aimed at saving the country from an invasion or belligerency that would jeopardize the hard-won achievements of the War of Independence and of the subsequent Kemalist revolution. This course put her in the anomalous position of having treaty and commercial relations with both sides; it also, admittedly, involved stretching the interpretation of some of her treaty commitments to the utmost limit. She remained stubbornly insensitive to any suggestion that she participate in military adventures either on the Axis side or together with the Allies. When the major danger of warlike involvement came from a possible German attack, her defensive capability to delay an invader provided an important deterrent. When the major danger came in the form of Allied pressure to join up, her lack of preparedness for a major offensive allowed her to procrastinate. The strains of six years' full mobilization and the interruption of her normal trade routes caused her considerable hardship, but she was spared the destructive effects of actual warfare.

IV.   Turkey's Foreign Policy Since 1945

The end of the second World War brought about a profound change in the balance of power in Eastern Europe and the Near East. Russian troops were on the Elbe, on the Adriatic, in the Balkans, and in Northern Iran. The Turkish Straits, coveted by Czars and Soviets alike, were within an easy 100 miles of Russian positions along the Bulgarian frontier. In fact Turkey's northeastern frontier (except for distant Afghanistan) remained the only point where Russian power had failed to expand beyond its prewar frontiers. It may well have been Turkey's obstinate and at times casuistical neutrality that spared her the fate of Rumania and Bulgaria or of Iran and Greece.

The Eastern Mediterranean, next to Europe and the Far East, was clearly a major objective of Soviet grand strategy in this immediate postwar period. At the Potsdam conference Russia tried to obtain a trusteeship over Libya, and in March 1946 her ambassador to Athens proposed the establishment of a Soviet refuelling station on the Dodecanese. The rapid Sovietization of the Danubian and Balkan countries in 1945-47 permitted the Red armies to give effective support to the Greek Communist guerillas. To the east, behind the screen of Russia's wartime occupation of Northern Iran, the Communists were setting up a puppet "People's Republic" of Azerbaijan, immediately on the Turkish border. Turkey was between the pincers of two thinly veiled Soviet military operations, but the frontal attack on Turkey herself was diplomatic. Even before the end of hostilities in

Europe Russia denounced her 1925 Treaty of Friendship and Neutrality with Turkey. By June 1945 Russia was naming her price for continued friendship: Soviet bases on the Turkish Straits and cession of the Eastern Turkish border districts of Kars and Ardahan. The territorial claim was elaborated in the Soviet press throughout the following year; and a Soviet proposal for revision of the Montreux convention restated the demand for what it euphemistically termed "joint defense of the Straits."

Turkey confronted the Russian demands at a time when she was in an exposed position not only geographically but also diplomatically. Public opinion in the Western countries was beginning to reexamine the overconfident wartime assumption that the German and Japanese defeat would ensure a more-or-less automatic reign of peace under United Nations auspices. Britain was continuing her military training and supply program in Turkey, which had also become eligible for American Lend-Lease shipments in February 1945. Yet Western diplomacy at the highest levels was still largely dominated by the ideal of "Big Three Unity." In view of her tardiness in joining the Allied war effort, Turkey had no reason to take for granted that Britain and America would give her full protection in the conflict that was shaping up with the third major ally.

Despite these factors of uncertainty, the Turkish response to Russia's expansionist designs was prompt and unequivocal; and increasingly Turkey's position received firm support in the West, where the true dimensions of Russia's postwar ambition came to be clearly appreciated. In the fall 1945 session of the Grand National Assembly President Inönü exclaimed amid prolonged applause: "We are saying it openly: We are under no obligation to give up Turkish soil or Turkish rights to anyone. We shall live with honor and die with honor." And the speaker of the Assembly coupled his plea for renewed Turco-Soviet friendship with a staunch warning: "Kars is the key to the gate of the Mediterranean, the only barrier to a big inundation. . . . If the Russians insist on their demand we shall fight to the last Turk." In February 1946 Foreign Secretary Bevin told the House of Commons that Britain would not allow Turkey to become a Russian satellite. Early in April the U.S. battleship *Missouri*, on which a few months earlier the surrender of Japan had been signed, paid a visit to Istanbul.[6] Meanwhile the Western powers were vigorously sup-

---

[6] The ostensible purpose of the visit was the return to Turkey of the body of her Ambassador to Washington who had died a year and a half earlier; but since a lesser vessel would have sufficed for this ceremonial purpose, the visit clearly had broader political implications.

porting Iran's complaint before the United Nations Security Council against the illegal continuation of Soviet occupation in Northern Iran. Responding to this firm pressure, the Soviets withdrew in early May; and by the end of the year the Teheran government had reestablished its authority in Azerbaijan. President Truman's proposal of military aid to Greece and Turkey, the so-called Truman Doctrine enunciated in 1947, was the logical culmination of this course. In thwarting Russia's immediate designs in the Eastern Mediterranean and the Near East, the new American policy of containment of aggression had borne its first important fruits. In 1948 Turkey was invited to participate in the European Recovery Program.

When the democracies of North America and Western Europe in the winter of 1948 were formulating arrangements for an Atlantic Alliance, the original plan was to supplement this structure at some later stage with a separate collective security treaty in the Eastern Mediterranean. But negotiations lagged, and a joint proposal for a Middle East Command, submitted to Egypt by the United States, Britain, France, and Turkey in October 1951, ran head-on into the resistance of Egypt, which had already resolved upon the unilateral abrogation of her 1936 alliance with Britain and which professed to see in the new proposal merely a back-handed scheme for perpetuating British control over the Suez Canal Zone. In the meantime Turkey, in June 1950, had been among the very first countries to respond to the United Nations' request for troops to Korea, and the Turkish brigade that joined the United Nations forces in the field received wide acclaim for its heroic conduct at the front. To the domestic critics who questioned whether Turkey was not recklessly exposing herself to Russia's wrath without adequate security guarantees from the West, Foreign Minister Fuad Köprülü replied with a classic statement of the case for collective security: "If I do not give help today how can I dare ask the United Nations for help when I am in need of it tomorrow?" Despite repeated Turkish pleas for admission to NATO, some of the European allies, particularly Denmark and Norway, proved reluctant to extend their commitments to the southern borders of Russia; and, for the time being, Greece and Turkey had to be content with associate status within the Atlantic organization. In the fall of 1951, however, the Scandinavian countries reconsidered their position, and after completion of the remaining formalities Greece and Turkey became full members of the North Atlantic Treaty Organization in February 1952.

Turkey has played an important role in the defense planning of the Western community. By virtue of her location she forms an essential barrier to Russian overland expansion in the direction of the Suez Canal or of the oil-rich Persian Gulf region. Although the land approach from Bulgaria is level, the Eastern Turkish mountains—linked by the Taurus chain in southern Turkey to the Mediterranean and by the Zagros chain in Iraq and Iran to the Persian Gulf—form a set of excellent natural defenses. At the same time Turkey's location is ideal for an effective counteroffensive. The new airfield at Adana is closer to the heart of Russian industrial strength in the Caucasus, the Donets region, and southern Siberia than any other NATO base. Turkey's land army is the largest within NATO. Although her twenty divisions —based on a two-year compulsory training period—have gradually been reduced in size from about 500,000 to about 350,000 men, they are being increasingly equipped and trained with modern mechanized weapons. To support this military build-up, the United States from 1947 to 1956 allocated in the neighborhood of a billion dollars of military aid to Turkey.[7]

Of almost equal importance has been Turkey's diplomatic role in helping to extend the Western defense system both into the Balkans and into the Near Eastern region—especially after the debacle of the 1951 Middle East Command scheme seemed to demonstrate that "no such system can be imposed from without." [8] Unlike the Balkan Entente and the Sa'dabad Pact of the 1930's which were erected on an isolated and hence highly unrealistic defensive basis, the corresponding regional security treaties of the 1950's have, through Turkey's NATO membership, a firm tie with a world-wide defense system. Nonetheless, developments of recent years have vividly demonstrated the difficulties of purely military arrangements in a region such as the Balkans and the Near East which have traditionally been riddled with internal political disputes and animosities.

Three years after his dramatic break with the Kremlin in 1948 President Tito of Yugoslavia indicated his desire for closer contact with the West by proposing a Balkan alliance of Greece, Turkey, and Yugoslavia. After prolonged preliminary contacts, a friendship treaty was signed in February 1953 and elaborated into an alliance in August 1954. Within a year, however, the foundations of the new pact were severely shaken by Greek-Turkish friction over Cyprus and

---

[7] The frugal habits of the Turkish foot soldier seem to have made him something of a favorite with economy-minded U.S. Congressmen. Summing up his testimony before a House Committee considering the Mutual Security Program for 1952, Major General William H. Arnold, chief of the American military mission to Turkey, said: "I know dollar for dollar you are getting more in Turkey than you are any place else in the world."

[8] In the words of John Foster Dulles' radio address of 1 June 1953.

by growing signs of a temporary *rapprochement* between Yugoslavia and Russia. The Baghdad Pact of mutual assistance (concluded on 24 February 1955 between Turkey and Iraq and joined before the end of the year by Great Britain, Pakistan, and Iran), on the other hand, has shown signs of continuing vigor. Its various committees—concerned with such problems as collective security, economic policy, and measures against subversion—have met regularly, and the United States, although not formally a member of the treaty organization, has fully participated in these committee meetings. At the two London conferences on the Suez Canal crisis of the summer of 1956, Turkey and other Baghdad Pact members successfully mediated between the European and Asian positions and suggested a crucial amendment which became the basis of the final 18-nation proposal. Following the Israeli-British-French attack on Egypt late in 1956, the four Near Eastern members continued their meetings, temporarily without British participation, and plans for closer military and economic cooperation were developed. The United States, although still unwilling to join as a member, has in effect undertaken to guarantee the security of the Baghdad Treaty nations.

Yet any hopes that the Baghdad Pact would serve as the nucleus for a wider defense scheme in the Near East were frustrated by the hostile attitude of the Egyptian government under Colonel Gamal Abdul Nasser. In 1954 Nasser had agreed to reactivation of the former British base at Suez in case of attack not only on one of the Arab states but also on Turkey. But following the signing of the Baghdad pact Nasser undertook to establish a rival joint military command with Syria, Saudi Arabia, Jordan, and Yemen. His subsequent purchase of large quantities of Russian arms and his increasingly intransigent attitude in the Palestine and Suez questions raised grave doubts whether, taken in isolation, the Baghdad Pact has resulted in a net gain in Western defensive strength in the Near East. Yet the problem of Near Eastern defense is primarily a question for the countries of that area, and next to that for the diplomatic skill of the powers of the free world in preparing a settlement of some of the thorny issues that have so far prevented any true regional consolidation. Happily for Turkey, her own ties with the Western defense system are secured through her membership in NATO, and thus unaffected by the adversities and intricacies of the West's Near Eastern diplomacy.

V.   The Survival of a Small State

Several underlying factors emerge from an examination of Turkish foreign policy in its historical context. First, Turkey is a comparatively small country with varied but limited resources. Her security therefore has depended on a combination of external circumstance and her own policy choices. Second, her policy has been based on nationalism—a nationalism as proud and assertive as any but more realistic in its purposes and more consistent in its method than young national movements elsewhere. Third, Turkish policy has been formulated and carried out by a governing elite with long experience and tradition behind it. Fourth, by a continuous process—gradual at first and more rapid of late—an ever-wider public has been admitted to the public arena and thus has come to be in a position to influence the choices of the policy-makers.

The application of the principle of nationality to Eastern Europe and the Near East led to a vast multiplication of sovereignties. The Serbian and Greek revolts early in the nineteenth century were the first step in this process; the peace settlements of 1918-20 were its culmination. The multinational Habsburg, Czarist, and Ottoman Empires left in their wake a score of new states from Finland and the Baltic countries in the north to the Arab Near East in the south. The fate that overtook most of these countries in the next three decades is a vivid demonstration of the perils of smallness in a world of continuing great-power conflict—and conversely a real measure of Turkey's accomplishment in the pursuit of her foreign policy. The Arabs shook off Ottoman rule as a result of the British campaigns of the first World War—only to see their hopes of unified or federated independence shattered against the rude reality of enforced partition into British and French mandates. The Balkan, East-Central European, and Baltic states in the 1940's fell prey in turn to Fascist, Nazi, and Soviet expansionism, and by the end of the decade most of them had been incorporated into the Soviet Union or its satellite Empire. Turkey alone among the post-World War I successor states survived this entire troubled mid-twentieth-century period without involvement in war, loss of independence, or diminution of her territory.

At several important points good fortune clearly played a decisive role in Turkey's survival. If Russia had not collapsed in 1917, twenty months before the Ottoman Empire, and thus relieved the military pressure on the retreating armies; if Allied statesmen in 1919 and 1920 had been alive to the true import and dimensions of the Kemalist movement and had moved against it with concerted effort; if Hitler in the spring of 1941, instead of embarking on his reckless Russian campaign, had grasped his advantage in the Near East, which seemed so close to his reach—these are some of the big if's that to Turkey might well have made the difference between independence and extinction.

But more was involved than good fortune alone. Turkey, through geographic circumstance, faces far more than the ordinary risk of attack. She is located near the intersection of land, sea, and air routes between Europe, Asia, and Africa. The air distance from Turkey to the Suez Canal or to the Baku oil fields is a mere 300 miles; the petroleum deposits of the Persian Gulf and the industries of the Donets and the southern Urals are well within a 1,000-mile radius. The Turkish Straits provide exclusive maritime access to the Black Sea ports of Russia, Rumania, and Bulgaria; they are the only natural international waterway located wholly within the sovereign confines of a single state. From the eighteenth century to the present Turkey and the Near East have played a major role in the diplomacy and strategic thinking of nearly every major world power—France under Napoléon and Clémenceau; Britain under Canning, Palmerston, Disraeli, and Churchill; Germany under the Kaisers and under Hitler; Russia under the Czars and under Lenin, Stalin, and Khrushchev; and the United States under Wilson, Truman, and Eisenhower. Of the three major imperialist threats in Eastern Europe and the Near East—the Anglo-French, the German, and the Russian—most of the World-War-I successor states have faced only two; Turkey alone faced each of the three in turn. Despite all this, Republican Turkey was able to turn the competitive power constellation in her favor, contributing to a balance of power in which she was a sufficient makeweight (by virtue of her control of the Straits and strategic land routes, and of strategic minerals such as chromium; and because of her own armed force) to adjust the scales in her favor at crucial points. Perhaps the contrasting fates of Turkey and Iran in the second World War provide a perfect illustration of the interplay of luck and of policy in Turkey's survival: When Britain and Russia in 1941 were determined to open a Near Eastern supply connection between them, Iran was the logical choice because German naval superiority disrupted communications in the Mediterranean. Yet Turkish armed force was sufficient that no two powers would have thought of unceremoniously occupying her as Iran was occupied in 1941.

VI.   Nationalism and Foreign Policy

Turkish nationalism originated only a little more than a half-century ago and found its first clear crystallization as recently as the postwar resistance movement of 1918-22. The Ottoman Empire was a dynastic and multinational structure. In view of its bitter experience with the Balkan separatist movements of the nineteenth century and with the imperial ambitions of nationalist Europe it tended to consider patriotism and nationalism as highly dangerous or even subversive emotions. The members of its administrative and military ruling class, though known as Turks to Europeans, were proud to call themselves Ottomans. The word "Turk" was reserved as a term of condescension for the illiterate peasantry of Anatolia. But the very success of the Balkan nationalisms, together with the continuing military defeats at the hands of Europe, prompted a gradual and painful conversion from an Ottoman to a Turkish consciousness. The vanguard in this change were the adherents of the constitutionalist movement of the turn of the century whom we know as Young Turks, but who, significantly, called themselves New Ottomans. Its contradictory allegiance to Ottomanism, Turkism, Islamism, and Westernism doomed this Young Turk movement to failure as much as did its reckless foreign policy. Yet by a fortunate dialectic the territorial losses of the Balkan wars (1912-13) and of the first World War for the first time made the Turkish-speaking population a majority within what remained of the Empire. Only at this point did its conversion into a Turkish nation-state, stripped of all imperial pretensions, become a tolerable—indeed a compelling—alternative.

In its tenacious and stubborn struggle against Western imperialism Turkish nationalism after the first World War might well have become the destructive, quarrelsome, and arrogant passion that we tend to associate with nationalism in the Balkans and in the Near East. The Turks, however, had a number of notable advantages over their former subjects, and thus they were able very largely to avoid any fixation on the negative phase of nationalism. After a dramatic and intense struggle they quickly attained independence within the limits they themselves had laid down in the National Pact. The new Turkish Republic was spared the Macedonian problem of checkered ethnic settlement. It also has been spared the type of corrosive conflict that has pervaded Arab nationalism in recent years: the conflict between allegiance to small, often artificially delimited states and a wider Pan-Arab loyalty. Above all, the impressive victory over Europe in the War of Independence gave Turkish nationalism a psychological sense of security which greatly facilitated Atatürk's policy of rapid Westernization; and that policy in turn injected a strong cultural internationalism which could not help but produce a moderating effect on political nationalism.

Turkey in the 1920's emerged as a nation-state, yet its boundaries did not coincide precisely with the limits of Turkish nationality. The National Pact in its broad reference to an "Ottoman-Muslim" majority included both Turks and Kurds, and in the 1920's and 1930's the Kurdish mountaineers, following their religious and tribal leaders in open rebellion against the secular government, posed a serious challenge to the political unity of the country. Since then the Kurds—only 6 per cent of the total population according to the latest official figures —have increasingly been absorbed into the Turkish majority as higher standards of living and education have spread to the Eastern Anatolian mountains. Other minority groups (chiefly Arabs in the South, and Greeks, Armenians, and Jews in Istanbul and other cities) constitute only about 3 per cent of the total, and except for intermittent friction with Greece over the treatment of Greek-speaking Turkish citizens, their presence has had little bearing on foreign policy.

Turkey's post-Lausanne policy firmly rejected the pursuit of any irredentist claims. The Alexandrette case was only an apparent exception; for the Turkish case rested on a special agreement with France which Turkey insisted on renegotiating at a time when France was ready to relinquish her Syrian mandate. Recent statements of Turkish policy on Cyprus have followed an analogous line of reasoning. Turkey has indicated her willingness to entrust the 100,000 Turkish Cypriotes to continued British, but not to Greek, rule, and hence has insisted on partition as the only acceptable alternative to the *status quo*. But here the Turkish argument has had no comparable legal basis, since the cession of Cyprus to Britain in 1923 (superseding the long-term lease of 1878) had been unconditional.

The more than twenty million Turkic peoples of the Soviet Union, speaking a variety of dialects closely or remotely related to Anatolian Turkish, constitute a far larger potential irredenta than the scatterings of ethnic Turks beyond Turkey's Near Eastern and Balkan borders. From the late nineteenth century a small but vocal group of Turkish nationalists, known as Panturkists or Panturanians, have advocated the political union of all these populations from the Bosporus to the Altai. The collapse of Czarist Russia in 1917 temporarily raised great hopes among the more venturesome Panturanians, and in 1922 Enver Pasha, wartime Young Turk dictator of the Ottoman Empire, lost his life in the pursuit of some such dream. Yet the Republic under Kemal and his successors, having resolutely turned its back on one lost empire, has shown no inclination to scatter its energies in the quixotic quest for a new one. If the Soviet Empire should ever crumble in external defeat or internal revolt Turkey might have to choose anew whether she is to go on building on Ottoman and Kemalist foundations in Anatolia or whether she is to follow Enver's example in a new Turanian adventure. For the present, Panturanism has its home only within a small and insignificant group at the fringe of Turkish politics.

The rediscovery of Turkey's Turanian cultural heritage has been an important ingredient in the upsurge of Turkish nationalism since the late nineteenth century; yet the country's political orientation has been westward to Europe rather than eastward to Central Asia. The aim of the Republic, in Kemal's words, has been to accord to the Turkish nation its rightful place wtihin the civilized world. And "civilized world" in modern Turkey has always meant Europe (as well as, more recently, North America). Turkish membership in such international organizations as the North Atlantic Treaty Organization, the Organization for European Economic Cooperation, and the Council of Europe has therefore been a point of deep pride with Turks. Nothing perhaps more sharply illustrates this Western orientation than the fact that Turkey took a leading role in negotiations leading up to the Baghdad Pact of 1955—but only after such a "Northern Tier" defense arrangement had been suggested by the American Secretary of State as an urgent desideratum. In contrast to the American journalistic habit of referring to Turkey, Iran, Iraq, and Pakistan as the "Muslim" members of the Baghdad Pact, Turkish commentators will protest against this term and insist that their policy is motivated by secularist considerations of enlightened national interest—not by religion.

VII.   The Formulation of Foreign Policy

Perhaps the most important asset in the foreign conduct of Turkey has been the presence of dedicated political leaders who were able to continue a tradition of responsible service dating back to the Ottoman Empire. Most other successor states have had to build up their administrative staffs from minute beginnings. Although the Turkish Republic did not find its administrative cadres ready-made, it could draw on a manpower pool that had been serving an Empire three or four times its size. Once the Turkish ruling class found itself relieved of the incubus of the decaying Empire it concentrated with renewed vigor on the far more manageable task of building up a small but viable Turkish state. The most important single link between the Ottoman leadership and that of the Republic was the army officers corps—not only the most Westernized service in Ottoman society, but also one of the few that was open to merit recruitment. In the initial period of rivalry between the Istanbul and Ankara governments the

civil servants often leaned toward the Sultan, while the military resolutely espoused the nationalist cause. Thus in the National Assembly
of 1920-23 the officers corps supplied roughly one-seventh of the membership, and held fully one-third of the cabinet posts. Yet once the
Republic was established, the military—and foremost Mustafa Kemal—
showed their foresight by effecting a firm understanding, as early as
1924, that active military service was incompatible with service in
the legislature or cabinet. During the remainder of the one-party
period political posts were increasingly held by career civil servants;
and Turkey has been spared the nefarious interference of the army
in politics that has troubled Near Eastern countries such as Iraq,
Syria, and Egypt.

The early diplomacy of the provisional nationalist government quite
naturally relied on a hastily improvised organization.[9] The first foreign
emissaries of the nationalists were a "Commission of Technical and
Scientific Investigation" dispatched by the National Assembly in August 1920 to report on recent events in Russia; and as late as the
time of the Lausanne Conference the Assembly in frequent secret sessions kept a firm and almost daily check on negotiations. But under
the long tenure of Tevfik Rüştü Aras in the Foreign Office (1925-
1938) the Republic built up an adequate and effective professional
foreign service. In the early years ambassadorships frequently went to
generals only recently retired from the front, and at later times ex-
cabinet members often took on the more important assignments such
as Paris, London, or Moscow. But even for these top diplomatic levels
there has been a gradual trend toward career foreign service.

The realistic attitude that has been so characteristic of Turkish
Republican foreign policy can probably be attributed to the rare combination of an imperial political tradition and its conversion to more
modest nation-state proportions. Turkish foreign policy-makers have
based their decisions on frank calculations of enlightened self-interest
—and they have generally assumed that other nations will follow
the same principle. Eagerly though the early nationalist leaders
received the Wilsonian doctrine of self-determination they knew that
they would have to fight for their independence; they did not expect
it as a gift from their victorious enemies. Thirty-five years later Turkish
statesmen were singularly unimpressed by such tactical Soviet slogans
as "peaceful co-existence" or the "Spirit of Geneva." When the Malen-

---

[9] For a vivid account by Turkey's first woman college graduate of the time
when she handled all diplomatic correspondence of the Ankara government on a
single decrepit typewriter see Halide Edib, *The Turkish Ordeal* (New York:
Century, 1928), pp. 146 ff.

kov government in 1953 formally renounced the earlier Stalinist territorial claims on Turkey the Turks were inclined to attribute this not
to any Soviet change of heart but rather to their own firm resistance
and to their strengthening ties with the Western defense system.

But considerations of statecraft not only have dominated foreign
policy itself; they have played an important role in domestic affairs
as well. The primacy of external over internal policy can be strikingly
illustrated from both the early and the more recent history of the
Turkish Republic—and nothing perhaps contrasts more sharply with
the situation among Turkey's Arab neighbors where internal upheavals
have time and again altered the course of foreign policy.

Throughout the War of Independence, Mustafa Kemal insisted that
all discussion of demands for internal reform must await full independence. It is symbolic of this attitude that the nationalist movement adopted its foreign policy plank—the National Pact—fully a year
and a half before it got around to drafting even a provisional constitution. At other times foreign considerations affected both the government's attitude toward various ideological movements and the timing
of major domestic policies. Unwilling to take a public stand against
the local sympathizers of his Russian allies, Kemal tried to undercut
their popular agitation in Anatolia by having some of his close associates form a so-called Turkish Communist Party (October 1920)—
which was given a legal monopoly of "agitation on behalf of Bolshevist
or Communist principles." In February 1921 Kemal, later to be known
as the archsecularizer, sponsored a Pan-Islamic Congress at Sivas in
a determined bid for Muslim support in the Near East and India.
The Sultanate was abolished three weeks after the armistice with
Greece (11 October–1 November 1922), partly to make it clear to the
Western powers that no separate representation from Istanbul and
Ankara would be tolerated at the forthcoming peace conference. And
the Republic itself was not proclaimed until after the Lausanne Peace
Treaty.

Similar examples may be cited from a later period. In 1944, when
wartime diplomatic relations with the Soviet Union had reached a low
point, the government tried to mollify Moscow by ostentatiously staging a political trial of various Pan-Turkist literateurs. A year and a
half later, when relations with the Soviets were clearly past repair,
a giant student demonstration, begun with the apparent blessings of
the authorities, resulted in the destruction of three left-wing newspapers whose publishers were widely suspected of being in the Soviets'
pay. Similarly the anti-Greek riots of September 1955 appear to have
started as a peaceful demonstration encouraged by the government

so as to strengthen its hand in negotiations with Britain and Greece on the Cyprus issue. The underlying assumption that the timing of domestic policy should be determined by foreign affairs is clearly revealed in a document that became a landmark in Turkey's transition from a one- to a two-party system—a proposal for democratic reforms submitted by the future founders of the Democratic Party on 7 June 1945: "In these days," the document states:

> . . . when the movements of democracy and liberty have won a complete victory in the entire world and when the principle of respect for democratic liberties is about to be internationally guaranteed, there can be no doubt that the entire nation, from the President of the Republic to the last citizen, is animated by the same democratic ideals.

The clearest and most far-reaching instance of the impingement of foreign on domestic affairs was, of course, provided by the economic policy of "etatism" (development of industry under state auspices) adopted by the Republic in the 1930's and '40's. The etatist preference for development of heavy industry over agriculture and consumer-goods industries was motivated to a considerable extent by the anticipated needs of military procurement and also by a vague desire for international prestige. Even in determining the location of some of the new plants, military considerations (such as remoteness from the coast and possible naval bombardment) seem to have competed with purely economic calculations of access to raw materials and markets. In the words of former President Ismet Inönü, "The policy of economic etatism, above all, by being a means of defense, appears to be a necessity of itself." [10]

VIII.   Foreign Policy and Democratization

Turkish political history over the last hundred years offers a spectacle of ever-wider participation by the population in the political process. The sultans of the early nineteenth century undertook their far-reaching attempts at reform in the face of the almost complete lethargy or opposition of their subjects. The Young Turk period brought the officers corps squarely into the political arena; it also stimulated the growth of an intensely political press and the proliferation of rather ephemeral party organizations. During the War of Independence the entire urban educated class became thoroughly politicized and firmly committed to the national cause. While the Republican

---

[10] Quoted in International Bank of Reconstruction and Development, *The Economy of Turkey* (Baltimore, 1951), p. 7.

People's Party after 1923 provided a valuable training ground for political talent, the party dictatorship of Kemal Atatürk and Ismet Inönü (1923-1945) set firm if broad limits to political discussion. Although political opposition parties were not formally outlawed, they were in practice tolerated only during two brief periods (1924-25 and 1930). There was no press censorship in peacetime, yet a press association, formed under semiofficial auspices and dominated by members of Kemal's Republican People's Party, provided general directives. In the interwar period the youthful, revolutionary assembly of the early 'twenties was gradually transformed into a more staid and bureaucratic body: The deputies' median age in two decades rose from 41 to 53, and the proportion of public servants among them from 61 to 73 per cent.

The constitutional framework of Turkish government has undergone little change since it was first laid down in the early days of the Republic. The constitution of 1924 provides for a strong, unicameral National Assembly elected for a four-year term by all adult men (and, since 1934, women). In addition to the customary legislative and budgetary functions, the Assembly is given the power to elect from its midst the President of the Republic; to confirm, by an initial confidence vote, the cabinet, which likewise is recruited from its midst; to conclude peace treaties and declare war; to confirm death sentences and to grant pardons, reprieves, or amnesties; and to dissolve itself, by simple majority vote, before the normal expiration of its term. The Assembly, moreover, on a motion introduced by one-third of its members and endorsed by a total of two-thirds, may amend any part of the fundamental law itself. Membership in the National Assembly ranks very near the top of the scale of social prestige, and even in the heyday of the Atatürk dictatorship the Assembly always preserved its role of discussion and criticism of detail. Roll-call votes were frequent, and occasional negative votes or demonstrative abstentions entailed no reprisals. Yet by the simple expedient of preventing the formation of opposition parties, the constitutionally prescribed *régime d'assemblée* was stood on its head and converted into a party dictatorship under the strong personal direction of Kemal Atatürk and, later, Ismet Inönü. Where the constitution envisaged the parliament as choosing a president, it was in fact the president who, in his capacity as party leader, determined the composition of the one-party Assembly. Despite the formality of parliamentary votes of confidence, it was in fact to the President-Dictator that ministers were accountable.

This *de facto* concentration of legislative and executive power in the presidential palace during the first two and a half decades of the Republic no doubt contributed to the stability of foreign policy. The chief architects of foreign policy during this period were Kemal Atatürk himself (President of the Republic 1923-38); Ismet Inönü (general and commander on the Greek front in 1921-22, chief negotiator at Lausanne, prime minister 1923-24 and 1925-37, President 1938-50); Tevfik Rüştü Aras (French-educated physician and foreign minister, 1925-38); and Şükrü Saracoğlu (teacher, Young Turk party official, cabinet minister in a variety of positions, including justice, 1933-38, and foreign affairs, 1938-42; and prime minister, 1942-46).

One of the characteristic features of the benevolent dictatorship of Atatürk and Inönü was that it rather consistently upheld wider political participation as a theoretical ideal to be carried into practice as soon as the level of popular education and other circumstances permitted. Following the end of the second World War President Inönü judged the time ripe. Opposition parties were allowed to form, the press was freed of previous restrictions, and after a hesitant start in the 1946 elections the adminstration pledged itself to even-handed dealing with government and opposition parties. The result was the spectacular landslide victory in 1950 of the newly formed Democratic Party, which had campaigned on a platform of economic liberalism, agricultural development, and partial restoration of religion.[11] In 1954 the Democratic administration of President Celâl Bayar and Prime Minister Adnan Menderes was confirmed in a second landslide election.

The experience since 1950 has shown that the tendency toward predominant control of a single party is more deeply rooted in Turkey's political system than the optimistic observers of her first free election in 1950 had assumed. The election system for the National Assembly itself, much like that for the presidential electoral college in the United States, tends to magnify the position of the majority (or even plurality) party and thus to impose a severe handicap on any opposition. In 1950 and 1954, for example, the Democratic Party won 85 and 92 per cent of the Assembly seats on the basis of only 55 and 58 per cent of the popular vote. More important perhaps, the Democratic Party, having been formed in response to Inönü's change of course in 1945 by individual dissidents from his Republican People's Party, lacked any prolonged experience in the fight for the right to democratic expression. Its leadership thus was ready to reimpose

---

[11] On the religious question cf. Dankwart A. Rustow, "Politics and Islam in Turkey, 1920-1955," in Islam and the West, ed. R. N. Frye (The Hague: Mouton, 1957), pp. 69-107.

many of the political restrictions whose temporary relaxation had originally brought the party into power. Shortly before the 1954 elections the government confiscated the assets of the Republican People's Party and closed the Nation Party (the second-largest opposition group). The government also began a systematic drive to curtail the freedom of the press and to rid the judiciary, civil service, and universities of elements alleged to be leaning toward the opposition. In fact, whereas the Atatürk-İnönü regime freely tended to admit its own shortcomings by democratic standards which it recognized in principle, its successor tended to see in the series of landslides that returned it to office sufficient proof of its democratic orthodoxy. Within the Democratic Party its leader Adnan Menderes soon established complete personal control, leaving the more vocal dissidents a choice of resignation or expulsion. Where the Republican People's Party had elevated its leaders to the presidency, Adnan Menderes to date has been content with the premiership.

The recent political changes, however, are not a simple reversion to the earlier one-party regime. In the National Assembly the bureaucratic element (down from 73 per cent in 1943 to 39 per cent in 1950) has made room for sizeable contingents of businessmen, lawyers, and other members of the professions. While the courts today impose more fines and jail sentences on journalists than they did in the 'thirties, the press in fact expresses a far wider range of opinion than ever before. In a series of competitive elections, moreover, the country's overwhelming peasant majority—although as yet supplying few parliamentarians or party officials—has emerged as a decisive factor in all political calculations. Although the government may ride roughshod over the urban critics, issues dear to the peasantry, such as religious restoration, development of rural roads and water resources, the level of wheat-support prices, and the demand for a moratorium on agricultural debts are beginning to overshadow the domestic political scene. For the present the peasant electorate seems to be the force most likely to impose any effective check on the autocratic leanings of its elected representatives.

The sharper tone of public debate in the press and on the campaign platform has entailed a more critical examination of the details of the government's foreign policy. Following Turkey's decision to support the United Nations' military action in Korea there was a major foreign policy debate in the National Assembly. And the government's more active policy on the Cyprus question since 1955 is to some extent due to the prolonged nationalist campaign of the newspaper *Hürriyet* (which boasts one of the widest national circulations) and to the agitation of the Cyprus Is Turkish Association. Yet the principle that politics stops at the water's edge has been faithfully and instinctively observed. Thus the debate on Korea dealt not with the substance of the decision; instead the criticism of the Republican and independent opposition was aimed (much as was the parallel American criticism) at the fact that the government had sent troops to Korea by executive decision without specific parliamentary approval.

There are definite indications that the earlier habit of primacy of foreign over domestic policy is slowly giving way to a more bilateral relationship. The etatist planners of the 1930's deliberately slowed the pace of economic development so as to avoid dependence on foreign assistance or foreign private capital. By contrast, the present Democratic administration, committed to rapid development of industry and agriculture, has encouraged foreign investment and has consistently pleaded with its American allies for vastly increased amounts of economic aid to enable it to complete its ambitious development projects.

Despite these sweeping domestic changes there has been no sign of deviation from the traditional line of Turkish foreign policy: absolute dedication to peace except in case of attack; a determination to defend Turkish territory whatever the odds; a search for allies in the face of potential aggression; and the pursuit of an increasingly active role in the cultural and political community of the free nations of the West.

Selected Bibliography

Atatürk, Kemal, A Speech Delivered by Ghazi Mustapha Kemal, 2 vols. (Leipzig: K. F. Koehler, 1929).

Davison, Roderic H., "Turkish Diplomacy from Mudros to Lausanne," in Gordon A. Craig and Felix Gilbert, eds., The Diplomats (Princeton: Princeton University Press, 1953), pp. 172-209.

Lewis, Geoffrey L., Turkey (New York: Praeger, 1955).

Thomas, Lewis V., and Richard N. Frye, The United States and Turkey and Iran (Cambridge: Harvard University Press, 1951).

Ziemke, Kurt, Die neue Türkei (Stuttgart: Deutsche Verlags-Anstalt 1930).

9 . . .

FOREIGN POLICY
OF MEXICO

. . . George I. Blanksten

IN 1910 FRANCISCO IGNACIO MADERO, a curiously quixotic lawyer, launched a rebellion that in the following year brought down the government of General Porfirio Díaz, who had ruled Mexico since the 1870's. Madero's action inaugurated a generation of turmoil and reconstruction. This Revolution—the celebrated "wind that swept Mexico" —has dominated the attention and energies of the people of Mexico during much of the twentieth century. To say that the Revolution lies central to anything in Mexican politics—whether domestic affairs or international relations—is not to exaggerate. The Revolution has given course and character not only to the country's internal politics, but also to its relations with the rest of Latin America, with western Europe, with the Union of Soviet Socialist Republics, and with the United States.

I. The Revolution

It would therefore appear to be in order to examine the Mexican Revolution briefly before embarking upon a discussion of the country's foreign policy.

So-called "revolutions" are, of course, frequent in Latin America. The bulk of these, however, are not genuine revolutions in the sense of bringing with them profound and thoroughgoing changes in the social and political structure of the states affected. But the Mexican Revolution stands apart. It has been as genuine a revolution as that which struck France in the eighteenth century or Russia less than a decade after the fall of Díaz. Although its initial goals were more limited, the Mexican Revolution came to constitute a frontal attack upon fundamental problems—such as land tenure, the temporal position of the Roman Catholic Church, the situation of the lower classes, and foreign economic influence in the country—that have historically troubled not only Mexico but also much of the rest of Latin America.

The Revolution's approach to the land question finds its antecedents in a century-long history of domestic struggle in Mexico. The Spaniards who conquered and colonized the country brought with them the quasi-feudal pattern of land tenure they had known at home. Throughout most of Mexico's subsequent history the country's economy was characterized by huge landed estates held by a small landowning aristocracy, with much of the rural population living and working on these estates in conditions reminiscent of the serfdom of medieval Europe. Some attempts at land reform had been made in Mexico before the Revolution, to be sure; the most notable of these occurred in the middle of the nineteenth century, when the "War of Reform" brought the remarkable Benito Juárez to power. With the passing of Juárez and the "War of Reform," however, the small landowning aristocracy resumed its role in the pattern of land tenure. Indeed, it has been estimated that in 1910, on the eve of the Revolution, about 1 per cent of the population owned approximately 70 per cent of the land surface of Mexico.

The Revolution was committed to, and has achieved, a basic change in the pattern of land ownership. Dedicated to the proposition that the large landed estates must be reduced, the Revolution has introduced two other land systems which are held to be mutually compatible. The first of these is designed to create a large group of individual owners of small parcels of land. The second is the *ejido* system, intended to deliver collectively owned lands to rural communities. Particularly in the early years of the Revolution, Mexico sought a solution to its historic land problem through these devices, notably the *ejido* system.

The place of the Roman Catholic Church in the temporal life of Mexico was a second historic problem challenged by the Revolution. Traditionally, the Church had played a dominant role in the affairs of this overwhelmingly Catholic country. The Church had at first brought formal education to Mexico, then stayed to monopolize its administration. Closely associated with the state in colonial days, the Church remained an arm of government after the achievement of Mexico's national independence in the 1820's. Against an historic background of frequent unions of Church and State, the Church had come, in the years before the Revolution, to be one of the major landowners in Mexico.

In the wake of the Revolution, the Church has been disestablished and placed in a weakened position. It has been deprived of much of the land it had acquired before the Revolution, and Church officials are forbidden to vote or to present themselves as candidates for public office. In short, much of the Revolution is distinctively anticlerical in nature.

The Revolution has, further, sought a redefinition of the place of the lower classes in the national life of the country. Historically, Mexico's class system has been made up of three rigidly separated groups, with interaction among them being held to a minimum. The small upper class, variously known as creoles or "whites," had long dominated the political and economic life of the nation, excluding from effective participation the two lower groups, the *mestizos* and the Indians. The Revolution has sought a new national role for these classes. A part of the answer is to be found in the *ejido* system, but the land issue is only a part of Revolutionary Mexico's handling of the Indians and *mestizos*. Illiteracy is fought by the Revolution, which has likewise endeavored to preside over a somewhat engineered *renaissance* of Indian culture. An attempt has been made with some success to destroy the older class system with a view to multiplying the opportunities available to the lower classes of the country.

And then there was the "foreign imperialist," another historic problem for Mexico. Particularly during the regime of Porfirio Díaz (1876-1911), foreign capital, especially from the United States, was encouraged to enter Mexico on a large scale and to develop and exploit its natural resources. Oil was the most important and the most dramatic of the sectors of Mexico's economy thus affected, but there were others, notably transportation, communication, and electrical energy. In rejecting the Díaz approach to foreign capital, the Revolution has endeavored to reduce outside economic influences in the affairs of Mexico. Restrictions and limitations have been placed upon the ability of foreigners to acquire most types of property in the country, with United States interests being primarily affected by these measures. Expropriation and other steps of the Revolution have deprived foreigners of their holdings in such areas of the Mexican economy as oil, land, and transportation. Foreigners attempting to do business in Revolutionary Mexico frequently find themselves discriminated against by the pattern of the laws.

Students of the process of revolution have advanced the hypothesis that all major revolutions experience a common set of steps or stages.

Attempts to test this hypothesis have thus far been largely restricted to research on the French and Russian revolutions.[1] The terminology of the French Revolution has given a name—"Thermidor"—to what is held to be one of the later stages experienced by all profound revolutions.

Insofar as this hypothesis is valid, the Mexican Revolution may well have entered the stage of Thermidor in the early 1940's. Thermidor is the time of the cooling off of revolutionary ardor, the stage in which the ideals of the revolution become impure, the phase in which its ideology accepts compromises. In this sense, the last "pure" President of Revolutionary Mexico was Lazaro Cárdenas (1934-1940). During subsequent administrations the Revolution has tended to cool down, its ardor has subsided, its programs have tapered off, its leaders have become more willing to make compromises of its principles. With Revolutionary Mexico at the stage of Thermidor, land reform has lost its fire and *ejidal* programs are pushed less vigorously than previously; the Revolutionary party's presidential candidate [2] can be elected after telling an anticlerical Revolution that he is a Catholic; it becomes easier to look down one's nose at the Indian once more; and a man who collaborated with the foreign invaders, the "Yankees," may head the Revolutionary party and be elected President.[3]

Thermidor is, no doubt, a subtle and sensitive proposition. It means a species of compromise on the principles of the Revolution, but it does not signify their rejection. Mexico in Thermidor has compromised on, but cannot reject, the Revolution. And it is this Revolution—Thermidor and all—that underlies contemporary Mexican national life. This condition lies central to Mexico's foreign policy, whether the issue at hand be relations with other Latin-American states, with western Europe, with the Soviet Union, or with the United States.

II.   Organization for the Conduct of Foreign Affairs

In examining the constitutional context in which Mexican foreign policy is conducted we should note that, as in the cases of most of the other countries of Latin America, the constitutional system of Mexico has been strongly influenced by that of the United States. Many of the arrangements, agencies, and practices of her northern neighbor have their counterparts in the Mexican system.

---

[1] See Crane Brinton, *The Anatomy of Revolution* (New York, 1938), and Lyford P. Edwards, *The Natural History of Revolution* (Chicago, 1927).

[2] Miguel Alemán, who was President of Mexico from 1946 to 1952.

[3] President Adolfo Ruíz Cortines (1952-58) aided the United States forces during the occupation of Vera Cruz.

The national history of Mexico is characterized by, among other things, frequent periods of domestic turbulence and political instability. Constitutions are occasionally among the casualties of these disturbances. Mexico's present Revolutionary Constitution of 1917 is a product of the Revolution. Thus, as compared with that of the United States, the Mexican Constitution is of quite recent vintage. Compared, however, with the basic laws of the other Latin-American states, where political instability is also a severe problem, the Mexican document enjoys considerable seniority. Of those nineteen other countries, only Argentina and Colombia currently maintain constitutions antedating Mexico's.

Like most of its predecessors, the Revolutionary Constitution of 1917 provides for a presidential system somewhat resembling that of its United States model, characterized by a separation of powers on the national level among executive, legislative, and judicial branches of government.[4] The chief responsibility for the conduct of Mexican foreign affairs is the executive's, under the Constitution; the legislative branch plays a more limited role in this field, while the international function of the Mexican judiciary is quite small.

The President of Mexico, who is elected for a six-year term, is normally the most powerful single individual in the determination of the country's foreign policy. Two chief considerations—one constitutional and the other political—underlie this condition. Constitutionally, the major powers relating to foreign affairs are the President's. He is responsible for the country's diplomatic negotiations with other states, and he is empowered to suspend the Constitution in the event of invasion. He is authorized to banish from Mexico, without previous trial, any foreign nationals whose presence he considers dangerous to the country. The President appoints his Secretary of Foreign Affairs and all members of Mexico's diplomatic and consular corps. Further, the President is Commander in Chief of the nation's armed services, and appoints their higher-ranking officers.

Politically, the President is usually a stronger figure than even these constitutional provisions suggest. The Mexican political tradition has historically involved a strong executive, and many areas of national life have long been conditioned to seek his favor and do his bidding. The country's history is replete with instances of dictatorship; Mexicans have become accustomed to expect their presidents to be strong men. Further—and this is also true elsewhere in Latin America—militarism has long been a key feature of Mexican political life. The

---

[4] Mexico has twice—once in 1822-23 and again in 1864-67—experimented with monarchy. Both episodes are generally considered to have been failures.

armed services are among the more powerful political groups in the country, and—with only three exceptions [5]—all of Mexico's presidents have been army officers who found their way to the office through their influence in, or over, the military. Organizational behavior in the Mexican executive branch frequently resembles military command patterns despite the constitutional proposition that government is theoretically a civilian function.

Some ramifications of this are obvious. Thus, although the Mexican resembles the United States constitutional stipulation that the President is Commander in Chief of the armed forces, in Mexico this is normally much more literally and directly true than in the case of the northern republic. Again, the Mexican President's power to appoint the higher-ranking officers of the military is more than a constitutional formality. Finally, any discussion of the power of the President of Mexico is unrealistic if it fails to take the country's political party system into account. Mexico has what has been called a "modified one-party system." [6] Although other political parties are legal and do exist in the country, only one, the Party of Revolutionary Institutions (PRI [7]) wins most elections and controls the overwhelming majority of the officials of the executive, and of the members of the legislative branches of the national government of Mexico. The role of the President in the leadership of the PRI varies somewhat from administration to administration. Sometimes he is recognized as the leader of the party. When this is not the case, he is at least a part of the PRI leadership. Thus the President of Mexico, for both constitutional and political reasons, emerges as a powerful political figure; foreign relations is but one of the areas of public affairs reflecting this condition.

Again resembling the prototype in the United States, the Mexican President is assisted by a Cabinet. In the southern republic this institution is composed of eleven members, all of whom are appointed by the President to administer executive departments, called "secretariats" in Mexico. One of these is the Secretariat of Foreign Affairs, the chief of which acts as the President's agent and lieutenant in the conduct of foreign policy. The Secretary of Foreign Affairs directs the secretariat, administers the country's diplomatic and consular corps, and advises the President on international matters.

Normally, the Secretary of Foreign Affairs is a major political figure

---

[5] Francisco Ignacio Madero (1911-13); Miguel Alemán (1946-52); Adolfo Ruíz Cortines (1952-   ).

[6] See Austin Ranney and Willmoore Kendall, "The American Party Systems," *American Political Science Review*, Vol. XLVIII (1954), pp. 480-81.

[7] After the initials of Partido Revolucionario Institucional.

in his own right. In terms of the pattern of domestic Mexican politics, two—Foreign Affairs and Interior—of the eleven Cabinet posts are normally more crucial than the rest. These two secretaries are frequently influential in the PRI leadership. Often, to be Secretary of Interior or Foreign Affairs is to be groomed for the presidency of the republic. Thus the Secretary of Foreign Affairs is often popularly regarded—albeit sometimes inaccurately—as the next President of Mexico.

Politically, then, the executive branch—particularly the President and his Secretary of Foreign Affairs—is even more critically important in the determination of Mexican foreign policy than the provisions of the Revolutionary Constitution of 1917 would suggest. This is in sharp contrast to the situation in the case of the legislative branch. Here the political pattern operates to reduce the foreign-relations powers of Congress to a measurably lesser role than a literal reading of the Constitution would seem to indicate.

The Mexican Congress—here again the constitutional influence of the United States is striking—is bicameral. The lower house is known as the Chamber of Deputies, and the second chamber as the Senate. The major constitutional functions of Congress relating to international affairs appear on their face to be impressive. The Mexican national legislature, for example, has the sole authority to declare war. Also, the power to admit new states and territories to the Mexican union is the legislators'. Further, Congress is empowered to create and maintain the armed forces, to establish rules for the regulation of the diplomatic and consular corps, to contribute to the definition of the legal status of foreign nationals in the country, and to establish the terms under which the President may negotiate loans on the credit of Mexico. Congress, of course, enacts tariff legislation. In addition, the Senate ratifies treaties and approves presidential appointments of the Secretary of Foreign Affairs and of members of the diplomatic and consular corps. Senatorial authorization is required to send Mexican troops outside the country, and the Senate's approval is also a prerequisite to the peaceful passage of foreign troops through Mexican territory. Foreign-relations and military-affairs committees are maintained by both the Chamber of Deputies and the Senate.

If it be assumed that the above, or some of them, might be crucial powers in certain types of international situations in which Mexico might become involved, a question still remains as to the extent to which Congress actually possesses independent discretion in the exercise of its constitutional functions. This question leads down two paths. The first is that of tradition: Mexican legislatures have historically been weak vis-à-vis the executive and the military. The second path stops at the door of the PRI. The two houses of Congress have a combined membership of 215 Deputies and Senators. Situations, of course, differ from election to election, but it rarely happens that fewer than 200 of the national legislators are members of the PRI. Little is as yet known by political scientists of the nature of party discipline within the PRI. It can be said, however, that since the establishment of the party in 1929 there have been no major instances of legislative revolt against the PRI leadership.

A further word may be in order with respect to the direction of the party. Founded by President Plutarco Elías Calles, the PRI [8] in its early years was essentially under the one-man leadership of the President of the Republic. This was especially true during the administrations of Presidents Calles (1924-1928) and Lázaro Cárdenas (1934-1940). Although the Revolutionary Constitution of 1917 prohibits the reelection of the President, both Calles and Cárdenas remained politically powerful after the expiration of their terms of office. In a real sense, ex-President Calles dominated the government party until 1934. Cárdenas was the central leader of the party not only during his presidency but also for some years after. Although he never became the powerful "boss" that Calles had been, Cárdenas remained a strong figure for more than twenty years after relinquishing the presidency.

Thus, none of the presidents since Cárdenas [9] have held as much power in the PRI as had he or Calles; indeed, post-1940 Mexican presidents have been characterized as relatively weak executives. During this period, basic power within the PRI has moved progressively into the hands of a central executive committee, composed in significant part of military men, some of whom had seen action in the Revolution. Ex-President Cárdenas sits with this group as a species of elder statesman. His party role since 1940 is somewhat reminiscent of, but not so powerful as, that played by Ex-President Calles from 1928 to 1934. Where Calles had been an active policy-determining leader, Cárdenas has preferred to perform more of what might be characterized as a veto function. PRI policies are initiated and, for the most part, decided by the central committee on a collective basis. Cárdenas is frequently consulted by the committee, which rarely makes a decision it believes him to oppose. Thus the role of Cárdenas is the

---

[8] Initially known as the National Revolutionary Party (PNR), the name was changed to Mexican Revolutionary Party (PRM) before the PRI acquired its present designation in a party reorganization of 1945.

[9] The subsequent Presidents have been Manuel Avila Camacho (1940-46), Miguel Alemán (1946-52), and Adolf Ruíz Cortines since 1952.

largely passive one of veto-wielder rather than that of active leader, as in the earlier case of Calles.

In view of the traditionally strong place of the executive in Mexican political life, and the fact that it was that branch of government around which the PRI was originally formed and through which men like Calles and Cárdenas rose to power, the PRI has tended to focus its attention upon the presidency. Thus, whether or not the President at any given time is an influential PRI leader, party control of his office is a "must" in Mexican politics. With the executive and the legislative branches of government sensitively responsive to the PRI, decision-making in many fields, including foreign policy, is concentrated upon the presidency, with the Congress exercising little independent discretion, constitutional permission to the contrary notwithstanding.

The Mexican judiciary has at best a minor part in foreign policy. This is, for the most part, jurisdiction over those cases in international law which happen, for one reason or another, to fall to Mexican courts. Where this occurs, it is worth bearing in mind that Mexico is a Roman- or code-law country, where the chief function of the judiciary is the application of relatively comprehensive legal codes laid down by the legislature.

Thus, the structure and operation of the Mexican government is such that the major policy-determining powers in the field of foreign affairs lie with the executive branch, the primary responsibility falling upon the President and his Secretary of Foreign Affairs, provided normally that their actions have the approval of the leadership of the PRI.

III.   Mexico and Latin America

A cardinal feature of contemporary Mexico's foreign policy is the circumstance that in a real sense the country functions as a diplomatic leader in a large part of the Latin-American community. Three major considerations are involved in Mexico's position as an inter-American diplomatic leader, and each of these is worth exploring.

First, there is the ever-present Revolution, which has markedly increased Mexico's stature in the Latin-American community. Emilio Portes Gil, who was President of Mexico in the late 1920's, and subsequently Foreign Minister in the cabinet of President Cárdenas, has described the Revolution as a phenomenon that "Mexico regards with pride, because she holds that [it has] been made, not for her own benefit, but also for that of the interests dearest to humanity." [10] This

---

[10] Quoted in José Angel Ceniceros, *Mexico's Attitude in Its International Relations* (Mexico City: Ministry of Foreign Relations, 1935), p. 11.

is no idle nationalistic boast. The fundamental problems with which the Revolution grappled were not peculiarly Mexican problems. All of them—land tenure, Church-State relations, class privilege, and the riddle of the "foreign imperialist"—recur in one form or another, and in various combinations, throughout the Western Hemisphere. The belief is widespread in the Americas that the Mexican Revolution provides a formula for the solution of basic problems common to most of Latin America, and that Mexico points the way. Through revolution, Mexico has acquired a distinguished position of leadership in the hemisphere, and this is recognized in an ever-increasing number of American nations. This writer was impressed, when he was in Ecuador, with attitudes in that country toward the Mexican venture. When Ecuador inaugurated a new President, the various governments with which Quito maintained diplomatic relations sent special delegations to attend the inauguration ceremonies. When the Mexican delegation, headed by Portes Gil, arrived, the Ecuadoran press assiduously interviewed the Mexicans on the progress of the Revolution. These interviews were given such publicity that they displaced even the inauguration of a new President of Ecuador from the front pages of the Ecuadoran press!

A second factor in Mexico's leadership in Latin America is the country's size. It is not the custom in the United States to regard Mexico as a significantly large country, but these matters are, of course, relative. "When Mexico is statistically assessed relative to the United States it is overwhelmed, as are its individual companions in the Latin-American community," Howard Cline has pointed out. "But when measured against other Latin-American countries and areas in the group as a whole, the outcome is quite different." [11] With a population approaching 30,000,000, Mexico stands among the major states of Latin America. In the area only Brazil is more populous than Mexico; and, with the exception of Argentina, the remaining states of Latin America have individual populations under 12,000,000.

A third consideration is Mexico's geographical proximity to the United States. "Poor Mexico!" Porfirio Díaz is said to have exclaimed. "So far from God—so close to the United States!" In the Latin-American world, Mexico is frequently viewed as a dyke obstructing various kinds of overflow from the United States. Mexico has suffered many difficulties arising from her northern neighbor and has, for the most part, withstood these hardships with what Latin Americans generally regard as dignity. Thus, in a sense, Mexico defends Latin Amer-

---

[11] Howard F. Cline, *The United States and Mexico* (Cambridge, Mass., 1953), p. 7.

ica's northwestern frontier, often regarded as the Hispanic-American community's most vulnerable extremity.

Finally, consider the situations of Mexico's rivals for the diplomatic leadership of Latin America. These are, for most purposes, two in number—Brazil and Argentina. Neither can stand as an unchallenged standard-bearer for the area. Portuguese rather than Spanish in its European origins, Brazil is a part of Latin America, to be sure, but it is not a member of the *Hispanic*-American community. In the United States, it may be difficult to see why this should make much difference. Nevertheless, Portugal and Brazil are indeed foreign to many of the concerns of the Hispanic world. Since the early years of the eighteenth century, for example, Portugal has been involved diplomatically in the British orbit; Portuguese and Brazilians view international problems from a different historical background than do Spaniards and Hispanic Americans. During centuries of international politics, Portugal was often aligned with Britain against Spain. Contemporary Brazil, with a population of over 50,000,000 and an area larger even than that of the United States, is a species of subcontinent in itself. Its life, its culture, its historical and diplomatic orientations differ from those of Spanish America. These perhaps subtle but nevertheless real considerations render Brazilians outsiders to a significant part of the world of which Mexicans are insiders. Argentina, with a population approaching 18,-000,000, was for many years a more serious bidder than Brazil. Argentina, however, has pursued a foreign policy opposed to inter-American cooperation. This policy reached its peak, and failed, during World War II. The events of the 1940's dealt severe blows to Argentina's diplomatic prestige in the Americas, and have detracted from that country's position of leadership.

Revolutionary Mexico, then, emerges as a diplomatic leader in the Latin-American community. To what uses has Mexican foreign policy put this prestigious position?

The Mexican Foreign Office is fond of describing its international policy as "traditionally peace-loving." [12] Most governments have come to advertise themselves as "peace-loving," especially since this has become a condition of membership in the United Nations. Again in the Mexican case, however, this is no idle boast. Consider the historical record. For more than a century, Mexico's dealings with the other states of Latin America have been almost uniformly peaceful. Where Mexico's foreign relations have been strained, the conflicts and difficulties have been not with other countries of Latin America but rather

---

[12] Ceniceros, *op. cit.*, p. 29.

with the United States and with Europe. Throughout her entire national history, Mexico has been involved in only two international wars. The first of these (1846-48) was fought against the United States; the second was World War II, with Mexico joining the anti-Axis cause in June of 1942. These were separated by almost a century in which the country suffered intervention on the part of France (1862-67) and was involved in renewed difficulties with the United States, particularly during the administrations of the "Yankee" President Woodrow Wilson, when Mexico was in the throes of the early stages of the Revolution. On the other hand, the record of Mexico's relations with the other states of Latin America has been one of virtually unbroken peace.

Stretched on a Latin-American rack, this background neatly divides Mexico's historic enemies from her friends. The enemies have been states larger and more powerful than Mexico, which has suffered invasion and intervention at their hands. The friends, on the other hand, have been the other states of Latin America, most of which—particularly Mexico's immediate neighbors—have been smaller and weaker than she. On this record, Mexico stands as a force for peace in Latin America. She has rarely threatened or attacked her neighbors, and she has uniformly stood ready to participate in arrangements for arbitration and in other projects designed to achieve peaceful settlement of such international disputes as have arisen within the Latin-American community.

The question of whether a Latin-American "bloc" exists in international affairs is both subtle and intriguing. Some types of problems divide the states of the area among themselves; other international questions tend to draw the Latin-American countries together in a bloc or united front. In situations conducive to bloc behavior, Mexico normally participates in these coalitions, frequently taking the lead in forming them. In general, there are two types of international situations in which Mexico plays a leading role in Latin-American blocs.

The first of these involves situations in which the Latin-American governments are in general agreement among themselves as to some international objective sought by all of them. In such cases Mexico normally leads—and where she does not lead, she usually joins—the bloc in pursuit of the common cause. Two illustrations of this type of Mexican international role may be cited. The first has to do with what international lawyers refer to as the "law of local remedies." Recognition of this "law" has long been sought by the governments of Latin America in bloc fashion, and Mexico has led the bloc. Briefly, the "law of local remedies" provides that foreigners doing business or otherwise being present in a country would have the same legal rights as the nationals or citizens of that country, and, in case of difficulty, would have recourse to the same courts or other remedies as they, but no recourse to remedies not available to them. Thus, a United States citizen doing business in, say, Guatemala and in legal difficulties there, would, were this principle acted upon, have recourse only to the remedies available to Guatemalan citizens, and would be denied the intervention of the United States Department of State or other forms of diplomatic protection. Latin America, led by Mexico, has sought recognition of the "law of local remedies"; the United States has in many cases been reluctant to accept it. A second illustration of this type of bloc behavior involves the thorny question of extending diplomatic recognition to revolutionary governments in the Americas. The problem of whether or not to recognize a given regime that has come to power in Latin America by nonconstitutional means is a difficult one. Latin America, led by Mexico, has sought the adoption of policies recognizing the right of revolution and permitting diplomatic relations with governments of questionable constitutional antecedents. Mexico's chief creative contribution in this field is the celebrated "Estrada Doctrine," advanced in 1930 by Foreign Minister Genaro Estrada, and supported by much of Latin America. Under this, Mexico would continue the practice of recognizing new states, but would discontinue the custom of recognizing new governments in states already recognized. Rather, Mexico's diplomatic mission in the affected state would do business with whomever the business was relevant.[13]

The second type of international situation in which Mexico plays a leading role in Latin-American bloc behavior involves the position of the inter-American community in the creation of new patterns of relationships among the Great Powers. Thus, when the United States launched its "Good Neighbor Policy" in the 1930's, Mexico, one of the first Latin-American states to respond positively, did much to forge a

---

[13] The Estrada Doctrine, a remarkable instrument, is worth quoting in full: "Mexico does not make any announcement as to granting recognition, because she holds that this is an offensive practice which, besides wounding the sovereignty of other nations, lays them open to having their domestic affairs judged in one sense or another by other governments, which assume a *de facto* critical attitude when they decide, whether favorably or unfavorably, on the legal status of foreign regimes. Consequently, the Mexican Government confines itself to keeping or withdrawing, whenever it shall deem it advisable, its diplomatic agents, and to continuing to accept, also when it shall deem it advisable, similar diplomatic agents accredited by such countries to Mexico, without judging, either hurriedly or *a posteriori*, the right of any foreign nations to accept, preserve, or change their governments or authorities." Quoted in Ceniceros, *op. cit.*, p. 25.

bloc pattern of response to Washington's new approach. Again some years later, on the eve of World War II, Mexico took the lead in aligning the inter-American coalition in the anti-Axis camp. Later, at the Inter-American Conference on Problems of War and Peace (popularly known as the "Chapultepec Conference") held at Mexico City in 1945, Mexico, under the skilful leadership of Foreign Minister Ezequiel Padilla, performed the remarkable feat of separating the inter-American community from Argentina, which was then pursuing a pro-Axis foreign policy. A few months later at the San Francisco Conference, also held in 1945, Mexico, still under the foreign-policy leadership of Padilla, assisted in the reincorporation of Argentina in the inter-American fold and the admission of that country into the United Nations.

IV.   Mexico and Europe

The pattern of Mexico's relations with the various states of Europe is complex. For purposes of simplification, it would be well to single out only three European states and to examine Mexico's relations with them. The three are France, Spain, and the Soviet Union.

A.   Mexico and France

France has long been regarded as a political and cultural leader of the Latin world, and Mexico normally falls into its orbit. French political, constitutional, and administrative ideas are aped throughout Latin America, with Mexico being no exception. Paris is looked to by Mexicans as the home of European culture and civilization, and most ideas or departures acquiring appreciable vogue in France soon find their repercussions and counterparts in Mexico, as well as elsewhere in Latin America.

The history of Franco-Mexican relations is, for the most part, a record of cordial dealings. One noteworthy exception is worth mentioning. During the Second French Empire, Napoleon III pursued the ambition of extending his holdings and influence to include Mexico. Under the pretext of forcing the collection of debts owed by Mexico, French troops landed in Mexico in the closing weeks of 1861. Mexico remained subject to the French intervention until 1867. This period marks the most strained relations that have occurred between France and Mexico. During the occupation, the French established a puppet monarchy, proclaiming Maximilian Hapsburg and his wife Carlotta Emperor and Empress of Mexico. Assuming this tottering throne in

1864, Maximilian remained in Mexico for three tragic years. The French troops were withdrawn in 1867, and the monarchy collapsed at that time. Throughout the intervention, Mexicans resisted the French and Maximilian, who was executed in 1867 by forces loyal to President Benito Juárez.

B. Mexico and Spain

Relations with Spain, the former mother country, have been cool and strained throughout most of Mexico's independent national existence. Difficult relations with Spain were, perhaps, to be expected in the period immediately following the achievement of Mexican independence in 1822. These, however, persisted throughout the nineteenth century. Plagued by controversy over succession to the throne at Madrid, Spain fell into the Carlist Wars in the 1830's, and civil war, instability, and near anarchy characterized Spanish political life for more than a generation. During this period Mexico exhibited little sympathy for any of the contending factions in the mother country. This remained the dominant Mexican attitude toward Spain until the closing years of the nineteenth century.

The Mexican position was altered somewhat, although not fundamentally, by the Spanish-American War. Mexicans, closely watching the controversy developing in Cuba in the 1870's, in general sympathized with the cause of the Cuban colonists against their Spanish rulers, and maintained this attitude when hostilities broke out in the island. With the entry of the United States into the fighting in 1898, Mexican bitterness toward Spain was mitigated somewhat by fear and resentment of the role of the "Colossus of the North" in the Cuban crisis.

After 1910, of course, the Revolution operated as a governing factor in defining Mexican policy toward Spain. Largely on revolutionary ideological grounds, Mexicans opposed the Primo de Rivera dictatorship which seized power in Spain in 1923 and paralleled developments in Fascist Italy until the fall of Primo de Rivera in 1930. Mexico was cheered by the abdication of King Alfonso XIII and the establishment of the Spanish Republic in the following year.

In all of Mexico's national history, the country experienced no more cordial relations with the former mother country than was the case during the period of the Spanish Republic (1931-1936). The doctrinal bases of the Madrid Republic struck responsive ideological chords in Revolutionary Mexico, and the period is remarkable for its rebirth of cultural and political intercourse between the two countries. In that epoch, trade and communication increased, tourists and students were exchanged, and the Spanish-Mexican *rapprochement* reached an unprecedented peak.

The Spanish Civil War, breaking out in 1936, exercised a dramatically divisive effect on Latin America. Some of the countries of the Western Hemisphere hailed the rise of General Francisco Franco. Mexico, however, took a leading position among the Latin-American states supporting the Loyalist cause of the Spanish Republic. When the Republic fell before Franco's onslaughts in 1939, Mexico opened her doors to political refugees from Spain; indeed, a Spanish Republican Government-in-exile was headquartered in Mexico for many years after Franco's assumption of power at Madrid.

With the outbreak of World War II the Spanish *Falange*, under Franco, became one of the major outlets for Axis propaganda and influence reaching the Western Hemisphere. Again largely on ideological grounds stemming from the Revolution, Mexico resisted these pressures. Two Mexican political parties—the National Action Party (PAN [14]) and the National Sinarquist Union—were receptive to wartime *Falange* influences. The government of Revolutionary Mexico, then under the presidency of General Manuel Avila Camacho (1940-1946), stoutly resisted these influences; indeed, the Sinarquist party was outlawed during the war. In the years since the end of World War II, relations between Revolutionary Mexico and Franco Spain have become somewhat less strained, although remaining cool.

C.   Mexico and the Soviet Union   *

Relations with the Soviet Union constitute one of the most intriguing chapters in Mexican foreign policy. Here again, the Mexican Revolution operates as a controlling consideration. More precisely, the central issue is the relationship between the Mexican and Russian revolutions. Three aspects are of high significance—the time differential between the two revolutions, the similarity in their ideological content, and the general developmental process of revolution.

Consider the time differential. The Mexican Revolution began in 1910, a full seven years before revolution came to Russia. These seven years were crucial. During that hectic period between the rise of Madero and the fall of Kerensky, the Mexican Revolution acquired its own course, character, and definition—its own identity as a major social and political movement. If anyone entertained the ambition, when the Bolsheviks came to power in Russia in the closing months of 1917,

---

[14] After the initials of *Partido Acción Nacional.*

of joining the Mexican and Russian revolutions together into one unified over-all international movement, he was doomed to failure. By the end of 1917 it was too late. The Mexican Revolution, with its own course, character, and identity already defined, was separate and distinct from the Russian upheaval; and separate and independent of each other the two have remained.

Nevertheless, a certain similarity between the ideological contents of the Mexican and Russian revolutions is inescapable. The similarity is largely coincidental, that is, there is little organizational relationship between them; but the similarity stands as a hard and present fact. The Mexican Revolution sought land reform, disestablishment of the Church, a change in the class structure, and the ejection of foreign capital.

So did the Russian Revolution.

Finally, there is the matter of the general process of revolution. It will be remembered that students of this process have advanced the hypothesis that all major revolutions experience a common set of steps or stages. One of these stages is variously known as the accession of the extremists, the reign of terror, the era of virtue, or the period of revolutionary dictatorship. Whatever the designation, this is the time when power is held by those revolutionists who are dedicated, often fanatically, to the social myth or the political philosophy of the revolution. They are, by their lights, rigidly honest men. They accept no compromise in the social myth, for they believe it immoral to compromise on political principles. Those who question these principles are ruthlessly dealt with; in the reign of terror the philosophical purity of the revolution cannot be attacked with impunity.

Thus the significance of the time differential between the Mexican and Russian revolutions is enhanced. In Mexico, the reign of terror began in 1913, and drew to a close in the 1930's. For a brief period the Mexican and Russian reigns of terror overlapped in time. This was the period when many observers saw similarities not only in ideological contents but also in process between the two revolutions, the period when books with titles such as *Soviet Mexico* were published in the United States. But, though the two reigns of terror overlapped briefly, they were essentially out of gear with each other, as was evidenced when Mexico entered Thermidor under Avila Camacho.

The two ships passed in the night. It was a close brush, but the essential point is that they *did* pass each other, to go in different directions. The seven years were crucial.

Perhaps because of this passing in the night, Mexicans maintained a more sympathetic interest in the progress of affairs in the Soviet

Union than was to be found in most of the other states of Latin America. Mexico was among the first in the Western Hemisphere to extend diplomatic recognition to the Soviet Government. Mexicans watched Lenin come and go; and, upon his death in 1924, they witnessed the power struggle between Joseph Stalin and Leon Trotsky with a fascinated neutrality. When Stalin's triumph drove Trotsky into exile, Mexico welcomed the distinguished political refugee. He lived among the Mexicans until his assassination in 1940.

When World War II began in 1939, only four of the twenty states of Latin America maintained diplomatic relations with the Soviet Union. Mexico, of course, was one of these.[15] In the years before the war spread to the Western Hemisphere, Latin America was divided in its attitudes toward the conflict, especially after the Soviet Union joined the anti-Axis cause. Some American governments, notably that of Argentina, sympathized with the Axis; and during the early phases of the war Mexico—under President Avila Camacho and his Foreign Minister, Ezequiel Padilla—played a leading role in aligning Latin America against the Axis. The success with which this endeavor was crowned was attested to by the fact that by the end of the war all of Latin America, including even Argentina, had declared war against the Axis, to become allies of Britain, France, the United States—and the Soviet Union.

The break between the Russians and their Western allies was in its early stages when the San Francisco conference met in April of 1945 to produce the Charter of the United Nations. As Mexico had been among the first in Latin America to enter into friendly relations with the Soviets, so—quite unexpectedly—she became, at San Francisco, one of the pioneers in the "cold war." Padilla, leading the Mexican delegation, clashed bitterly with Vyacheslav M. Molotov, who headed the Russians at San Francisco, originally on questions relating to the organization of the conference, and later on more fundamental issues. The ensuing "cold war" found Mexico aligned with the West. This remained the country's position in the closing years of the 1950's, although Mexico still maintained diplomatic relations with Moscow.

Mention should be made of the Mexican Communist Party, known since the late 1940's as the Popular Party. In the years since the Madero Revolution this group has played a curious role. Its influence in Mexican domestic politics has, in general, been small, especially since the administration of President Avila Camacho (1940-1946). Nevertheless, the Mexican Communists have included among their

---

[15] The other three: Chile, Cuba, and Uruguay.

numbers such outstanding figures as Diego Rivera, the great artist, and Vicente Lombardo Toledano, leader of the Confederation of Latin-American Workers (CTAL).[16] Perhaps more significant than its internal role in Mexico is the Popular Party's international function. Especially since the close of World War II, it has served as a point of liaison between Moscow and the Communist parties of other Latin-American countries, particularly those in Central America and the Caribbean islands. Although the evidence of this is not as complete as the careful student might wish, there is considerable indication that communications and information from Moscow have passed from the Communists of Mexico to those of neighboring states, notably Guatemala and Cuba. Since the end of World War II, meetings of the Communist leaders of these countries have on occasion been held in Mexico.

V. Mexico and the United States

There is no country in the international community with which Mexico has had more difficult relations than with the United States. In a sense, this was perhaps inevitable. "Mexico and the United States are constantly aware of each other's presence because they share an unfortified transcontinental boundary of 1,500 miles," it has been pointed out. "In the broadest sense, international relations are constantly occurring." [17]

Moreover, a sizable chapter in the territorial expansion of the United States has been written at the expense of Mexico. Texas was a part of Mexico when that country achieved its independence in 1822. Under the leadership of "North Americans" who had settled there, Texas seceded from Mexico in 1836. The secession was bloody, and the Texan War ended with the independence of Texas recognized by Mexico, but with the precise location of the boundary between the two still in dispute. Following its annexation of Texas in 1845, the United States inherited this dispute. It was resolved through additional bloodshed. The United States won a decisive military victory in the Mexican War (1846-48), and, in the ensuing Treaty of Guadeloupe Hidalgo, relieved Mexico of approximately half its territory, constituting the later states of Arizona, California, Nevada, New Mexico, and Utah. The present frontier between the United States and Mexico was rounded out through the Gadsden Purchase of 1853, when the "Colossus of the North" acquired additional land from Mexico.

---

[16] After the initials of *Confederación de Trabajadores de América Latina*.
[17] Cline, *op. cit.*, p. 10.

This episode has long colored Mexicans' attitudes toward the United States. The bitterness, however, was mitigated by events of the 1860's. The Civil War left the United States temporarily unable to enforce the Monroe Doctrine, and France embarked upon her military occupation of Mexico in the closing months of 1861. The French intervention revolutionized Mexican policy toward the United States. The change was best expressed by Matias Romero, Mexican Minister at Washington:

> Before the Civil War commenced in the United States it appeared that they were the only enemies which Mexico had, because their ideas and usurping policy had deprived us of half our territory and were a constant menace against the integrity of what we had left. Nothing therefore was more natural than to see with pleasure a division which by a fortunate continuation of circumstances would render almost impotent against us each of the parts which remained. . . . But unfortunately the sedition from which we expected such favorable results had hardly begun when we discovered another danger from which the power of this country had freed us and against which its present unity would be the surest guaranty. . . . We therefore find ourselves in the presence of the hard alternative of sacrificing our territory and our nationality at the hands of this country or our liberty and our independence before the despotic thrones of Europe. The second danger is immediate and more imminent; in evading the first we may count upon the future and the lessons of experience.[18]

Six figures stand out as the major architects of Mexican-United States friendship, as born in the 1860's: Romero; his chief, President Benito Juárez; Porfirio Díaz, then Juárez' key military commander; Abraham Lincoln; Andrew Johnson; and their Secretary of State, William H. Seward. Together they struggled against the French and their puppet Emperor, Maximilian I. United States assistance to the Juárez government was, of necessity, limited for the duration of the Civil War. After 1865, however, Washington gave impressive military, financial, and diplomatic aid to the Mexicans. The withdrawal of the French and the collapse of Maximilian in 1867 was a victory for Lincoln, Johnson, and Seward as much as for Juárez, Díaz, and Romero.

The "Big Stick" era of President Theodore Roosevelt (1901-09) damaged Mexican-United States relations somewhat. But a far more severe blow was dealt them by Washington's policies toward the early stages of the Mexican Revolution. After 1910, the Revolution became

---

[18] Quoted in J. Fred Rippy, *Historical Evolution of Hispanic America* (New York, 1940), pp. 492-493.

controlling in the business the two states conducted with each other.

The Revolution has not only governed Mexican attitudes and policies toward the United States, but it has also exercised an impressive influence upon Washington's view of Mexico and, indeed, of revolutionary movements in general. "From its genesis to the present," Cline has said, "the Mexican Revolution has affected the United States, its attitudes toward Mexico, and toward social change in general." [19]

In the view of the Revolution, there were two terrible *gringo* villains. Both were named Wilson.

The first was Henry Lane Wilson. He was named United States Ambassador to Mexico by President William H. Taft (1909-13), and he remained at that post for some time after Woodrow Wilson assumed office at Washington.

Ambassador Wilson was in Mexico when the Revolution began. He developed a penchant for acting on his own initiative, frequently disregarding instructions from the State Department. He acquired a strong personal antipathy for Madero shortly after the fall of Díaz in 1911, and the feud between H. L. Wilson and Madero, today regarded by Mexicans as the leading hero of the Revolution, assumed the proportions of a personal vendetta. Ambassador Wilson supported the political ambitions of General Victoriano Huerta, a revolutionary rival of Madero. H. L. Wilson signed a general agreement, known as the "Pact of the Embassy," with Huerta. Subsequently, in 1913, President Madero was assassinated. Most students of the affair place the primary responsibility for the murder of Madero at Huerta's door. Such satisfaction as Ambassador Wilson drew from the assassination of Madero and the rise of Huerta was short-lived: Huerta fell in 1914.

Meanwhile, the second Wilson had arrived upon the scene. Assuming office in 1913, President Woodrow Wilson pursued an anti-Huerta policy. Following the fall of Huerta, the Mexican Revolution entered a phase of general civil war and near-anarchy which endured for almost two years, that is, until the rise of President Venustiano Carranza in 1915. Mexico's became the first of Latin-American "revolutionary" regimes to taste a new departure in Washington's recognition policy inaugurated by President Wilson. Whereas previously the United States had pursued a generally *de facto* recognition policy, accepting the right of revolution and maintaining diplomatic relations with Latin-American governments that had come to power by force, President Wilson replaced this with a *de jure* policy. Much interested in constitutionalism, W. Wilson was reluctant to recognize a govern-

---

[19] Cline, *op. cit.*, p. 5.

ment of questionable constitutional antecedents, and withheld recognition from regimes that had not come to power through a pattern of "constitutional legitimacy." Mexican revolutionary administrations, of course, could not meet this test; and, under President Wilson's leadership, the United States entered a period of suspended diplomatic relations with Mexico. An immediate result of this was the recall of Ambassador H. L. Wilson to Washington. Thereafter, the first Wilson did not plague Mexicans.

But the second was still with them. During the course of Mexico's general civil war and near-anarchy of 1914-1915, the Tampico area became a theater of hostilities among revolutionary factions. A number of oil installations, operated for the most part by United States companies, were located there, and the companies became fearful of the safety of their property. To save the installations, the United States Navy occupied Vera Cruz in April of 1914. Thus occurred President Wilson's first "intervention" in the Mexican Revolution.

Despite his views on constitutionalism and recognition, W. Wilson was persuaded to establish diplomatic relations with the government of President Carranza (1915-20). However, this did not help the situation much, and President Wilson soon found himself feuding not only with Carranza but also with other Mexican revolutionary leaders. One of these was General Francisco ("Pancho") Villa, who had initially supported Madero and later came to be counted among Carranza's chief enemies. Villa led a guerilla army of considerable size, which warred against Carranza and, at times, against President Wilson. In March of 1916, Villa's guerillas crossed the United States border to raid the city of Columbus, New Mexico. W. Wilson, quite naturally, was incensed, and sent a detachment of the United States Army, under the command of General John J. Pershing, into Mexico on a punitive expedition. Pershing and his troops spent much of 1916 and the early months of 1917 wandering around in northern Mexico looking for Villa. Thus the second "intervention."

Then came the sensational Zimmerman Note, which, thanks to the British Government, was brilliantly timed. World War I, of course, had been in progress since 1914. Mexico remained neutral throughout the war, and in 1917 the United States, concerned with the submarine menace, was forced to choose between continuing in neutrality or entering the war against Germany and the Central Powers. The Zimmerman Note had been sent by the Germans to the Mexican government. It had been intercepted by the British, and released by them in time to help the United States in making its decision on war or peace. In the celebrated note, Berlin offered Carranza what the

German Foreign Office said it regarded as an opportunity for Mexico to escape from its difficulties with the "Colossus of the North." If Mexico were to enter the war on the side of Germany, Berlin would see to it in the peace settlement—assuming, of course, that the Central Powers would be the victors—that Mexico would regain from the United States the territory lost to it during the middle years of the nineteenth century. Carranza told the Germans that he regarded the imaginative project as inopportune; and the United States went to war. Pershing, withdrawn from Mexico, was sent to Europe to chase other villains.

The era of the two Wilsons has left its mark on the relations between Mexico and the United States. It has colored "North Americans'" views of Mexico, of revolution, and of social change; it has affected Mexicans' understanding of their northern neighbor. Nevertheless, relations between the two countries have improved measurably since the end of World War I.

The United States' "Good Neighbor Policy," coinciding generally with the administrations of President Franklin D. Roosevelt (1933-45), signalized a marked and probably long-lasting improvement in relations between the two countries. Mexico led among the states of Latin America in responding positively to these new and friendly overtures. This general trend toward more cordial dealings between the two countries was disturbed somewhat by the expropriation of the oil fields in Mexico. Responding primarily to the continuing process of the Revolution, the Mexican government in 1938 nationalized the oil industry, which had previously been worked by foreign companies, principally headquartered in the United States. This gave rise to renewed bitterness in some quarters in the United States. Relations with Mexico did not deteriorate over this issue as much as could have been expected in other times and in other contexts: the "North Americans" were beginning to learn to live with the Mexican Revolution, and the "Good Neighbor Policy" and a more understanding United States Ambassador in Mexico held the damaging consequences of the incident to a minimum.

This increased cordiality between the United States and Mexico was reflected by the latter's role in World War II as an ally in the anti-Axis cause. Since that period, Mexico has in general cooperated with her northern neighbor. A few minor difficulties between the two states remain, to be sure. There is, for example, the so-called "Chamizal" question. This is a small piece of land which the United States claims to be a part of El Paso, Texas, and the Mexicans claim to belong to Ciudad Juárez on the Mexican side of the frontier. Again, questions occasionally arise over matters of irrigation and flood control affecting the two countries. And then there is the problem of the so-called "Wetbacks," Mexican workers who, on a largely seasonal basis, illegally cross the border to take employment in the southwestern part of the United States. These issues are occasionally cause for friction, but in general they are minor problems in the over-all pattern of relations between the two countries. As of the close of the 1950's, the United States and Mexico were essentially firm friends. As the Revolution in its Thermidor phase has become more respectable in the northern republic, so the *gringos* since the "Good Neighbor Policy" have, in Mexican eyes, gone a long way toward graduating from the role of threatening bully to that of understanding comrade in facing the increasingly complex and difficult problems of the international community. Each has grown, each has matured; and in maturation each not only finds the other easier to live with but also relies more heavily on mutual cooperation and friendship in resolving the remaining problems common to the two countries.

VI.   Mexico and International Organization

A major point serves as the focus of contrast between Mexico's policies toward international organization and other aspects of her foreign affairs. In much of the latter, surveyed in the foregoing pages, the Revolution has been controlling during much of the twentieth century. In the case of international organization, however, Mexican policy finds its roots not so much in the Revolution as in other factors.

Like many another Latin-American state, Mexico presents what appears superficially to be a curious paradox. The record of Mexican internal politics has been one of violence, of turbulence and revolution. Disorder has been the rule rather than the exception. In international affairs, however, Mexico and other members of the inter-American community have long campaigned for order and the rule of law, have long condemned violence as an instrument of international policy.

Thus Mexico—and this was equally true before as it has been since the Revolution—has traditionally been counted among those states advocating and participating in international organization and other devices designed for the resolution of international difficulties by peaceful and orderly means. In assessing Mexico's policies in this area, a distinction should be drawn between two types of international organization—regional and universal.

The Western Hemisphere has enjoyed an impressive record of successful experience in regional international organization, a record not equalled in any other area of the world. The Second International Conference of American States, which met at Mexico City in 1901 and 1902, provided for the establishment of the Union of American Republics. This became the nucleus for the later Pan American Union, the transformation being formalized by the Fourth International Conference of American States, held at Buenos Aires, Argentina, in 1910. In the ensuing thirty-eight years, the Pan American Union functioned as a major instrument of inter-American cooperation. Through this regional international organization, cultural, economic, and political mutual understanding was promoted among the states of the Western Hemisphere.[20] By the close of World War II it could be said—thanks in appreciable measure to the Pan American Union—that regional international cooperation was more advanced among the American Republics than within any similar area of the international community. The inter-American system was again revamped by the Ninth Conference of American States, which met at Bogotá, Colombia, in 1948. Since then, the regional organization has been known as the Organization of American States, conceived primarily as the regional agent in the Western Hemisphere of the over-all United Nations.

Historically, Mexico has played a central and frequently leading role in the affairs of the Union of American Republics, the Pan American Union, and the Organization of American States. Mexican policies toward the other American nations have normally been channeled through these organizations, and Mexico has supported their proposals directed toward peaceful cooperation within the hemisphere, introducing many of them herself.

A similar Mexican record is to be found in the field of global international organization. A member of the League of Nations, created at the close of World War I, Mexico contributed to the attempts of that institution to deal with world problems through the machinery of international organization. Likewise, Mexico has participated since World War II in the work of the United Nations, occasionally leading Latin-American bloc action in that organization.

Although it is true that this phase of Mexican policy antedates the Revolution, and responds not so much to it as to other factors of longer historical standing, it would be an error to conclude that the Revolution has not affected Mexico's role in international organization at all. Much of what Mexico has done in that context, and many of

---

[20] Although repeatedly invited to join, Canada has refused to become a member of the Pan American Union or, later, of the Organization of American States.

the policies pursued by her in the League of Nations and the United Nations have been colored by the Revolution. Thus, the effect of the Revolution could be found, for example, in Mexico's contribution to the work of the International Labor Office, affiliated at first with the League of Nations and later with the United Nations. Again, especially in the latter organization, Mexico has supported much international work designed to raise standards of living in underdeveloped areas of the world, and other programs whose objectives have been, at least in part, in conformity with the values emerging from the Revolution. However, historically considered, these values have not been so controlling in Mexico's role in international organization as in other areas of the country's foreign policy.

VII. Conclusion

In summary, during much of the twentieth century the Madero Revolution has underlain, and given course and character to, many of Mexico's policies in the international field. That upheaval bears an integral relationship to Mexico's position as a diplomatic leader of Latin America, with many of the country's American neighbors believing that through revolution Mexico has resolved many of the fundamental social, economic, and political problems common to most of them. The Revolution has also been crucial in Mexico's relations with many of the states of Europe, especially Spain and the Soviet Union. In the case of Spain, the Revolution has contributed an ideological orientation essentially hostile to the regimes of both Primo de Rivera and Francisco Franco. In the Soviet situation, the Mexican Revolution has been controlling in policies that have earned for Mexico a record of having been more sympathetic toward the Russians than has been any other American government, especially during the 1920's and the early half of the 1930's. So far as the United States is concerned, the Revolution has affected significantly not only Mexican policy toward the northern republic, but also United States policies toward Mexico and toward revolution and social change in general. The role of the Revolution is not so great in determining Mexican policies toward, and participation in, international organization. These stem not so much from the Revolution as from forces with deeper historical roots, although the Revolution has, of course, given a somewhat selective coloration to the types of projects and measures Mexico has supported in the Pan American Union, the Organization of American States, the League of Nations, and the United Nations.

Two final points should be made with respect to Mexico's role in international affairs, particularly as it affects the United States. First, Mexico has been the leading Latin-American state with which Washington has had to deal. In this context, United States policies toward Mexico are basic in Washington's attitude not only toward Latin America but toward other areas of the world as well, particularly the underdeveloped regions where revolution looms as an active ingredient of the political scene. "The states of Europe and Asia within the United States' sphere of influence are going to be as touchy as the Latin-American states," the distinguished historian, Arnold J. Toynbee, has said; "and the United States is likely to handle them by a diplomatic technique that she has learned from her Latin-American experience." [21] Evidence already abounds of the tendency of the United States to apply to other areas of the world policies and techniques first tested in Latin America, particularly in Mexico.

Finally, although much of the history of United States-Mexican relations has been a record of difficulty, of war and intervention, both the United States and Mexico have matured. They have not only learned to live with each other, but have also—especially since the "Good Neighbor Policy"—developed a relationship of solid and sound mutual respect and cooperation. As of the closing years of the 1950's, Mexico and the United States were genuinely firm friends. "The points of contention that might lead to serious friction have been largely eliminated in recent years. Mexico is not a major pawn in the struggle between Russia and the United States. . . . Recent United States dealings with Mexico have proved amazingly successful. In the international field we are discussing success, not failure." [22]

It is a human characteristic that success commands less attention than failure. There is no major crisis in the contemporary relations of Mexico with any state of the world. Mexican foreign policy, therefore, today rarely merits a front-page headline in the reporting of the progress of world politics. Nevertheless, success stands, at least as much as failure, as a significant lesson in foreign policy.

Selected Bibliography

Ceniceros, José Angel, *Mexico's Attitude in Its International Relations* (Mexico City: Ministry of Foreign Relations, 1935).

Cline, Howard F., *The United States and Mexico* (Cambridge: Harvard University Press, 1953).

---

[21] Cline, *op. cit.*, p. 6.
[22] *Ibid.*, p. 1.

Gregg, R. D., *The Influence of Border Troubles on Relations Between the United States and Mexico* (Baltimore: Johns Hopkins University Press, 1937).

Parkes, Henry Bamford, *A History of Mexico* (Boston: Houghton Mifflin Co., 1938).

Schurz, William Lytle, *Latin America: A Descriptive Survey* (New York: E. P. Dutton and Co., Inc., 1949).

Tannenbaum, Frank, *Mexico: The Struggle for Peace and Bread* (New York: Alfred A. Knopf, 1950).

Turlington, E., *Mexico and Her Foreign Creditors* (New York: Columbia University Press, 1930).

10 . . .

THEORIES AND PROBLEMS
OF FOREIGN POLICY

. . . Kenneth W. Thompson

I.   Two Approaches to Foreign Policy

TWO APPROACHES to foreign policy have vied with one another in
Western thought at least since the days of the French Revolution.
One is the *ideological* approach, according to which the policies of
states vis-à-vis the rest of the world are merely expressions of prevailing political, social, and religious beliefs. In this approach, foreign
policies are classified as democratic or totalitarian, libertarian or
socialist, and peace-loving or aggressive. The second approach to foreign policy is *analytical.* At the heart of this viewpoint is the proposition that policy rests on multiple determinants including the state's
historic tradition, geographical location, national interest, and purposes and security needs. To understand foreign policy the observer
must take into account and analyze a host of factors.

In the twentieth century it has been commonplace for critics to
proclaim that the United States or Britain or France has no foreign
policy or has been unfaithful to liberal or socialist or conservative
principles, as the case may be. This is one way to think about foreign
policy; to the present day it is perhaps the prevailing approach. Periodically the domestic political arena rings with angry charges that a set
of political leaders, a political party, or an administration is opportunistic and morally derelict to its political creed or ideology in foreign
affairs. Governments are condemned for not supporting democracy
or free enterprise or a particular social class everywhere around the

world. This dominant approach views the conduct of foreign relations primarily in psychological terms; it looks to the motives or ideologies of leaders or governments as the essential if not the sole determinant of policy. It maintains that a democratic regime pursues one type of foreign policy, an autocratic government another, a communist government a third, and a democratic-socialist administration still another. There is a fairyland-like simplicity about this that makes it widely acceptable and easily understood. Foreign policy is considered a function of a political system in action or of the preferences or convictions of political leaders who carry out its programs.

There is a second approach to foreign policy, however, which has at least as respectable a heritage. It was a ruling point of view throughout much of the eighteenth and nineteenth centuries whether in doctrines of "raison d'état" or in broader historical interpretations, and it is being revived in our day by a handful of analysts and scholars.

Its renaissance is partly an outcome of the apparent shortcomings of the psychological or ideological approach, especially in accounting for present-day international developments. For this approach has been shaken and discredited by inner contradictions and has faltered and failed in describing the continuities of objective and purpose in the policies of states. That is to say, regardless of the party in power or the leaders and their private or public philosophies, British and American and French and Russian foreign policies display unities that transcend individual beliefs or ideologies. In the early postwar period the Labor government in England, despite long-standing protests against Tory imperialism and power politics, turned inevitably to the protection—in Western Europe, in the countries of the British Commonwealth, in the Iberian Peninsula, and in the Near and Middle East—of substantially the selfsame interests that Tories and Whigs had considered vital for several centuries. In the United States, the Dulles-Eisenhower foreign policy has looked to the central goals with which the administrations of Roosevelt and Truman were concerned. The means or methods or techniques may have changed, but the interests and objectives have been relatively constant.

Therefore in a period of a little more than a decade the study of international relations has witnessed a reaction against the ideological approach. It should perhaps have been obvious that a conception in which foreign policy is nothing more than a by-product of domestic politics could hardly do justice to the elements of continuity in national policy. At some point recognition was needed that objective requirements of the national interest place certain irremovable limits upon any statesman seeking to formulate foreign policy. That is, regardless of the intentions, social philosophy, or religious outlook of individuals, there are broad strategic interests intimately bound up with a nation's geographic position and its international role that must be safeguarded if its independence is to be preserved. Not only are these interests permanent, say, for Bolsheviks as well as Tsars, but in addition continuity appears in the approach of a nation's statesmen who stand guard over their country's security and whose conception of that security has been formed and molded by the same institutions and traditions. However intangible, the "national mind," which interprets the national interest, is itself a factor in the permanence of foreign policy. Thus out of the interplay of a durable international position with permanent traditions and institutions the larger nation-states have fashioned foreign policies which, in broadest outline, have been consistently maintained over long periods, even in the face of drastic changes on the domestic political scene.

According to this second approach, foreign policy demands of policy-makers choices and discriminations of a basic order. Not only are the interests of a nation permanent in character, but they range themselves in a hierarchy of greater and lesser interests. In a classic statement intended as a guide in the formulation of Belgium's foreign policy but with relevance for all foreign policy, Monsieur Paul-Henri Spaak observed:

> There must be a hierarchy in international obligations. The nations of a continent cannot reasonably be asked to consider with the same realism and sincerity of judgment affairs which directly concern them and events which are taking place thousands of kilometres away in regions where they have neither interests nor influence.

Certain interests must be defended at all costs; others should be safeguarded under particular circumstances; and certain others, although desirable, can almost never be defended. It is the task of foreign policy, in the first instance, to determine its own hierarchy of interests and, next, to examine the scale of interests revealed in the principles or practice of other nations' foreign policies. Even when national leaders forswear the formulation of hierarchies of interests, the hard tests of practice often evoke underlying conceptions of vital interests, as when the United States saw fit to fight the second World War in Europe and the North Atlantic to a successful conclusion before turning to destroy the enemy in the Pacific, or when Britain at the turn of the nineteenth century saw Poland attacked and other nations invaded before forming active coalitions against Napoleon as it became clear the security of the Low Countries was at stake.

The interests of states and their power to pursue their claims are of course immutable for any given historical period only in the sense that they set broad limits within which choices in foreign policy are made. They set the framework within which the domestic political contest over external policies must be waged. In the same way that no German political party today can afford to ignore the sometimes latent but ever-present demands for German reunification, no American government can take steps that would compromise the security of the Western Hemisphere. It is obvious that both power and interests can be made responsive to the forces of change. For example, a so-called "peace-loving" nation faced by emergent threats to its security can translate its resources into military power, its influence into foreign bases and real estate, and its industrial and military potential into forces in being. This has in effect been the trend of postwar American foreign policy. Or a state may suffer a loss in power as Britain did in World War II with the consequent need for revising its estimates of national interest. Technology can demand continuing reappraisals of national security and of the means of preserving it and may lead to changes in the ranking of the great powers. Britain may fall in the hierarchy of powers as other nations belatedly experience the industrial revolution, but it may recapture at least some of its vaunted supremacy in an era of atomic energy and hydrogen bombs. The existence of continuities in the foreign policies of states is admittedly more subject to debate in an era when one of the few certainties is the continual unrelenting pace of technological change.

Yet students of international politics are in the main persuaded that those recurrent patterns of the foreign policies of nations which most diplomatists appear to take for granted are amenable to study and analysis by the modern scholar. These patterns have been approached along several distinct if parallel lines. Scholars have engaged in more general studies of the geographical, industrial, and physical position of nations; the peculiar historical circumstances in which these conditions have operated; the actual adjustment of nations on the basis of their objective position to successive historical circumstances; and the claims and declarations made by statesmen engaged in pursuing a certain historic foreign policy. Obviously the intent of the studies in this volume is not to do basic research in any or all of these areas, but significantly and almost without exception each separate inquiry starts with an examination of one aspect or another of the objective patterns and conditions of foreign policy in the respective countries. At the same time, successive chapters go on to consider the role of ideology, of those changing institutions and domestic political factors which give to the policies of states that endless subtlety and richness that throws in question every simple generalization about the conduct of states. In effect, the theme of the book is one of continuity and change, of unities and coherences alongside the unique and particular in foreign relations. The authors, although wary of what Burckhardt described as "grand simplifications," are nevertheless compelled by their interests as political scientists to examine what can be said in general about foreign policy. This provides a unifying theme or central core of intellectual interests not everywhere made explicit but unquestionably at hand for those who seek understanding in this complex and fascinating realm.

II.   The Elements of Foreign Policy

The study of foreign policy despite the two major approaches provides no ready-made taxonomy or set of categories that can be examined for every nation. Perhaps even in the physical sciences the effort to uncover total systems, at least in these terms, is less fruitful than is sometimes imagined. In any event, there is marked diversity in the categories of analysis by which foreign policy has been studied in the present volume. To a considerable extent this results from differences in national context. For example, social stratification has implications for the making of foreign policy in Britain that it seems not to have in the Soviet Union, and the policy-making process in Britain has greater continuity and tradition even than the American system. A *fortiori* the newer states cannot point to the same political experience and diplomatic tradition in which the older nations can take pardonable pride. Despite these individual variations in the species, the nation-states whose policies are described have considerable in common. Their foreign policies are susceptible of analysis in terms of a check list of elements that exist and can be identified and that merge and comprise the bases of foreign policy.

The elements of foreign policy may be thought of in terms of concentric circles. At the center are certain elements that are more or less material in character. Of these some are relatively permanent, such as geography and natural resources. Others, like the economic, industrial, and military establishments, are more responsive to change and human manipulation. Then there are human factors, largely quantitative in the case of population, and qualitative as regards national character, social structure, national morale, political institutions and experience, and an effective tradition of diplomacy. From these elements and the instrumentalities of the policy-making process, the substance of foreign policy derives and major historic policies and the vital interests of countries emerge.

It may be worth at least passing mention that students of international politics have for the most part concentrated their attention on the elements of foreign policy. By contrast, writers on comparative politics have dealt more particularly with the policy-making process including the influence of political parties, interest groups, effective political ideologies, and the peculiar executive-legislative relations in a country. The attempt has been made in the present volume to marry these two approaches and to combine the study of objective factors in foreign policy and the study of processes by which decisions are reached and policies implemented. An enterprise of this kind, although probably not unique, is clearly exceptional in the literature of international relations.

A.   The relatively permanent material elements

The more or less permanent elements of foreign policy obviously include geography, perhaps the most stable factor undergirding a nation's policies. It is not without significance that "except for Japan . . . Britain is the only major power of modern times to be based on an island rather than a sizeable continental area."[1] Its separation from the European continent by a narrow but strategic body of water, the English Channel, proved as decisive in frustrating the designs of Hitler and Napoleon as it had those of Julius Caesar or Philip II. No less an authority than Sir Eyre Crowe observed: "The general character of England's foreign policy is determined by the immutable conditions of her geographical situation on the ocean flank of Europe as an island State with vast oversea colonies and dependencies, whose existence and survival as an independent community are inseparably bound up with the possession of preponderant sea power."[2] This passage gives a clue to an important source of one of the most successful foreign policies in history. Going back to the fifteenth and six-

---

[1] See Chapter III.
[2] Sir Eyre Crowe, "Memorandum on the Present State of British Relations with France and Germany, January 1, 1907," *British Documents on the Origins of the War 1898-1914*, ed. G. P. Gooch and H. Temperley (London, 1938), Vol. III, pp. 402-3.

teenth centuries, England, with but two exceptions, has neither been invaded nor defeated; and the exceptions—the American Revolution and the Afghan Wars—are hardly impressive evidence to challenge the importance of its geographic position. Even today England remains an island with what Winston S. Churchill described as threefold commitments to Europe, the British Commonwealth, and the "New World." Historically and down to the present, it has striven to retain for itself sufficient freedom of action to harmonize its commitments in each of these orbits, and only at points where they overlapped have new undertakings been possible. It is true that technology, through inventions like the airplane and submarine, has transformed the character of Britain's location, and there are signs that its interests today are drawing it ever closer to Europe. In part political factors have prompted this trend, including the British failure to pursue a successful independent foreign policy when its interests were in conflict with those of the super-powers as in the autumn of 1956 with the Suez crisis. But in Arnold Toynbee's apt phrase, "in this postwar age, the English Channel is no broader—in the subjective human terms of measurement which have to be applied in this context—than a Dutch dyke in the age of Alva and William the Silent; and the Atlantic itself is no broader than the Channel at the time when Napoleon's army of invasion was encamped at Boulogne." [3] Nonetheless, there are reasons for treating with some reserve claims about the annihilation of distance, for this statement dates back to 1934—only a few short years before the backbone of Nazi strategy was broken by an island state whose geography continued to make a difference.

No one would doubt that communications and modern warfare have shifted the emphasis that can properly be laid on geographic location, but its influence continues in various ways, not least in the case of the great powers. The territorial expanse of the Soviet Union with its land mass extending over one-seventh of the land area of the earth, or the vast reaches of the Chinese empire—both make military conquest and control problematical even with absolute weapons. The policies that the United Nations was able to pursue in Korea were circumscribed by the magnitude of the military effort of fighting a successful war on the seemingly endless terrain of the mainland of China. At the same time the difficulties of maintaining communication networks in these vast areas can be a source of weakness in defense. For Russia the lack of natural frontiers in the west or of natural obstacles to invasion across the plains of Poland and Eastern Germany

---

[3] Arnold J. Toynbee, *A Study of History* (London, 1934), Vol. III, p. 353.

has been a source of conflict and weakness from the fourteenth century up to the present day. This condition must be considered at least partly responsible for Soviet policies toward the satellites and for the insistence of the late Premier Stalin that "Poland is a matter of life and death."

Consequently, experienced diplomats like Ambassador Charles E. Bohlen warn that the most probable *casus belli* for the Russians would be a sudden change in the status of Eastern Europe. Short of a general settlement, they would fight to preserve their position in this area.

The crisis in the Middle East provides a reminder that natural resources continue to be a vital element in foreign policy. The decisive importance of the countries in the Arabian peninsula rests largely in the control they exert over oil. In practice modern technology has made Middle Eastern oil production an increasingly vital necessity, especially for regions like Western Europe. Instruments of production, transportation, and war require oil as a source of energy—Clemenceau once observed that "one drop of oil is worth one drop of blood of our soldiers"—and its importance has led to a shift in the relative power of major regions of the world (as in the rise to importance of the Middle East) and of some of the major nations. Self-sufficiency in this natural resource has enhanced the power of Russia and the United States while Britain and other European nations have been made weaker by their want of oil. The Middle East furnishes about 80 per cent of Western Europe's oil supplies, and barring major conflicts this figure was expected to increase to 90 per cent by 1959. Other estimates suggest that with the expansion of industrial production and national income and in the face of the flagging output of Europe's coal industry, Western European oil consumption may be trebled in twenty years. Hence control of oil becomes a crucial stake in world politics, and oil diplomacy has emerged as a term of art among policy-makers.

Similarly other natural resources influence foreign policy; the most basic has tended to be food production. Germany's military and political strategy in two World Wars was influenced by the need to gain a comparatively early victory before its limited food reserves were exhausted. For much the same reason Britain, which before World War II produced only 30 per cent of its food, ran the risk of destruction when its lines of communication with other regions were threatened by submarines and air power. In the degree that Britain's economic enterprise extended its influence until by the 1930's there was no part of the world not linked in some way with London, its security became more precarious in proportion to its dependence on tenuous and extended lines of communication. Liberals prompted by their zeal for international trade frequently decry a nation's quest for autonomy and self-sufficiency, yet in wartime this becomes a decisive source of strength. Food and energy are the lifeblood of a nation; its leaders must find ways, whether domestically or internationally, to satisfy these needs.

B.   Less permanent material elements

The twin forces of the industrial revolution and the contemporary political revolution, symbolized by the twenty new nations gaining recognition since World War II, underscore the vital importance of another element of foreign policy. In the nineteenth and twentieth centuries the industrial establishment of countries has been the most basic index of world power. So long as Britain had no equal as an industrial power, its weight in the balance of power was bound to be decisive. With the increase in industrial strength of Germany and the Soviet Union or of Italy and Japan, to say nothing of the United States, Britain's capacity to influence the course of world politics was substantially reduced. Britain having lost its industrial supremacy also lost its capacity to serve as a balancer. France is a dramatic example of a state whose industrial decline in relation to Germany meant that it was no longer able to resist German expansionism. Industrial capacity in both World Wars even more than peacetime military preparedness proved to be the *ultima ratio*. It was the latent power of the United States reflected in its industrial resources that tipped the scales and gave the victory to the allied powers. "In any comparison of the potential resources of the Great Powers the United States, even before Hitler's war, far outstripped every other nation in the world in material strength, in scale of industrialization, in weight of resources, in standards of living, by every index of output and consumption. And the war, which all but doubled the American national income while it either ruined or severely weakened every other Great Power, has enormously increased the scale upon which the United States now towers above its fellows." [4]

The realities of industrial capacity can therefore be ascertained and measured at least in approximate terms. India, for example, seems to have been lacking in the industrial resources essential to a great power. Although it has substantial deposits of coal and iron and ranks high in manganese production, it has in the past lagged far behind the

---

[4] *The Economist* (London), May 24, 1947, p. 785.

first-rate powers in the level of its industrial establishment. Only a tiny percentage of its total population has been engaged in industry, and its industrial plants have been severely limited. However, India is but one of a number of new nations whose rising political expectations carry with them demands for expanded industrial capacity. Its Five Year Plans are in part the expression of the drive for economic development and industrialization. Most of the nations that only recently have attained independence regardless of their natural resources seek economic growth as the indispensable prerequisite of status in the international society. For some the quest for rapid industrialization cannot be other than abortive. Indeed there is more than a touch of pathos in the headlong rush of many of these states to industrialize and thus identify themselves with powers of the first rank. The "objective observer" can suggest that they might play a more significant role if they held to a more modest view of their destiny and cast their lot with neighboring states in a regional development program. In so doing, however, they would accept a permanently inferior position in which their freedom of action would be hedged about, and this they are unwilling to do.

The military establishments of nations comprise another and possibly the most explicit element of foreign policy. Diplomacy and military strength go hand in hand. In an earlier day, the great powers sent gunboats up the rivers of states they were seeking to influence, while today a show of strength involves air forces, fleets, and satellites. The postwar distribution of power was an outcome of the position of the Red Army at strategic points in the heart of Europe. Germany's demonically successful diplomacy in the interwar period was clearly the direct outgrowth of superior military preparedness. The explosion and testing of atomic weapons by the Soviet Union has been joined with strategic moves in the cold war. Oftentimes the frontiers separating the spheres of influence of warring states demarcate the limits of their effective military forces, for example, in Korea. As long as force remains the final arbiter of rivalries among nations, the comparative strengths of their military establishments set boundaries to their actions in foreign affairs.

Military strength quite obviously lacks the permanence of the elements of geography or natural resources. Throughout history it has been subject to the compulsions of technological change. Military history is replete with examples of military techniques that have supplanted one another and brought far-reaching shifts in power. The phalanx was the key to Sparta's victory over Athens in the Peloponnesian War of 431-404 B.C. Its effectiveness lay in the use of heavy infantry in close-order formation and in reliance upon shock techniques. The Athenians recovered from their defeat and thirty-three years later employed swarms of light infantry to conquer the Spartans. Somewhat later the Thebians improved the phalanx by distributing its power in depth, thus introducing an element of surprise which had been missing. The Macedonians revamped the Spartan phalanx, made use of Greek mercenaries, and put their stress on a war of movement. But Macedonia was succeeded by the military genius and mobile legions of Rome. Hardened in civil and border wars, the Roman army proved versatile enough to fight as skirmishers or heavy armed infantrymen in open country and in villages and towns. However, the battle of Adrianople against heavy armed cavalrymen from the east brought the challenge Roman military leaders had foreseen but for which they were unprepared. In modern times, technology has given dramatic opportunities to those military leaders who proved capable of adaptation and innovation. By contrast, failure to respond to change has usually meant failure even for those whose traditional military resources appeared to be adequate. Thus the Germans were defeated in World War I by using the strategy of 1870 against their opponents' order of battle of trench warfare and economic blockade. The French in the 1930's, expecting another costly and brutal war of attrition, built the Maginot Line to fight the kind of struggle that military technology had already rendered obsolete. Short of warfare itself, the failure of military establishments to keep pace with fast-moving technological changes can also reduce nations' influence in the chancelleries of the world. This in effect was the tragedy of France before World War II.

The difficulties inherent in maintaining military establishments that will not suffer defeat are more complex than mere responses to technological change. A nation may recognize the need for military organs capable of supporting the foreign policies it pursues but be limited in the margin of its economic resources that can be turned to military use. Some countries exhaust their resources in attaining a viable economy; others, like the United States, have a surplus with which to meet foreign military and political commitments. Belgium cannot afford to devote the same part of its gross national product to military ends as can the Soviet Union or the United States. Thus, both in absolute and relative terms, the military establishment of smaller powers including the newer states must lag behind.

Three errors are commonly made in appraising the military component of foreign policy. First, military power is often confused with national power, and a nation's capacity to impose its will is equated with its military establishment. By contrast, military power is like the fist whose force depends on the health and vitality of the body politic and the whole society. Troops in being are an important determinant of a successful foreign policy, but without other foundations they will not suffice. Second, the military element is often viewed in more static terms than is appropriate. The democracies in two World Wars, although the last to arm, have rallied their forces to gain the victory in the end. Third, it is difficult to analyze and foresee in advance of a particular war the most effective distribution of the components of military force. For example, what comprises a strong military force today? Is it large ground forces, hydrogen bombs, or intensive research? Is a small, highly specialized army more desirable than a large number of ground forces, or are both essential for a nation that seeks to be strong? The answers to these questions will probably be decisive in determining a state's future influence in the world, yet it is sobering that estimates must be made on the basis of contingencies that cannot now be foreseen. We know in a general way that an effective foreign policy must be supported by a military program that can safeguard national security. But this leaves those who make decisions with the painful task of distributing resources among alternative means of defense without any certainty of the kind of war they may have to fight.

Beyond this, the weapons of today may not be used in future wars because technology has rendered them obsolete. It is said that conventional weapons are fast being supplanted by new and more deadly weapons and therefore traditional armaments fail to provide an adequate basis for foreign policy. On the other hand, there are military experts who question whether atomic and hydrogen weapons will ever be used, given the prospect of mutual annihilation. Is it not fair then to ask whether the stockpiling of an unlimited supply of weapons that no nation would dare to use furnishes a state with the requisite military support? A military establishment grounded in conventional weapons may fall short of providing a defensible military posture, but so may a military program aimed at superior atomic capacities. These are the horns of the dilemma on which defense strategists could be impaled.

C.   The human elements: quantitative and qualitative

Students of foreign policy have stressed another set of elements that make up a third concentric circle of factors of policy. They constitute the human forces—both quantitative and qualitative. Population is a

quantitative factor that obviously must be considered in every calculation of the capacity of states. The Middle East provides an example
of the weight that policy-makers give to numbers of people and to
the fact that Arabs are more numerous than Jews. The importance at
the end of the second World War of China and India rests partly at
least in the size of their populations, which exceed 400 million people.
Both the Soviet Union and the United States, numbering less than
half the populations of these countries, have shown respect for their
potential. Conversely, nations with falling birth rates have lost influence among the society of nations, as France did after World War I.
In the past the wide diversity in technological skills, say, between an
Englishman and a Chinese, meant that population was not a factor.
In recent years this situation has been undergoing change—especially
in the last decade. The 50 million people now living in the United
Kingdom enjoy a high degree of scientific skill, but there is no longer
any certainty that the peoples of underdeveloped areas may not eventually approach them or that the combined skills of so large a population may not compensate for a persistent technological lag.

The use of population statistics and of the forecasting of trends
suggests that the science of estimating and predicting the numbers
in states relative to one another is simple and precise. Yet demography
is subject to many of the vicissitudes to which scientific research is
exposed in other social spheres. For example, World War I had the
effect of virtually wiping out a whole generation of Frenchmen.
France's casualties from 1914 to 1918 numbered 1,400,000 young men.
By 1938 the French birth rate no longer compensated for the death
rate; and in World War II France lost 625,000 men, almost three
times America's losses in a country one-fourth America's size. Yet
since World War II the French birth rate has reversed itself, and
since 1946 the surplus of births over deaths has been 300,000 a year—a
surplus greater than that of Italy or West Germany. France, which had
been static and immobile between the wars, has witnessed a renewal
of its rate of growth. In more general terms, then, population as an
element of foreign policy is lacking in absolute predictability and
certainty and depends on other related elements. It may enable or
prevent a state from achieving its national purposes, but in either role
it is also subject to change and fluctuation.

D. Diplomacy: national purposes

Another human element of foreign policy is the quality of a nation's
diplomacy. At one level, this involves a clear conception of national
purposes; at another, it involves prudence and skill in the use of the

tools of statecraft. For purposes of analysis, both can be examined in the context of American foreign policy.

It is well to remind ourselves that issues confronting the makers of American foreign policy compete for attention, crowding out and succeeding one another in headlines of the daily press. Korea, Indochina, Formosa, Israel, the French elections, and Germany flash kaleidoscopically across each of our horizons as we seek to understand international affairs. Sensing this process, it is tempting to second-guess the future. When one is asked what will be the most compelling and troublesome problems of the next six months or a year, he can prophesy the threat of war in the Middle East, orderly transition to independence or self-government in former colonial areas, or agreement on atomic controls. But behind these issues and affecting their resolution are deep-seated, underlying questions relating to this country's basic goals and national purposes. What do Americans seek in the world? Is it peace? Power? Prosperity? Each of these goals in turn often is set forth as a national fundamental aim. Sometimes peace, especially in this atomic age, is made an absolute purpose; again prosperity seems to emerge as the one end Americans seek above all others in the conduct of their affairs in the world. We shall look in turn at each of these goals, seeking to ascertain its relevance to the real issues in America's foreign affairs.

It is sometimes considered a mark of bad judgment, not to say bad manners, to recite at the outset of any discussion a succession of "great generalities." They may be construed as insults to the reader's intelligence. However, the present crisis imposes upon us responsibilities of perceiving more clearly the ebb and flow of certitude and truth with respect to the root principles of world affairs. Recent events have shaped and molded the dimensions of the international problem in a manner that few anticipated. Take as an example the issue of peace. For the first time in centuries rational men have been claiming, apparently with some accord, that war has become obsolete as an instrument of national policy. President Eisenhower has reiterated this view, and he maintained again at the First Geneva Conference that victor and vanquished alike would be casualties in any nuclear or hydrogen war. At the end of such a war they would look out upon the charred ruins of civilization itself. If Geneva settled anything, we are told, it registered a tacit agreement—founded on the stalemate in atomic production—outlawing this form of warfare. But does this mean that peace is inevitable? Does it suggest that atomic warfare is impossible? Apparently not if we consider recent policy statements, the informed opinions of experienced leaders, or events in Hungary, Suez, and Syria.

The most celebrated and controversial policy statements in the mid-'50's were those attributed by *Life* writer James Shepley to Secretary of State John Foster Dulles. In discussing the policy of "massive retaliation," Mr. Dulles observed: "The ability to get to the verge without getting into the war is the necessary art. If you cannot master it, you inevitably get into war. If you try to run away from it, if you are scared to go to the brink, you are lost." Earlier he had said that a potential aggressor must know that his acts would be met by such retaliation and that he would lose more than he could gain. Specific targets for retaliation had to be selected and agreed upon in advance. "The way to deter aggression is for the free community to be willing and able to respond vigorously at places and with means of its own choosing." Its response should be massive and overwhelming.

If we separate the chaff from the wheat, the political from the inescapable truth in this contested statement, it seems clear that the possibility of resort to military measures has not been cast out from the armory of American foreign policy. Since the Eisenhower administration has stressed wherever possible the replacement of manpower with decisive weapons, the risk of warfare with ultimate weapons can hardly be said to have passed. Nor is this possibility made any less ominous by the boasts of Soviet leaders that they too have developed a strategy of retaliation. In this situation an accident, a miscalculation, or an act of desperation could easily set off the conflict that Geneva was said to have made impossible.

Turning to the issue of prosperity, we enter the presence of the most appealing of the current trends of informed thinking on our foreign affairs. This trend of thought maintains with varying reservations that most of the tensions between the West and the non-Soviet but uncommitted countries of the world are the result of mutual suspicions, and that these can be composed through economic cooperation and aid. Put in the proper perspective, a policy of contributing modestly and consistently to prosperity and the raising of standards of living in the world is a viable if not an utterly essential goal for American foreign policy. Its emphasis is all the more crucial because of the neglect of this facet of American thinking in the past. However, prosperity, like peace, is at best a proximate guide to action. It offers no panacea to all the ills that engulf the world. Tensions may be eased when the fruits of economic development and growth are more widely shared at home and abroad. Yet American experiences of intense strife and division nationally during the past decade should caution against excessive optimism. The wounds of the worst bitterness and rancor in the lifetime of some Americans are a sobering reminder that 60,000,000 employed is scant guarantee of peace and tranquility among peoples and parties.

On a world scale, the limits of a form of inverted Marxism that looks to economic development as a miraculous device for purging tensions and strife are even more graphic. India and the United States have not been deterred from misunderstandings by India's phenomenal economic growth. The fact that India has literally raised herself by her own bootstraps, that she increased real income 15 per cent in the period from 1949 to 1954 and attained in 1953-54 the highest rate of economic growth in the world, has if anything prompted her to press claims more vigorously, even when they conflicted with those of the West.

Furthermore, those who would lay the disparities in standards of living throughout the world on the conscience of the West sometimes seek to exact a heavier tribute than any nation or civilization can fulfill. For these developments in other countries are intimately bound up with cultural traditions, with political order and stability, with resources and attitudes and population pressures and a thousand local conditions that Western powers can shape or affect but slightly. If Western efforts can assist others to inch their way to a happier and more promising state of economic well-being and political justice, this will be enough; and it may even stem the advance of hostile forces. However, it can lead at best to public disillusionment and perhaps a deep and festering embitterment with the West's role in the world if public justification of these programs claims more than is warranted.

That the West should be left to find its way gropingly, painfully, and with uncertainty can come as a shock only to those who forever seek simple absolutes and the easy pathway. Peace more than ever before in America's history is a paramount goal of American foreign policy. However, it is a goal that knows its limits. Power throws a spotlight on those dark corners of American action which throughout the era of intellectual pacifism and political neutralism were but dimly lighted. Prosperity—especially in Asia, Africa, and the Middle East—must be as much America's aim as military security, particularly since the foe becomes ever more cunning and resourceful in his pursuit of this enterprise. Yet prosperity is a means and not an end. The interests of progressive no less than oppressed states clash and must be accommodated. Diplomats and not the experts in technical assistance must be called to this task.

We will be on surer ground if we recognize that peace, power, and prosperity are rough guidelines to action. They show us the perimeters within which to work. They in no way remove the demands placed on leaders for political judgment and practical wisdom.

E. Diplomacy and democracy

In diplomacy, the choice of methods and techniques is no less vital than clarity about objectives. Democracies sometimes assume that the demands of coherence and consistency in diplomacy fall less heavily upon them than upon other states. In part this goes back to a prevailing outlook about democracy and foreign policy.

The first two decades of the twentieth century witnessed the flowering of a philosophy of international politics that was unambiguously simple, straightforward, and capable of engendering widespread popular appeal. This philosophy looked in a spirit of buoyant optimism to democracy and national self-determination as the twin sources of international peace and order. The creation of popular regimes on the Anglo-American model everywhere throughout the world was heralded as a sure corrective to the harsh conflicts that for centuries had wracked international life. New nations brought into existence at the will of a self-conscious community of peoples would dissolve the rivalries and frictions that had always led to conflict among contiguous social groups. The faith of modern Western *homo sapiens* in man's potentialities for unending progress found its expression on the international scene in the assurance that a brave new world merely awaited the fulfillment of these goals.

It is ironic that this illusion based on an excess of faith in essentially divine-right *vox populi* has in the recent past been rudely shaken on numerous fronts. The phenomenon of totalitarian democracy, unknown in the nineteenth century, has not only left political rivalries and conflict intact but has heightened and made virtually irreconcilable the disputes among the new collectivities. Inflamed public passions playing on statesmen have made moderation and compromise more difficult of attainment. National leaders by pandering to popular passions have often reduced the alternatives open to responsible makers of foreign policy. Nationalism has led not to more peaceful relations among peoples who rested content with their political status but has bred the most embittered antagonisms between new nations and their former colonial masters or between non-Western states and their erstwhile exemplars in the West. National self-determination and democracy can hardly be said to have ushered in a new era; and our more serious observers find deep anguish in the steep and sudden decline of influence and self-confidence of the Western democracies. The West succeeds in engendering resentment and suspicion more often than it earns respect. Yet many students and statesmen insist on talking in bated breath about the causes and conditions of our decline. The bulk of those who assume leadership in intellectual and political life are singularly inhibited when it comes to diagnosing the source of our ills. It is commonplace to respond to a critical evaluation of the conduct of foreign policy in a democracy by pointing the finger of scorn at non-democratic societies that are still more obviously the authors of our most recent historic catastrophes. The key to this difficult problem is surely not loss of faith in democracy. It is rather a deeper awareness of the methods of diplomacy.

Democratic diplomacy, like all diplomacy, must adhere to certain sound principles and rules. It must prove its consistency with the diplomatic tradition and the imperatives of effective negotiation. Majority votes in multilateral conference or dialectics, invective, or propaganda may hold a certain fascination for the spectators of world affairs. But more often than not their effect is to sow international distrust and increase rather than alleviate world conflicts. The first principle worth noting is that diplomacy and foreign policy historically have not been considered identical. Foreign policy has been viewed as the legislative aspect and diplomacy as the executive aspect of managing foreign relations. Diplomacy has called for experts with freedom of action; policy is a matter for the most responsible branches of government, including at some point the legislature. Diplomacy is not the framing of policy but rather its execution. It is no more a point of focus for public attention than is the execution of the national budget as distinct from its authorization.[5]

The Oxford English Dictionary states that: "Diplomacy is the management of international relations by negotiation; the method by which these relations are adjusted and managed by ambassadors and envoys; the business or art of the diplomatist." This definition suggests a second principle. The test of diplomacy is not the vindication of some abstract moral principle or the rewarding or punishment of virtuous or evil forces. It is rather the most effective accommodation of state relations that are sometimes in harmony but other times in conflict.

Third, diplomacy calls for an intimate knowledge of the mechanics of negotiation, for endless patience in the use of numberless expedients in working out agreements, and for consummate skill in adjusting na-

---

[5] See Chapter 3.

tional proposals and making them acceptable at home and abroad without sacrificing vital ojectives.

In recent years many serious writers have questioned whether or not diplomacy has measured up to the standards inherent in these principles. Hugh Gibson, who has few peers among twentieth-century American diplomatists, wrote:

> What we have come to call diplomacy in the course of the past twenty years has failed to achieve results and has led into all sorts of disasters. But it wasn't really diplomacy. It was the usurpation of diplomatic functions by politicians and inept amateurs; it was the new method of having the negotiation of infinitely complicated world problems handled by politicians, amateurs, and adventurers; the forcing on the world in critical times of new and untried methods; publicity stunts and hurried personal discussions between the political leaders, who should stay at home and be the heavy artillery in reserve rather than trying to direct operations on hurried visits to the front-line trenches.[6]

These words have even greater relevance today than they had a little more than a decade ago.

For nearly four centuries the statecraft of Europe had certain salient features. It sought, in theory at least, to mitigate and reduce conflicts by means of persuasion, compromise, and adjustment. It was rooted in the community of interests of a small group of leaders who spoke the same language, catered to one another as often as to their own people, and played to one another's strengths and weaknesses. When warfare broke out, they drew a ring around the combatants and sought to neutralize the struggle. The old diplomacy, so-called, carried on its tasks in a world made up of states that were small, separated, limited in power, and blessed, ironically enough, by half-hearted political loyalties. Patience was a watchword; negotiations were often as protracted during war as in peace. It was taken for granted that talks would be initiated, broken off, resumed, discontinued temporarily, and reopened again by professionals in whose lexicon there was no substitute for "diplomacy."

Today not one of these conditions any longer prevails, and the search for new formulas in diplomacy has gone on apace. The first and most novel pattern to crystallize after World War II found expression in the United Nations and in what is called "popular diplomacy." It looked to international forums and to majority votes in the General As-

---

[6] Hugh Gibson, *The Road to Foreign Policy* (Garden City, New York: Doubleday, Doran and Company, Inc., 1944), p. 63.

sembly as a substitute for the tortuous paths of traditional diplomacy. It must be said that this choice was expressed more rigorously in practice than in the United Nations Charter, which emphasized talks among the parties to a dispute before placing an issue on the agenda. Popular diplomacy reflects the faith in parliamentary procedures, in the rule of the people, and in straightforward, rational, and open discussion. It is jointly the product of an age of rationalism and an age of popular government. It translates into global terms supreme political attainments of free people within the democratic state. Popular diplomacy, despite the role of the Great Powers in the Security Council, marks a swing of the pendulum to diplomacy by all the peoples of most of the nations. It is the antithesis of secret diplomacy by a concert of leaders of the preeminent countries.

Because popular diplomacy is the keyboard on which much of our postwar diplomacy has been played, we are able to make a modest estimate of its success. To use Lester Pearson's phrase, we find that the problems of "diplomacy in a gold fish bowl" are more intractable than we had supposed. Publicity has been both a virtue and a vice. It has kept the spotlight of public opinion on world affairs, but it has encouraged the actor in world politics, in striking a pose, to take inflexible positions from which it is difficult to retreat. Majority votes on Korea have demonstrated who controlled greater support; they have left conflicts of interest unaffected or have actually contributed to their increase. When this new pattern of diplomacy has worked, it has been savored with more ancient techniques as with the private diplomacy of Mr. Ralph Bunche in Palestine and of Mr. Jessup on Berlin, and the "quiet diplomacy" of the Secretary General.

These successes, however noteworthy, have failed to arrest the sharp swing of the pendulum to another type of international diplomacy. The Eisenhower administration has espoused personal diplomacy as a means of correcting the excesses of public negotiations. The first Geneva Conference, the United States-Canadian-Mexican Conference at White Sulphur Springs, and the meeting with India's Prime Minister Nehru and with Prime Minister MacMillan of England illustrate a new and emerging pattern. It is a pattern based upon the President's partiality "for talking things out rather than negotiating things out" in an atmosphere of genial informality. It reflects the view that some of the roots of conflict will dissolve when leaders from other nations, sitting across a table from Mr. Eisenhower, become persuaded of his good intentions. The personal touch of a famous personality has been placed on the scales of world diplomacy.

The two novel approaches—personal and parliamentary diplomacy

—are at opposite poles of the spectrum. One emphasizes public speeches, mass assemblies, and resolutions emerging from open forums; the other stresses informality and man-to-man conferences free of protocol, agendas, and advance preparation. (At White Sulphur Springs the Canadians on the eve of the Conference didn't know the topics to be discussed.) Yet these new patterns, so divergent in conception and design, share one thing in common. They constitute a revolt against traditional diplomacy.

For diplomatists historically the first rule has been that negotiations are essential when national interests are in conflict. Since such conflicts arise from causes more basic than personal hostility, personal amiability can hardly resolve them. Sir Harold Nicolson has argued:

> Diplomacy is the art of negotiating documents in a ratifiable and dependable form. It is by no means the art of conversation. The affability inseparable from any conversation . . . produces illusiveness, compromises, and high intentions. Diplomacy if it is ever to be effective, should be a disagreeable business, and one recorded in hard print.

The trouble with approaches that set aside the lessons of the past is that history has a way of returning to haunt us. Both popular and personal diplomacy have their place, especially if we safeguard them against their excesses. The best way of doing this is to remember that foreign policy has a memorable tradition, not all of which is folly in the present.

III.   The Mood of Foreign Policy and the Cold War

The elements of foreign policy and the forces of international politics may seem abstract, remote, and distant when conceived of in principle or viewed in the light of an historical past. However, the present conflict between the Soviet Union and the United States is approached more meaningfully if seen in terms of the scheme of the basic factors that lie at the roots of foreign policy. The cold war is more than a decade old by now, and is plainly visible as a conflict with at least two dimensions. At one level, the struggle is for men's minds; the vitality and universality of communism and democracy are at stake. At the other level, the struggle engages two great configurations of power who by reason either of necessity or of design reach out to influence others. A treatise on foreign policy is perhaps not the most appropriate place to analyze the comparative strengths and weaknesses of democracy and communism, for in one sense this is chiefly an issue in political theory, albeit theory in action. Soviet-American rivalry, however, is more clearly a problem in foreign relations.

Both the Soviet Union and the United States have been blessed with the most favorable of geographic situations. The United States is surrounded in the north and south by friendly and weaker states and bounded and safeguarded in the east and west by two great ocean moats. The geographic area of the Soviet Union, constituting about one-seventh of the earth's surface, has historically swallowed up any would-be invader, although its western boundaries are exposed by the open terrain of the European plains. The natural resources of both powers are immense, and their technology is far advanced. In conventional military weapons Russian strength probably exceeds American, but in the production of new weapons—first of an offensive type but more recently of a defensive kind—the Russians despite their progress with satellites have lagged behind. Russia's population is greater than America's, although their per capita technical skill is probably less. American political institutions should in the long run prove superior, but the Russians may temporarily enjoy the advantages that flow from a system in which instantaneous decision-making and kaleidoscopic initiative are possible. National morale, particularly in the hydrogen age, is difficult to measure before a crisis. The quality of diplomacy on both sides is subject to the broader tendencies and problems that have been described.

Americans live by the faith that other peoples will come to embrace a political creed involving a decent respect for the dignity of mankind, and that an international order may be founded on respect for the rights and interests of other sovereign states. However, there are three obstacles that confound American policy-makers and that must at least be mitigated if the struggle is to be won.

The first obstacle is inherent in the problem of marshalling support domestically for American policies while at the same time putting America's best foot forward in the eyes of the rest of the world. To mobilize support for policies, Americans say things to themselves that from the standpoint of other peoples might better be left unsaid. (In this the United States is of course not unique.) America is a vast sprawling continent of great diversity of political and religious beliefs; in its constitutional system power and responsibility are broadly diffused, although less so in foreign affairs than in the conduct of domestic affairs. Thus Americans speak in many voices, some raucous and strident, as they seek to persuade one another of the right course to follow. The language of domestic politics is not the language of political theory. It aims to unite as many as will join to support policies or programs. It looks to a common denominator that can more often be found in broad principles and moral generalities than in specific directives of strategy, which like military policies must be cast in practical alternatives to meet circumstances. It prefers militant slogans to qualified truths and a crusade to public conversations on a problem.

Above all, it is a permanent part of the landscape of international relations that American foreign policy must draw its support from a union of the experts, the public, and friends and allies abroad. History demonstrates that no American statesman can ignore any point on the triangle without courting disaster. Before World War II, the public ostensibly lagged behind the thinking on foreign affairs of experts and allies. Following World War II and up to 1950, American policy—especially for Europe—was acceptable alike to the authoritative views of the experts, to the public, and to the members of the postwar grand alliance. This day has passed; and demands of the three groups have tended increasingly to go their separate ways. America's allies have more and more viewed their national interests as not necessarily identical with the United States', and ironically, at a time when American policies are vulnerable to criticism by experts at home and abroad, they enjoy broad endorsement at all levels of American life to the point of becoming virtually untouchable. By stressing one side of the triangle and striving above all for harmonious domestic political relations, the Eisenhower administration created difficulties for itself at the other points on the triangle. In this way it illustrated a perennial problem in the conduct of foreign relations.

Another obstacle stems from the colonial dilemma, which reaches beyond America's national life and touches conflicting interests at work throughout the rest of the world. We know that the colonial problem stands at the top of every agenda for discussion of American foreign policy. Responsible officials are encouraged to issue proclamations and to throw America's weight behind popular revolutions. In this setting it is tempting to take general and sweeping positions and to express an American doctrine on the rights of peoples everywhere to independence and self-government. This is particularly true because Americans' own experience is so rich in its lessons and apparently pregnant with meaning. The fruits of attempts thus far made to propound a dogma should serve, however, to give us pause, for the record of America's efforts to align itself squarely with either colonial or anticolonial powers is sprinkled with as many failures as successes.

Nevertheless, Americans face new situations today and demands crowd in upon them for new and more vigorous policies. We are reminded that Senator Vandenburg with his emphasis on Europe and Western unity never disparaged the rights of colonial or former colonial peoples. Nationalism is on the march in Asia, the Middle East, and

Africa, and Americans implore one another to identify their country with these movements rather than appearing to stand in their pathway. Unhappily, the colonial problem is less tractable than those exhortations suggest. For at the same time as the fight is waged to end old imperialisms, a new and more demoniac expansionism threatens. To meet it, some feel that America must cleave to its trusted friends and allies with whom it has interests and military bases in common, striving to preserve a more stable world balance of power. Yet, in itself, this is not likely to be enough. The present equilibrium of power will be upset unless America can join with new forces in the so-called under-developed areas. We may say, therefore, that the United States faces the triple challenge of stemming the tide of Russian imperialism and world Communism, uniting the other Western states, and drawing closer to non-Western peoples only recently emerging as independent states. In a manner of speaking, policy-makers must keep three balls in the air. This is the unenviable task of American statesmanship.

The pathos of our present position may be illustrated briefly from recent events. First there was the statement on Goa recognizing Portugal's authority in the tiny enclave in India, prompted doubtless by the zeal of European officers in the State Department to display a sense of community with Portugal. This provoked deep resentment in India and perhaps throughout much of Asia. Next came the expression of "sympathy" for Greek feelings in the Cyprus dispute by the United States Ambassador to Greece, Cavendish W. Cannon, which loosed a torrent of British protest. Then the Dutch voiced dismay at Mr. Dulles' warm and friendly comments during a visit to the Indonesian Republic. More recently the United States aroused its European friends by appearing to take sides with Egypt, and Middle Eastern friends by reassuring Turkey against Syria and Russia. Taken together, American efforts to cement ties of community and good will with one side in the colonial struggle threatened or ruptured the bonds of unity with the other. Possibly the one exception was Ambassador Dillon's speech supporting France's search for "liberal solutions" of her problems in North Africa, and even this was challenged by the moderate Tunisian nationalist leader Bourguiba.

Perceiving these problems, can we say anything about this perplexing picture that will offer some guidance to the juggler or policy-maker of whom we have spoken? Are there guidelines or principles we can enunciate to spotlight a few of the darker corners of this colonial problem? Perhaps there are. First, we must start with the presumption that the colonial problem is fraught with dilemmas with which America must learn to live. Nor will dogmas for or against colonialism waft them away. Solutions must be worked out case by case; and as, for example, Tunisia is not identical with Algeria, policies must be shaped to meet individual needs. Second, timing is of the essence. The statement supporting Indonesia stirred up a hornets' nest because of Dutch-Indonesian tensions at that time over the trial of a former Chief of Dutch Military Intelligence charged with plotting to overthrow the Indonesian government, the conflict over Netherlands New Guinea, and the unilateral abridgment by Indonesia of certain financial and economic treaties. Third, if any general solution can be found it rests in the coordinating or mutual interests, not in the wholesale sacrifice of one set of interests to another. In North Africa, French, American, and African interests appear to coincide as respects "liberal solutions." Likewise in other regions the goal should be the harmonizing of interests. This calls for a judicious balancing of claims. Fourth, it is one of the ironies of history that force may be necessary to preserve colonial arrangements not in order to perpetuate them but that their orderly liquidation may be achieved. Fifth, it will not do to call every conflict of view between America and its European allies a colonial issue. On October 2, 1956, in what one commentator called a Freudian slip that betrayed the main lines of American thinking, Mr. Dulles noted that Britain and America were at odds over Suez on the question of the "shift from colonialism to independence." He treated Suez as an issue between the "colonial powers" and " the powers which are primarily and uniquely concerned with the problem of getting their independence as rapidly as possible." Walter Lippmann was prompt to point out that Egypt could hardly be considered a colony, especially as it sought to expand its national power. A British journal observed: "The American desire to keep the goodwill of the Arab states is good sense . . . but it will defeat itself in the end if, in pursuing it, the Americans think in anti-colonial conventions which are current. . . . In that way they will merely seek to please everybody, committing their strength to the support of local weak men, and overlooking that the conflicts which trouble the region, being real conflicts, require solutions of substance which are bound to give offense to some." [7] Finally, conflicts of interest—as in the past between Britain and India or the Dutch and the Indonesians—may be swept along by powerful historical movements until one side emerges supreme. Here it may be necessary for American policy-makers to choose sides and in this way inevitably give offense. These facts need not preclude prudence and restraint.

---

[7] *The Economist* (London), December 8, 1956, p. 853.

A final obstacle has roots in the moral problem. The question of right and wrong is continuously raised in international relations as in all the other social orders. Nations as individuals either seek to do, or claim to have done, what is right. The nature of Western values as embodied in American culture assures that far from being an exception, America persistently aspires to justice and to the goal of international order. We are pained when we are told that some aspect or another of national conduct cannot be justified in broader international terms, yet we can take comfort from the fact that historically this has been among the most baffling philosophical problems. The question is whether an action shall be called good if it serves the group of primary loyalty or whether it must serve a more inclusive purpose. Political morality as distinct from pure law or justice answers this question in terms that give it a unique flavor. It looks for the point of concurrence between the particular and the general value or interest, rather than calling for the sacrifice of the part to the whole. Politics can count on a residual egotism or self-interest which represents the creative potential of individuals and groups. The nascent international community must guard against extreme forms of parochial loyalty that claim too much and reserve to themselves the right to suppress and overwhelm weaker neighbors. Short of this, however, the larger community is able to harness, beguile, and deflect the more limited national purposes even though it cannot easily transcend them. In Reinhold Niebuhr's words: "The individual or the group may feel called upon to sacrifice an immediate value for the sake of the more ultimate or general interest. But the community cannot demand this sacrifice as its right." Nor, one might add, can another sovereign state.

The American credo of political morality, especially in recent years, has been more pretentious and less modest than this. It has oftentimes called upon others to sacrifice local advantage to some nobler and higher cause. Some of the statements we have had from French, Israeli, Egyptian, and British leaders on the Suez crisis have thrown a dash of political realism on the standards that the United States sought to impose. Justice and international order are properly considered the broad framework of political morality, but their relative emphasis in any decision and the particular content they should receive can never be determined in advance. The values of community and order are frequently in tension with the principles of justice, which are liberty and equality. In the fall of 1956, the international order suffered a threat to the peace. At the same time three of the nations invoked the principle of justice, which in equality calls for giving each man his due, including his right to survival. If the national community cannot assure a tolerable measure of justice, even though as a despotism it maintains order, in the long run its authority tends to erode. Similarly, if the international order lacks the power and prestige to safeguard all its members, they will be tempted to seek justice in other ways. There is an indefiniteness in political morality resulting because "various and frequently contradictory values are involved in political decisions and the preference which is given one value and end over another, must be determined by historical contingencies rather than fixed principles. There are fixed principles and norms in the political realm, but there is no fixed principle for relating the norms to each other. It is possible to define as 'bad' only those situations in which one or more norms are completely wanting. . . ." [8]

America's policy-makers by contrast look for shortcuts to the moral problem. They talk a great deal more about promoting the impact of morality than about determining its content. They seize on the most readily available expressions congenial to their tastes and interests, like "majority rule" and "the will of the United Nations." The workings of political machinery are invested with all the trappings of a religious exercise and political pronouncements are equated with the glorification of God. Repelled by all the talk of "missions" and "crusades," one of our most sensitive critics has said: "I would rather *be* moral than claim to be it; and to the extent we succeed in lending moral destruction to the conduct of our affairs, I would rather let others discover it for themselves." The deep pathos of the moral problem calls more for Christian humility than for a moralistic self-righteousness, which can win few friends abroad and serves only to lower the currency of moral principles.

IV.   Conclusion

The analytical approach to foreign policy as distinct from the ideological approach is no miracle-working device for understanding the complex problems of international affairs. It gives no clue to the specific decisions that must be reached daily in the cold war. It is not a cookbook with recipes for action to fit every contingency. It does, however, provide a way of thinking about the foreign policy of any country and ordering the factors that contribute to the conduct of foreign relations. If prediction is still beyond the reach of scholars, analysis in the face of varying contingencies may be attainable. In some form or another, this method is useful in studying the acts of great and small

[8] Reinhold Niebuhr, unpublished manuscript on "Theory of International Politics," p. 11.

powers. With all the variation of individual scholars writing about unique national policies, the present book serves to demonstrate the role and the limits of the systematic analysis of foreign policy.

Selected Bibliography

Raymond Aron, *A Century of Total War* (New York: Doubleday & Company, Inc., 1954).

Louis J. Halle, *Civilization and Foreign Policy* (New York: Harper and Brothers, 1955).

George F. Kennan, *Realities of American Foreign Policy* (Princeton: Princeton University Press, 1954).

Hans J. Morgenthau, *Politics Among Nations* (New York: Alfred A. Knopf, 1954).

Harold Nicolson, *The Evolution of Diplomatic Methods* (New York: Harper and Brothers, 1955).

Charles de Visscher, *Theory and Reality in Public International Law* (Princeton: Princeton University Press, 1956).

11 . . .

AMERICAN FOREIGN POLICY

. . . Bernard C. Cohen

AMERICAN FOREIGN POLICY—the objectives of the United States in a world of other nation-states, and the courses of action chosen and the means or instruments employed to try to attain these objectives—is, like the foreign policy of any country, a product of history and tradition, of political institutions and processes, of prevailing attitudes and the nature of emerging problems. In the sections of this chapter that follow, we shall examine some of the more enduring of these factors that help to shape American foreign policy in our time, and some of the general substantive characteristics of contemporary policy itself.

I. History and Tradition as Factors in Contemporary American Foreign Policy

To be concerned with history and tradition in this context is to be interested ultimately, not in impersonal forces relentlessly and inevitably pushing foreign policy in any particular direction, but in the American people themselves and in the things that have helped to make them what they are: their social and cultural backgrounds, their economic and political traditions, and their diplomatic experiences. These features of the growth and development of the United States are part of the intellectual heritage of the American people today, their values, attitudes, and predispositions—their likes and dislikes. Thus they have a significant influence on contemporary American foreign policy.

379

A.   The social-cultural background

An ethnically mixed population is one of the important features in the cultural heritage of American society. At every stage in the history of the United States there have been large, often strategically situated groups with interests in or emotional ties to other nations. The concept of the "old country" is widespread, although its significance naturally varies from group to group and from generation to generation. As examples of the foreign policy consequences of this heterogeneous population may be noted the disinclination of persons of German ancestry in the midwestern states to support a foreign policy of intervention against Germany in both World Wars; the support of Israel and of a pro-Israeli policy in the Near East by American Zionist groups; and the rapid formation of organizations for the aid or relief of nations suffering political hardships or natural disasters.

Another element in the social background is the "classless" aspect of American society, or rather the ease with which it is possible to move from one socio-economic level to another. One can readily discern a stratification of American society, but the place of any individual in it is in considerable measure a matter of achievement rather than birth. But the "self-made man" in the United States is not always able to comprehend status-bound societies in other countries, or to have much sympathy or tolerance for the political manifestations of social systems more rigid than his own.

The religious composition of the American social order has a continuing political and policy significance. In a world where religious values and interests of all sorts play a major and occasionally decisive role in international politics, it is important to remember that most Americans uphold the values and ethics of a Protestant secular state, and make judgments on the basis of attitudes partially derived from them.

B.   The economic tradition

Strands in the economic history of the United States and in the economic philosophy that has accompanied it combine in a thread that is visible in the current fabric of American foreign policy. From the earliest days of the Republic this has been a bourgeois society, with a capitalist tradition that has been strengthened by adaptation to changing political and social conditions. There is a deep—frequently unconscious—commitment on the part of Americans to the concept of private property, and to its attendant political, economic, social, and legal institutions and the values they embody. American foreign policy feels the impact of this commitment in many ways—most obviously, perhaps, in the form of negative attitudes in Congress and elsewhere toward European socialist governments, or toward the nationalization by foreign governments of property owned wholly or in part by Americans, but also in subtler and more indirect forms, such as a distrust of domestic economic controls as an adjunct to or a consequence of foreign policy measures.

This economic philosophy has been nourished by the phenomenal growth of the American economy. The ready—and in some cases seemingly unlimited—availability of resources, a vast and expanding internal market, and a skilled population have together helped to create an optimism about the American capacity for achievement and an expectation of progress that have spilled over from the domestic to the foreign policy field. They have also contributed to the development of military attitudes reflecting this abundance—for example, a high ratio of equipment and firepower to manpower. In the social realm, this mass prosperity conditions the way Americans react to less fortunate peoples in foreign countries—some with a moral revulsion against poverty and apparent laziness, and a distaste for "substandard" plumbing, others with an impulse of generosity in the face of extensive requirements for economic development.

During its own long period of economic development the United States imported large amounts of capital, balancing it with the export of agricultural products and some manufactured goods. In the twentieth century the process of economic growth, combined with the repatriation of European investment as part of the financing of two World Wars, altered the position of the United States from debtor to creditor on capital account. But the attitudes that were appropriate to the debtor status have not been as quickly supplanted by attitudes appropriate to a creditor; an import psychology, for example, has not yet struck deep roots. A major consequence for foreign policy is the chronic world shortage of dollars in the post-World War II period, and the continuing necessity for programs of economic assistance.

C.   Ideology and the political tradition

The American people have cherished a distinctive set of political attitudes for many generations; they are so much a part of the culture that they are transmitted through the primary educational systems. And because these beliefs touch on the fundamental questions of where power is to reside and how it is to be controlled and exercised, their foreign policy impact is obvious, direct, and cumulative.

One of the key elements in the American political tradition is the importance attached to constitutionalism and to stable, resilient political institutions, which in the American view often seem to travel together. In both general and pedagogical discussions, heavy attention is paid to the formal aspects of government—to its structural features and its legal foundations and products—as against the political aspects, which despite their significance are less well understood and command less respect. "A government of laws and not of men" is both an American ideal and an ambiguous standard that is often applied—though not always with consistency—in judging the governmental and political practices of other countries. Cabinet instability in France is, to many Americans, both incomprehensible and reprehensible, despite France's status as a constitutional republic; whereas the prospect of Western-type—and especially American—constitutions and political institutions in newly independent non-Western countries attracts much sympathy and support, despite reasonable doubts as to their practical workability in these cultures.

Another ideal that is part of the American political tradition is equality of political opportunity, which is sometimes passed on to a new generation in the form of "log-cabin egalitarianism"—any man, no matter how humble his origins, may become President. Although one may question the validity of such a generalization, this element in the American ideology nevertheless does have a substantial foundation in reality. The social mobility that was mentioned earlier helps to underpin this equality of political opportunity. As there is no social caste system, there is no narrow political class, but rather a wide base of political recruitment. Thus the more general social and political values become embodied in governmental and political practitioners, and the notion of equal opportunity nourishes itself. The foreign policy implications of this are as vast as the foreign policy ideas that circulate throughout the body politic. The tradition itself, however, seems to encourage in Americans a predisposition toward democratic institutions in other countries as values worth supporting in themselves and for no other necessary reason.

The American political tradition has a further impact on contemporary foreign policy in the form of rather concrete attitudes about power and responsibility. One important cluster of attitudes concerns the role of the professional military group in a democratic society, and has long assigned to it a narrow, carefully circumscribed authority. Only in recent years, and then only partially and with the greatest reluctance, have popular attitudes of distrust of the military been modified in the face of mounting evidence that in many foreign policy problems military and political considerations are inextricably mingled, and that military advice and analytical skills are often required in foreign policy-making.

D.   The diplomatic experience

The political and diplomatic circumstances attending the creation of the United States were responsible for a set of anticolonial attitudes which are still a vital force in international politics. After 180 years, and from a position of unparalleled power in the world, the American people, confronting contemporary struggles between imperial powers and colonial peoples, are still instinctively sympathetic with the latter.

In the different circumstances of international politics and American diplomacy in the nineteenth century was created a philosophy of foreign policy some of the elements of which still affect current thinking, even though the philosophy itself no longer has a wide circulation.

The successful pursuit of a policy of isolation from European politics for nearly a hundred years after the promulgation of the Monroe Doctrine has been attributed to several conditions, among them the workings of the European balance of power, and the protective shield of the British fleet, which kept that balance-of-power system from expanding to include the United States. This situation prevailed for several generations—long enough to be regarded as a fact of life, a condition at once both fundamentally normal and profoundly right. And its causes were attributed by many, perhaps through misunderstanding or a process of generalization, to the qualities of the nation and its people rather than to the configuration of international politics. Thus a conviction grew that the United States was a nation not only separate from, but also morally superior to, other nations.

Some of the contemporary manifestations of this isolationist tradition might be mentioned briefly here. One can on occasion still discern in foreign policy debates an implicit assumption that it is possible for a nation to attain perfect security in this world, and thus that involvement in international politics is a matter of national choice, governed inevitably by moral values appropriate to individuals in the American culture. Even more common in the American approach to foreign policy is a rejection of "power politics"—that is, actions that are overtly political in inspiration and objective—as savoring too much of an international immorality supposedly characteristic of European states. Some specific antiforeign sentiments can perhaps be traced back to these elements in the isolationist tradition.

The twentieth century has witnessed a rude break in the continuity of American diplomatic experience. Twice in one generation the United States became involved, reluctantly, in what started out as major European wars, as the American interest in the European balance of power became manifest. And in the Far East, too, the steady accretion of political commitments and, concurrently, an expanding conception of vital interests drew this country steadily into political involvement and then into war. With an understanding of the fundamental breakdown of the nineteenth-century political order has come, slowly, a breakdown of its basic isolationist assumptions. But the old tradition has not yet found a coherent replacement; current thinking is tentative and exploratory, moving from uncertain policy gains to equally unsure losses. The present condition of the United States is one of unprecedented involvement in the politics of a world that is itself new. More than the lessons of experience and the precepts of tradition may be required to solve the problem of how to survive and progress in this new international environment.

II.   The Foreign Policy-Making Process

America's political institutions, like many of its traditions and attitudes, do not seem ideally suited to the requirements of the United States' international political position in the second half of the twentieth century. The foreign policy-making institutions, and the system of separated powers in which they are set, were designed to meet the needs of a simpler, more stable era, in which the functions of government were fewer in number and narrower in scope. True, the early Presidents on occasion also found themselves under constraints imposed by the system, but the foreign policy consequences were not far-reaching. But in the present period of explosively rapid change, in which foreign policy considerations span the entire range of governmental activities—themselves vastly enlarged—and in which there is often need for quick decisions, long-range commitments, and flexibility in both objectives and operations, the American foreign policy-making process suffers obvious, and sometimes grave, disadvantages. Arguments range freely on both sides of the question whether the system as now constituted is too anachronistic to be able to weather the present challenge. Experience seems to demonstrate, however, that it is highly adaptable in actual performance.

A.   The governmental agencies

One of the most important facts about the political system in the United States is the constitutional separation of governmental powers among three coordinate branches of the national government. Perhaps the major consequence, as far as our present purposes are concerned, is that the necessary governmental functions in the foreign policy field are divided between, or shared by, the executive and the legislative branches, and that they cannot be formally integrated without violating or overturning the constitutional structure. The President has major responsibility for foreign relations, and is the Commander in Chief of the armed forces, but only Congress can declare war, and Congress maintains and supports the armed forces. This is but one example of the division of power and responsibility between the executive and legislative branches, but it suffices to illustrate the imperative character of collaboration between them.

1. *The executive branch.* Constitutionally, and by Constitutional interpretation, vast foreign relations powers reside in the President. In brief, and most important, he possesses the "executive power," and "shall take care that the laws be faithfully executed"; he is the Commander in Chief of the Army and Navy, and of the state militia when they are called into federal service; he has the power to "make treaties" ("Provided two thirds of the senators present concur"); he nominates "ambassadors, other public ministers and consuls" (and appoints them by and with the advice and consent of the Senate), and he receives "ambassadors and other public ministers." He has, further, a wide range of statutory powers, and especially in the case of executive agreements, which have the force of treaties but do not require Senatorial approval, he has large customary powers supported by Supreme Court interpretation.

Administratively, the President's powers in foreign relations are shared by the numerous agencies in the executive branch that have been established by law to assist the President. The leading one, of course, is the Department of State, which directs the political relations of the United States with foreign nations. As the problems of American foreign policy have multiplied in recent years, the State Department has grown in functions and size. Economic aid and technical assistance, constituting major instruments of contemporary foreign policy, are administered by the State Department through the International Cooperation Administration. The Department of Defense, created after the second World War as part of the process of unifying the armed forces, is a partner of the State Department in those ever-widening areas where foreign policy and military considerations converge. The military chiefs themselves, organized as the Joint Chiefs of Staff, give the President military advice on foreign policy matters. Military and political aspects of foreign policy come together in the National Security Council, which advises the President on national security policy, and serves as a point of coordination for the State Department, the Defense Department, and other agencies involved in major security policy. The National Security Council is located administratively in the Executive Office of the President, and is the highest-level interdepartmental policy-advising and policy-coordinating body. Very many other agencies and offices are also involved in the formulation and administration of American foreign policy—in the Executive Office of the President, in other Departments in the executive branch, and as Independent Offices. The Bureau of the Budget, the Operations Coordinating Board, the United States Information Agency, the Central Intelligence Agency, the Office of Defense Mobilization, the Atomic Energy Commission, the Tariff Commission—these are the more important ones, and simply to list them is to suggest the operational range and complexity of the executive foreign relations power.

Politically, the power of the President in foreign affairs may be even greater than the powers he derives from the Constitution. The power to act, and to get others to act, in order to accomplish desired objectives is the ultimately significant power, and in this respect the President can take the initiative that is inherent in his position. In other words, the real power of the President depends, at any given time, not only on the Constitutional situation and the qualities of leadership in his administration, but also on the nature of the foreign policy problems to be solved, and on the prevailing domestic political configuration. His power in foreign policy is part of his general power as President, and his capacity successfully to extend its scope wherever it is not already clearly defined depends heavily on his political standing and his policy objectives. If his standing is high and his objectives are widely shared, his capacity to act without political challenge may be very great. The argument between President Truman and members of the Senate in 1951 over whether the President had the authority to send American troops abroad to bolster Europe's defenses was to a large extent a political debate over the wisdom of the policy at issue, even though it was couched mostly in terms of Constitutional power and prerogative.

2. *The Congress.* Specific Constitutional grants of foreign policy powers to Congress are impressive by themselves, even though they do not exhaust the capacity of the Congress as a legislative and a political body to influence American foreign policy. We have already noted that treaties must be approved by a vote of two-thirds of the Senators present, and that Presidential appointment of Ambassadors, other public ministers, consuls, and other officers of the United States also requires Senatorial consent. Furthermore, Congress has the power

to "provide for the common defence"; "to regulate commerce with foreign nations"; "to declare war"; "to raise and support armies"; "to provide and maintain a navy"; "to make rules for the government and regulation of the land and naval forces"; "to provide for calling forth the militia to execute the laws of the Union, suppress insurrections, and repel invasions." In addition to these explicit foreign relations powers, there are other legislative powers that are being used to shape foreign policy. The most important of these is the appropriations power, which has acquired a wholly new meaning since the second World War as economic and military assistance have become major pillars of American foreign policy. The regulation of immigration is another Congressional function that has acquired a general and a continuing foreign policy significance.

The Constitution gives greater foreign relations powers to the Senate than to the House of Representatives; the Founding Fathers argued, for example, that only the Senate had the stability of membership and the wisdom of experience to exercise properly the treaty-making power. But the real powers of the House are increasing, also as a result of the changing character of foreign policy; the most obvious example is provided by appropriations bills, which originate in the House of Representatives.

The most important committees of Congress in the foreign policy field are the Senate Committee on Foreign Relations and the House Committee on Foreign Affairs, and the Armed Services Committees in both houses. To these one has to add immediately the House Appropriations Committee and the Senate Finance Committee. Most major legislation dealing with foreign policy matters is referred to one of these committees in each house; often two committees may be involved before all aspects of a policy matter are finally disposed of. The policy recommendations of a committee to the Senate or House are given great weight in subsequent legislative action, particularly if the committee records a unanimous or near-unanimous vote. Other committees play a minor but not insignificant part in Congressional consideration of foreign policy; for example, the Committees on the Judiciary, Ways and Means, Merchant Marine and Fisheries, Government Operations, and Interstate and Foreign Commerce frequently handle matters that may properly be regarded as affecting United States foreign policy.

Legal and institutional descriptions of policy-making responsibilities must be complemented by descriptions of role and policy tendencies before the political process leading to a decision takes a recognizable form. Thus, one can spell out the official arrangements for foreign policy-making in the executive branch of the government in great detail, but the real functioning of the executive branch depends on the way these arrangements are operated by real people. In this connection one need only mention in passing that the State Department under the Secretaryship of John Foster Dulles worked differently—which is to say, was a different policy-making institution—from the State Department under the Secretaryship of Dean Acheson, as that of Acheson differed from that of General George Marshall.

Constitutional and political powers relating to foreign policy have tended to be used by government officials in certain specific ways for the performance of routine or new functions. Executive powers are used chiefly to initiate and formulate policy proposals, to advocate their adoption by legislative bodies where necessary, and to execute and administer them if they are approved. Congressional powers are used chiefly to test executive proposals against the standards of constituent opinion, to modify proposals, and occasionally to keep a watchful eye on the administration of approved policies. This is an over-simplification, to be sure; nevertheless, this functional division of labor approximates present reality, and is regarded as proper by persons in both the executive and legislative branches.

B. *The nongovernmental agencies.* The heart of foreign policy-making is naturally in the government, for there lies the real authority to make and enforce decisions. But nongovernmental agencies play a very important part in the American foreign policy-making process: directly, by participating or intervening in a governmental process that is remarkably "open," sometimes even by operating the formal governmental institutions; and indirectly, by conditioning the political atmosphere and expectations within which governmental decisions are hammered out. Either way they constitute a significant influence, not merely on the process, but within it.

1. *Political parties.* The role of the party in American foreign policy-making is somewhat obscure, partly because party influence in the American political system is uneven, varying from person to person and from situation to situation; and also because party influence merges with other influences when it begins to flow in formal institutional channels. Furthermore, there are no coherent theories of foreign policy that are characteristically distinctive of either of the major American parties. Nevertheless, party leaders and others who speak under the name of the party do articulate positions on foreign policy issues, positions that tend to be shared in greater or lesser degree by large numbers of the people who repair to the standards of the party, whether in the voting booth or in public office. The minimum common

denominator of agreement may be reflected at intervals in national party platforms.

We can discuss only the general foreign policy tendencies of the American parties here. In the Republican Party, an "Eastern internationalist wing"—a misleading sectional label that has recently yielded some ground to the phrase "Eisenhower wing"—has been dominant since the overwhelming Republican defeat in 1936. These national leaders of the modern Republican Party accept the premises of an active involvement in foreign affairs. But there is a large section of the Republican Party, including many members of Congress, that has a stronger nationalist orientation and, to the extent that it favors an active foreign policy at all, is more interested in the Far East than in Europe.

The Democratic Party has been more unified on questions of foreign policy than the Republican Party. The Democrats have long been predominantly "internationalist" and the advocates of lower tariffs and freer trade; they have also tended to advocate the assumption of new international responsibilities, placing less emphasis than the Republicans on the costs involved. To an as yet undetermined degree, however, this pattern of Democratic attitudes is undergoing change, partly as the result of an economic and social transformation within the South. The Southern wing of the Democratic Party, always more conservative than other sections of the party in domestic policy, shows signs of a lessening ardor for internationalism; and the party platform in 1956 reflected a growing favor for protectionism among Democratic ranks.

Still, one should not exaggerate the foreign policy differences between the two major parties; in actual fact, Republicans and Democrats seem to agree on many of the important aspects of current American foreign policy. Political competition requires some kind of opposition, however, and so party differences in the tactical aspects of foreign policy—in styles of diplomacy, for example, and in approaches to the instruments of policy—tend to become magnified in the course of political debate, suggesting major strategic disagreements where they do not always exist.

2. *Interest groups.* Interest-group activity in the foreign policy sphere may be less confusing and more meaningful to the observer if it is put in some kind of order; hence we might usefully distinguish three types of interest groups and discuss their impact on American foreign policy.

The first type consists of the major, large-scale, national organizations in American public life: business associations, labor unions, church groups, veterans' organizations, women's groups, and the like. Almost all of these organizations are interested in a broad range of foreign policy subjects, and—except where their own group interests are at stake—have supported in general terms the major aspects of American foreign policy since World War II. When their own interests are felt to be involved in policy matters, however—on international labor matters, for example, or a military reserve policy, or a rearmament proposal—the general frame of reference often becomes specific, and these groups mobilize what political power they can command in order to influence the policy-making process.

The second type is composed of smaller or special-purpose groups— for example, trade associations, private firms, regional and local associations—that participate in the foreign policy-making process only when their own rather narrowly circumscribed interests are touched. This may happen when the question of a tariff is raised, or in connection with specific economic aspects of major foreign or defense policies. But these interests are not only economic: they may be concerned with certain ideological attitudes and aspirations, for instance, or with certain sections of the country.

The third type consists of normally unpolitical groupings that come together—or are brought together—when people's imaginations are caught by a foreign policy problem, or when they discover common interests in a given policy situation. Perhaps the best illustration is provided by the political appearance of ethnic associations when events involve the United States and the mother country. Another example is the formation of *ad hoc* groups, such as the Committee on the Present Danger, in response to crucial foreign policy situations.

The pursuit of group interests of all types is an important feature of American policy-making, foreign or domestic. Interest groups constitute a major sector of the politically active public, and their competition, even in the foreign policy sphere, is a common phenomenon of American political life. Sometimes the outcome of this competition may be restrictive and cramping, and sometimes it may be broadening. Where narrow interests effectively dominate policy, the range of choice that is available to the policy-maker is restricted. But when a number of large national organizations lend their weight to major foreign policies, the policy-maker gains the added measure of discretion that comes with the security of this kind of support.

3. *Media of communication.* The communications media are an important element in the process of foreign policy-making in the United States. One way to measure their significance is to imagine how the process might function in the absence of any large-scale and rapid

means of communicating knowledge about events and opinions among the various participants in the process and the observers of it. The media of communication work in a number of different ways to shape this process of foreign policy-making.

By means of expressions of editorial opinion, the media provide an intangible link between the policy-maker and the ordinary reader or listener. On the one hand, they reflect a specialized segment of informal "public opinion" to the government official and, on the other hand, they help to give some structure and content to the opinions of a wider public. In one motion, as it were, they both create and report a body of opinion.

By means of general news-coverage, the media help to define the salient events of the day. In other words, they communicate *importance* to government officials, to legislators, to interest groups, and to the public. Many policy events and opinions acquire an added significance by virtue of the fact that they exert a claim on everyone's attention simultaneously.

By means of mass circulation the media assist in quickly standardizing interpretations of the meaning of events. The place that the national newspaper occupies in other countries is filled in the United States by the national wire services, by national radio and television networks, by national-circulation news magazines, by syndicated columnists, and by a few high-quality media, part of whose contents may be reproduced by other newspapers. Through these manifold channels a large majority of the population is rapidly exposed to an inevitably limited range of views as to the significance of foreign policy developments.

Through writers and commentators specializing in foreign affairs, the media sometimes originate policy ideas; these are then circulated among both the public and the governmental audiences, perhaps stimulating some intellectual explorations on the part of government officials. And the ordinary performance of their duty by persistent and determined reporters serves to force a measure of accountability on the policy-maker; whatever his personal inclinations, it is difficult for him to withhold relevant policy information for very long, or to cover up his own tracks in the face of a resourceful group of correspondents.

Finally, the media supplement existing lines of intragovernmental communication, informing policy-makers in all branches of the government of what is transpiring in other branches that might be relevant to themselves. In this way the media actually are a part of the governmental communications process, and may even be deliberately exploited in this way for internal political purposes, as, for example, when one office seeks by calculated indiscretions to build up its own position or to undermine a competing viewpoint.

No hasty generalizations about the policy tendencies or preferences of the media of mass communication in the United States can be made with safety: there are too many trees in this forest to warrant making rough estimates of that sort. Clearly, where media do take editorial positions, they are found on all sides of foreign policy questions. Elsewhere than in editorials, however, one can discern in foreign policy coverage what might be called an orientation—generally implicit—toward the brand of international involvement and responsibility that has been characteristic of successive American administrations for the last two decades.

4. *Characteristics of public opinion.* American public opinion on foreign policy, as on most other subjects, has a high degree of heterogeneity. There are important gradations in the level of interest in foreign policy matters among the American people, in the amount of information they possess about these matters, and in the degree of their personal involvement. At the lower ends of these scales there is either apathy or simple elemental responses to foreign policy situations, without stability or intellectual structure. At the higher levels there is continuous exposure to communication on foreign policy, discrimination in the selection of responses to policy situations, and elaboration of policy-related ideas.

It follows from these variations that there is also considerable diversity of specific attitudes and opinions on foreign policy issues among the American people. However, the prevailing consensus includes an acceptance of large-scale American participation in international affairs, and a willingness to pay a high price for a reasonable and enlightened security policy. Commitment to this general policy direction is undoubtedly less firm on the lower levels of interest and involvement, where policy is judged, if at all, on the basis of moods that may change rapidly as a result of events or conditions that may not even be relevant to the policy matter. Stability of mood and judgment in the search for effective policy formulations is more characteristic of those on the higher levels of interest and information—leadership groups and the "attentive public." These are the sources of policy- and opinion-articulation and thus the chief architects of the consensus.

Public opinion plays a continuous role in the process of American foreign policy-making, even though it is not always manifest. Quite apart from the specific influence on policy of identifiable individuals and groups, the state of public opinion in the aggregate helps to define the area of discretion that is available to governmental foreign policy-makers, and also to set the political context within which Executive-Congressional relationships take place. These functions are performed no matter what the specific content or nature of public opinion may be on any particular issue at any given time; rather, variations in the character and substance of public opinion will affect the *manner* in which the functions are performed. In other words, public opinion will in all cases have some effect on the discretion of American policy-makers in dealing with foreign policy problems, but the precise character of those effects will depend on the nature and dimensions of public opinion.

III.   The Substance of American Foreign Policy

Before we attempt to generalize about the substance of American foreign policy, it may be useful first to give an account of what is so often called the "revolution" in that policy that has occurred since the close of World War II.

A.   Recent history

By early 1945 the second World War seemed to be nearing its end, in Europe at least; the power of Hitler's Germany was nearly broken, while Mussolini's Italy had capitulated in mid-1943 and later had assumed a co-belligerency status in the Allied camp. The Allied coalition was on the verge of complete and total victory on the European continent, and was preparing to swing its mighty war machine around to the Far East where it could participate in the final assault on the Japanese home islands. In this military context, American statesmen began to move ahead on the major political problem confronting the postwar world as they saw it—the creation of an international security system that would preserve the peace that was being so strenuously won. Their plans for such a system were based on the two assumptions, or hopes: (1) that the Allied coalition would endure in the postwar period, and (2) that if an international security organization could be created while the wartime unity of purpose was still alive, the chances of establishing a successful security system to protect the postwar peace settlements would be enhanced. Thus the United Nations was created in the spring of 1945, requiring Great Power unanimity on all questions of substance brought before the Security Council; and the United States looked forward to Allied cooperation in devising peace settlements that would dispose of the "German Problem" for several generations.

This approach to the postwar international problems limped along for about two years, when it finally collapsed under the weight of the manifest evidence that both the major problems and the chief assumptions were not the relevant ones. In the first place, the war itself had finally ended with the spectacular demonstration of the potentialities of nuclear weapons, and it was made clear within a very short time that possession of an atomic technology for military purposes could not remain an American monopoly for more than a few years. Second, with the end of the war came the precipitate demobilization of the American armed forces, in response to a tremendous variety of public and political pressures. Third, the Soviet Union quickly demonstrated—in its treatment of the Eastern European nations it had reconquered from Germany, and in its negotiations with the Western Allies on a multitude of military and political issues developing at the end of the war—that rather than extending the limited wartime cooperation with its allies, it was determined to extend its political influence far beyond its own borders. Repeated meetings of the Foreign Ministers of the United States, Great Britain, France, and the Soviet Union (the Council of Foreign Ministers) produced little more than an increasing frustration on the part of the Western three at Soviet strategy and tactics; and after fourteen months of negotiations—from October 1945 to December 1946—had been required to draft the Treaties of Peace with Italy, Finland, Bulgaria, Rumania, and Hungary, the machinery of Big Four cooperation to liquidate World War II became rusty and scarcely operable.

The rapidity with which American relations with the Soviet Union disintegrated may be appreciated by noting these events of 1946: In February, Stalin made his first postwar public address to the Russian people, in which he indicated that hostility and tension were the prime features of Soviet-Western relationships. At the beginning of March, President Truman sat with former British Prime Minister Churchill on a platform at Fulton, Missouri, as the latter told his American audience that an Anglo-American alliance was needed to contain the Soviet Union. Also in March, Soviet troops began their withdrawal from Iran after heated United Nations Security Council debate and direct United States-British protests. In August, two American planes were shot down over Communist Yugoslavia; survivors were released and an indemnity paid only after the U.S. threatened to take the case to the Security Council. And in December, as final agreement on the "satellite" peace treaties was being painfully achieved, the U.S. and the U.K. finally merged their occupation zones in Germany, in an effort to seek at least partially the economic unity of that country which the Soviets had succeeded in blocking.

By early 1947, after months of patient but fruitless efforts to patch up the wartime coalition in order to achieve the system of security envisioned in 1944-1945, it was apparent to policy-maker and private citizen alike that the fundamental premises and objectives of American foreign policy had slowly, subtly, but effectively, shifted. The Soviet Union, rather than the Axis Powers of World War II, was now recognized as the real threat to the present and future security of the United States and the Western world—indeed the entire non-Communist world—and as a corollary it was felt with increasing urgency that the United Nations, rendered largely ineffective on the political level by Soviet-Western antagonism, needed to be supplemented by new security arrangements among the Western powers designed to meet this new threat. The form that these new arrangements might take was suggested by the Inter-American Treaty of Mutual Assistance signed at Rio de Janeiro in September 1947, a regional collective security arrangement within the framework of the United Nations Charter.

The watershed of policy may be said to have been the enunciation of the Truman Doctrine in March 1947, by which the United States took over the military and economic responsibilities in Greece and Turkey which the British felt themselves no longer able to afford. Here, for what seems to have been the first time, a United States foreign policy pronouncement at the top level was couched almost explicitly in anti-Communist terms, as President Truman told a joint session of the Congress that the imposition of totalitarian regimes on these countries would represent a threat to the security of the United States. From that point on, the chief problem of American foreign policy was how to protect the United States and the rest of the free world from the menace of Soviet Communism—a difficult problem at best, but one made even more complex (a) by the developing revolution in military technology, (b) by American inexperience in the front lines of international political and military involvement in peacetime, (c) by the rapidly changing political and economic relationships within and among the dependent and underdeveloped areas of the world, and between them and the major Western powers, and (d) by the differences among all these non-Communist nations as to the real nature of the Communist threat, i.e., whether it was political, economic, military, or ideological, and as to the most effective ways to deal with it.

As one of the first steps in the process of constructing an effective security system to protect the West, the United States chose to attack in a massive way the persistent economic difficulties that had gripped Europe since the end of the war. Economic recovery from the devastation of war and the attendant disruption of trade was a long-standing interest of the United States, expressed formally in the midst of war by the agreement establishing the United Nations Relief and Rehabilitation Administration (UNRRA). Yet four years later real recovery had not taken place. Recognizing that military strength required political stability, and that both of these required productive economies and economic relationships, Secretary of State George Marshall stated in an address at Harvard University in June 1947 that the United States would welcome the initiative and cooperation of the European countries in the elaboration of an economic program of self-help combined with American assistance. The free European nations quickly responded to this "Marshall Plan," forming as their vehicle of cooperation a Committee of European Economic Cooperation, which laid the foundation for the establishment the following year of the Organization for European Economic Cooperation (OEEC), still in existence in the late '50's. In April 1948 the Congress approved the bill creating the Economic Cooperation Administration (ECA) as the instrument for channeling billions of dollars to the nations of Europe over a four-year period in an effort to revitalize the European economy.

With the machinery for economic cooperation and assistance thus created, attention turned to the military aspects of the security problem. On June 11, 1948, the Senate adopted the "Vandenberg Resolution" (Senate Resolution No. 239, 80th Congress, 2nd Session), which advised the President of the Senate's feeling that among the policy objectives of the Government should be the "Association of the United States, by constitutional process, with such regional and other collective arrangements (for individual and collective self-defense, in accordance with the purposes, principles, and provisions of the United Nations Charter) as are based on continuous and effective self-help and mutual aid, and as affect its national security." Supported by this expression of Senatorial opinion, the Administration immediately undertook exploratory conversations with the Western powers on an appropriate form for military cooperation and assistance. After President Truman's reelection in November 1948, the United States turned its conversations into formal negotiations, and by April 1949 the North Atlantic Treaty was ready for signature. Approval of the Treaty by the Senate in July 1949 represented an historic reversal of the traditional American policy against participation in peacetime military alliances in Europe.

The Marshall Plan and the North Atlantic Treaty were the major economic and military aspects of American policy in trying to create a stable and secure international environment in Europe in the face of Soviet expansionist pressure. On the political-psychological side, the Soviet blockade of Berlin instituted in the summer of 1948 gave the United States an opportunity to demonstrate—by means of the year-long airlift into the city that followed—both its intention and its capability to resist Soviet moves of that type against free peoples in Europe. And as the lines between the United States and its allies on the one hand, and the Soviet Union and its satellites on the other, were more tightly drawn, the United States government began to build up its own international information services, and to encourage the related activities of private organizations such as the National Committee for a Free Europe, which ran Radio Free Europe.

The military component in American foreign policy was further stimulated first by the Soviet detonation of an atomic blast in the late summer of 1949, and then by the outbreak of the Korean war on June 25, 1950, when North Korean forces crossed the 38th parallel into South Korea. The commitment of American troops to the defense of South Korea carried the United States policy of containing Communism onto new ground—direct military intervention. The war situation in the Far East, and the fear that similar trouble might start in Europe, brought military and defense policy to the forefront of American foreign policy. The Marshall Plan emphasis on economic aid was gradually shifted to military assistance, first through the Mutual Defense Assistance Act of 1949, which followed the passage of the North Atlantic Treaty to give it military substance, and later, in 1951, through the Mutual Security Act. And at the same time the North Atlantic Treaty Organization (NATO) rapidly sought to attain an operational condition. Communist aggression in Korea was also responsible for the spread of United States military commitments from the Western Hemisphere and Europe to the Far East; in 1951 the United States signed collective security treaties—according to which each party regarded an armed attack on any party as dangerous to itself and promised to act to meet the common danger "in accordance with its constitutional processes"—with Japan, the Philippines, Australia, and New Zealand; in 1953 with South Korea, and in 1954 with the Republic of China. Also in 1954 a similarly loose-knit collective security arrangement (commonly called SEATO) involving the United States, the United Kingdom, France, Australia, New Zealand, the Philippines, Thailand, and Pakistan, was brought about by the Southeast Asia Collective Defense Treaty.

When the Eisenhower Administration took office in January 1953, new conditions and new perspectives combined to produce new directions in American foreign policy. By that time rapid progress had been made in the development of thermonuclear weapons, with a capacity for destruction far exceeding that of the original atomic bombs. At the same time the atomic weapon was being adapted to a wider range of military uses, as the problem of nuclear scarcity yielded to a situation of nuclear plenty. Both of these factors, together with the rapid rise in the size of the "conventional" military budget owing to the demands of the Korean war and the inflation that accompanied it, served to raise the costs of defense to a level where a "new look" at the entire problem of military policy seemed justified. Two other conditions were also relevant to the new developments in foreign policy. The first was a widespread public and political reaction against the Korean war, among other reasons because it was a "limited war" without a clear prospect of quick termination through victory, and because it was fought as a United Nations "police action," seeming thereby to transfer control over the predominantly American military forces to an international organization (which also favored the limited-war concept). The second was the death of Stalin in March 1953, and the almost immediate adoption in the Soviet Union of more moderate methods in the conduct of political and international affairs.

Both in the United States and in the Soviet Union, then, there was an apparent desire to do something tangible in the way of reducing international tensions, and in the United States, at least, and possibly in the Soviet Union, a feeling that there was an immediate and compelling need to adjust basic defense policies to fit the changing nature of warfare. One of the early results of these new perspectives was the truce in Korea, which was tantamount to a *de facto* settlement of the Korean war. This left the struggle in Indochina as the only direct military conflict involving Communist and Western powers, but this too was liquidated after another year of French reverses and much discussion about American intervention; when it became clear that the United States was not disposed to risk another Korea—although it did enlarge its mutual defense commitments in the Far East at this time, in an attempt to deter Communist China from further military moves—the French Government made its peace in Indochina.

On the diplomatic, cultural, and economic levels, too, American policy moved to reduce tensions and "normalize" international relationships. In December 1953 President Eisenhower made his "Atoms for Peace" address to the United Nations, proposing that an International Atomic Energy Agency be established to receive and allocate fissionable materials for peaceful uses. Increased cultural contacts between the United States and the Soviet Union were also a feature of Eisenhower's first administration, particularly in its later years. The high-water mark of this policy was the Geneva meeting in 1955 between President Eisenhower, Soviet Premier Bulganin, British Prime Minister Eden, and French Premier Faure. The major achievement of this "summit" meeting can perhaps be described as a mood of international tolerance; this "Geneva spirit" lasted for just a few months, after which the customary political competition between East and West was resumed, in the Near and Far East especially.

The fundamental changes in American defense policy that were launched during these years propelled the United States deeply into the nuclear age. In a first attempt to reconcile the American comparative advantage in nuclear weapons as against manpower, and the Administration's unwillingness to get involved in Korean-style wars on the periphery of the Soviet Empire, Secretary of State John Foster Dulles advanced the policy of "massive retaliation," according to which the United States, in case of such peripheral attacks, would have the capacity—and presumably the intention—to retaliate wherever and whenever it chose, including, presumably, the Soviet or Communist Chinese "center." This policy, enunciated in 1954, was rather quickly modified by reinterpretation, as its distinguishing features came under attack from those who argued that by implication any small war would be converted into a general atomic war. But the passage of time and the concomitant accumulation of nuclear weapons and nuclear technology have ineluctably contributed to the evolution of a nuclear strategy, in which even "limited wars" are likely to be fought with atomic weapons.

In the late '50's, with thermonuclear weapons and delivery systems available to the United States, Great Britain, and the Soviet Union, and with intercontinental missiles poised on the edge of reality, major efforts were still required to maintain the state of deterrence averting major war between East and West. With their first earth satellites the Soviets launched a more intense competition with the United States in all fields contributing to fundamental economic, political, and military strength. Accepting the challenge, the U. S. began to increase the scope and pace of its security planning. Talk of disarmament and "summit" meetings continued, but the essential policy question was unchanged: how to protect the U. S. and the rest of the free world from the menace of Soviet Communism?

B.   Means and objectives in American foreign policy

It is a rather simple matter to say, in the above fashion, what American policy has been at a particular time and in specific circumstances; it is quite another thing—and a much more difficult one—to describe "American foreign policy" satisfactorily in general terms covering a longer time span and a host of circumstances. United States foreign policy is inevitably a mixture of the interests, objectives, and actions of both government officials and all of those persons and groups outside of government who have some part in the foreign policy-making process. No wonder, then, that United States policy is often full of inconsistencies and contradictions, as various groups try to achieve different objectives. It is possible to talk about a coherent body of foreign policy only after viewing the subject from an analytical distance, where the common elements among the various policy claims and approaches can be seen in sharper outline, but even then the conflicts and inconsistencies—for example between ideology and security considerations—do not really disappear.

The major interests and objectives of United States foreign policy may be summarized as peace, security, the expansion of world trade and prosperity, and the enlargement of the scope and the area of human freedom. If these policy aims sound suspiciously altruistic, it is perhaps because they reflect the belief—rather new for Americans —that the fate of the United States will be in large part determined by what happens in the rest of the world.

More specifically, these interests might be stated as follows: (1) The maintenance of world peace, and concomitantly, the establishment of conditions deemed necessary or appropriate thereto—for example, a workable system of disarmament, effective international organizations, and any other institutions that might serve to minimize or even eliminate the occasions when it seems necessary to resort to force as a means of resolving international disputes. The Near East presents a ready illustration of the American interest in preventing international violence that, if left unchecked, might engulf the United States and the Soviet Union. (2) The development of an adequate security system for the United States, by independent means and in concert with other nations in the free world, in order to deter acts of aggression and to protect against their worst consequences if deterrence fails. As the recent developments in the international environment outlined above indicate, military conflict with the U.S.S.R. must still be regarded as a major contingency, imposing an inescapable security objective on American foreign policy. (3) The fostering of an active and expanding system of international trade, and of large-scale economic and technical development, in order to raise levels of real income and standards of living in the United States and the world at large. Economic growth and the expectation of a better life on the part of underdeveloped countries, and the prospect of an increasing level of trade on the part of the more developed nations, are some of the economic goals that are associated, rightly or wrongly, with political stability. This emphasis on development and growth is a logical amplification of the wartime and postwar interest in economic relief and recovery. (4) The extension of free institutions in the world, especially in areas that are groping toward self-government. Nationalist and independence movements in Asia and Africa have struck a responsive chord in the anticolonial tradition in American thinking about foreign policy, although in practice American anti-colonialism has often been diluted when it conflicted with one or another of the American foreign policy objectives, especially the security goal.

These objectives, formulated in various ways, are shared to a greater or lesser extent by all the significant elements that participate in the foreign policy-making process. There are fluctuations, however, in the emphasis that various groups place on the different objectives, and also on the degree of their commitment to them. To repeat the previous example, for some people the American security interest is generally paramount, while others do not always accept the proposition that the security objective requires American interference with the progress of colonial areas toward independence. France's fight against Algerian Nationalists in 1956–1958 raised in an especially acute form this anti-colonialism vs. security dilemma in U.S. foreign policy. These broad, rather stable, and long-term objectives of American foreign policy are sought by means of a combination of specific policy instruments designed to achieve short-run and intermediate as well as long-run effects. This necessity to choose methods in order to implement higher goals introduces another element of competition into the making of American foreign policy: for not only do some foreign policy methods promise advantages to some groups in society and not to others; even further, there are real limits to the capacity of men to predict the consequences of their choice of policy means, and even with the best of intentions basic disagreement on such matters is common. Some of these problems will be explored in the following discussion of aspects of American foreign policy.

1. *Security foreign policy.* A historical review of U.S. policy such

as that given above clearly demonstrates that security policy is the most important aspect of American foreign policy, as well as the most evident. National security is the shield protecting men's pursuit of other values, and when men agree that security is threatened, they readily assign the highest priority to its protection. In the absence of a war situation, however, the nature of a possible threat to the nation's security cannot be determined with great precision; ambiguity of this sort has been one of the novel features of the "cold war" competition between the United States and the Soviet Union. But it is the case at the present time that the threat seems sufficiently manifest to warrant paying close attention to the security elements of American foreign policy, but not quite so imminent as to preclude important differences of opinion on how a security policy ought to be implemented.

Since 1947, as we have seen, the United States has helped to create a world-wide web of military alliances for defensive purposes, under the United Nations Charter provisions allowing regional arrangements for collective self-defense. This network of military alliances is unprecedented in scope and form; it represents the massive use of a policy instrumentality that is essentially new to the American experience. Not only has the United States overturned completely its respected historical tradition against alliances that contain or imply advance commitments to employ military force. What is also unprecedented is the extent of public agreement on this development in American security policy. The significance of the new consensus may be appreciated, perhaps, by noting the character of the criticism it meets. The recent American attempt to stabilize an area militarily—by unilaterally asserting the defensive arrangements of an alliance against the possibility of Communist aggression in the Near East—ran into some opposition not because this extension of security policy was deemed inappropriate, but rather because it was thought to be insufficient: only half a loaf, so to speak, instead of one loaf too many.

On another major pillar of security policy, however, there has been rather less agreement: the military and defense policies that the United States has been evolving by itself and in association with those few—mostly European—allies with whom it conducts joint military planning are much more subject than is alliance policy to the competing claims not only of political calculation but also of technical development. On the technical side, the rapid progress of weapons development that has had such a radical impact on strategic planning has in the process upset traditional notions about the uses of force and traditional divisions of responsibility for its use. Thus recurrent and semi-public attempts on the part of the military services to establish new divisions of responsibility in the face of extremely rapid technological obsolescence have contributed to the general uncertainty over the direction that military policy should follow. On the political side, the movement in the direction of a nuclear strategy has not been without fundamental conflicts also. The costs of maintaining both a conventional military strategy and a nuclear one are now regarded as excessive; but the risks involved in making a choice, or in setting priorities, between these alternative policies are exceedingly difficult to calculate and have thus been subject to varying estimates. While the major trend of policy has been an increasing reliance on nuclear instruments at the expense of conventional ones, important political dissents have been registered, questioning whether it is wise to rely on a nuclear strategy if it saves money but in the process requires that even "limited wars" be fought with nuclear weapons.

In its present character, military policy, like alliance policy, is new to the American foreign policy experience; in fact, only recently has military policy been regarded as a proper concern of foreign policy analysts, and there are even now only a few specialists in the subject outside of the armed services. In other words, the basic elements of contemporary security foreign policy are those for which tradition and experience have not adequately prepared the United States. Here, indeed, is the crux of one of the major United States foreign policy difficulties of our time: the necessity to use and to perfect military instruments when America's whole orientation in the past has been to avoid or reject them. Neither the problem nor its ramifications will soon disappear.

But the American search for security does not follow the military path exclusively. All the channels of politics and diplomacy, including the extraordinary personal channels that run to the Presidency, are utilized to exploit the possibilities of reaching settlements of major and minor disputes between the United States and other countries, including the Soviet Union, whenever the chances for agreement seem real enough to justify the undertaking. The political resources of the United Nations, too, are given an important, though not a commanding, part to play in the American search for peace and security. But diplomacy, even United Nations diplomacy, can do no more than capitalize on the willingness of foreign statesmen to come to some understanding, and to create that willingness the United States has to exploit all the other means of foreign policy—political, military, economic, and "psychological."

2. *Economic foreign policy.* Economic instrumentalities play an

increasing part in American foreign policy, building on their past successes in helping in the relief and reconstruction of Europe after the second World War and in the recovery of its productive capacity: they are an essential ingredient in the cement that binds the alliance system together; they assist in the enormously difficult task of economic development abroad; and they aid in the endeavor to expand the world trading system. But the realm of economic foreign policy is also the arena for extensive political competition: few values, to secure which men engage in political activity, are as extensively desired and as obviously scarce as purchasing power. Every attempt to use economic means in the furtherance of American interests abroad—whether economic, political, or other interests—is the occasion for extensive debate, as various groups, both private and governmental, try to influence the allocation of resources in ways that will benefit them the most or harm them the least. This conflict between special economic interests and national political interests, and between those who wish to bend economic devices to political purposes and those who are chiefly economic conservatives, has been a constant feature of American foreign policy debate ever since economic means became a major instrument of United States policy abroad in the second World War.

The most spectacular and significant devices of economic foreign policy over the past decade have of course been "economic aid," which is the massive provision of American dollars to foreign nations to meet balance-of-payments difficulties as well as for reconstruction and recovery, and "military assistance," to further the American-led effort to strengthen the defenses of many nations in the free world. Closely related to foreign aid of these types is "technical assistance," most commonly made available to underdeveloped countries engaged in elaborate development plans. The foreign policy purposes of these economic instruments have been varied, but they might be summarized as an effort to create in the recipient countries a stronger military posture and a prospect of economic growth and betterment, valued for itself as well as for its contribution to political stability and the development of free institutions. The annual provision of several billion dollars for foreign aid and technical assistance has carried the world a long distance from the desperate postwar days; recovery has been succeeded by growth, and with the change the longer-range political objectives of American aid have come to the fore. The Soviet Union has also adopted foreign aid as an instrument of foreign policy in areas outside the Soviet orbit, and thus is in competition with the

United States, particularly in development projects in underdeveloped countries. American economists are beginning to argue, however, that if economic development is the immediate objective of American policy, it makes little difference whether the funds for that development come from the Soviet Union or the United States. In this view, rather than competing with the United States, the Soviet Union is contributing to American long-run goals of growth, stability, and free political development.

The tariff has traditionally stood at the borderline between American domestic politics and foreign policy; its importance in economic foreign policy has been overshadowed in recent years, however, by the tremendous volume of foreign aid. The Reciprocal Trade Agreements Act of 1934, and its periodic renewals, have brought tariffs down significantly from the heights they reached in the Hawley-Smoot Tariff of 1930. Every debate on the extension of the Act, however, has been the occasion for a fresh struggle between the supporters of the principle of progressive tariff reduction and the defenders of particular domestic economic interests that might be damaged by competition from foreign concerns, providing new illustrations of the connection between domestic politics and foreign policy. With the lowering of tariff rates and the postwar rise in world productivity, the volume of international trade—and, with it, of American foreign trade—has gone up. But there is still a wide gap between the values of American exports and imports: in 1956, exports were at a record high of nearly $18,500,000,000, while imports, also at a record high, were nearly $13,000,000,000. The gap between the two is partly closed by means other than trade—for example, tourism, private investment, and military aid—but direct economic aid has also been necessary to help provide the dollars required for balance-of-payments purposes. Partly, then, foreign aid may be regarded as an alternative to a lowered tariff schedule, one that spreads the costs over the entire economy through the mechanism of a higher tax rate. Although trade policy is still an important feature of American foreign policy, tariff adjustment is only rarely used now as a means of achieving political objectives. It has been replaced by more efficient instruments—quantitative trade controls, for instance—or more generous forms of economic blandishment.

Neither the Constitutional provisions governing appropriations, nor traditional American business-minded attitudes, are conducive to the large-scale and long-run exploitation of economic instrumentalities for foreign policy purposes. Instincts of generosity and short-run calculations of necessity have created the current dimensions of economic foreign policy, but a bolder and more enterprising approach is required if there is to be any exploration of the further political potentialities of economic means.

3. *Cultural and ideological foreign policy.* The United States also tries to achieve its foreign policy ends by "psychological" means, which do not seem to be quite as obviously political in character as military and economic instrumentalities, even though their ultimate objectives may all be the same. By a wide variety of techniques involving social, cultural, and ideological relationships, the United States tries to broaden the area of international understanding and welfare, and to influence the attitudes of friendly, uncommitted, and hostile groups in whatever directions policy suggests. By their very nature these devices have a disconcerting intangibility; and when used by themselves, rather than in concert with other instruments, they are not notably successful in achieving significant policy objectives. Nevertheless, they reflect a widespread American desire to find substitutes for "power politics," and also to break through the hard crust of intergovernmental relations and establish contacts between "peoples."

The American government itself participates in many organizations and activities that are designed to further our general interests on the social, cultural, and ideological levels. Some of these are specialized, functional agencies of the United Nations, having the purpose of improving the conditions of life of ordinary peoples—for example, the World Health Organization. The United Nations Economic, Social and Cultural Organization (UNESCO) receives extensive American support, governmental and private, in its efforts to construct the "defenses of peace" in "the minds of men." The Department of State, by itself and in cooperation with other government departments, encourages exchange-of-persons programs in order to help spread a first-hand knowledge about everyday living in this and other countries among influential persons not in high government positions. And the government, through the President, the State Department, and other offices, assists a myriad of private organizations—service groups, civic education groups, labor unions, and the like—in their own programs aiming at cultural interchange. These few examples hardly do justice to the range of activities within the purview of official American foreign policy that have the purpose of forging bonds of understanding and friendship between Americans and citizens of other countries.

As for the use of "psychological" means to shape the attitudes and opinions of individuals and groups in foreign countries, this is one of the many functions of American political representation abroad, and of major foreign policy personnel at home; it is also the chief assignment of the United States Information Agency (USIA), which runs the Voice of America and other informational and cultural programs directed to foreign populations.

President Truman stressed the importance of these varied means of international communication for purposes of what is sometimes called "psychological warfare" by creating a high-level Psychological Strategy Board to advise on and to coordinate programs of this kind. And President Eisenhower, recognizing that psychological efforts are more likely to be effective if they are related to and coordinated with actual policy, converted the Psychological Strategy Board into the Operations Coordinating Board. But although there is widespread recognition that a psychological offensive is no substitute for sound American policies in search of peace, security, and welfare, there is still a general conviction that the United States would benefit from an ideological offensive on behalf of the free world that matches in inspiration and in novelty the American security and economic initiatives.

IV. Conclusion

Perhaps the most fitting conclusions to this discussion are some general observations about the conditions of foreign policy-making and of policy itself in the United States today. For it would be misleading to leave an impression that U.S. foreign policy is customarily clearly defined, well structured, and logical. It is so—if at all—only in retrospect, and after much analytical refinement.

Foreign policy-making is marked above all by indeterminacy; the practical world of policy-making is one where men are always groping, in different directions at once, to find ways to influence the course of events, even while they have to make hurried responses to events shaped by people or policy-makers in other countries. And as long as the American people are interested in achieving more than one value or set of values in the international arena at any one time, it is inevitable that policy-making will have its share of contradictions and compromises—and perhaps it is even desirable that it should. Americans find themselves supporting the European colonial powers, even in some of their colonial problems, while they try at the same time to create an image of the United States as anticolonial, and to give positive policy encouragement to areas struggling to pass from colonial status to independence; and it is rather easy to defend the proposition that it is better for the United States to do both of these things than to do either one of them alone. The same holds true of the inconsistency between America's ideological attachment to free institutions throughout the world, and its maintenance of political, economic, and military connections with regimes such as those in Yugoslavia, Spain, and countries even closer to home that by American standards are more authoritarian than democratic.

If policy-making is often indeterminate, foreign policy itself is rather unstable, except in the most general terms and in the very broad sweep. Political events and situations are constantly in a state of flux—and the more successful American policies are in shaping events, the more quickly are new policies required to meet the new situations. In its days of isolation the United States could get a lot of mileage, so to speak, out of most of its specific policies; to maintain its position of free-world leadership today, however, this country has had to get accustomed to a rapid rate of obsolescence in its foreign policies, and consequently to an almost constant need for new ideas and new proposals. Today, for example, the American alliance structure seems to be stable, having weathered a severe crisis of confidence as a result of the Anglo-French invasion of Egypt in November 1956. But alliances do not remain forever unchanged, and the conditions that define the present structure may well be modified sometime in the future by new and fundamental developments in military technology. The widespread opposition in Europe to American proposals to locate missile bases in Britain and on the Continent may turn out to be a forerunner to more far-reaching changes.

American foreign policy-making has rarely been characterized by bold inventiveness and a willingness to take large risks; there is little of this in the nation's past history, and it is almost discouraged by her institutions of government. Yet both of these attributes would seem to be prerequisites to survival in a long drawn-out competition with the Soviet Union. America's adaptation to changing conditions over the past decade has been remarkable; but the circumstances of the past decade, despite their unprecedented challenge, have been essentially within the compass of experience of the Western state system. The next ten years, and the ten that follow that, are very likely to present problems utterly new to the Western tradition; and if they do, the requirements of courage and intellectual resilience and imaginativeness on the part of American foreign policy-makers will be extraordinarily high.

Selected Bibliography

Almond, Gabriel A., *The American People and Foreign Policy* (New York: Harcourt, Brace and Co., 1950).

Bailey, Thomas A., *The Man in the Street* (New York: The Macmillan Co., 1948).

Dunn, Frederick S., *War and the Minds of Men* (New York: Harper and Brothers, 1950).

Key, V. O., Jr., *Politics, Parties, and Pressure Groups* (2d ed.; New York: Thomas Y. Crowell Co., 1948).

Millikan, Max F. and W. W. Rostow, *A Proposal: Key to an Effective Foreign Policy* (New York: Harper and Brothers, 1957).

Perkins, Dexter, *The Evolution of American Foreign Policy* (New York: Oxford University Press, 1948).

Public Opinion Quarterly, Special Issue on International Communications Research, Vol. 16, No. 4, Winter 1952-53.

Snyder, Richard C., and Edgar S. Furniss, Jr., *American Foreign Policy* (New York: Rinehart, 1954).

Truman, David B., *The Governmental Process: Political Interests and Public Opinion* (New York: Alfred A. Knopf, 1951).

INDEX . . .

C

contributors:

Gabriel A. Almond

Vernon V. Aspaturian

George I. Blanksten

Bernard C. Cohen

Karl W. Deutsch

Lewis J. Edinger

Leon D. Epstein

Roy C. Macridis

Dankwart A. Rustow

Robert A. Scalapino

Kenneth W. Thompson

Allen S. Whiting